Protecting Human Rights in Africa

University of Pennsylvania Press
Pennsylvania Studies in Human Rights
Edited by Bert B. Lockwood

A complete listing of the books in this series
appears at the back of this volume

Protecting Human Rights in Africa

Roles and Strategies of
Non-Governmental Organizations

Claude E. Welch, Jr.

University of Pennsylvania Press

Philadelphia

Library of Congress Cataloging-in-Publication Data
Welch, Claude Emerson.
   Protecting human rights in Africa : roles and strategies of non-
governmental organizations / Claude E. Welch.
       p.   cm. — (Pennsylvania studies in human rights)
   Includes bibliographical references and index.
   ISBN 0-8122-3330-1 (alk. paper)
   1. Civil rights—Africa.   2. Human rights—Africa.   3. Non-
governmental organizations—Africa.   I. Title.   II. Series.
JC599.A36W45   1995
323′.096—dc20   95-30107
                                                          CIP

To Jeannette—present always in spirit, if not in person, while I travelled through Africa researching this book

Contents

Preface: Setting the Stage

Many of the pages that follow are written in dry academic prose, but the concerns that led to them are deeply emotional. Any author brings to his or her subjects a series of personal interests and attitudes. It is best to be "up front," revealing in advance how these concerns have developed, and how they in turn may have affected the analysis.

Protecting Human Rights in Africa continues my personal involvement in seeking to understand, and to present to others, informed, sympathetic analysis of political change south of the Sahara. My quest has lasted well over three decades. It started in the heady years of rapid decolonization and ascendant nationalism. A profound transformation of the map of Africa came in 1960, when the pink of the British Empire, the green of the French Empire, and the varied colors of Belgian and Portuguese possessions shifted to the multiple hues of independent Africa. New names sprouted inside borders drawn long before. These events seemed to promise a new beginning. The process was fascinating. I first started to follow it as an undergraduate; thoughts of a possible State Department or international organization career heightened my interest in the new-born nations. For my baccalaureate thesis, I delved into the fate of Namibia (then called Southwest Africa) under United Nations supervision; one benefit was a nodding acquaintance with international reporting systems. Several of my college classmates chose the nascent Peace Corps as their first post-BA experience of Africa; others of us decided that further study was our forte; my doctoral work in England included close to a year's field research in West Africa, my first chance to experience directly the charms and challenges of the region. The State University of New York at Buffalo, where I started to teach in 1964, encouraged my continued learning and writing about Africa, her people, and her politics.

The subject of this book is human rights, specifically human rights nongovernmental organizations that focus on contemporary Africa. It is not a new area of analysis for me, for, like Molière's famous character, I have been speaking this sort of prose all my adult life without fully realizing it. My earlier research (be it my undergraduate analysis of Southwest Africa under the Mandates and Trusteeship systems; my doctoral work on tensions between Pan-Africanism and nationalism in West Africa; my subsequent analyses of causes and consequences of military involvement in

African politics and of relationships between human rights and development) involved crucial aspects of human rights: self-determination; civil and political rights, including government legitimacy; unfulfilled basic needs that cry out for economic and social development. All this research required showing how domestic and international actors shaped the African context. I presented the results in detached terms, concentrating on "political modernization" or "civil-military relations" or "civil society." The men and women whose ideas, ideals, energy, resources, personal commitment, and struggle fueled these changes remained largely in the background. This time, I have tried to be more personal (though not less analytical!), by depicting the inner workings of interesting but little-known organizations. The Inter-African Committee on Traditional Practices Affecting the Health of Women and Children, or the African Centre on Democracy and Human Rights Studies, or the Namibian Legal Assistance Centre are known only to small numbers of persons. Yet what they seek to accomplish could improve the lives of millions. Their strong commitment was evident at all points in my research.

Many individuals and offices have helped me in the research and writing of this book. Field work was facilitated by sabbatical leave from the University at Buffalo and by grants from the Fulbright Commission and the United States Institute of Peace. Many persons made me feel welcome in my travels across the continent. I am especially grateful to the leaders of organizations who discussed in frank detail how they sought to bring about change, and the informed observers who shared their ideas. A partial list of those willing to be recognized publicly includes the following: in Ethiopia, Abraham Abebe, Ambassador Mark Bass, Almaz Eshete, Almaz Haile-Selassie, Dr. Azeb Tamrat. Andreas Eshete, Assefaw Gebre-Egzebier, Melaku Wolde-Mariam, Mesfin Wolde-Mariam, Brother Gus O'Keefe, Shongizaw Chane, Tadelech Wolde-Michael, Teshome Asrat, Steven P. Tucker, Yacob Haile-Mariam, Yitayew Alemayehu, and Daniel Woubishet; in Namibia, Andrew Corbett, Joshua Forrest, Bience Ganawas, M. O. Hinz, Dianne Hubbard, I. Kaakunga, Frans Kapofi, Peter Koep, Theunis Keulder, Ilenikelao Latvio, Anneli Lindahl-Kenny, Gwen Lister, the Reverend Samuel Mbambo, Magdalena Shamena and the Reverend Ng. Nakhamehla of the Council of Churches of Namibia, Ambassador Marshall McCallie, Phil Ya Nangoloh, Hilgard Patemann, Nashilongo Shivute, David Smuts, Hon. Ngarikutuke Tijiriange, G. Tötemeyer, Arnold Wehmhörner, and Ilse van der Westhuizen; in Nigeria, M. Ajo Ajomo, Jadesola Akande, Amah T. Amah, Remi Anifowose, Chom Bagu, Ambassador Walter Carrington, Robert Downey, Oraze Lanre Ehonwa, Gani Fawehinmi, Tokunbo Ige, Glory Kilanko, Clement Nwankwo, Mora McLean, Isabella Okagbue, Derin Ologbenla, Abdul Oroh, Beko Ransome-Kuti, Adesina Sambo, Dr. Irene Thomas, and Ambassador M. Yahya; in

Senegal, Marcele Basenne, Mariane Coulibaly, Boubacar Kanté, Jacques-Mariel Nzouankeu, Babacar Sine, Papa Moussa Félix Sow, and Bakary Traoré. In the United States, I benefited from interviews with Janet Fleischmann and Aryeh Neier of Human Rights Watch/Africa; Julia Harrington of Harvard Law School and Astrid Danielsen of the Danish Ministry of Foreign Affairs reviewed my analysis of the African Commission and provided many helpful suggestions. In Geneva, that wonderful center for human rights NGOs, I profited from discussions with Philip Amoah, Adama Dieng, David and Dominique Johnson, Berhane Ras-Werk, Berth Verstappen, and Peter Wilborn. Mike Dottridge, Christopher Hall, Martin Hill and Gillian Nevins of Amnesty International (London) furnished valuable suggestions. Other help in Europe came from Wolfgang Benedek and Gerd Oberleitner (Graz), Salem Mezhoud (London), Zdenek Cervenka (Uppsala), and Theo van Boven and Cees Flinterman (Maastricht). Special thanks are also due to USIS officials who smoothed my way in several African cities: in Addis Ababa, Isaac Russell; in Dakar, Thomas Hodges; in Lagos, Sophie Folly and James Warren; in Windhoek, Robert Sartori and Helen Picard. The draft manuscript was read in its entirety by Abdullahi A. An-Na'im, Karla Cunningham, Rhoda Howard, and Aimée Verdisco, whose comments were most helpful in making final revisions. My Buffalo colleague Peter Ekeh has always been a fine stimulator of ideas. I am especially grateful to Virginia Leary, who was both mentor and friend, in Buffalo and Geneva. The ultimate responsibility for the accuracy, persuasiveness, and academic merit of what follows remains mine, however. It is a responsibility I gladly accept.

Claude E. Welch, Jr.
Geneva, Switzerland, and many parts of Africa, 1993/94

Part I
Setting the Scene

Chapter 1
The Context of Human Rights in Africa: Issues in Four Countries

Central to this book are two assumptions. First, Africans are well aware of human rights issues. They are working hard (often with external encouragement or support) to reduce or eliminate abuses. Organized human rights groups can now be found in most African countries, unlike the situation barely a decade ago.[1] Consciousness of the global, continental, and national dimensions of human rights has added a new, important dimension to the struggle for justice. Second, non-governmental organizations (NGOs) play critical roles in resolving human rights issues. NGOs gather information, seek to influence public opinion, provide assistance to individual victims of abuses, and press governments and international supervisory bodies for action. If these NGOs lack political space within which to operate, or resources necessary for fact-finding and publicity, it stands to reason that human rights abuses will continue. Governments unchecked by civil society become major threats to their societies — a lesson recent African history teaches.

Widespread abuses of human rights have occurred, and continue to occur, south of the Sahara. Take some historic examples. Slavery has been widely practiced by societies[2]; however, the scale of enslavement in tropical Africa (especially in the seventeenth and eighteenth centuries) and the disruption thereby engendered have no parallels. The division of the continent over a century ago among grasping colonial powers also had precedents, but not on such a scale. The authoritarianism marking European colonial rule was not unique, but was mammoth in its impact. These abuses of individual and collective rights echo to the present. Harmful effects of the periods of slavery, partition, and colonial rule have yet to be totally overcome.

But we need not delve only into history for evidence. Contemporary examples of abuses abound. Customary practices, and especially the actions of many governments, mock the high hopes with which independence was attained. Slave-like practices continue in a few states.[3] Throughout a wide belt of countries in the Sahel, young girls continue to be subjected to genital operations, thereby denying, critics comment, their right to the integrity of their bodies. Some governments wage war on groups of their citizens, based on ethnic or ideological differences, or on simple lusts for power. Corrupt, power-hungry leaders remain intransigently in office, having hijacked or ignored popular pressures for free, competitive, and democratic elections.

Events of this sort sadden Africans and Africa watchers. The aura of pessimism that now marks much of Africa stems in large part from continued denials of human rights. More important, these demands contribute to a widespread popular belief that the continent as a whole is retrogressing. The marginalization of Africa, an economic fact of the 1980s and 1990s, has been accompanied by its political sidetracking, especially since the end of the Cold War. As the situation seems to have darkened, so too the attention has diminished.

It would be presumptuous to place blame for the human rights abuses that have occurred on one factor alone.[4] Rather, a combination of factors accounts for the problems in many states. Among these are historically searing colonial experiences, failures in the leadership of centralized governments, a high level of military involvement in politics, severe economic deprivations, cultural fragmentation, and weak regional means to promote and protect human rights. Lack of knowledge compounds the problems. Without understanding the obstacles and opportunities confronting those who want to bring change, we cannot comprehend fully how justice can be achieved in Africa.

There are important rays of hope, nonetheless. Such events deeply concern Africans of many backgrounds and interests. They seek to rectify the situation through human rights organizations. They face difficult tasks, for which they merit sympathy and support. *Protecting Human Rights in Africa* focuses on NGOs and their multiple roles. A look at the membership and goals of human rights organizations will illuminate the road travelled to date, and the steps still remaining, for protecting human rights.

This book generalizes through induction. It is deliberately comparative. It looks at specific organizations, showing how they have addressed specific human rights issues. The issues are varied: combatting female genital mutilation through consciousness-raising; incorporating human rights into school curricula; using *pro bono* lawyers to file suits; showing activists how to write communications and complaints to international agencies. These case studies, presented within a general framework of analysis, lead to overall conclusions about strategies to promote and protect human rights in Africa. Thus, this book is intended to deepen knowledge about NGOs and their roles, to acquaint the reader with a range of human rights matters, and to draw out policy implications.

I have selected four countries and major human rights NGOs within them for detailed analysis. The remainder of this chapter summarizes salient features of these countries (Ethiopia, Namibia, Nigeria, and Senegal). They represent a broad spectrum of issues and contexts. The countries represent diverse regions of Africa — Ethiopia to the northeast, Namibia in the south, Nigeria and Senegal in the west. While Ethiopia defended itself successfully against European colonialism (with the exception of the late 1930s) Namibia was shaped by German and then South African rule, Nigeria by British, Senegal by French. Namibia achieved independence early in 1990; Ethiopia lost it only briefly; Nigeria and Senegal gained full self-government in 1960, that unique year of African independence.

The human rights situations for all are complex. Three of the four experienced turbulent political transitions involving widespread violence; yet all are committed, at least constitutionally, to impressive ranges of civil and political rights, and to broadly worded social, economic, and cultural rights. They have pledged to the international community to promote and protect these rights. The states' ratification of major human rights treaties, such as the International Covenant on Economic, Social, and Cultural Rights or the African Charter on Human and Peoples' Rights, exemplifies their official commitment. Democracy with freely-contested elections is the official format for all. In reality, however, political choice has been circumscribed by the heritage of struggle, the interests of the armed forces, and ethnic and regional factors. Development represents another fundamental policy objective for the four governments. In reality, once again, the aspirations far outstrip the accomplishments.

In short, these four countries represent much of the spectrum of contemporary Africa, historically, socially, economically, and politically. Evidence drawn from Ethiopia, Namibia, Nigeria, and Senegal can thus be used as the basis for understanding sub-Saharan Africa as a whole.

None of them has achieved all its desired human rights goals. Major economic indicators declined in the late 1980s and early 1990s, exacerbating social and political tensions. This economic decline entailed cutbacks in education, and hence the possibility of spreading a "human rights culture" through widespread schooling. In terms of enforcement of human rights norms, as pledged in their constitutions and treaty ratifications, the four governments have fallen short to varying degrees. But in all these cases, government performance has been subjected to open domestic and international criticism. Human rights NGOs have emerged as sharp critics of national policies — and leaders of some of them have been imprisoned on flimsy charges. NGOs in Ethiopia, Namibia, Nigeria and Senegal have met with varying degrees of success in appealing to domestic courts or international supervisory bodies in order to have governments translate constitutional provisions or treaty commitments into clear policies. And finally, all four governments seemed to shrink from empowerment of previously quiescent groups, save under conditions they can dictate. Education, empowerment, and enforcement of human rights have all been circumscribed.

Ethiopia

Ethiopia's violent political history makes protection of human rights there both more difficult and more necessary. Ethiopia is a textbook case of political transformation from below, with the successful guerrilla struggle of the Ethiopian People's Revolutionary Democratic Front (EPRDF) in the late 1980s potentially transforming what had been an autocratic, Addis Ababa-centered political system. Some of the EPRDF's actions since taking power raise the specter of renewed centralized repression; others presage a markedly better future. A critical set of choices is now being made.

Between the early 1970s and the early 1990s, Ethiopia changed profoundly. It moved from the remnants of a feudalistic system ruled by a modernizing autocrat, through a creeping coup d'état culminating in a military dictatorship and self-proclaimed Marxist-Leninist republic, to a civil war ending in 1991 with the triumph of regionally-based groups and installation of a transitional government rhetorically committed to ruling democratically. It is a chronicle, in other words, of years of nearly continuous denial of human rights, of an atmosphere in which organized expressions of popular discontent had no legitimate role in the eyes of the rulers, followed by a rocky and as yet incomplete transition toward civil society and a widespread human rights culture.

My first visit to Ethiopia came in late 1973, when the International Congress of Africanists met in Addis Ababa. Emperor Haile Selassie I presided at the opening session in the impressive setting of Africa Hall. A few days later, the Emperor welcomed all participants at the most elaborate luncheon I have ever been served. Although Ethiopia was then racked by a severe drought which had driven hundreds of thousands from their homes in search of food, the capital (and certainly the demeanor of the royal court) bore little evidence of this social disaster. Security forces had removed thousands of semi-starved Ethiopians from the streets of Addis a few days earlier. The Emperor seemed unconcerned about the spreading social disaster. At the conference, I presented a paper on types of pre-colonial, colonial, and post-independence military organizations and their implications for Africa.[5] Little did I or other participants understand the tensions then building within the Ethiopian armed forces. Its members were sullen about their salaries and privileges. Younger officers and many enlistees were incensed by the Imperial Government's seeming paralysis in the face of widespread famine. On a broader level, resentment simmered among Eritreans, Somalis, Oromo, and other groups against the Amharas' political, economic, and social dominance. These tensions — an explosive mixture of ethnic, class, and corporate grievances — were to spell *finis* to Ethiopia's imperial government in the next few months.[6] Nearly sixteen years of harsh, centralized rule under military auspices were about to start. But the Emperor, his entourage, and most of the visiting Africanists seemed oblivious to the gathering storm.

Almost exactly twenty years later, I returned to Addis Ababa as part of the field work for this book. The trappings of royal power had been replaced by Kalashnikov-toting, fatigue-clad TPLF soldiers, discreetly guarding public buildings. The *Ethiopian Herald* (known in the early 1970s as the one-minute wonder, that being the amount of time necessary to extract any real news it might carry) no longer had to feature the head of state in all major stories but still conveyed the official government line; on the other hand, a host of other newspapers competed for readers' attention, more often through sensationalism than detailed, accurate reporting. Scores of political parties and NGOs operated out of crowded offices; in 1973 or 1985, by contrast, such organizational pluralism would not have been tolerated. A constitutional drafting committee was putting final touches on its product, drawing liberally from international human rights ideals, some Western constitutions, and the "Transitional Period Charter of Ethiopia," issued a few weeks after military dictator Mengistu Haile Mariam was overturned in June 1991. During Haile Selassie's reign, the constitution had been a gift from H.I.M. ("His Imperial Majesty"), intended to legitimize and reinforce power at the top rather than to provide for democracy from below; in Mengistu's day, the 1987 constitution was also imposed from above, despite rhetorical flourishes about popular sovereignty, and enshrined dictatorial power unchecked in any meaningful way. Then came the ouster of Mengistu. Human rights and civil society were subjects of widespread discussion, at least among intellectuals.

Contrasts between the political atmospheres of 1973 and of 1993 were thus stark. Deliberate reinforcement of the imperial system, with preservation of the emperor's powers, had marked the early 1970s and previous decades; dictatorial attempts to build power in the name of the people through a self-proclaimed Marxist-Leninist party had marked the late 1970s through mid-1980s. Conscious remaking of the political system, with institutionalization of democratic practices, was now the official goal. The term "human rights" did not occur in political dialogue under

Haile Selassie and Mengistu. By contrast, reference to the Universal Declaration of Human Rights peppered political conversations under the "transitional" EPRDF government. Its Charter ambitiously proclaimed

the overthrow of the military dictatorship . . . provid[es] the Peoples of Ethiopia with the opportunity to rebuild the country and restructure the state democratically . . . equal rights and self-determination of all the peoples shall be the governing principles of political, economic and social life. . . the proclamation of a democratic order is a categorical imperative. . . . Based on the Universal Declaration of Human Rights . . . individual human rights shall be respected fully, and without any limitation whatsoever. . . . [The Transitional Government] shall make special efforts to dispel ethnic mistrust and eradicate the ethnic hatred that have been fostered by the previous regimes.[7]

Ethiopia stands at the threshold of being able to establish, recognize and implement human rights to an unprecedented degree. Compared to other regimes in the country's history, the EPRDF has made more detailed verbal commitments to a democratic society than any of its forebears. As Human Rights Watch indicated in its 1993 report, "there has been significant progress toward respect for human rights in Ethiopia, and the Transitional Government remains more accountable on human rights matters than any other government in Ethiopian history."[8] More than 130 political parties had come into existence following the violent end of one-party rule, for example. Nonetheless, for reasons explored below, the process of establishing the requisite values and institutions will be prolonged. "The development of other institutions necessary for a flourishing civil society promises to be a slow process, despite the government's gradual enactment of legislation that is largely respectful of civil and political rights."[9]

The rich, complex history of Ethiopia defies easy (though not simplistic) analysis.[10] The basic outline can be quickly sketched. Unlike almost all the rest of Africa, Ethiopia experienced direct European colonial rule over its territory for only a few years (1935–42). Ethiopia was instead an indigenous African empire, its core in the mountainous central area inhabited by the Amharas and Tigreans. Much of present-day Ethiopia passed under Amhara rule during the late nineteenth century as a result of military conquest. As European powers seized control elsewhere in Africa, ambitious emperors (particularly Menelik II) pushed Abyssinia's frontiers outwards, rewarding effective soldiers with grants of land (including power over already-settled peasants).[11] Emperors used Imperial favors to reward or punish persons. *Shum-shir*, literally "up-down," described well how this feudalistic, personalized system operated for many decades. The country as a whole was (and remains) fiercely pluralistic. Recent estimates count upwards of eighty ethnic groups, with the Oromo

(30–50 percent), Amhara (15–20 percent) and Tigreans (just under 10 percent) among the most numerous.[12]

As Emperor, Haile Selassie prized institutions largely for their effectiveness in buttressing his control. He sought simultaneously to modernize the society and to maintain personal power. The constitution that came into force in 1956 resulted largely from Haile Selassie's own initiative.[13] One of the most important institutions was the army, simultaneously highly professionalized and directly linked to the Imperial person. The bureaucracy, under the general guidance of the "Minister of the Pen," served as well to reinforce central power. Political parties had no formal role, at least as Haile Selassie conceived of the system. Nor did organized interest groups. The press (to the extent one existed in Imperial Ethiopia) showed few stirrings of journalistic independence. Education remained a privilege rather than a right; location in or near a major town essentially determined whether a child would be schooled. The Imperial bureaucracy swallowed up the relatively few high school and university graduates. Though university students became more critical as their numbers grew, the attractiveness of government employment — and the astute use of *shum-shir* — kept them largely in line well into the 1960s. Ethiopian society was, in essence, a poor, rural peasant society dominated by a small, urbanized, and largely Amharic-speaking minority. The mosaic of autonomous associations typical of civil society scarcely existed in Ethiopia during the Imperial period.

The rule of the "Lion of Judah" — indeed, the power of an entire generation and class of largely Amhara officials and nobility — crashed in 1974. Haile Selassie was unceremoniously dethroned, stuffed into a Volkswagen, and taken away to prison in February 1974, where he died seven months later. Power passed to military officers. After several months of bloody in-fighting, the mantle of power was assumed by Mengistu Haile Mariam, head of the mysterious Derg ("committee") within the army.

Radical military rule in Ethiopia started with a great deal of popularity. This was a measure primarily of the ancien régime's unpopularity. Simply revising many of Haile Selassie's policies brought support for the Derg. The Imperial regime had shown fatal shortcomings, especially in handling the 1973 drought. Grievances had developed over the decades-old policy of settling demobilized soldiers in the south. The extinction of Eritrean autonomy[14] had aroused tensions in that area. Somali desires for unification under one flag had heightened tensions in the Haud and Ogaden sections of the east. The new regime not only inherited these problems, but multiplied them through errors of its own.

As an Afro-Marxist state, Ethiopia under Mengistu's rule did seek, and in its early years did find, a degree of popular popular legitimation. The

Derg's conception of human rights derived from a Soviet model, emphasizing economic development through highly centralized control. Ethiopian society would have to be transformed, according to this perspective.
Since all history was the history of class struggle, and since Imperial rule
had fostered a parasitic, feudalistic class, wiping out its remnants would
supposedly directly advance the good of others. Wresting land away from
landlords, particularly in the south (Keffa, Gemu Gofa, Sidamo), and
redistributing it to the original inhabitants won the Derg much local
popularity. This good will was rapidly squandered, however, by forcing
these peasants to pool their newly-(re)acquired lands for collective farms,
often under the guidance of urban ideologues. "Procedural" civil and
political rights were seen as marginal to the greater tasks of popular
mobilization around economic development and the vanguard political
party, the Workers' Party of Ethiopia. As the 1985 State Department
report on human rights practices commented, "The country remains
without civil or political freedoms and without institutions or laws to protect its citizens' human rights."[15] No safety valve of grass-roots participation existed, save through instruments (such as the ubiquitous *kebeles*)
designed to control the populace. Mengistu and his close associates exercised power "through arbitrary arrest and intimidation."[16] Their marked
emphasis on centralization and ready reliance on the use of force —
leading to the largest standing army in sub-Saharan Africa — were to have
disastrous consequences for human rights. Mengistu ruled with an iron
fist. As various regions sought to slough off centralized, largely Amhara
rule, he ordered massive attacks. His counter-insurgency strategy, as de
Waal has documented in detail, consciously involved starving rebellious
areas into surrender. At least one million lives, and potentially 1.5 million, were lost as a consequence.[17] This human toll was accompanied by
another cost: "the stifling of any initiatives towards democracy, the rule of
law, and the development of civil society."[18] The years of Derg rule were
without question dark ones indeed for Ethiopia.

The Achilles heel of the Mengistu government proved to be its inability
to cope with regional insurgencies, themselves intensified by the lack of
effective, responsive political institutions. The exactions of the regime
sapped its legitimacy. The more the Derg tried to maintain Ethiopia as a
centralized state, the more it aroused antagonisms, and the more powerful initially small guerrilla groups became. Regional sentiment grew, with
resentment of Amhara dominance.[19] Vigorous military pressure against
the Eritreans, Oromos, and Tigreans thus backfired, resulting in greater
support for the rebels. The swollen Ethiopian army, which benefited
from billions of dollars worth of Soviet equipment and the forced con-
scription of hundreds of thousands of young men, found its logistical and
numerical superiority ultimately counter-productive. Policies of central-

ized control, extensive use of force, and denial of human rights were central to Mengistu's rise to power, his control of it, and his ultimate loss of it. Having taken control by palace coup, the Mengistu regime was to perish by popular revolt.

The end of the Derg's power was at hand by the end of 1990. While other states in Africa were renewing political authority through sovereign national conferences and other steps toward strengthening civil society, Ethiopia was crumbling. The regime confronted a coalition with growing strength. The Ethiopian Peoples' Revolutionary Democratic Front (EPRDF) was formed in 1988 as an alliance among insurgent groups. Its forces, comprised largely of Eritreans, Tigreans, and Oromos, by that point controlled essentially all Eritrea, plus Gondar, Welo, and Tigre regions. Armed EPRDF units reached the outskirts of Addis Ababa by mid-May 1991. The disgruntled, alienated Ethiopian military put up little resistance. In a whirlwind of behind-the-scenes deals, Western diplomats arranged for Mengistu to go into exile in Zimbabwe, and for the EPRDF to form a transitional government pending national elections, a new constitution, and other trappings necessary for democracy and future peaceful transfers of power. Thus ended a sorry chapter in Ethiopia's history.

The timing of the change in regime was important. Tropical Africa as a whole turned an important political corner with the advent of the 1990s. The model of the one-party centralized state had become discredited, as had rule by military officers. The collapse of the Soviet Union, following the sweep of democratic movements across eastern Europe in 1989, removed the major international backer of Afro-Marxist governments. Erstwhile military regimes faced a bitter choice between voluntary and forced withdrawal.[20] A choice existed between peaceful transitions of power (as inaugurated in the West African republics of Benin and Cape Verde, where incumbent heads of state were defeated in open elections in 1990), and violent removal of presidents (as occurred in neighboring Somalia, Mali, and Liberia as well as Ethiopia). Competitive elections and other attributes of democracy — including human rights and encouragement of civil society — became the order of the day.

Human rights entered the Ethiopian political vocabulary in part through external influences at this time of critical regime change. As Communist governments in Eastern Europe had collapsed through their economic and political failings, so non-democratic systems in Africa seemed ripe for replacement. In mid-1991, the Bush administration was putting finishing touches on a major new policy initiative toward Africa. Governments would be judged not necessarily by the "stability" they imposed, but by effective "governance" they practiced, including popular participation. Economic assistance was to be conditioned, in large part, on steps toward free elections. Democratization became both objective and measuring rod. This more activist American policy, centered on democracy and human rights, found one of its first applications in Ethiopia. The U.S. Embassy was perceived as a center of strong support for a quasi-competitive political system, although the EPRDF's de facto domination gave little encouragement to opposition movements.[21]

Domestic factors were more significant than international factors in the lurch toward democratization, however. The Transitional Government of President Meles Zenawi wished to do more than satisfy external powers; it had an internal agenda to implement as rapidly as possible. The new EPRDF government wanted to enhance regional autonomy.[22] Conditions in 1991 made this imperative. Provincial and ethnic awareness had been intensified by the guerrilla struggle. Peaceful secession for Eritrea had to be arranged, for (despite grumbling in the capital) there was no way it could be reintegrated into Ethiopia. Dismantling the hated institutions of the Mengistu period was imperative. Within a few weeks of taking power, as noted earlier in this chapter, the Transitional Government of Ethiopia (TGE) issued its charter, with immense potential implications for human rights. All military and police forces were fired, their places taken by EPRDF fighters. Within Ethiopia itself, major change was underway.

Issuing the Charter and replacing the security forces were simple. Translating Charter commitments into legislation and litigation proved far more complex than the TGE had anticipated, however. Basic questions about human rights had to be answered. How could, and should, the TGE deal with the abuses of the past? What trials should be held for persons who committed extra-judicial killings? How would the new rulers cope with the accumulated grievances and frustrations brought by decades of authoritarianism and ethnic or regional discrimination? Might the aspirations enhanced by policies of the new regime, especially in proposing greater ethnic autonomy, outstrip its ability to deliver? Questions of this magnitude affected the context within which the first significant human rights organizations in Ethiopia took shape.

One of the most difficult issues with which governments all over Africa must deal is meeting popular expectations while institutional capacity may be waning. With the collapse or removal of authoritarian rule, aspirations for improvement explode. Feeling about a "second independence" bringing immediate benefits could not be denied. But while the *political* resources available to rulers may have increased (albeit temporarily) as a result of promising better human rights performance, their *economic* resources and *administrative* capability may ironically have shriveled. The demand for better protection of rights and freedoms has not

come at a easy point in the continent's history, given Africa's marginalization and decline of recent years. Leaders invite credibility gaps, promising more than they can deliver. The commitments of the EPRDF to collective rights illustrate this point well. The political space within which
Ethiopian human rights NGOs operate has been expanded by the Transitional Government's commitment to the Universal Declaration and to
greater ethnic autonomy (self-determination); yet this high-stakes gamble could involve changes in Ethiopia beyond the already accomplished
independence of Eritrea. It could result in a substantial dismantling of
Ethiopia as a single state and fundamental challenges to the revolutionary government.

The TGE Charter broke new ground (at least in Africa) by recognizing
collective rights of ethnic groups, including their right to secession. To
quote specifically from Article 2:

> The right of nations, nationalities and peoples to self-determination is af-
> firmed. To this end, each nation, nationality and people is guaranteed the right
> to:
> a) Preserve its identity and have it respected, promote its language and his-
>   tory and use and develop its language;
> b) Administer its own affairs within its own defined territory and effectively
>   participate in the central government on the basis of freedom, and fair and
>   proper representation;
> c) Exercise its right to self-determination or independence, when the con-
>   cerned nation/nationality and people is convinced that the above rights
>   are denied, abridged or abrogated.[23]

No other African country has taken such far-ranging steps, although
many have espoused decentralization of power and far greater exercise
of local power. (Indeed, democratization, to meet popular expectations,
necessitates such moves away from top-down administration, as Owusu
illustrated.)[24] It is a set of assertions well beyond Nigeria's creation of new
states and commitment to the country's "federal character," or Senegal's
rhetorical commitment to greater regional powers, for example.

The newly-installed Ethiopian government made these sweeping promises out of a combination of political realism, idealism, and desire to break
with the past. The coalition that militarily overturned the Mengistu regime comprised several regional movements, linked not only by their
opposition to the Derg and its punitive policies,[25] but also by their wish to
move power away from the Amharas with whom the ousted government
had increasingly identified itself. Political sensitivity dictated that the
Eritreans, Tigreans, Oromos, and others who fought successfully would
redistribute power. The secession of Eritrea was a foregone conclusion; it
remained only to let a two-year transition pass, arrange for international

monitoring, then welcome the new Eritrean state as Africa's youngest country. But how far might this precedent apply to other parts of the country?

Self-determination as a collective right poses extremely ticklish issues in tropical Africa. To compress a vast literature to its essentials, two forms are commonly recognized: "external" and "internal." The former has now been achieved south of the Sahara; the latter remains a subject of sharp dispute.

"External" self-determination involves achieving independence from foreign rule. It is a once-and-for-all-times change. It is recognized in the International Covenants on Economic, Social, and Cultural Rights (ICESCR) and on Civil and Political Rights (ICCPR) at their very beginning. Article 1 of the ICESCR and the ICCPR states, "All peoples have the right to self-determination. By virtue of that right they freely determine their political status and freely pursue their economic, social and cultural development." The sentiments that motivated this article were drawn from the 1960 UN resolution on the granting of independence to colonial countries and peoples. Once independence was achieved, leaders in Africa and elsewhere held that inherited boundaries were to be preserved. The principle of self-determination should not be invoked for secession. The Organization of African Unity, established in Addis Ababa in 1963, set preservation of independence, maintenance of inherited boundaries, and national unity as basic principles.

"Internal" self-determination differs. It refers to steps taken domestically to provide measures of administrative, fiscal, and political power to groups or regions. It does not — at least according to almost all African leaders until the independence of Eritrea — mean that existing sovereign states should be carved up on ethnic or regional lines. This sentiment is deeply rooted. "Balkanization" was explicitly rejected by the Organization of African Unity when it was founded in 1963. Strong resentment was expressed earlier against the leaders of Katanga, Biafra, and the "homelands" in South Africa for seeking to destroy inherited boundaries. There is no question that African leaders feared that their newly-independent countries would fragment along social fault lines such as ethnicity. They strengthened central governments (many of which soon decayed into one-man regimes) as a consequence. Ethiopia was typical. The Mengistu administration fought against any type of secession or even regional autonomy, and thus helped dig its own grave. Its EPRDF successor recognized Eritrea's irreversible march toward independence, but had to question whether other sections of the country could, would, and should claim the same opportunity.

In contemporary Ethiopia, then, salient issues of human rights exist on several levels. First is the macro issue of collective rights, notably self-determination. What limits does the EPRDF government have in mind with its encouragement of ethnic autonomy? This concern is greatest with respect to the Oromo. The Oromo Liberation Front (OLF) formed part of the triumphant EPRDF. Within a few months of the change of government, the OLF had withdrawn from the coalition and refused to participate in elections. Open conflict erupted, and 19,000 OLF fighters were detained by the government in mid-1992. If the Oromo seek empowerment through various means, will this lead them out of the multi-ethnic Ethiopian state? Second is the continuing problem of impoverishment. Lack of development, particularly in rural areas, means the lives of many are "nasty, brutish and short." Higher popular expectations unleashed by the defeat of the Derg collide with the limited resources available to the government (even if external donors are generous). Does this mean that, without economic growth and improved distribution, other human rights will be undercut? Third is the establishment of civil and political rights, in a context historically marked by authoritarianism. Can effective enforcement of rights occur where the legal system is so weak?[26] Can the prosecution of officials of the former Derg reinforce nascent human rights awareness?[27] If major international human rights treaties are not ratified, can Ethiopian NGOs use fora outside their country to bring pressure on the government? The efforts of EHRCO (Ethiopian Human Rights Council), the Inter-Africa Group, Forum-84, the Ethiopian Congress for Democracy and other nascent human rights groups are thus being made in a politically charged environment, with highly limited economic resources, with widespread popular expectations for major improvement, and with limited opportunity for rectification through the legal system. Human rights NGOs in Ethiopia confront a complex situation indeed.

Namibia

Next to Eritrea, Namibia is Africa's youngest state. It too experienced major political violence in its transition to independence, from the brutal days of German occupation through the conquest by South Africa early in World War I, up to the guerrilla struggle led by SWAPO (South West Africa People's Organization) in the 1970s and 1980s. Independence, which came on March 21, 1990, resulted from both domestic and international struggle against a determined occupier.

For 75 years, South Africa administered Namibia as, in effect, a "fifth province," imposing apartheid-style laws contrary to evolving norms of international human rights law. Other external powers, working with and through the United Nations, played direct roles in Namibia's political evolution. In a real sense, Namibia was, and is, a showcase for international pressure bringing substantive political change. Namibia's success as a color-blind, democratic, and developing society can teach a lesson to the world, and in particular to neighboring South Africa.

Namibia's small population is scattered over vast distances. Most of Namibia is uninhabited desert. Agriculture is possible only along the Okovango River of the north, where members of the country's largest ethnic group, the Owambo, have long resided. Mining and ranching dominate the economy. Namibia figures among the world's major producers of uranium and diamonds. Government offices and most manufacturing are centered in Windhoek, the spacious capital. People are separated not only by tremendous geographic distances, but also by significant economic and social gulfs. While whites and a growing number of blacks enjoy the pleasant life of the capital, working class Africans are overwhelmingly concentrated in the adjacent township of Katatura — in the Herero language, "the place we do not want to settle."[28] Patterns of racial discrimination were enforced by decades of apartheid legislation. Economic and political power were concentrated in white hands. Afrikaans-, English- and German-speaking whites constitute five percent of the population, but dominate major industry, large-scale farming, and professional positions. Old habits of presumed racial superiority persist among some whites, and discrimination continues to be "a very sensitive political issue."[29] This inherited pattern cannot immediately be overcome. Color-blind guarantees in the Constitution, prohibition in Article 23 of the "practice and ideology of apartheid," and a December 1991 law banning race as a criterion for eligibility for membership in a cultural society were hence important steps. For in Namibia as elsewhere, the establishment of a propitious human rights climate takes time and conscious effort. Building popular confidence in the legal system, and belief in a color-blind rule of law, stand as primary tasks.

Namibia experienced, one could argue, a longer period of international involvement in its domestic politics than any other contemporary African state. Oversight started shortly after World War I, when a treaty between the Union of South Africa and the League of Nations created a "mandate."[30] The former German colony of Southwest Africa was to be administered as an "integral part" of South Africa. Nonetheless, regular reports had to be submitted to the Permanent Mandates Commission (a nine-member [later expanded to 10] committee of experts established by the League of Nations to monitor conditions in former German and Ottoman possessions) on how the goals of the treaty were being met. In reality, very little changed. South Africa regarded Southwest Africa as a for-all-times addition to its territory. Hence, when the Permanent Mandates Commission lapsed with the birth of the United Nations, South Africa refused to report to the new international body, arguing that the goals of the mandate had been accomplished. A decades-long legal and political tussle ensued, involving (among other events) important advisory decisions by the International Court of Justice,[31] General Assembly resolutions, and eventually even action by the Security Council.[32]

But while diplomats and international lawyers argued about Namibia in the marbled halls of New York City, The Hague, and elsewhere, residents of the territory carried out their own major push from below. The independence of Namibia ultimately resulted from guerrilla struggle, intensifying the pressures on South Africa by major international actors.

SWAPO started its guerrilla action in the late 1960s, as potential peaceful steps toward autonomy ran headlong into South Africa's intransigence and the failure of global institutions to change its attitude. In particular, the 1966 advisory judgment by the International Court of Justice — a highly disappointing 8–7 decision (in which the President of the Court voted twice to break a tie) that the Court lacked jurisdiction to determine whether the territory was being administered in the "best interests" of the inhabitants — caused SWAPO to reconsider its *modus operandi*. In addition to pressing for international recognition of the justness of its call for self-determination, SWAPO decided to recruit and train guerrilla fighters for a people's war. Troops for PLAN — People's Liberation Army of Namibia — were drawn largely from the Owambos. Modest military assistance came from China, the Soviet Union, and some African countries. The long border with Angola provided, for a few years, a zone of refuge, training, and regrouping. Their direct military successes were limited. Determined resistance by South Africa stalled the small number of SWAPO fighters. The Botha government, following a "forward" strategy, occupied southern Angola to flush out SWAPO troops and threw increasing numbers of South African forces, plus troops raised in Namibia itself (the South West Africa Territorial Force, or SWATF; special groups of trackers, drawn from the Bushmen; others) into the battle. The armed struggle was long and bloody.

As already noted, the international community took an exceptionally prominent role in the twisting path to Namibia's independence. The UN General Assembly established a Council for Namibia in May 1967 (Resolution 2248), eight months after voting to terminate South Africa's mandate (Resolution 2145). The UN Security Council set a framework for evolution in Resolution 435 of 29 September 1978, by means of which a five Western-nation contact group (Canada, France, West Germany, the United States, and the United Kingdom) engaged in intense negotiations with South Africa and SWAPO, on behalf of the entire UN. This effort soon foundered on the shoals of Great Power competition. The eruption of the Cold War in an adjacent part of southern Africa changed the American tune in particular, and resulted in the near-collapse of the

contact group's effort. As civil war in Angola flared, its MPLA government received extensive Soviet and Cuban military assistance, raising the
specter of east-west confrontation; the United States became involved.
President Reagan vigorously supported UNITA, the chief domestic opponent of the MPLA, because of its "anti-Communist" pretensions. The
whole contact group process slowed, nearly shuddering to a halt.

It took nearly a decade for new international negotiations to succeed.[33]
During this period, SWAPO's guerrilla forces grew in tandem with global
disapproval of South African policies. Diplomats finally hammered out a
plan of phased Cuban disengagement from Angola and South African
withdrawal from Namibia. The path was cleared for the agreement on
Namibia's independence. A new start could be made, free from the incubus of apartheid. The United Nations took a major role through UNTAG
(United Nations Transition Advisory Group) and appointment of a su-
pervisor to watch over the South African administration during the specified interim period. In keeping with a 1982 set of principles endorsed by
the Security Council,[34] free elections were held for a constituent assembly, SWAPO holding 41 of the 72 seats. A constitution featuring strong
human rights clauses was drafted and promulgated; the constituent assembly was transformed into a national assembly; Namibia started its
independent life as a functioning democratic system.

With this, I am tempted to write, the most difficult human rights work
began. Translating the words of the constitution into a vibrant reality
does not come easily, given the decades of inequalities fostered by apartheid, the gap between resources and desires, and the nascent state of civil
society in Namibia. Transforming liberation-oriented groups that had
struggled against the regime into potential partners for development
and legal enforcement required time and sensitivity.

In the largest sense of human rights, the first issue to be confronted was
that of self-determination. Not, as in the Charter of the Transitional
Government of Ethiopia, for ethnic groups, but for the country as a
whole. As already noted, Article 1 of both the International Covenant on
Civil and Political Rights and the International Covenant on Economic,
Social, and Cultural Rights places the achievement of independence as a
prerequisite to determining political status and economic, social, and
cultural development. The struggle for self-determination lasted decades, but was fulfilled in March 1990. The new government of Namibia
was immediately recognized, and a relatively large flow of foreign aid
(relative to the population) started.

The human rights situation in Namibia in its early years of independence has been among the most favorable in all of Africa, as shown in
recent reports. Namibian citizens enjoy significantly higher levels of human rights protection than do citizens of the 11 African countries dis-

cussed in detail by Human Rights Watch in its 1993 report.[35] Amnesty International gave a little more than one column to Namibia in its 1993 report, noting that reports of torture or ill-treatment by police had been met by investigations ordered by government authorities.[36] In other words, ordinary citizens did not have to fear police shakedowns or beatings, a situation rare in much of Africa. The United States Department of State report applauded the country's functioning multi-party, multi-racial democracy, with its constitutionally entrenched bill of rights.[37] The rancor and strains inevitable from decades of guerrilla struggle against a racist regime thus appeared to these observers to have been largely overcome. Although accounting for disappearances during the liberation struggle concerned some human rights NGOs, the accommodating attitude of the government was held by others to have defused the situation.[38]

How can this semingly auspicious start in terms of human rights be explained? Can it be maintained? Is Namibia benefiting on a short-term basis from the international publicity and assistance it has received, or are human rights already firmly embedded in its socio-political setting? What roles do Namibian NGOs play in implementing the constitution's guarantees? We shall analyze the activities of the Legal Assistance Centre in detail later. A few comparative points should be made at this juncture, however.

Compared with Ethiopia, Namibia's context for human rights seems far more favorable. Civil war ravaged Ethiopia much more than Namibia. Accommodation among groups seems marked in Namibia, although Owambo dominance (a demographic and political fact) arouses some concern. Ethiopia is racked by sharp ethnic tensions, perhaps inadvertantly accentuated by the Charter of the Transitional Government, the independence of Eritrea, and disputes between Amharas, Tigreans and Oromos. Owambos hold most significant positions in Namibia, but others have been welcomed; by contrast, some Amharas in Ethiopia feel marginalized relative to their position under Haile Selassie and Mengistu, and the Oromos (the largest of all groups) remain restive. Small arms are widely diffused throughout Ethiopia, and both dismissed soldiers of the Mengistu regime and Oromo Liberation Front members harbor resentments against the EPRDF. By contrast, the new Namibian army is a composite entity, deliberately constituted from elements of both PLAN (the armed branch of SWAPO) and the SWATF (the security force established to safeguard South African rule). Namibia has experienced open democratic elections, under international monitoring, considered free of fraud or intimidation. Ethiopia had no real history of political party competition under the Emperor or the Derg; its 1992 local and regional elections were flawed by numerous irregularities and the withdrawal of opposition parties a few days prior to balloting.[39] The National Assembly is perceived by many as little more than an EPRDF fief-dom. By contrast, the main opposition party to SWAPO, the DTA (Democratic Turnhalle Alliance), remains active in parliament, openly debating with the government. Whites continue to hold core economic power, and account for a high share of senior government positions.[40] Although Namibia remains heavily dependent on mining, global recession has not impacted as heavily on it as on Ethiopia, which is classified by the United Nations among the world's 25 poorest countries.

Both countries are building on new political and social foundations: Namibia through SWAPO members, Ethiopia through the TPLF (Tigrean Peoples Liberation Front) and other members of the EPRDF coalition. At the same time, however, leaders of both states risk alienating other groups whose support they must eventually acquire, if the more favorable human rights climate of early independence / post-military triumph is to continue. The challenges to both must not be minimized. Significant problems exist in both democratization and development.

Nigeria

Armed revolt from below appeared, in the instances of Ethiopia and Namibia, to have fostered human rights. Military direction of politics from above, in the case of Nigeria, seems instead to have jeopardized human rights.

No analysis of contemporary Africa can overlook the "sleeping giant" of Nigeria. It is Africa's most populous country, accounting for nearly a fifth of the continent's more than 550 million people. Nigeria has sought to lead at regional, continental, and global levels, for example in giving impetus to ECOMOG (a military observer group drawn largely from the Nigerian armed forces) during the Liberian civil war, and has actively campaigned for a permanent seat on the United Nations Security Council. It enjoyed a brief economic boom during the 1970s as a result of burgeoning petroleum revenues. As a result, ambitious development schemes were accelerated, including Universal Primary Education (UPE). Nigeria's 1979 Constitution and 1989 revision set forth both entrenched civil and political rights and fundamental principles of state policy including economic and social development. In short, the country has unmistakable importance.

A vast literature on Nigerian politics exists.[41] Yet the most significant political disputes in the country have remained hidden from scholars' eyes. Members of the officer corps have ruled Nigeria for nearly two-thirds of its independent history. Details of discussions within the various military governments — at various times, called the Federal Military Government, the Supreme Military Government, or the Armed Forces Ruling Council — have not leaked into the media. Plots and failed coups have been brutally crushed. Unsuccessful intra-military challengers have been tried in camera and usually executed after procedurally flawed trials.[42] Electoral campaigns have on occasion exacerbated tensions; and inept responses by the armed forces to democratic pressures from below have further worsened the situation. Clearly, the long-term good health of Nigeria requires a stable, orderly, effective, and democratic means of changing governments, with adequate protection of human rights.

The promises of Nigeria have not been matched by its performance. Squandered opportunities and resources mark the Nigerian malaise. The fault lies largely with military officers who have fallen short in their self-proclaimed task of reforming the economic and political systems. As Human Rights Watch wrote, "The blame for many of the human right abuses during [1992] can be tied directly to the failure of the Armed Forces Ruling Council (AFRC) to leave office as promised."[43] Human rights "remained circumscribed" as the military haltingly loosened its grip on power.[44] Removing the men in khaki from political power has become the fundamental goal for many Nigerian activists. The most vexing human rights issue is accordingly the armed forces' centrality to the political process. As long as they remain in power, it can be argued, democracy and the rule of law are jeopardized.

Popular participation in Nigerian politics has been episodic and negligible, dependent on the twists and turns of intra-military politics. A rhythm of expectation followed by deeper disappointment and cynicism has developed. Although a regime newly installed by a coup d'état may enjoy temporary popularity, its welcome soon fades. Nigerian history is littered with the wrecks of military governments, several having been displaced by colleagues in arms, others having retreated voluntarily to the barracks after handing over control to civilians. The first coup-installed government, led by Brigadier J. T. A. Aguyi-Ironsi, ruled from January 15 to July 27, 1966, before being ousted by intra-military revolt. The successor regime, under General Yakubu Gowon, lasted until mid-1975, fighting a bloody civil war en route. Proposals for redemocratization remained unimplemented. Public resentment grew. Gowon was deposed by fellow officers led by Colonel Murtala Mohammed on July 29, 1975; they were motivated in part by the increasingly tarnished popular image of the armed forces. Stability proved difficult to establish. The assassination of Murtala in February 1976 revealed how ethnic and regional tensions had spilled over from society into the military. Murtala's successor, Brigadier Segun Obasanjo, implemented Murtala's disengagement program. The Second Republic was installed October 1, 1979, after hard-fought competitive elections, conducted under rules intended by the outgoing soldiers to reduce ethnic and regional tensions. This return of civilians to power occurred at the crest of petroleum revenues — which politicians wasted no time in squandering on pet projects. As Schatz observed, "Access to, and manipulation of, the government spending process has become the golden gateway to fortune."[45] (A temptation, to be certain, to military officers as well as civilian politicians!) The boom lasted but a few months. The new civilian government appeared incapable of coping with the massive collapse of oil revenues in the early 1980s. It proved far easier to expand than to rein in expenditures. Rampant corruption disgusted many military officers. On December 31, 1983, yet another coup was staged. The authoritarian government of General Muhammadu Buhari assumed office, using what were, by Nigerian standards of the time, draconian measures against opponents. It was in this context of disappointed public expectations in the rule of both civilians and officers that Major General Ibrahim Babangida (number three in the hierarchy) seized control August 27, 1985.[46]

Babangida reduced restrictions imposed by his predecessors. As a leading specialist observed, "From its initial statements and actions and the enthusiastic popular reception it received, the Babangida coup appeared to mark a decisive rejection of the previous authoritarian trend."[47] For example, he repealed a widely-protested press decree, formed a committee to look at detainees, named an outspoken human rights advocate as Attorney-General and Minister of Justice, and ordered the release of about 150 persons held without charges.[48] Because of parlous financial conditions, he declared a state of economic emergency, although he refused to accept an IMF loan because of the stringent conditions attached.[49] He promised to set in motion a process of reconstitutionalization, returning the military to the barracks in a few years. A so-called "Political Bureau" was inaugurated in early 1986, concurrent with reforms in local government. Babangida's early steps did not mean he was willing to allow a return to "politics as normal," however. He warned many times that democracy could not function in Nigeria without substantial changes in the ways politicians operated, and advocated change in terms he frequently altered. The date of effective recivilianization retreated and retreated and retreated.

In other words, Nigeria had to be reformed *to the military's satisfaction* before disengagement could be completed. The armed forces, in turn, had little reason to stand down. Babangida perceived major weaknesses in civilians who sought to succeed him: widespread corruption used to gain elective office; mammoth fraud and favoritism that marked the exercise of power; unwarranted criticism of those in power; inflaming of ethnic, regional, religious, and class antagonisms. He should have examined his own actions critically! Most of these were rooted in Nigeria's political culture, but were exacerbated, I am convinced, by the Babangida government's policies. Powerful economic and political incentives existed for the armed forces to retain their grip on power. Shrinking resources could entail severe budget cuts; disputes among civilian groups could spill over into the military. Hence, the transition to elected government went through numerous fits and starts, suffered unexpected delays, and ended up as an exercise in political frustration rather than legitimation. In the process, human rights remained severely abridged and NGOs became increasingly vocal critics of the government.

The most blatant examples of Babangida's direct involvement in politics came in reshaping the system of political parties and annulling elections.

The federal nature of Nigeria under colonialism, and the presence of dominant ethnic groups in the three Regions, resulted in an unusual structure of political competition. No overarching grand coalition or single nationalist movement arose, unlike the majority of African states. Each region had, at independence, its own home-grown party based on the largest group (in the East, the NCNC [National Council of Nigeria and the Cameroons], identified with the Igbo; in the West, the Action Group, identified with the Yoruba; in the North, the NPC [Northern Peoples Congress], identified with traditional Fulani rulers). There was, in addition, at least one significant opposition party in each region, identified with minority groups. Electoral and governmental alliances were thus liable to complex combinations of ethnic and regional loyalties. Politics allowed the winners to dine at the golden trough of government; losers were shut out. Patronage became a central function of parties; the various levels of administration were staffed by the faithful; ethnicity provided an undercurrent. That these patterns were deeply entrenched emerged clearly in the run-up to the 1979 elections when, despite the banning of "old breed" politicians, supposedly new parties turned out to resemble their banned predecessors. Efforts to ensure "federal character" fell short.[50]

When Babangida reopened opportunities for party formation in May 1989, the old script was replayed, even with what were supposed to be totally new casts of characters. They were not. Personality, region, and basic belief were too deeply rooted in Nigerian political culture to be eradicated by military dictum. Within a few months, 49 political associations had surfaced, 13 of which sought registration with the National Electoral Commission. On October 7, two days after the National Electoral Commission had recommended official recognition of six parties, President Babangida exploded the bombshell planted earlier by the Political Bureau, which had suggested the possibility of a two-party system. He dissolved all the aspirant groups and ordained the creation of two new ones. As he stated, "The prevailing attitude appeared to be that every Nigerian wanted to be a 'founder' and no one wanted to be a 'joiner.' " Everyone wanted to be a leader of a party, or a close associate of the leader."[51] He also faulted the supposed lack of distinct ideologies and the links to erstwhile politicians. As an alternative, the new system would be comprised of the NRC (National Republican Convention, "a little to the right of center") and the SDP (Social Democratic Party, "a little to the left of center").

Quasi-controlled competition hence emerged by military administrative fiat, rather than by "natural" evolution. Presidential candidates would have to be cleared by a powerful National Electoral Commission, and politicians identified with previous governments disqualified. To reduce the likelihood of fraud, voters would queue up publicly in lines for their choice and be counted, rather than cast secret ballots. The parties themselves would be financed by the government. Their officials would be trained in the techniques of democracy by the Centre for Democratic Studies (an entity to which we return in a later chapter). The NRC and SDP would have to provide tangible evidence of national support, based on complicated electoral rules for Presidential elections. Appeals to regional, religious, ethnic, or sectional interests would be barred. No aspect of party organization seemed to be left to chance. Rhetorically, Babangida wanted to march out of power proudly, certain his successor would embody a new beginning in political values for Nigeria's Third Republic. It was to be inaugurated October 1, 1990; it was not. For behaviorally as opposed to rhetorically, Babingida moved in the contrary direction. He was far more concerned with maintaining his grip on power than with surrendering control to elected officials. There were four postponements of the official hand-over date. Babangida and his cronies distrusted change along lines other than those they prescribed from on high, their prescriptions often taking the form of ex post facto denial of political party registration, cancellation of party primaries, and removal of candidates. Evidence mounted of the increased restiveness of hardliners within the military administration. A tug-of-war between hawks wanting to hold onto control and doves arguing that failure to disengage would seriously harm the armed forces took place in "The Villa," as the sprawling presidential compound in the capital of Abuja is known. The hawks won; Nigeria lost. The cancellation of the 1993 vote mid-way through ballot counting aborted progress toward democracy. The role of human rights NGOs became even more complex.

In the judgment of observers, Nigeria enjoyed a generally fair, open presidential election election June 12, 1993. Nonetheless, Babangida annulled the results less than two weeks later. He claimed that the balloting had been "hopelessly flawed," but he seriously misread the national mood, and in particular the sense in the Yoruba southwest that it was "their" turn to provide the president. Babangida and his coterie of advisers were surprised by the vehemence of the popular response in Lagos — indication of his government's distance from public opinion. (In a similar vein, as will be discussed subsequently, leaders of the Campaign for Democracy were themselves amazed by the extent to which the people of Lagos answered their call to strike.) Denying the validity of the election galvanized a coalition of NGOs into action, linked by their rejection of the regime's action. Under pressure from the same military colleagues who had counselled him to "hang tough," Babangida had to concede the formal reins of power and go into retirement. His farewell address, given August 27, seemed long on words, short on understanding the political dynamic:

the administration took the painful decision [to annul the elections] in good faith and in the interest of [the] stability and security of the nation as well as for the enhancement of democracy. The annulment might have created tension and a sense of frustration in some quarters, but it was most certainly not intended as a sabotage of the expectations of the electorate. . . . We are determined not to let temporary setbacks upset the building blocks of unity set by our past heroes.[52]

The ignominious collapse of Nigeria's lengthy, costly experiment in democratization came as a disappointment on several fronts. Efforts to bring a new generation of leaders into existence failed. The regime's efforts with a mandated two-party system, "Grassroots Democracy," and explicit training through the Centre for Democratic Studies, seemed to come to naught. Democratization from above was jerry-rigged on a slippery foundation. Empowerment from below also met with setbacks. Despite massive protests, examined below in Chapter 8, the Campaign for Democracy (a coalition of NGOs supporting rapid removal of the military government) failed to carry the day. The CD ran up squarely against serious obstacles: only in the southwest were their strike calls heeded; pro-government groups castigated the CD as a "front" for tribal (Yoruba) interests; the coalition splintered, as leaders disagreed on the best strategy; the fevered political pitch of summer 1993 could not be sustained. Human rights groups faced the dilemma of deepening their political involvement or of narrowing their focus; in any event, it was a cruel choice.

Thus, while broader political participation and greater protection of human rights came about in Ethiopia and Namibia as a result of guerrilla struggle from below and international pressure from above, greater democratization and human rights in Nigeria remains a domestic political matter, pitting an incumbent military against various civilian groups. The difficulties Nigeria's most recent military government confronted in fulfilling its promises of disengagement brought human rights NGOs to the center of the political vortex. ˙

Perhaps the most active assemblage of human rights NGOs in tropical Africa can be found in Nigeria. They are among the oldest and most active. The struggle for a transparent electoral process, with results honored by those in power, has been pressed by the Campaign for Democracy, an umbrella for several organizations. Many other human rights issues have come to the fore. For example, the Constitutional Rights Project and the Civil Liberties Organisation have highlighted prison conditions, arbitrary arrests, and police brutality. They and other groups have encouraged training of paralegals and legal aid clinics. The Legal Research and Resources Development Centre has enlightened the public through a series of easy-to-understand brochures. Women's groups have fostered steps toward gender equality. Other efforts could be highlighted. There is no question that the difficult human rights situation in Nigeria requires active indigenous monitoring groups, ready and able both to report the abuses they observed and to take corrective actions.

But there is also no doubt that the off-again, on-again nature of national elections and full hand-over of government reins to elected officials has weakened Nigerian civil society. The tasks of political construction remain immense. I carried out my field work in Nigeria early in 1994. The official handover of power from the "transitional" government had yet to take place. Babangida had stepped down from power August 27, 1993, and installed an "interim" civilian-headed government. However, a fellow officer, Sani Abacha, had taken over the presidency November 17, 1993. Political decay continued unabated. Nigerians by this time were thoroughly disheartened by the obstacles to democratization. Their country's economy, despite its petro-dollars, was in shambles. Major cities were torn by strikes and demonstrations. Violence flared in rural areas, particularly over land claims by competing groups and religious squabbles. Corruption within the police and among other underpaid government employees continued the parasitic nature of the ruling cliques and their followers. Human rights activists still faced enormous challenges. Unlike the relatively hopeful atmospheres in Windhoek and Addis Ababa, Lagos (the economic capital) and Abuja (the political capital) were marked by sullen resignation. Yes, change in government leadership theoretically would be for the better, but how could long-standing basic political problems be resolved? Most notably, could the armed forces be persuaded definitively to leave power? Could the institutions of civil society be constructed in the face of widespread, continuing military involvement in politics?

Some hope might lie in the Nigerian constitution, were it ever allowed fully to function. The 1960 Nigerian Constitution, designed specifically to meet the problems of independence, was among the first in the British Commonwealth to include a specific bill of rights. Rather than trust to parliamentary sovereignty, fundamental freedoms would be entrenched (that is to say, non-amendable or non-derogable save by constitutionally difficult means). Independence settled the question of "home rule." It did not, however, settle the question of "who shall rule at home" to the satisfaction of all. Numerous minority groups — that is to say, non-Hausa, non-Igbo and non-Yoruba — feared the domination of the traditionally prominent ethnic groups would shut them out of effective government roles. Their agitation for special consideration led the British Government to appoint a special Minorities Commission in 1958. It recommended inclusion of a bill of rights in the independence constitution, believing this would suffice to meet popular demands. By ensuring non-discrimination and embedding a series of rights applicable to all Nigerians in the 1960 constitution, so the Commission hoped, future problems might be avoided. Hence, Chapter III of the independence constitution drew heavily from the (European) Convention on Human Rights and Fundamental Freedoms; and, as a noted Nigerian scholar comments, "these rights have since then generally remained the same in substance except for minor alteration in arrangement, nomenclature and amplification here and there."[53]

These human rights clauses, as later pages will show, proved ineffectual against successive Nigerian military regimes. Quite simply, they ignored or overrode them. Arming themselves with "ouster" decrees which precluded any judicial review of the actions taken in contravention of the constitution, Nigeria's various juntas rode roughshod over individual and group rights. NGOs responded in various ways, many by pressing political mobilization against the armed forces (empowerment), others by seeking popular enlightenment about rights (education), still others by pressing for a strengthened legal and constitutional system (enforcement). The NGOs recognized that the root cause of human rights abuses in Nigeria came from non-responsive governments, able to muscle through their political, economic, and social agendas without effective legal challenge, but differed in their prescription for improvement. By cutting off recourse to courts and by clamping down harshly on political opponents, the Nigerian military undercut human rights protection. It was the overweening obstacle. Without democratization, restoration of the rule of law, transparency and accountability in government operations, and the like, the human rights situation in Nigeria remained seriously flawed. NGOs had succeeded in raising issues; the governing junta had not responded. As the Campaign for Democracy (CD) and the Movement of Solidarity of the Ogoni People (MOSOP) were to demonstrate, political mobilization of only a segment of the populace will not bring victory over a determined opponent. As the Legal Research and Resources Development Centre (LRRDC) was to illustrate, creating a "human rights culture" required long periods of time. And, as other Nigerian human rights groups showed, the legal framework required considerable strengthening.

Senegal

The fourth country whose human rights record and groups is closely examined in this book is Senegal.

Just as the generally positive picture of human rights in Namibia contrasts with the mixed setting of Ethiopia, so the human rights performance of Senegal seems brighter than that of Nigeria — even despite the deaths of up to 250 persons in early 1993, associated with ethnic violence in the southern Casamance region. The openness of its political system has often been commented upon. Senegal is one of a handful of African countries where competitive elections have long featured in the political culture. Voting has occurred regularly, even if the leading party has yet to be supplanted. The reluctance with which Nigerian military officers acceded to pressures for an open party arena contrasts sharply with the multi-partyism of Senegalese leaders (at least since 1980 when President Léopold Sédar Senghor moved away from single-party dominance). Of course, a realist might retort, the dominant position held by the Parti Socialiste means that elections do little more than confirm the incumbents in power. Many of the 20 active parties (1994) are little more than personality cliques. Nonetheless, the political transparency and accountability shown in Senegal puts it in a small band of long-time democratic African states.[54] And, despite some disturbing signals examined later in this chapter, the framework of laws and government control of the military remain strong. There are other favorable points. Even though separatist sentiment in the southern Casamance region has flared into open fighting at various points, ethnic, regional, and religious divisions seem far less marked than in Nigeria or Ethiopia. Extensive overseas economic aid has helped the government maintain social peace. The foundations of a human rights culture appear to exist in Senegal — leading to obvious questions. Why? Can it be sustained? Does it really exist? Can economic development satisfy growing popular demands, given that Senegal lacks the mineral resources of Namibia or Nigeria, being heavily dependent on peanuts and tourism?

Senegal's commitment to democratic competition and its rich array of citizen organizations draw in some respects from deep historical and cultural roots. French rule in Senegal was inspired — in theory, and sometimes in reality — by human rights ideals. For a privileged few Africans in the Dakar/Cap Vert area, the concepts of *liberté, égalité, fraternité* were translated in the short-lived 1848 French constitution into their being granted French citizenship. Deputies from the region were elected to the French National Assembly, with Africans holding the seat from 1911 until independence. Political parties were organized, focusing increasingly on issues concerning the African majority rather than the handful of French expatriates. The experience proved useful in terms of avoiding massive disruption. Major Senegalese politicians — Blaise Diagne, Lamine Guèye, Léopold Sédar Senghor — focused on achieving rights within a franco-centric framework. Diagne recruited troops from West Africa for the trenches of World War I, assuring them that military service was part of their patriotic duty[55]; Lamine Guèye used his French legal training and his political convictions to found a Senegal section of the socialist party (SFIO) and successfully lobbied for a law establishing similar conditions of service for French and for African government employees; Senghor, crowned with his *aggrégation de grammaire*, was a leading wordsmith of the 1946 constitution of the Fourth Republic, within which he worked to diminish differences between "citizens" and "subjects" in the newly-titled French Union. Leaders of this sort, examples of French assimilation policy, never concealed their admiration for French culture and institutions. Though each had painful personal experiences with the racism of *petits blancs* in Senegal, each nonetheless sought the best, the universal, within the rich texture of French civilization.

(As a parenthetical note here, readers should be aware of the prominence of Senegalese in the world of human rights, at least as of early 1994. The senior figure is undoubtedly Kéba Mbaye, member of the International Court of Justice, former Chair of the UN Commission on Human Rights, and recipient of many honors. We will encounter him again in a later chapter, in his role as a leading advocate for the "right to development." Adama Dieng, one-time registrar of the Senegalese Supreme Court and personal assistant to Mbaye, presides over the Geneva-based International Commission of Jurists (ICJ).[56] The ICJ will also figure in this book, being the most active proponent of strengthening the African Commission on Human and People's Rights. Heading the United Nations Centre for Human Rights in his capacity as Assistant Secretary General of the UN is yet another Senegalese, Ibrahim Fall. The UN Centre provides essential services to most human rights treaty bodies, and offers governments important technical assistance. The United Nations special rapporteur on arbitrary detention is Lamity Kama; El Hadji Ibrahima Guissé served as co-special rapporteur for the Sub-Commission on impunity; Bacre Waly Ndiaye was special rapporteur on extra-judicial, summary or arbitrary executions; Jacques Diouf headed the FAO (Food and Agriculture Organization, a UN specialized agency). Finally, Amnesty International, the world's largest human rights NGO, selected Senegalese Pierre Sane its head in June 1993. Amnesty's manifold actions on behalf of human rights, though not examined in detail in this book, have been extraordinary. Certainly in international terms, Senegal stands tall in the world of human rights.)

But it would be shortsighted to attribute Senegal's policies of democratic pluralism solely, or perhaps even primarily, to a few leaders, or to human rights ideals imported from France. Attention must be given as well to indigenous values, in particular a spirit of compromise that strikes observers of the country. Atmosphere cannot be quantified, but it can be experienced. Senegal — at least within the dominant Wolof culture — appears relatively at ease with cultural and religious diversity, political and ideological differences, and ethnic pluralism (even with the Casamance issue, explored in greater depth below in the chapter on empowerment). Though over 90 percent of its inhabitants profess Islam, for example, a Catholic president held power for the first two decades of independence. Introduction of shari'a law was not (at least in the early 1990s) a goal of any major groups. Though the streets of Dakar witness frequent political demonstrations, these are usually met with clouds of tear gas, not with rifle fire. Press freedom, ample opportunity to organize political parties, extensive trade unions with a labor code (though the code is not applicable in the agricultural or informal sectors), and an independent judiciary mark the country. I would assert that such aspects reflect not only choices made by leaders, but also deeply implanted roots of civil society, nurtured over time. This record is matched by adherence to global conventions. Among our four states, Senegal has ratified the largest number of international human rights treaties, as shown in Table 1.

All is not sweetness and light in Senegal, however. A sharp dispute between Senegal and Mauritania in 1989 resulted in the expulsion of thousands of persons from both countries. Tensions in the southern Casamance region surfaced in 1982, and erupted into serious open conflict between government and insurgent forces just over a decade later. To introduce what is discussed more fully subsequently, one should note that Casmance is physically separated from the bulk of Senegal by the enclave of The Gambia and has long suffered from its geographic isolation. While Wolof (together with Toucouleur, Peuhl, Serer, and other groups) live in the economically-vital peanut-growing area and along the Senegal River, Diola dominate Casamance. Wolof are gradually establishing farms and charcoal-burning enterprises in the area. Educational opportunities remain limited in Casamance; few Casamançais sit in politically powerful positions. A sense of economic neglect, political disadvantage, and ethnic distance underpin the Diola-based Mouvement des Forces Démocratiques Casamançais (MFDC), to which we shall return in later pages. Periodic peace accords are signed, then violence breaks out again. Self-

TABLE 1. Treaty Ratification[57]

	Ethiopia	Namibia	Nigeria	Senegal
African Charter on Human and Peoples' Rights		x	x	x
Covenant on Economic, Social and Cultural Rights	x		x	x
Covenant on Civil and Political Rights	x		x	x
Convention on the Elimination of Racial Discrimination	x	x*	x	x
Convention on Discrimination Against Women	x		x	x
Convention Against Torture	x		s	x
Convention on the Rights of the Child	x	x	x	x

s=signed; *=ratified in 1982, although Namibia had not yet formally achieved independence

determination, at least in terms of some degree of regional autonomy, is a desired goal.

The population of Dakar is politically turbulent. President Diouf and the Parti Socialiste enjoy wide support in rural areas, thanks in large measure to strategic alliances with traditional leaders. Muslim brotherhoods have played prominent roles as props of the government. By contrast, the opposition Parti Démocratique Sénégalais (PDS) commands a large following in Dakar and among advocates of change. When PDS national electoral fortunes wane, or are perceived as being manipulated to the advantage of the incumbent PS, many residents of the city take to the streets. (The parallels with Lagos are striking.) The multi-party system in Senegal has moved steadily toward a two-party struggle, but there is little likelihood the PDS will gain control, because of the power the governing group enjoys.[58] The PS has the inside edge, and does not hesitate to use its muscle behind the scenes to remain in power. Case in point: the February 1993 presidential election. The Constitutional Court, presided over by the highly respected Kéba Mbaye whom we met a few paragraphs back, had the responsibility of certifying the returns. Tremendous controversy swirled around the results. Their credibility was called into question by the resignation of Mbaye early in the presidential count, and his leaving the country for an extended period. The head of the all-party National Tabulation Commission also resigned. The Court took a full three weeks to certify results from the first round, ruling 1) that Diouf had received 53 percent of the votes, PDS leader Wade 32 percent (minor candidates divided the rest), thereby making a run-off election unnecessary, and 2) that voting irregularities did not affect the integrity and validity of the election.[59] Vaunted Senegalese democracy was fraying around the edges.

Economic adversity increased the political temperature. A few days before I reached Dakar for field work in late February 1994, serious disturbances erupted there. Five policemen trapped in a vehicle were stabbed or beaten to death by mobs. A few days later, despite their parliamentary immunity, four deputies belonging to opposition parties were arrested.

Observers of Senegal were shocked by the killings, though not surprised by the discontent. The violence reflected, to a substantial degree, the unavoidable frustrations of an impossible financial situation. Senegal had been living well beyond its means; bitter medicine had been prescribed, for which the populace and government were ill-prepared. After years of haggling and delay, officials of the West African economic community (CEAO, the bank of issue for most French-speaking countries in the area) had devalued the currency by 100 percent. Some imported goods, to which the Senegalese are highly attached, doubled in price. Unemployment rates continued to climb. Graffiti proclaiming "We need jobs" appeared on Dakar walls. The usual mechanisms of coping and adjustment were close to being overwhelmed, and new extremist groups took advantage of the turmoil. Thus the once highly-tolerant climate was under severe pressure, politically by the disputed results of the 1993 presidential election, economically and socially by the continued budget deficit, the drastic change in the exchange rate, and the increasing malaise in the job market. The question was whether Senegal was sliding down a slope of increased violence and restriction of human rights.

What was the response of human rights NGOs to the violence in Casamance and on the streets of Dakar? With one exception, they sat on the sidelines. Senegal sports a relatively large number of self-styled human rights groups, but unlike the three other countries assessed in detail in this book, they were (at most) muted in their criticisms of the government and lacksadaisical in their preparation of reports. Only one — run by professors of linguistics at Cheikh Anta Diop University — has built any record of documenting abuses. The contrast with Nigeria could not have been more marked. A substantial portion of Nigerian human rights NGOs prided themselves on their opposition to the military-based regime, seeing it as the preeminent challenge to the rule of law. Few Senegalese groups strongly criticized the Diouf regime, even during the dark days of the presidential election controversy, of the Casamance killings, or of the economic riots. While Nigerian groups turned out detailed studies or informative booklets, Senegalese groups (despite external funding) were slow or non-responsive in their actions. I was puzzled, indeed surprised.[60] Senegal's proud record of human rights accomplishments and the prominence of Senegalese among the world's leaders of human rights work seemed at odds with passivity of many local NGOs and the events of the early 1990s. The lessons are indeed important, and I shall return to them in the concluding chapter.

This survey of the four countries underscores several important points. First, all four governments have faced growing international interest in their human rights records. Human rights NGOs such as Amnesty International, Article 19, or Africa Watch, together with the US State Department and a series of liberal North Atlantic democracies, published regular analyses of governments' human rights performance. No longer could any country remain fully isolated from external scrutiny by other governments, by NGOs, or by its own citizens. Namibia and Senegal have benefited from relatively generous outpourings of foreign aid linked to their generally strong human rights records and political stability. Ethiopia and Nigeria, by contrast, received many outside criticisms of their human rights performance: Ethiopia under the Derg, Nigeria in the bumbling disengagement of the Babangida and Abacha administrations. As will be discussed more in the following chapter, major Western states and international financial institutions shifted policies in the late 1980s-early 1990s, consciously stressing political accountability, transparency, and human rights as criteria for aid or loans.

Second, each country has set forth laudable human rights goals in its constitution. Guarantees appear in all with respect to freedom of association, independence of the judiciary, prohibition of torture, periodic free elections, and the like; all mention government responsibility for minimum levels of health care, social welfare, education and the like. The enforcement of these — well, that may be another story. Similarly, the record in ratifying international human rights treaties has been spotty, as shown in the table above. Ratifications bind the governments to adopt legislation consistent with the aims of the respective treaty, and to report regularly on implementation. The results have not been striking. Weaknesses in constitutional enforcement and reporting have been marked.

Third, noticeable gaps remain between aspirations and accomplishments. Economic difficulties mark all four countries. Social antagonisms of various sorts, some of which have been sketched above, complicate the goal of equal, non-discriminatory treatment. And, where certain groups have enjoyed historic privilege, the possibility of affirmative action arouses criticism. Worsening financial situations for all and the claims of the armed forces (certainly for Ethiopia and Nigeria) further complicate matters.

Fourth, human rights groups in Ethiopia, Namibia, Nigeria, and Senegal are almost all relatively recent creations. Their fiscal underpinnings are weak, with external funds accounting for the bulk of their resources. They face government pressures, and in many instances societal skepticism. Several of them stand in the forefront of political struggle; others have taken much less prominent positions, working instead with socially or economically disadvantaged groups in rural areas, or seeking to implement human rights education, thus building a human rights culture from below; some have been quiet, printing a letterhead and seeking funds but giving little evidence of other activity. We must explore how, through strategies of education, empowerment and enforcement based on documentation, democratization and development, these NGOs function. The strengthening of civil society in Africa by means of NGOs lies at the root of promotion and protection of human rights in that continent.

Notes

1. In the late 1980s, more than a third of the human rights NGOs based in Africa were located in South Africa; in nearly twenty countries, the assiduous researchers of Human Rights Internet could not identify a single organization working directly for human rights or social justice, while in another dozen countries they could find only "one or two somewhat peripheral organizations." (Specifically, no nationally-based and -focused NGO [apart from branches of entities like Amnesty International or the Inter-African Committee] could be found in Angola, Burundi, Central African Republic, Chad, Comoros, Congo, Djibouti, Eritrea, Ethiopia, Gabon, Guinea, Guinea-Bissau, Liberia, Libya, Madagascar, Malawi, Mozambique, Rwanda, Seychelles, Somalia, and Western Sahara! From Laurie S. Wiseberg and Laura Reiner, *Africa: Human Rights Directory and Bibliography* (*Human Rights Internet Reporter* 12, 4 (1988/89), 105–264. I count 93 nationally-based and -focused NGOs, excluding South Africa and branches of NGOs based in other African states, but including NGOs focused on more than one country. In addition, some 28 organizations focused on Africa generally, two on northern Africa, seven on southern Africa. As the authors observed,

> Human rights, as a concept around which people are prepared and permitted to organize, has not yet gained adequate legitimacy or potency in many parts of the continent, despite the history of egregious violations Africans have suffered both in the colonial and post-independence period. . . . In many countries, the political space necessary to organize human rights groups does not exist. Organizations which attempt to monitor government behavior and hold officials accountable to international human rights standards are considered subversive. . . . those courageous enough to speak out for human rights, or to defend those whose rights are violated, may be severely sanctioned: isolated, and lacking sufficient popular support in their societies, they may be imprisoned, tortured, killed, or forced into exile. (6)

By mid-1993, as should be apparent to all readers of this note, the situation had dramatically changed. Compilers of the new Internet directory found scores of NGOs. The number had swelled to 53 NGOs focused on specific regions of the continent (of which 33 concentrated on Southern Africa), plus 102 based in individual African countries (58 of which were headquartered in their country of focus, all but one of the others in Western countries). Among the countries with the largest numbers were South Africa (163), Egypt (30), Nigeria (26), Morocco (20), Ethiopia and Tunisia (18), Uganda (17), and Tanzania and Zimbabwe (16). Figures calculated from Human Rights Internet, *A Listing of Organizations Concerned with Human Rights and Social Justice Networks,* supplement to *Human Rights Internet Reporter* 15 (1994), 143–210.

2. Orlando Patterson, *Slavery and Social Death* (Cambridge, MA: Harvard University Press, 1982).

3. Most active in this respect is Anti-Slavery International (formerly the Anti-Slavery Society); founded in the early nineteenth century, it claims to be the world's oldest continuously-functioning human rights NGO.

4. Ali Mazrui accounted for the current difficult condition of Africa (in personal correspondence) with the following breakdown: historical causation (legacy of colonialism, the bondage of colonial boundaries, the clash of cultures and its aftermath), 40 percent; global causation (impact of the contemporary capitalist world economy and implications of the new world order for Africa), 25 percent; ecological causation (environmental factors), 15 percent; personality factors (including quality of leadership), 15 percent; other factors (chance, accident), 5 percent. Mazrui thus sought to counter the widespread tendency to place most blame for Africa's post-independence problems on its leaders.

5. Claude E. Welch, Jr., "Continuity and Discontinuity in African Military Organization," *Journal of Modern African Studies* 12 (1975), 224–45.

6. In discussions in 1973 with members of the Political Science Department at what was then Haile Selassie I University, I mentioned that I had just published a book on how and why armed forces seized power. My Ethiopian colleagues were quite interested, and requested copies. None of the copies I sent arrived — and within a few years those persons who had requested copies had fled or been killed. Did my publication *Military Role and Rule* play some minor role in the political tumult of Ethiopia at the twilight of the Imperial regime?

7. "Transitional Period Charter of Ethiopia," mimeographed copy prepared by the Ethiopian Embassy, Washington, DC.

8. Human Rights Watch, *Report 1993* (New York: Human Rights Watch, 1993), p. 10. There is no writeup about Ethiopia in the 1994 report.

9. Human Rights Watch, *Report 1993,* p. 14.

10. Among the most useful sources for Ethiopian politics over the years have been (in chronological order) Margery Perham, *The Government of Ethiopia* (New York: Oxford University Press, 1948); Donald N. Levine, *Wax and Gold: Tradition and Innovation in Ethiopian Culture* (Chicago: University of Chicago Press, 1967); Robert L. Hess, *Ethiopia: The Modernizing of Autocracy* (Ithaca, NY: Cornell University Press, 1970); John Markakis, *Ethiopia: Anatomy of a Traditional Polity* (Oxford: Clarendon Press, 1974); David and Marina Ottaway, *Ethiopia: Empire in Revolution* (New York: Africana, 1978); Fred Halliday and Maxine Molleyneaux, *The Ethiopian Revolution* (London: Verso, 1981); John Markakis, *National and Class Conflict in the Horn of Africa* (Cambridge: Cambridge University Press, 1987); Harold Marcus, *Haile Selassie* (Berkeley and Los Angeles: University of California Press, 1987); and Christopher Clapham, *Transformation and Continuity in Revolutionary Ethiopia* (Cambridge: Cambridge University Press, 1988).

11. "The period of [Menelik II's] reign (1889–1913) is a milestone in Ethiopian history. It witnessed the culmination and consolidation of the vast territorial expansion launched by Menelik while still King of Shoa which turned Ethiopia into an empire in fact as well as name. In a burst of furious energy, the Ethiopians

overran the southern part of the plateau, doubling the domain of the Solomonic throne and imposing its rule on a large number of peoples of diverse origin and cultures. As a result, the composition of the society found within the enlarged boundaries of Ethiopia changed radically. The Christian group, the Abyssinians of old, found itself a minority, albeit dominant, in its own state." Markakis, *Ethiopia: Anatomy of a Traditional Polity*, pp. 22–23.

12. Figures from *An Evaluation of the June 21, 1992 Elections in Ethiopia* (Washington, DC: National Democratic Institute for International Affairs, 1992), p. 8.

13. The "revised" Constitution of Ethiopia included a chapter entitled "rights and duties of the people," whose provisions contrasted markedly with actual implementation. For the text, see James C. N. Paul and Christopher Clapham, eds., *Sourcebook of Ethiopian Constitutional Law* (Addis Ababa: Faculty of Law, Haile Selassie I University, n.d.), Vol. 1, esp. pp. 10–13.

14. Seized by Italy in 1888, Eritrea (the cradle of much of Abyssinian history) became a political orphan after World War II, as Italy's colonial possessions were stripped away, their fate decided by the United Nations after the four victorious powers failed to reach agreement. A UN Commission established in 1950 advocated federation with Ethiopia, which the General Assembly then voted. What had been distinctive Eritrean institutions were incorporated into Ethiopia; use of Arabic and Tigrinya was banned in 1956, replaced by Amharic; full annexation came in 1962, following election of a parliament under Ethiopian control. How the resultant discontent took form in the Eritrean Liberation Front and Eritrean Popular Liberation Front can be followed in Haggai Ehrlich, *The Struggle over Eritrea 1962–1978: War and Revolution in the Horn of Africa* (Stanford, CA: Hoover Institution, 1983); also see Richard Sherman, *Eritrea: The Unfinished Revolution* (New York: Praeger, 1980) and Robert Machida, *Eritrea: The Struggle for Independence* (Trenton, NJ: Red Sea Press, 1987).

15. *Country Reports . . . 1985*, p. 103.

16. Ibid.

17. Alex deWaal, *Evil Days: 30 Years of War and Famine in Ethiopia* (New York: Human Rights Watch, 1991), p. 16.

18. Ibid., pp. 7–8.

19. Precise documentation is not available. However, while the Derg sought in its early years to represent wide sectors of Ethiopian society, it became more and more Amhara dominated subsequently. In a vicious circle, government efforts to maintain unity meant greater use of appeals to Amhara, less to opponents. The greatest "losers" appear to have been the Oromos, numerically the largest ethnic group. For more details on the growing Amharization under the Derg, see Claude E. Welch, Jr., "The Military and Social Integration in Ethiopia," in Henry Dietz, Jerrold Elkin, and Maurice Roumani, eds., *Ethnicity, Integration and the Military* (Boulder, CO: Westview, 1991), pp. 151–78.

20. Claude E. Welch, Jr. "Changing Civil-Military Relations," in Robert O. Slater, Barry M. Schutz and Steven R. Dorr, eds., *Global Transformation and the Third World* (Boulder, CO: Lynne Rienner, 1993), pp. 71–90.

21. Influential American political scientist Samuel P. Huntington spent a few days in Ethiopia early in 1993, for example, on a USAID contract; his paper for the Constitutional Commission, "Political Development in Ethiopia: A Peasant-Based Dominant-Party Democracy?" indicated that "the makings of a dominant-party system [i.e., EPRDF dominance] appear to exist in Ethiopia and such a system could have many advantages for the country" (p. 10).

22. While in Ethiopia in November 1993, I heard numerous explanations,

among them: 1) only by strong regionalism based on ethnicity could the Tigreans protect themselves from a resurgence of Amhara dominance; 2) lingering Marxist influence within the TPLF pressed it toward stressing "nationalities"; 3) the impending separation of Eritrea had to be rationalized; 4) the old order had been highly centralized, making a clean break with the past through ethnicity attractive. I shall return to the consequences of ethnic sentiments later in this chapter.

23. "Transitional Period Charter of Ethiopia," p. 2.

24. Maxwell Owusu, "Democracy and Africa: A View from the Village," *Journal of Modern African Studies* 30, 3 (September 1992), 369–96.

25. For details about the regime's murderous counter-insurgency steps, see deWaal, *Evil Days*.

26. *Ethiopia in Transition: A Report on the Judiciary and the Legal Profession* (Washington: International Human Rights Law Group, 1993).

27. Trials opened in mid-December 1994 for 73 former government officials, 45 of whom were in custody. They were charged with the killings of over 1800 persons and the enforced disappearances of more than 200 others. The Special Prosecutor's Office, to which reference will be made later in this book, had amassed more than 300,000 documents to buttress its efforts.

28. David Lush, *Last Steps to Uhuru* (Windhoek: New Namibia Books, 1993), p. 5.

29. *Country Reports . . . 1992*, p. 186.

30. The mandates system represented a creative solution to conflicting claims for self-determination for parts of the former Austro-Hungarian, German, and Ottoman empires. In Umozurike's words, "The First World War brought the principle of self-determination to the fore of international politics." Umozurike Oji Umozurike, *Self-Determination in International Law* (Hamden, CT: Archon, 1972), p. 11. War propaganda had its effects; by the time of the Versailles conference, the principle was already generally accepted by all the belligerents (ibid., p. 20). The principle could be far more readily applied, statesmen believed, in central Europe and the Middle East than in Africa and the Pacific. One of the most influential figures at Versailles was South African leader Jan Christian Smuts, author of "The League of Nations: A Practical Suggestion." He asserted that German colonies in these areas were "inhabited by barbarians, who not only cannot possibly govern themselves, but to whom it would be impracticable to apply any ideas of political self-determination in the European sense" (quoted in ibid., p. 31 and in H. Duncan Hall, *Mandates, Dependencies, and Trusteeships* [Washington, DC: Carnegie Endowment for International Peace, 1948], p. 13). Tremendous controversy swirled around the proposed mandates system, almost causing the breakdown of the Versailles Conference, with President Wilson and Prime Minister Lloyd George standing against the annexationist claims of other powers (Umozurike, *Self-Determination*, pp. 32–33). Former German Southwest Africa was appended to South Africa, which became responsible for submitting a detailed annual report. Officially, the mandatory power had to report on slavery, labor, arms traffic, trade and manufacture of alcohol and drugs, liberty of conscience, military clauses, economic equality, education, public health, land tenure, moral, social, and material welfare, public finances, and demographic statistics—to which were added "the text of all the legislative and administrative decisions taken . . . in the course of the past year." No wonder the annual report for 1939 submitted by South Africa was 250 folio pages long, in small type and with 1,368 numbered paragraphs! Hall, *Mandates*, pp. 190–91, 188.)

31. Key documents, including the ICJ's 1966 and 1971 decisions, appear in John Dugard, ed., *The SouthWest Africa/Namibia Dispute* (Berkeley: University of California Press, 1973). Also see Solomon Slonim, *South West Africa and the United Nations: An International Mandate in Dispute* (Baltimore: Johns Hopkins University Press, 1973). Other helpful works include Peter H. Katjavivi, *A History of Resistance in Namibia* (London: James Currey, 1988); Geise Maria Rocha, *In Search of Namibian Independence: The Limitations of the United Nations* (Boulder, CO: Westview Press, 1984); Peter Katjavivi, Per Frostin, and Kaire Mbuende, eds., *Church and Liberation in Namibia* (London: Pluto, 1981); and, for a glimpse of the post-independence scene, Donald L. Sparks, *Namibia: The Nation After Independence* (Boulder, CO: Westview, 1992) and Lush, *Last Steps to Uhuru.*

32. As one indication of the extent of UN interest in Namibia, take publications. No less than 362 specific documents on the Namibian issue are listed in the *Human Rights Bibliography: United Nations Documents and Publications 1980–1990* (New York: United Nations, 1993), Vol. 1, 139–54.

33. For details about the negotiations and "linkage" issues of Cuban disengagement from Angola and South African withdrawal from Namibia, see Chester A. Crocker, *High Noon in Southern Africa: Making Peace in a Rough Neighborhood* (New York: Norton, 1992). Writing about the emergence of the linkage formula, Crocker argues:

> The decision to engage in Southern African peacemaking in 1981 was less a commentary on the "ripeness" of the region for peace than on the urgency of Western leadership there. . . . One thing was certain: the future of this region would depend on whether we participated actively in shaping it. We engaged because we had a clear vision of our interests, a readiness to run the risks of taking a major initiative, and a desire to limit the damage of letting nature take its course.
>
> But we also entertained the illusion, in 1981, that we might be able to pull the Namibia and Angola tracks together some time over the next eighteen months (by the end of 1982). That seemed like an eternity in a professional environment where a six-week scenario represents long-term planning. As it was, we were off by a few years. (73)

34. "Principles concerning the Constituent Assembly and the Constitution for an independent Namibia," UN Document S/15287, Annex, 12 July 1982. Among the central provisions were election of a Constituent Assembly, which would adopt a constitution by two-thirds majority; a declaration of fundamental rights "consistent with the provisions of the Universal Declaration of Human Rights"; and "balanced structuring of the public service, the police service and the defense services."

35. Human Rights Watch, *Report 1993*, pp. 5–65. Because of limited resources, Human Rights Watch/Africa does not attempt to cover the entire continent in detail, but focuses instead on countries with significant levels of human rights abuses and reasonable prospect that American pressure could rectify the situation. For more details on Human Rights Watch/Africa's work, see Chapter 7 below.

36. Amnesty International, *Annual Report 1993* (New York: AI USA, 1993), pp. 218–19.

37. *Country Reports . . . 1992*, p. 182.

38. Some Namibian human rights NGOs such as the National Society for Hu-

man Rights (NSHR) and the Parents' Committee were established to determine the fate of persons missing behind SWAPO lines. The government's own investigation into missing persons was criticized by some groups, especially the NSHR, which claimed many detainees were still being held in Angola. SWAPO agreed in June 1990 to lead an all-party parliamentary investigation into allegations; the motion was proposed by National Patriotic Front leader Moses Katjiuongua, backed by the Prime Minister, and eventually led to a request to the International Committee of the Red Cross. *Country Reports . . . 1990,* p. 263. A detailed paper written by Richard Dicker centers on both South African and SWAPO violations of the laws of war: *Accountability in Namibia: Human Rights and the Transition to Democracy* (New York: Africa Watch, 1992). David Smuts also took up the theme in a recent article: " . . . reconciliation pre-supposes a knowledge of the past. . . . The policy of national reconciliation cannot, if honestly applied, form a justification for precluding thorough investigation of past abuses. . . . In the almost three years which have passed since Namibia's independence, little has been done by the government to address the issue of past human rights abuses. . . . Without an acknowledgement of past abuses and addressing them in a principled manner, the elaborate steps taken in the constitution to prevent their recurrence are undermined." Dave Smuts, "Accounting for Violations in the Context of National Reconciliation," *Namibia Brief* 16 (March 1993), 12–13. Also see Chapter 7.

39. In the judgment of the major observers, "the June 21 elections did not contribute directly to Ethiopia's development as a democratic state. At best, the elections were premature . . . Less kindly judged, the elections were ill-conceived, dubious and counterproductive in their contribution to the democratization of Ethiopia. The elections, moreover, exacerbated existing tensions, reinforced the hegemonic power of the EPRDF while marginalizing other fledgling parties, and were a central factor in the withdrawal of the OLF from the TGE and the return to war in the Oromo region. Finally, the elections created new 'political facts' — EPRDF-dominated regional and district assemblies — that will remain controversial in regions where the elections are mired in doubt and suspicion." *An Evaluation of the June 21, 1992 Elections in Ethiopia* (Washington, DC: National Democratic Institute for International Affairs, 1992), p. 7.

40. As of late 1992, approximately 45 percent of senior administrative positions were held by whites, who constitute less than 5 percent of the Namibian population.

41. Among the best sources, in chronological order of appearance, are James S. Coleman, *Nigeria: Background to Nationalism* (Berkeley: University of California Press, 1958); Richard A. Sklar, *Nigerian Political Parties: Power in an Emergent African Nation* (Princeton, NJ: Princeton University Press, 1963); John Mackintosh, ed., *Nigerian Government and Politics: Prelude to the Revolution* (Evanston, IL: Northwestern University Press, 1966); Robin Luckham, *The Nigerian Military: A Sociological Analysis of Authority and Revolt 1960–67* (Cambridge: Cambridge University Press, 1971); Richard Joseph, *Democracy and Prebendal Politics in Nigeria: The Rise and Fall of the Second Republic* (Cambridge: Cambridge University Press, 1987); Larry Diamond, *Class, Ethnicity and Democracy in Nigeria: The Failure of the First Republic* (Basingstoke: Macmillan, 1988); Toyin Falola and Julius Ihonvbere, *The Rise and Fall of Nigeria's Second Republic, 1979–1984* (London: Zed, 1985).

42. Julius O. Ihonvbere, "A Critical Evaluation of the Failed 1990 Coup in Nigeria," *Journal of Modern African Studies* 29 (1991), 601–26; Africa Watch, "27 New Executions for Coup Attempt" (September 20, 1990), "42 Executed After

Unfair Trial" (July 31, 1990), and "Aftermath of Abortive Military Coup" (May 10, 1990).

43. Human Rights Watch, *Report 1993*, p. 37.

44. *Country Reports . . . 1992*, p. 196.

45. Sayre P. Schatz, "Pirate Capitalism and the Inert Economy of Nigeria," *Journal of Modern African Studies* 22, 1 (1984), 145–57.

46. For a more detailed study of the military's role in Nigeria politics, see Claude E. Welch, Jr., *No Farewell to Arms? Military Disengagement in Africa and Latin America* (Boulder, CO: Westview, 1987), pp. 98–125; and "Civil-Military Agonies in Nigeria: Agonies of an Unaccomplished Transition," *Armed Forces & Society* 21, 4 (summer 1995), 593–614.

47. Larry Diamond, "Nigeria: Pluralism, Statism, and the Struggle for Democracy," in Larry Diamond, Juan J. Linz, and Seymour Martin Lipset, eds., *Democracy in Developing Countries: Africa* (Boulder, CO: Lynne Rienner, 1988), 57.

48. *Country Reports . . . 1985*, p. 238. The man named as Attorney-General, Bola Ajide, later fell out of favor with human rights groups for his defense of the Babangida government's actions; his election to fill an unexpired term on the International Court of Justice was sharply criticized by Nigerian activists.

49. Nonetheless, the country's parlous economic situation necessitated an equally onerous structural adjustment plan. Its social consequences have been immense, assuredly a major part of the widespread delegitimization of the Babangida government.

50. The 1979 Constitution (Article 14) specifically indicates, "the composition of the Government of the Federation or any of its agencies and the conduct of its affairs shall be carried [out] in such a manner as to reflect the federal character of Nigeria . . . ensuring that there shall be no predominance of persons from a few ethnic or other sectional groups."

51. Quoted in Oye Oyediran and Adigun Agbaye, "Two-Partyism and Democratic Transition in Nigeria," *Journal of Modern African Studies* 29 (1991), 226.

52. Reprinted in *West Africa* (6–12 September 1993), 1577.

53. M. Ayo Ajomo, "The Development of Individual Rights in Nigeria's Constitutional History," in M. Ayo Ajomo and Bolaji Owasanoye, eds., *Individual Rights Under the 1989 Constitution* (Lagos: Nigerian Institute of Advanced Legal Studies, 1993), p. 5.

54. John A. Wiseman, *Democracy in Black Africa: Survival and Revival* (New York: Paragon House, 1990).

55. For details, see Myron J. Echenberg, *Colonial Conscripts: The Tirailleurs Sénégalais in French West Africa, 1857–1960* (London: Currey, 1991); G. Wesley Johnson, *The Emergence of Black Politics in Senegal: The Struggle for Power in the Four Communes, 1900–1920* (Stanford, CA: Hoover Institution, 1970).

56. A brief biography of Dieng, entitled "The Passionate Advocate," appears in *West Africa*, 10–16 May 1993, p. 769. Also see Howard B. Tolley, Jr., *Global Advocates for Human Rights: The International Commission of Jurists* (Philadelphia: University of Pennsylvania Press, 1994).

57. United Nations, "Human Rights International Instruments: Chart of Ratifications as at 30 June 1994 (New York: UN Document HR/94/21) for all except the African Charter.

58. Babacar Kanté, "Senegal's Empty Election," *Journal of Democracy* 5 (1994), 96–108.

59. *Country Reports . . . 1993*, pp. 243–44.

60. But, I must add, many of those I interviewed were not. Senegal's long

record of relatively open competition has helped create and sustain a set of assumptions: Senegal is a democratic, rights-protecting state. There has been, they argued, a tendency to coast on reputation. The sixth ICJ workshop on NGO participation in the African Commission on Human and Peoples' Rights (April 1994) criticized Senegal (along with Rwanda, Burundi, Djibouti, Algeria, Nigeria and South Africa), thereby causing a stir in the country's press.

Chapter 2
Civil Society and Human Rights NGOs: Themes for the 1990s in Africa

Decades seem to cry out for titles or dominant themes. The 1990s are no exception. It bids fair to be the decade for examining "civil society" in Africa.

The thirty-plus years since 1960 — the *annus mirabilis* of African independence — have taught an important lesson. Strongly centralized states were tried, and found wanting.[1] Relative to the tasks they promised to accomplish, governments fell short. Their rhetorical promises far outstripped their actual performance. Many negative consequences flowed from over-emphasizing the personalities, institutions, and interests of the capital. Authoritarian African regimes failed to protect human rights, foster economic development, or promote national integration. Hence the reaction to failure by moving to a new paradigm. A shift in emphasis has occurred. The grassroots, rather than the elites of the capital, have become the focus of increased policy and scholarly attention. The demands of democratization, development, human rights, and the like require a different approach, not confined to the chief cities and their political/military elites, but more widely focused on people or groups throughout the country. Society more than state has become the watchword for analysis.

Such an emphasis is not new, however. An alternating emphasis on state or society has long characterized studies of African politics.

In the 1950s, for example, emphasis lay on social institutions. Nationalist movements, the major concern of the period, were generally — and correctly — perceived as wide-ranging coalitions of ethnic associations, improvement unions, proto-political groupings, and trade unions.[2] The movements were diverse. Drawn together by dislike of colonial policies, and convinced that self-government would help resolve most issues, members of a wide variety of groups coalesced in congresses, often led by charismatic individuals. The governments of the time were under European control, but societies were vibrantly African. Opposition between colonial administration and popular groups existed naturally.

With independence in the 1960s, emphasis shifted from the societal to the political side, and in particular to the new African-led states. The conversion of loose-knit congresses and nationalist movements into would-be "vanguard" single parties became the central theme for scholars. Governments now reflected the interests of the majority, not the colonizing minority. Specific country studies documented this quick transformation.[3] By the end of the decade, as bullets replaced ballots as the chief means of governmental change, the causes and consequences of coups d'état became the central subject of study. Analysts focused on political shortcomings of the state and specific characteristics of the armed forces as institutions.[4]

Decay within African governments (whether newly installed by the armed forces or maintained in power by various means by the "founding fathers") became an increasingly common theme in the 1970s, despite (or, paradoxically, because of?) efforts to strengthen their structures. Conditions started to worsen. By the 1980s, with massive social dislocation brought by famine, civil war, systematic exclusion of groups from access to power, and accelerating economic decline, a pessimistic tone increasingly marked analyses by Africans and Africa specialists. Withdrawal from the state became a central theme. Only by turning to the protection of kinship groups or similar institutions could persons cope with decline. The African state, in short, lost legitimacy.

A further nail in the coffin of the centralized state came from events outside Africa. The collapse of supposedly monolithic eastern European regimes underscored the fragility of African governments. The end of the Cold War entailed the rapid collapse of external support for many authoritarian governments. The state having failed, so it seemed, a new focus for effort was needed for the 1990s. Accordingly, the extraordinary (in retrospect) series of changes inside and outside Africa, linked to democratization, helped reintroduce the time-honored question of the relative significance of state and society. But at this point, society might rescue the state from its own inadequacies.

Civil society now draws the attention of Africa-watchers.[5] To quote Alfred Stepan, civil society is an arena "where manifold social movements . . . and civil organizations from all classses . . . attempt to constitute themselves in an ensemble of arrangements so that they can express themselves and advance their interests."[6] More simply, Michael Bratton defines civil society as "public political activity that occurs in the realm between the state and the family."[7] Its functioning concerns policy-makers, scholars, and, above all, Africans themselves. They recognize that the dramatic political shifts in the continent at the start of the 1990s can be sustained only with vigorous civil societies. Contrasts in their vigor can have direct, significant political consequences.[8] A remarkable agreement on the importance of democracy and human rights, central to the institutions and values of civil society, has thus emerged in sub-Saharan Africa.

Human rights non-governmental organizations (NGOs) form a crucial part of civil society. NGOs, in the words of Philippe Schmitter, are "intermediary organizations and arrangements that lie between the primary units of society — individuals, families, clans, ethnic groups of various kinds, village units — and the ruling collective institutions and agencies of the society."[9] They occupy a special place. They are integral, in short, to civil society. NGOs differ in principles, membership, and goals from families (including extended families), from ascriptive groups based on real or presumed descent, and from other face-to-face groupings. They are not primarily involved in market relationships, although they may promote the economic interests of members. They differ from government institutions in not directly making and implementing authoritative decisions, based on a monopoly of legitimate coercion (to reword Max Weber's classic definition). Yet NGOs interact extensively with governments. That, indeed, is their reason for existence.

NGOs link the complex, unfamiliar world of government to the familiar terrain of existing or nascent social and economic groups. They are not primarily interest or pressure groups, however. These groups lobby bureaucrats or elected representatives for favorable actions. They prepare legislative proposals, organize public opinion around specific issues, inform broader publics about various concerns, and seek favorable actions for their members. Pressure groups provide, as well, a continuous source of feedback about the impact of government policies. The NGOs examined in this book have a broader purpose. They seek to benefit society, or at least a significant portion of it, without necessary direct benefit to themselves. They constitute both a precondition for, and a supplement to, the constitutionally defined political process and the formal political bodies of the democratic state.[10] As voluntary organizations in large measure, they often pursue idealistic causes. But these causes are crucial to the functioning of a modern society. As Wiseberg recently stressed, human rights NGOs perform "two absolutely indispensable functions": information gathering, evaluation, and dissemination; and keeping the political process open or creating political space for democratic forces.[11]

The importance of these tasks cannot be underestimated. A would-be modern democratic society rests upon an underpinning of citizen-based associations, voluntarily established to pursue their interests, relying upon a government that implements policies relatively equitably, and reasonably responds to pressure from below. A democratic state and a civil society are two sides of the same coin. Likewise, an NGO and a government are complementary: fulfilling different functions, both presumably dedicated to improving society.

NGOs, like political parties, are "modern" entities.[12] They have proliferated since World War II, and especially in the 1980s. In 1939, according to Dunér, there were fewer than 800 worldwide; by 1948, 41 NGOs enjoyed consultative status with ECOSOC (the United Nations Economic and Social Council); researchers estimate that between 18,000 and 20,000 NGOs currently exist.[13] Several reasons account for their growth in numbers. They are linked, as already pointed out, with democracy, which has expanded dramatically in less than 50 years. They correspond to the needs of increasingly complex societies. They have emerged as vital sources of information. In the useful summary of Morten Kjaerum, Director of the Danish Centre for Human Rights, NGOs 1) articulate citizen demands through active participation and consciousness-raising, 2) encourage diversity and the growth of different opinions, 3) assist in integrating groups in civil society and within the political process, 4) serve as early warning mechanisms (usually in conjunction with international networks), and 5) serve as buffers against both the state and the market structure.[14]

The "NGO revolution," as I am tempted to label it, has swept through all parts of the world. Within Africa, NGOs have multiplied because of urgent relief, development, and political needs. The trend first became obvious in the early 1970s. With the diminished efficiency of African governments in providing services, external governments and private aid-givers sought to bypass or supplement patently weak regimes by turning to NGOs. The reasons were obvious. Famine, civil war, and political failings made global partnerships essential. The disastrous Sahel drought of the early 1970s made rapid relief imperative — beyond the capacity of governments to deliver. African and international NGOs started to play increasingly prominent roles as governments, national economies, and political parties collapsed. NGOs took a significant part in relief efforts. Beigbeder defines these relief entities as "non-governmental, autonomous, non-profit organizations, initiated by private citizens for a stated international relief assistance purpose, supported mainly by voluntary contributions in cash and kind from private purposes."[15] Their prominence accelerated in the 1980s; meanwhile, their purposes tended to shift from relief to development and to political or social mobilization. NGOs — both linking citizens to government and protecting them from government — had thus emerged prior to the 1990s wave of democratization. They were further encouraged by increased governmental openness and the end of Cold War confrontations.

The growth of NGOs took place at several levels. Domestic developments were enhanced by international impacts. Within the United Nations, ECOSOC opened the way. Article 71 of the UN Charter permitted ECOSOC to grant organizations "consultative status," and thereby gain access to the system. UN human rights activities take place to a substantial extent under the aegis of the Commission on Human Rights, within the

ECOSOC framework. Consultative status thus became an important means of entry for NGOs into direct contact with Geneva-based UN treaty bodies and the Commission, as will be discussed later in this chapter. Major aid-givers, such as the Nordic countries, sought out local NGOs (especially those concerned with development) as foci for their grants. Grants from the United States Democracy and Human Rights Fund (so-called Section 116e funds) have been directed heavily toward indigenous NGOs. International NGOs such as Oxfam have (in the face of government opposition or shortcomings) also turned to partnerships with indigenous NGOs. Indeed, the great majority of African NGO budget support comes from Western (or, if you prefer, Northern) sources, a point to which we shall return.

The most important level of NGO development was and remains national, however. By establishing NGOs, Africans have sought to cope with domestic problems. What should citizens do in the face of massive economic, political, and social issues? The problems of the state encouraged many Africans not to "exit" but to engage. Seeking, in Hirschman's terms, "voice," NGOs have enriched and deepened opportunities for widespread political involvement. They function within societies in which citizen participation is — at least in theory! — accepted by leaders and within the culture, but in reality is denied or abridged in many ways. They form a vibrant, active, crucial part of civil society. They press for the interests of their members. Without NGOs' actions, individuals and groups would be more susceptible to negative government pressures, or to neglect in the distribution of political goods and services.

Why may NGOs succeed in tasks such as disaster aid, grassroots development, or human rights advocacy where other types of organization have apparently failed? They have strengths where governments have weaknesses. Although Beigbeder's study focuses only on relief entities, its conclusions are more broadly applicable. NGOs enjoy: 1) the ability to involve the intended beneficiaries of a particular project; 2) greater readiness to perceive disasters, report on them, and respond; 3) greater ability to identify, formulate, and publicize problems and needs without excessive caution or exclusive reliance on official diplomatic sources of information; 4) light administrative structures, which make them more cost-effective; and 5) personnel deemed to be highly motivated by humanitarian dedication.[16]

In human rights matters, where regimes in power both threaten some citizens and selectively enforce rights for others, can non-governmental organizations tip the scales toward non-discriminatory treatment? Are NGOs effective in meeting their self-proclaimed goals? Can they satisfy the aspirations of their intended audiences? of their chief supporters? Funding for many African NGOs has come from external foundation and governmental sources, raising questions (especially among critics) about the NGOs' political motivations and organizational independence.

Tension inevitably exists between African governments and NGOs. NGOs attempt to safeguard their autonomy; states try to control them.[17] Governments confront NGOs simultaneously as partners and potential opponents. Their relationship, especially in the thorny area of human rights, oscillates between wary linkages and sharp antagonisms. Common ground may exist in socio-economic development; there, NGOs and governments can cooperate. Tension is bound to arise when NGOs monitor and report on governments' human rights abuses, however. As should be apparent, NGOs occasionally work in the lacunae of government, using their own and outside resources; sometimes, however, NGOs perceive the regimes in power as the source of problems, and lead efforts for change. There is no simple, consistent relationship; much depends on the nature of the problem.

Analyzing the effectiveness of NGOs means giving attention to several aspects. Among the most important are the political "space" within which they work, the resources on which NGOs draw, and the objectives their leaders (and major donors) seek to achieve. No one of these factors can explain their relative effectiveness. Nonetheless, I strongly believe that NGOs can, over time, have a direct, beneficial impact on their societies, based on choice of strategies and careful appraisal of the opportunities for change. They can, in short, help deepen the level of civil society in sub-Saharan countries.

As Bratton suggests, contemporary Africa differs from other areas because of the limits to civil society and to the power of governments. "Because of the shallow penetration of society by weak state institutions, there is a relatively larger realm of unoccupied political space in Africa than anywhere else in the world."[18] This presents challenges and opportunities to NGOs. The quality of leadership, strategies selected, and the resources and organizational maneuvering room available limit what they can accomplish.

We can envisage four ways in which relations between NGOs and governments determine the extent and nature of political space. Both entities can be relatively active or relatively passive; they can cooperate, or they may oppose each other. For mnemonic ease, think of the acronym CUTS: space can be Created, Unoccupied, Taken or Surrendered. These interactions appear in Table 2. Examples of each type will come later.

The number of NGOs has risen dramatically, a sign, I argue, of their increased significance.[19] Early in the 1980s, Human Rights Internet started to compile directories of human rights NGOs. Few were focused on Africa — and of these, the majority concentrated on southern Africa.[20] By the early 1990s, the situation had changed dramatically.[21] Many NGOs

TABLE 2. Government/NGO Relationships over Political "Space"

	NGO/government cooperation	NGO/government opposition
Government active	Space created	Space taken
Government passive	Space unoccupied	Space surrendered

had been founded elsewhere in Africa, although figures for South Africa remained high. (A private group recently estimated that South Africa in mid-1993 housed 54,000 NGOs [defined as nonprofit private sector organizations]).[22] A USAID list for the far smaller, less developed neighboring state of Namibia included 153 NGOs plus an additional 141 CBOs (community-based organizations) and projects.[23] And in poor but populous Ethiopia, the Christian Relief and Development Association expanded from less than 20 NGOs in 1983 to 64 by the end of the decade; by late 1992, membership had increased to 77.[24] Recall, finally, Dunér's estimate of between 18,000 and 20,000 NGOs in the early 1990s.

NGOs and Human Rights

Human rights NGOs around the globe have developed in tandem with human rights awareness and treaty obligations. Indeed, the process has been symbiotic and interdependent. All the "regimes" of human rights identified by Donnelly[25] — declaratory; promotion; implementation; enforcement — have involved NGOs. But it is in the last area in which their contributions have been most notable in recent years. But NGOs need research and publicity. By drawing attention to abuses, human rights NGOs serve not only the interests of their immediate supporters, but also the broader needs of civil society. The documentation and networking NGOs undertake make them central to the promotion and protection of human rights.

Let me illustrate these points by first discussing the annual August meeting in Geneva of the United Nations Sub-Commission on the Prevention of Discrimination and the Protection of Minorities. The three-week-long session takes place in a large chamber of the new wing of the Palais des Nations. The 23 experts elected to the Sub-Commission sit at facing tables, perpendicular to a long podium for Sub-Commission officers. The experts are ringed, in concentric circles, by desks for government representatives (most of whom do not bother to attend), for representatives of UN functional agencies (again, conspicuous by their absence), and, in the outer rings, for scores of NGO representatives, all anxious to have their concerns heard and attended to. When the agenda item for public discussion is reached, NGOs have an opportunity — presuming they have registered in time and are present in the chamber — to speak briefly. After each speech, limited to ten minutes, other NGO representatives flock to pick up the text that has just been read; copies are hand-carried to Sub-Commission members and to the media covering the session. There is a fever pitch of activity. Extensive caucusing and networking occurs in the corridors, lounges, and hotels. How to influence the Sub-Commission figures in most conversations. Can we get a resolution passed, condemning (say) Indonesia's repression in East Timor? criticizing Chinese actions against Tibetan cultural and political aspirations? deploring pressures against Native Americans, shouldered aside in their supposedly protected reserves by gold seekers? Obtaining UN endorsement of a national NGO's concerns seems to make the costly trip to Switzerland a triumph. For in this fashion the world has borne witness to the concerns of one small part. On the other hand, there can be, and perhaps has been, too much of a good thing. NGO speeches at the Sub-Commission run far into the night. The meeting room empties. Speaker after speaker repeats wearisome stories of abuse. The high costs of travel keep away the great majority of national human rights NGOs. The result, at its worst, is a recycling of oft-studied concerns, spoken largely on behalf of the Third World by First World-based organizations.

However one may assess the Sub-Commission spectacle, the central role of non-governmental organizations stands out. In the words of one noted Sub-Commission member, NGOs play a

forceful and creative role. . . . Their representatives engage in substantial lobbying behind the scenes. Sometimes they circulate drafts of resolutions which are subsequently modified and presented by Sub-Commission experts; they provide written and oral submissions; and they present allegations of violations. They have been of particular assistance in the elaboration of principles and other forms of standard-setting.[26]

Herein lies a key to grasping the importance of human rights NGOs. Documenting the plight of victims, and pressing governments for corrective action, are crucial tasks. They speak and act for victims. At the same time, human rights groups also contribute significantly to the development of new human rights standards[27] (Donnelly's "declaratory" regime) and to the promotion of human rights, as well as to their enforcement. But it is their voice on behalf of those who suffer that makes NGOs indispensable. As Alston writes, "In terms of protection activities it has always been the NGOs that have applied the real pressure for reform of the Commission [on Human Rights]'s procedures and the great majority of the 'evidence' of violations continues to be generated directly by NGOs."[28]

As important as the Sub-Commission and other United Nations bodies may be on the global human rights scene, however, the most significant focus for NGO actions comes "back home." Ultimately, the strategies that NGOs utilize need to impact on their own states, altering the policies that led to the abuses they document and protest. Action must be taken at the national level for a human rights group to be credible and effective. The choice of strategy is thus of paramount importance.

Six Strategies and Means of Promotion and Protection

NGOs can choose among several strategies and means, depending on their resources, objectives, and political "space." Most concentrate their efforts on documenting and publicizing abuses — in other words, acting directly on behalf of victims through calling attention to the human suffering involved. They monitor, in short. Some NGOs focus on the longer-term, less glamorous task of promoting human rights awareness, usually through education. They seek long-term attitudinal change, making for a "culture" of respect for others. Some human rights NGOs work in partnership with governments, recognizing that while political authorities may abuse their powers, they also have the responsibility and resources to protect citizens' rights. Still other human rights NGOs perceive particular governments as enemies that must be replaced, or at least radically modified, to improve the situation. They work in highly politicized environments, seeking democratization or perhaps greater autonomy for a specific group. And, finally, yet other NGOs labor for development. Many came into existence as short-term, relief-distributing entities; they have shifted toward longer-term, growth-oriented organizations.

In reality, the ways in which NGOs operate shift over time. This has proven particularly true for human rights NGOs. An abrupt change in the national political climate — such as occurred in Ethiopia with the triumph of the EPRDF — can permit their rapid sprouting and flowering, or conversely, their extinction. Establishment of democratic institutions in formerly authoritarian settings poses challenges to NGOs to change their ways of operating.[29] Global changes play an important part as well. International emphasis on human rights, as through support by major governments and aid-givers, may permit groups to be formed and obtain support. NGOs can choose to act in internal and/or international arenas: they can pressure their own states for action; they can seek attention in Geneva, New York, or other world centers. In brief, they must be alert to changes in the political context, permitting (or indeed requiring) new approaches.

In the paragraphs that follow, I sketch six overlapping strategies that human rights NGOs in Africa and elsewhere have chosen. This listing is not exhaustive. It does, however, provide a basis to compare NGOs' effectiveness. What they accomplish must be measured in relation to groups' specific objectives, leadership, resources, and political space. Papayas must not be compared with mangoes. Little good is served, for example, if an organization dedicated to raising awareness about the harmful effects of genital operations is criticized for not pressing for release of unjustly jailed political activists. We must examine what human rights NGOs actually accomplish in terms of their specific purposes and strategies. Further, citizens' associations cannot accomplish major changes by themselves, save under highly unusual circumstances. They must work in tandem with others. Human rights NGOs, as part of an increasingly dense, rich network in civil society, can nonetheless improve the situation.

Education

Education classically forms part of promotion. This strategy recognizes that involved, aware citizens serve as the chief foundation for human rights.

Education constituted a central part of human rights action long before the establishment of the United Nations. Abolitionists and suffragists — persons who now would be called human rights activists — raised public awareness about the evils of slavery and the inequities of denying the vote to women in earlier centuries. Proponents of democracy such as John Dewey or Charles Merriam advocated civic education for all Americans, and, by extension, for citizens of all countries. Unfortunately, there is neither time nor space to pursue these forerunners. Let us narrow in on post-1945 steps taken explicitly in connection with the human rights norms advocated by and through the United Nations.

The UN itself pledged, in Article 1 of its Charter, "*promoting and encouraging* respect for human rights and for fundamental freedoms." The Universal Declaration of Human Rights (UDHR) was proclaimed "as a standard of achievement for all peoples and all nations," and called on "every individual and every organ of society . . . *by teaching and education* to promote respect for these rights and freedoms" (italics added). Education, according to Article 26 of the UDHR, would serve to strengthen respect for human rights and fundamental freedoms. UNESCO, the relevant UN specialized agency, has convened conferences on education for human rights, sponsored special publications and adopted specific conventions (such as the 1960 Convention Against Discrimination in Education or its 1978 Declaration on Race and Racial Prejudice) advancing human rights goals. In addition, UNESCO has since 1978 allowed individuals and NGOs a limited opportunity to raise complaints about denial of educational or cultural rights covered by its treaties.[30]

These international efforts, laudable in their intent, remain far removed from the true centers of action. Human rights education must be pursued primarily within individual states.

The task is mind-boggling. Nothing short of a goal of transforming society lies at the heart of human rights education, and of the groups that press for it. Building a "human rights culture," in broad terms, provides the *raison d'être* of NGOs focused on education. They operate on the assumption that students in the late twentieth century must be informed about the "fourth R" — rights. Influence over school curricula is central. Hence, one logical target for action are ministries of education. Another prime focus is law schools or training legal defenders. Yet another potential focus lies in military and police academies; their graduates surely need to be informed about the limits to their coercive powers.

For NGOs focused on human rights education, governments are not potential opponents, but necessary partners. Geographically, such NGOs naturally congregate in capital cities. Their personnel come overwhelmingly from the ranks of the well-educated. Their task is both long-term, from the bottom up in terms of influencing youth through curricula, and short-term, focused on specific critical audiences such as lawyers or police. Success (though far from readily measurable) must usually be calibrated in the broad realm of public opinion over decades. On the other hand, specific professional training can reap rapid benefits. A lawyer or paralegal trained to use the country's court system to protect human rights, or a policeman or soldier conscious of criminal procedure or of the laws of war and therefore less likely to abuse a person he has detained, constitutes a clear and immediate gain for human rights. The need for human rights education is thus both chronic and acute.

There has been little research on human rights education in developing countries, with one major exception. Thanks to Claude's excellent monograph, human rights education in the Philippines has been analyzed in interesting detail. The "People's Power" revolution of February 1986 made an indelible stamp on human rights in the country. Overturning the dictatorial rule of Ferdinand Marcos (in a manner not unlike the ouster of Moussa Traoré in Mali in 1991, though far less violent than the removal of the Derg from power in Ethiopia) gave the new Philippine government policies and constitution a decidedly pro-human rights nature. One Executive Order required military and police personnel to study human rights "as an integral and indispensable part" of their training; another Executive Order obligated the Ministry of Education, Culture and Sports to "include the study and understanding of human rights in the curricula of all levels of education in all schools in the country." The 1987 constitution of the Philippines incorporated all the civil and political rights found in the Universal Declaration, plus many economic, social, and cultural rights; an independent Commission on Human

Rights was established, charged with setting up "a continuing program of research, education, and information to enhance respect for the primacy of human rights"; NGOs were galvanized into activity and gained unprecedented access to government decision-makers. As Claude observes,

In the annals of political science, bureaucracies so accessible and open to input from NGO's are rare. EDSA [the four-day revolution] made a difference by energizing the NGO's and affording the established bureaucracies little publicly defensible basis for resistance.[31]

Such a profound, rapid opening of political space — perhaps possible only through widespread popular mobilization and the fluidity linked to profound upheaval — comes rarely. The Philippine case thus has potential relevance to Ethiopia. The legitimacy of both the Corazón Aquino and Meles Zenawi governments was directly linked to their improving human rights conditions. Aspirations in the two cases outran accomplishments. Despite a highly favorable context, the Aquino government's ambitious goals proved difficult to implement. Limited resources, resistance within the armed forces, bureaucratic inertia, and turf protection played their part. The hoped-for close cooperation between NGOs and ministry officials in designing programs broke down. Implementation of human rights education was undermined by organizational behavior, doctrinal disagreements about how to present issues of human rights violations, and blame for shortcomings within the government and the military.[32] Administrators did not respond well to constitutional and presidential mandates. Advances came primarily as a result of initiatives from NGOs and funding from outside the Philippines.[33] Rather than a comprehensive national program of human rights education, the country has had a series of piecemeal efforts — though undoubtedly more significant than in any African state with which I am directly acquainted.

There are, at this time, relatively few human rights NGOs in Africa for which education forms the primary strategy. The Nigeria-based Legal Research and Resources Development Centre (LRRDC) provides one example, the Society for Human Rights Education (SAHRE, based in Ethiopia), and the Inter-African Committee on Traditional Practices that Affect the Health of Women and Children (IAC) provide others. They pursue different goals with separate audiences. The LRRDC, given greater attention in Chapter 6, reaches out to the public through publications written in easy-to-understand English, largely on themes directly relevant to its poor, heavily female constituency. SAHRE had barely gotten off the ground in early 1994, bureaucratic caution and miniscule funding limiting its effectiveness. The IAC, examined in Chapter 3, combats female genital mutilation by holding seminars in selected countries and publicizing the negative consequences of "circumcision." While the

Nigerian LRRDC works with paralegals, community organizers, and others, SAHRE remains confined to the Ministry of Education in Addis Ababa; the IAC reaches out to traditional midwives, village chiefs, and government officials in many countries.

Empowerment

Empowerment is a second strategy used by human rights NGOs. It entails deliberate political mobilization of the community the NGO seeks to serve. Far more than education, empowerment confronts the status quo. Of the various strategies examined in this book, empowerment poses the most serious political challenges to governments. Deliberately so, I am tempted to add. Empowerment refers to politically (as well as historically, socially, and economically) disadvantaged groups. Typical groups for whom empowerment has been sought include landless peasants, uneducated rural women, and ethnic minorities with long-standing grievances. They thus challenge the status quo in class, gender, and/or social terms.

Efforts at empowering such groups seem to wave a red flag in front of many presidents, in Africa and elsewhere. Rather than halt or reconsider, national leaders charge directly at their critics; rather than examine the policy issues raised, they perceive threats to their authority, and react viscerally. Those at the top of the government see themselves as the true embodiment of popular wishes, and hence unquestionable in their decisions. NGOs disagree. By claiming to speak for "the people" contrary to the political leaders, NGOs seeking empowerment often find themselves liable to sharp repression. Accordingly, they may find it advisable to mask their aims, preferring instead to speak about "enablement" or "development." They may flourish better in rural areas, removed from the direct eye of government, than in cities. (This geographical separation diminishes their ability to affect central policy, however.) They may seek to minimize contacts with government, but when they occur they are more likely to be confrontational than cooperative.

Clear examples of empowerment as a strategy come from NGOs lobbying on behalf of specific ethnic groups. Three cases, two of them West African, deserve mention here, and lengthier discussion in Chapter 4.

In Nigeria, the Movement for the Survival of the Ogoni People (MOSOP) has skillfully drawn international attention through publications, lobbying, (especially within the United Nations) and high-profile leadership. The Movement's message is direct: the Ogoni people (who live in a major oil-producing section of Delta state) face severe threats to their continuation as a distinct group; they argue they should receive a greater share of petroleum revenues; self-determination and greater political rights must be provided. MOSOP crystallized around a determined

leader. Noted Ogoni novelist Ken Saro-Wiwa had been alert to discrimination against "his people" from the late 1960s on. No Nigerian has
wielded a pen (or plied a typewriter) more effectively in recent years
than Saro-Wiwa. He was among human rights leaders rounded up by the
Nigeria government in 1993 and again in 1994; his arrests provided the
Ogonis with an imprisoned martyr.

In Senegal, the Mouvement des Forces Démocratiques Casamançais
(MFDC) has pressed for greater regional autonomy—a claim based to a
substantial degree on social and historical factors. Casamance has been a
physically isolated, less developed section of Senegal, inhabited primarily
by Diola, it will be recalled from the previous chapter. Feelings of both
neglect and exploitation have buttressed the MFDC's regional/ethnic
appeal. Its separatism has been vigorously countered by the Senegalese
government. More than a decade of episodic armed confrontation has
brought resolution barely closer. The Casamance issue remains Senegal's
most sensitive, persistent human rights problem.

In Ethiopia, a coalition of ethnically-based resistance movements un-
seated the authoritarian regime of Mengistu Haile-Mariam. The Charter
of the Transitional Government (TGE) promised various Ethiopian peoples the right to self-determination. Once Eritrea had established its
independence after a referendum and new provincial boundaries had
been delineated, however, Ethiopian officials were far less willing to
countenance talk of secession. In particular, pressure for greater Oromo
autonomy posed an acute dilemma for the TGE. The Oromo Liberation
Front (OLF) formed an important part of the EPRDF coalition. A few
days before the 1992 election, the OLF pulled out, and conflict erupted.
It was unclear how far OLF leaders wanted to press for autonomy, but it
was abundantly clear that they distrusted the primarily Tigrean leaders of
the Transitional Government. Whether the proclamation of the Charter
was wise became hotly disputed. Could the genie of separatism be pushed
back into the bottle? The OLF was a movement of armed resistance,
distinct in its means of operation (if not necessarily its chief objective)
from some "standard" human rights NGOs.

The handling of Ogoni, Casamance, and Oromo concerns casts light
on the most complex issue many African countries confront: resolving
internal claims for self-determination. For (the argument goes) if one
group gets much greater autonomy or government rewards, won't others
be tempted to put on pressure as well? Won't the entire system be undermined? Fears of this sort in the early years of independence led to single-
party systems. Similar concerns were voiced by military leaders, as they
installed one-man rule. Analogous issues are already arising in would-be
democratic Africa. Empowerment is central to democracy, but irreconcil-
able group claims can tear it apart. At least rhetorically, Ethiopia's Transi-

tional Government permitted the greatest scope for ethnic differentia-tion. Article 2 of the Transitional Charter, the TGE's guiding philosophy, vested major powers in regions whose boundaries were redrawn to estab-lish a dominant group in each. Will Ethiopia become a more effective pluralistic democracy because of the Transitional Government's recogni-tion of collective rights for ethnic groups? What should happen when regimes imposed by the military talk about stepping aside? How can democratic processes be instituted? Will new forms of democracy take root? I shall return to these dilemmas of empowerment several times more in this book.

Enforcement

The third major approach used by African human rights NGOs, *enforce-ment* through national court systems and international treaty bodies, is a sophisticated, highly important, but rather limited strategy. It is the most familiar means of protecting human rights in developed countries; it faces significant obstacles in most African states. Nationally, it requires several crucial institutions: 1) a framework of laws and constitutional norms (the "rule of law"); 2) a functioning court system, whose judges are not subject to strong pressure to skew their decisions ("indepen-dence of the judiciary"); and 3) a functioning system of legal assistance, giving the less affluent access to the legal system as a whole. Interna-tionally, the strategy of enforcement also depends on three conditions: 1) specific conventions ratified by governments; 2) willingness by these gov-ernment to honor their treaty commitments, notably by submitting de-tailed periodic reports, incorporating necessary changes in their consti-tutions and legal frameworks, and acting in accordance with their treaty commitments; and 3) supervising committees, staffed by informed per-sons with professional support, who are ready to take an active role when human rights violations are called to their attention by NGOs or can be discerned from official reports.

Many human rights NGOs focus on enforcement. I could have chosen examples from any of the four states. The levels of activity vary markedly, however, depending on a congeries of factors. In Ethiopia, decades of authoritarian rule seriously weakened the judicial system. Marked prob-lems remain, as highlighted by the International Human Rights Law Group.[34] The concept of legal assistance is at an early stage, with informal caucuses of lawyers the chief avenue.[35] In Nigeria, by contrast, the Civil Liberties Organisation, the Constitutional Rights Project, FIDA (Interna-tional Federation of Women Lawyers), the Legal Research and Resource Development Centre and other groups all provide legal counsel or train paralegals. They press as well for the rule of law. In Senegal, the Association des Jeunes Avocats Sénégalais (AJAS) has proposed voluntary involvement by its members and a small clinic has been established in Dakar by another group; only rudiments of legal assistance currently exist, however.

But in Namibia the links among enforcement, human rights, and public interest law can be discerned most easily. There, the Legal Assistance Centre (studied in Chapter 6) occupies a unique position. During the struggle for independence (which took place on diplomatic and military levels, as well as in the psychology of individual Namibians), "law" played a curious role. The government of South Africa took great care to follow legal niceties in implementing its apartheid policies. The legal system, in other words, was used to define individuals' rights based on their race. Whites enjoyed far more legal privileges and rights than did Blacks. The apartheid system was systematically biased against the majority. However, the court system could also be used to gain victories against apartheid. Litigation could move Namibia closer to independence and a constitution guaranteeing equal rights for all. The techniques used by the Legal Assistance Centre (LAC) exemplify enforcement at the national level.

A rather different timetable and set of constraints marks international enforcement of human rights. By the mid-1970s monitoring of human rights through UN bodies started to take off. Several treaties were negotiated, then ratified by individual states. Central to all were reporting mechanisms. Governments agreed to provide periodic analyses of the legislative, judicial, and other measures taken to protect the rights specified in the particular documents. These reports were examined by independent experts, specially convened for the task, who questioned state representatives in public meetings. This has become a relatively successful means, at least under some treaties, lying "at the very heart of the international system for the promotion and protection of human rights."[36] Many of the achievements have been, I assert, the direct consequence of NGO monitoring and pressure. Human rights groups have supplemented, countered, updated, and generally provided alternative perspectives to official reports. To an increasing extent, NGOs have developed alternative fact-gathering and fact-presenting means. Their documentation has been absolutely crucial in the global human rights movement.

To understand the impact of reporting as a means of enforcement, we could focus on the seven major human rights treaties drafted by the UN and the reports submitted to their respective expert committees. (These treaties include, in chronological order of adoption and entry into force, the International Convention on the Elimination of Racial Discrimination, the Convention on the Suppression and Punishment of the Crime of *Apartheid*, the International Covenant on Economic, Social and Cultural Rights, the International Covenant on Civil and Political Rights [plus two Optional Protocols], the Convention on the Elimination of All Forms of Discrimination Against Women, the Convention Against Torture and Other Cruel, Inhuman or Degrading Treatment or Punishment, and the Convention on the Rights of the Child.) As of early 1993, no fewer than 678 ratifications had been officially deposited for these, meaning an average of 113 States parties to each treaty; a year later, the figure had climbed to an average of nearly 122 States per treaty.[37] Almost all African countries have ratified at least two of these conventions. They have accordingly taken on specific obligations, opening up opportunities for NGO input.

How have governments and non-governmental organizations responded to the challenge offered by the public discussion of reports? To be brutally honest, many governments have done little of a positive nature. They regard reporting as a nuisance, and have shirked their obligation, as will be discussed in Chapter 5. Tardy or non-existent reports have been common. Those submitted are often inadequately detailed or unresponsive to guidelines. Official representatives sometimes fail to attend meetings to which they are invited. Or, once there, they pettifog, stonewall, engage in diplomatic doubletalk, or dissimulate. Experts on the respective committees seem reluctant, on some occasions, to press hard questions. The task has been left in part to NGOs. Non-governmental organizations have (as an earlier quotation from Alston illustrates) put the screws on official delegations and members of the UN treaty bodies. Some NGOs have prepared statements specifically for the committees of experts. Such documentation has proven a useful corrective to the partial information offered by the governments. On occasion, representatives of African human rights NGOs have flown to Geneva (or, for the Women's Convention, to New York or Vienna) to listen to the remarks of their government's spokesperson, the questions of individual experts, and the responses, if any, from the representative — all in order to have greater influence through the reporting process and to shape their own responses. They have lobbied for greater attention from the supervisory bodies. Most important, they have sought to inform the committees of issues governments may conveniently have overlooked or minimized. By presenting the seamy side of human rights, NGOs provide a necessary corrective to the official stories received from governments.

Little is known in Africa about the process of reporting and public discussion by treaty bodies. It is a dull, costly, relatively unproductive and valueless effort, from the point of view of many NGOs. Their members cannot intervene in the discussion, although they may informally circulate written material, but few have availed themselves of this opportunity. After all, the major struggle is at home, not in the marble rooms of the United Nations. But some NGOs may be missing an important opportunity. Those that lobby with the treaty bodies (such as the Movement for the Survival of the Ogoni People) have sometimes reaped surprisingly large rewards in publicity. Treaty-based reporting systems have grown in significance far beyond the expectations of their initial proponents, in large part because NGOs have pressured for the process to be taken seriously. Accordingly, attention must be given to how reporting actually works. Here, we shall focus on the African Commission on Human and Peoples' Rights.

In some respects, the African Commission has proven more accessible to African human rights NGOs than have Geneva-based UN treaty bodies, in terms of enforcement through reporting.[38] The major reason is easy to discern: access to the group of experts (even if they work within a treaty widely perceived as weak) has been eased by a major international human rights NGO. The International Commission of Jurists (ICJ) has spent a great deal of money and time to bring upwards of 65 such groups (in the 1991–94 period) to African Commission sessions and pre-meeting workshops. The ICJ wants to make the reporting process a significant, open opportunity for constructive dialogue between States parties and individual commissioners, and between Commissioners and NGO representatives. Individual NGOs have become acquainted with the Commission's members, procedures, objectives, and values as a result of the ICJ's efforts. NGOs have learned how to inform the African Commission's work. Information-sharing networks have taken shape. At the same time, the Commission has come to appreciate NGOs' special strengths in gathering information about human rights abuses.

While carrying out research for this book, I attended several meetings of the African Commission over a two-year period. At each, mutual understanding between the Commission and NGOs increased. Combatants at the first ACHPR session I attended (Tunis, March 1992), they had become wary antagonists; seven months later (Banjul, October 1992) the distrust was ebbing; within 25 months (Banjul, April 1994) they acted like cautious partners. To some extent, they jointly determined issues to probe with reporting states and recommendations to make to the parent Organization of African Unity to strengthen the Commission. Detente turned into entente. Mutual understanding of their respective roles meant the Commission and NGOs found areas for cooperation. Their roles were not identical — nor should they be. However, an area of constructive overlap existed. NGOs could supplement, and occasionally correct, information provided by reporting states. NGOs could legitimate the Commission's work to wider audiences. NGOs shared the Commission's fundamental goal of *promoting* human rights, and wished it to take fundamental steps toward *protecting* them in ratifying countries. But is this latter desire feasible, at least under the means of reporting?

A basic problem exists with enforcement based on reporting as a strategy. Simply put, who enforces the findings of a committee of experts? The state, obviously. But if a government has systematically abused human rights, it is not likely to write a detailed, accurate report of these shortcomings, nor will it engage in constructive dialogue with the relevant treaty body. It may treat the occasion as a public relations exercise; the experts themselves rarely have the ability under the particular treaty, or the influence built over time, to compel better performance. But my impressions, built primarily on observing the African Commission and some Geneva-based treaty bodies at work, may be incomplete. A careful analysis of the Human Rights Committee (the 11-member group that examines reports submitted under the International Covenant on Civil and Political Rights) showed that several States parties changed national laws in response to Committee comments or Covenant standards.[39]

Having now looked at the our three E's, let us consider three D's as NGO means. Education, empowerment, and enforcement overlap with the means of documentation, democratization, and development. These latter two correspond to two primary African concerns of the 1990s. Making governments responsive to society requires democratization. Making the lives of Africans less exploited or economically degraded requires development. They are interdependent. The emergence and expansion of democracy is linked to the desire and need for better economic distribution. The reinforcement of human rights culture in Africa will require a combination of democratization and development. At the same time, however, it will rest to some degree upon the ability of NGOs to monitor governments' performances. Human rights performance must be documented. Official reports may tell one story, NGO analyses another. Both are essential. Hence, documentation, democratization, and development must all be considered.

 Documentation

Documentation by human rights groups logically complements states' reports. But the studies prepared and published by NGOs are far wider. Governments are supposed to prepare their reports on regular schedules. The documents follow frameworks set by the particular treaties. Between two and five years elapse between official submissions. Sometimes, these will be discussed within twelve months of submission; often, longer delays occur. Little public attention will likely be paid either to the "official story" or to its presentation to the supervising committee.[40] The reports can be, at worst, uninformative bureaucratic twaddle; at best, cautious expositions of what governments do, or intend to do.

It is not the official reports that are important; it is the reporting *process.*

The process element comes largely from NGOs' studies. Their documentation and pressure can put states on the defensive. Their links to the media may result in front-page or prime-time coverage of human rights abuses. In short, NGOs provide crucial elements of information and publicity. Public awareness of human rights problems arises largely as a result of NGO efforts.

NGO reports are designed to pressure governments into action, through the "mobilization of shame." NGO networks spread information. Documentation is, as Wiseberg notes, "a precondition for stopping abuses and a prerequisite for effective action in the human rights field."[41] Human rights NGOs begin to flourish south of the Sahara as the independence of the media grows. In this connection, recent media developments in Africa stand out. The number of newspapers has grown markedly since 1990 or so, as official restrictions and requirements have been eased. Far less private initiative has been permitted for radio and television, however. This should be expected. In tropical Africa, newspaper circulation remains largely confined to urban areas, usually among persons literate in the official languages. Radio listenership is much more widespread. The surest way to reach a large audience south of the Sahara is via early-morning broadcasts in indigenous languages. No wonder few states have ended official monopolies over the radio. Ending the official monopolization of the airwaves is proving more complex than opening the newspaper market to new entries.

Accusations may be bandied about, but credibility must be established. Human rights NGOs that engage in gathering evidence and publicizing abuses must evaluate their information. Reputations for effective, accurate reporting require long times to build. NGOs that have established their credibility (Amnesty International, with its cadre of well over 200 full-time researchers in its London offices, is the best example) become forces to reckon with. Truth — especially in detail — is the strongest weapon human rights NGOs can wield. Their pens challenge the state's swords.

Documentation is a duty of all human rights NGOs. Some have made information gathering, evaluation, and dissemination their primary objective. Geneva-based HURIDOCS (Human Rights Information and Documentation Systems International), to take one example, concentrates on developing documentation centers. Its training programs and publications, to which attention is given in Chapter 7, have started to have an impact on Africa. A second example located outside Africa is Ottawa-based Human Rights Internet (HRI). Since the mid-1970s, HRI has specialized in collecting and summarizing NGO reports. Such ephemeral "gray material" is rarely obtained by libraries, and likely has limited distribution even in its country of origin. HRI's publications, including its master list of NGOs, have dramatically increased awareness of NGO activities. But it is to the African human rights groups that we must give primary attention. Accordingly, much of Chapter 7 is devoted to the documentation they have prepared and distributed, with Nigerian prisons and police as the centers of attention. NGO monitoring lies at the heart of protecting human rights.

Democratization

Democratization builds upon the belief that civil society requires governments committed to freedom of association, competitive elections, independent courts and media, and other civil and political rights. The 1990s, as suggested at the start of this chapter, is the African decade for democratization, based on the expansion and deepening of civil society. A conjuncture of internal and external factors opened this opportunity. NGOs can facilitate democratization in several ways — as well as themselves benefit from the process.

Domestically, a majority of African countries experienced serious political refocusing early in the decade. Particularly in French-speaking countries, "sovereign national conferences" were convened to attempt to preside over political transitions from authoritarian rule.[42] If the system worked, change could be smooth and new leaders peacefully elected, as occurred, among others, in Benin, Central African Republic, Congo, Madagascar, and Niger. In others, demonstrations or riots broke out in protest against the continued clutch of the anciens régimes in power; the (re)birth of competitive politics and inauguration of new leaders in Mali, for example, came with some difficulty. Some leaders remained in control through astute use of coercion or divide-and-rule policies, despite national conferences or analogous rallying of opposition groups; some profited from divisions within the opposition. Cameroon, Gabon, Ghana, Kenya, Togo, and Zaire were countries in which (as of early 1994) bumbling by the challengers and/or various levels of fraud by the incumbents left the status quo in place.

International interest in democratization has been evidenced by all major aid-givers, and endorsed by various global gatherings. I shall cite a few examples. At the 1990 "Francophonie" summit, French President François Mitterrand stated that France would link continued economic aid to institutional progress toward democracy. Evidence would include free elections, universal suffrage, freedom of the press, independence of the judiciary, multipartyism, and abolition of censorship. Members of the Commonwealth declared at Harare in October 1991 that democratic systems should henceforward mark its members. Recent non-binding guidelines for aid from the OECD (Organization for Economic Cooperation and Development) were prefaced with the observation, "There is a vital connection between open, democratic, and accountable systems of governance and respect for human rights, and the ability to achieve sustained economic and social development." As a result, the report from OECD's Development Assistance Committee noted, "participatory development and good governance must be central concerns in the allocation and design of development assistance."[43] U.S. policy steps have been numerous. In December 1990, USAID launched its "Democracy Initiative." Participation and democracy were incorporated as criteria into AID's economic, social, and environmental programs. The State Department has placed renewed emphasis on democracy and human rights activities under the 116(e) Democracy and Human Rights Fund, supporting programs in legal assistance, human rights, electoral assistance, and constitutional reform and democratic institution building. Almost all these grants in Africa are made directly to NGOs or universities. Although the amounts are small, usually under $25,000 each, they can determine an NGO's success, even its survival.[44] The National Endowment for Democracy has made substantial grants for workshops and research on democracy. International election monitoring has become a staple of political change in many African countries; entities like the National Democratic Institute (NDI) and the African-American Institute (AAI) have documented the tortuous path of establishing multi-party competition.[45] Without question, developed countries have increasingly expected aid recipients to establish the basic institutions of civil society, thereby enhancing democracy.

Many world statesmen have linked democracy and development with human rights. UN Secretary-General Boutros-Ghali, in opening the June 1993 Vienna World Conference on human rights, spoke specifically about the need for responsive government. Speaking later that year at the meeting of the African Society of International and Comparative Law, he emphasized the importance of development.[46] States that protect civil and political rights (in almost all cases, democracies) advance economic, social and cultural rights better than those that abridge such rights.[47]

The movement toward democracy has many fathers. Surprisingly, perhaps, one of the strongest claims to paternity comes from a global economic organization. The staid World Bank in some respects led the bandwagon. Its 1989 publication, *Sub-Saharan Africa: From Crisis to Sustainable Growth*, had "a tremendous impact in reorienting attention to the need for political accountability, public debate, press freedom, political participation, pluralism, decentralization, consensus building and hence legitimacy in order to achieve real economic development."[48] Coming from an unexpected source that had sedulously avoided "political" pronouncements in the past, the World Bank's statement aroused wide interest — an interest intensified later that year by the collapse of Communist governments in Europe. "Governance" became a new watchword. To cite other analysts, "The new focus [on governance] has more explicitly political concerns with legitimacy, participation, pluralism, a free press and human rights, and these factors have become for the Bank a key factor in explaining Africa's current crisis."[49]

The magnitude of change is highly significant. Authoritarianism was on the retreat in tropical Africa from the start of 1990. Between January 1990 and July 1992, thirteen African heads of state were replaced, four of them voted out of office in competitive multiparty elections.[50] We have already noted Ethiopia's and Namibia's critical drafting of constitutions, in which human rights and democracy figured prominently. The reluctant, partial political disengagement of the Nigerian military was, without question, pressured by the emergence of democracy as a continent-wide goal, as was the greater willingness of the Senegalese Parti Socialiste to consult opposition groups about revising the electoral code.

Democracy, in short, has made significant, if irregular, progress through tropical Africa. Still further evidence comes from the annual publication of Freedom House, *Freedom in the World*. (As this title suggests, the publishers concentrate on civil and political rights.) In 1989, Freedom House rated 34 African states "not free," 15 "partly free," and three "free" (that is, democratic). In 1992, the numbers had shifted dramatically: The number "not free" had been cut in half to 17, while 23 were rated "partly free," eight "free."[51] The Carter Center's map, published quarterly in *Africa Demos*, conveys a similar lesson. By February 1993, it rated 11 African countries as democratic systems ("wide competition between organized groups, numerous opportunities for popular participation in government, and elections that are regularly and fairly conducted. Constitutional guarantees of civil liberties and human rights are effectively enforced."), only four as authoritarian ("highly restricted opportunities for political mobilization. Power is exercised by a leader or small group not formally accountable to an electorate. There are no effective constitutional limits to the exercise of political power."), four as directed democracy ("formal institutions and practices are present. In practice, however, the extensive powers of the ruler, party, or regime severely limit contestation by individuals, organized groups, legislative assemblies, and the judiciary."), no fewer than 20 at a "moderate" stage ("formal commitments to a democratic transition are accompanied by only measured, cautious, and preliminary steps toward institutionalization or pluralism. Promises reflect a sense of democratic purpose, but deeds are not yet comensurate with pledges."), and a dozen "ambiguous" ("Ruling elite's commitment to democracy is at best precarious, at worse a ruse and at most times unclear. On the one hand, stated commitments are often suspended due to the exigencies of the moment. On the other hand, the construction of elaborate democratic structures suggests little more than political maneuvering.").[52]

The upsurge of democratic efforts south of the Sahara has led to an explosion in publication.[53] The *Journal of Democracy* carries frequent articles on sub-Saharan Africa. A volume on Africa was the first to appear in the Diamond-Lipset-Linz trilogy on democracy in the Third World.[54] Academic conferences have proliferated. Election monitoring has turned into a small industry.

Most significant, democracy has been adopted by Africans as something they consider inherently valuable, and universal in its importance: African in its roots and significance, not merely an imposition of powerful outside countries. This fundamental belief undergirds the commitment of African human rights NGOs to democratization. For a global consensus exists, with the possible exception of some Asian states. Democracy is the preferred political form. Governments are responsible for establishing and maintaining the necessary electoral systems that can allow peaceful change. The rule of law requires effective administration. Other countries have the right to object when the rule of law is abridged. Regimes that circumvent or abridge steps toward democracy face criticism, both domestically and internationally. For example, when President Babangida annulled the results of the June 1993 Nigerian presidential election, the United Kingdom and the United States suspended their aid programs and issued strong statements; human rights groups and the Nigerian Labour Congress organized stay-at-homes; for a few days, the bustling confusion of Lagos lapsed into uneasy quiet because of the protest organized by the Campaign by Democracy (unfortunately shattered by violence and repression, as will be discussed in Chapter 8). Although the Babangida regime weathered the crisis temporarily, its claim to be fostering democracy was smashed irretrievably. Babangida's resignation on the eve of the eighth anniversary of his coup d'état evidenced the importance of the "second wind of change" across Africa.

The rising demand for democratic political participation through Africa has reinforced human rights NGOs of whatever strategy preference. Calls for further democratization have become central to their other goals. Prophetically, some joined with other NGOs at Arusha in February 1990 to issue the "African Charter for Popular Participation in Development and Transformation," published by the Economic Commission for Africa, demonstrating once again the links between economics and policy.[55] The Arusha Charter illustrated the linkage Africans draw among democracy (expressed here as popular participation), development, and future well-being. If current political leaders fail to open up new channels for political involvement, the NGOs warned, Africa as a whole would be the loser.

To exemplify the work of African human rights NGOs for democracy, I have selected the Campaign for Democracy (CD), which led the storm of protest against Babangida's action, and contrasted it with the government-sponsored Centre for Democratic Studies (CDS) as the major subjects for Chapter 8.

The CDS was established to train "newbreed" politicians belonging to the two officially-recognized political parties. Members of the NRC (National Republican Convention) and SDP (Social Democratic Party) would practice "grassroots democracy" and learn the political and economic facts of life from the Centre's programs. Further, CDS researchers (in conjunction with University of Michigan specialists) would document Nigeria's return to constitutional government. These aspirations were smashed. The multi-million dollar effort in training and research ran aground on the shoals of Babangida's resistance to military disengagement. He and a coterie of top brass feared that M. K. O. Abiola, democratically chosen by the people in the June 1993 president election, would launch a full probe into their financial manipulations. The CDS effort from above to reform political behavior seems to have focused on the wrong people: on party officials who aspired to power, rather than on military officers who actually held it. Democratization and empowerment from the top down fell short. The changes in attitude individual party officials may have gained through their study at CDS were not complemented by changes in attitude by the real rulers of Nigeria.

Equally, however, the bottom-up efforts of the Campaign for Democracy failed to reach their goal. As shown in the preceding chapter, the long-term reluctance of the armed forces to restore full constitutional government severely circumscribed human rights in Nigeria. Pressure on the military to return to the barracks and hand over power to Abiola came from a coalition of groups organized into the CD. Democratization should not, the CD argued, become a veil for renewed dictatorial rule. The CD's efforts nettled the military government. It struck back, playing the tribal trump card. Babangida and his immediate supporters accused the CD, which is based in Lagos and which draws much of its support from Yoruba in the southwest, of playing up ethnic solidarity at the expense of national unity—as defined by the military government. The CD's effort failed, at least in terms of bringing Abiola to Abuja as President. On the other hand, Babangida was forced to resign. The CD's pressure did convince senior military officers that "IBB" had to go, and that rule through an interim, largely civilian government was preferable. Nonetheless, the armed forces remained in effective control, as confirmed by Abacha's coup d'état of November 1993. Democratization and empowerment from the bottom up, through the CD's attempts at mass mobilization, failed to transform the basic contours of the Nigerian political system. The umbrella CD split; Abacha played cleverly on the widespread desire of prominent Nigerians to join the self-enriching political class; he also made sufficient promises of reforms to come to reduce the level of tension. Empowerment of "the masses" remained a distant goal. One hopes that Nigeria's peaceful but aborted presidential election of 1993 was not a one-time event.

Development

Development is the final broad means to be outlined. NGOs emphasizing this approach tend to operate at the margins of classic human rights activity, at least from the perspective of those emphasizing democratization or enforcement, and which draw quintessentially on "first generation" civil and political rights. For them, the primary tasks involve creating and sustaining effective governance, based on popular participation in open, competitive elections, and establishing and maintaining the rule of law, based on an independent judiciary, an even-handed police force, and functioning courts. Pro-democracy NGOs naturally cluster around policy makers in major cities. By contrast, pro-development NGOs tend to focus on farmers, rural women, or other marginalized persons — in short, on groups near the bottom of the economic and social hierarchy. They concentrate on goals that in most African countries receive fewer constitutional protections, a not uncommon situation for "second generation" rights.[56] The agenda of these development-oriented NGOs thus overlaps with empowerment. But while empowerment seeks to raise political consciousness and translate numbers into power, development emphasizes increasing economic welfare. Human rights begin with breakfast, after all! A person denied minimum levels of food, shelter, health care, or personal safety may not survive; and surely the right to life is the most basic of all. Man-made disasters such as civil war or induced famine make constitutions hollow mockeries of human rights.[57] Conditions through most of Africa make development, as well as democratization, imperative. However, the basic conditions are far from favorable.

Africa occupies a tangential and worsening position in the global economy. Despite special programs for development announced with great fanfare, economic indicators have moved from grim to horrifying. The World Bank estimated the average annual per capita growth of GDP for sub-Saharan Africa in the 1982–92 period was *minus* 1.1 percent.[58] This should be contrasted with a positive 2.9 percent for South Asia, 6.3 percent for East Asia and the Pacific, 0.5 percent for Latin America and the Caribbean, and 1.5 percent for all low and middle income countries.[59]

Africa accounts for a shrinking percentage of world trade. In the 1960–65 period, Africa accounted for 12 percent of the total income for developing countries of $801 billion; by 1988–89, when this overall figure had grown to $3 trillion, Africa's share had shrunk to 7 percent.[60] A huge debt overhang threatens growth. By 1989, total external debt for sub-Saharan Africa of $147 billion represented 99 percent of the countries' annual gross domestic products![61] The UNDP's profile split 173 countries among three categories. In the "high" category (55 countries), there were no African states; in the "medium" (56 countries), only Mauritius, Seychelles, South Africa, Tunisia, Botswana, Algeria, and Gabon appeared. However, in the "low level" (62 countries), the majority were African. Indeed, of the lowest 20, only two (Bhutan and Afghanistan) were non-African.[62] No wonder African leaders have long pleaded on international platforms for major boosts in aid. They perceive development as a right needed by most, and a duty incumbent on all.

Undoubtedly the most important African contribution to setting standards for international human rights standards has been in development. The "right to development," identified with the eminent Senegalese jurist Kéba Mbaye, moved from lecture topic to General Assembly resolution under his inspiration. Mbaye first publicized the concept in the 1972 inaugural lecture at the International Institute of Human Rights in Strasbourg.[63] As presiding officer at the 1977 session of the UN Commission on Human Rights, he was instrumental in resolution 4 (XXXIII), which supported the concept, and which called for a report from the UN Secretary General. Two years later, this report[64] advanced a series of legal, moral, and economic arguments on behalf of development as a human right. It was publicized as central to the "third generation" of human rights. The African Charter on Human and Peoples' Rights made direct reference to it in Article 22, indicating that all peoples "shall have the right to development" and that ratifying states "have the duty, individually or collectively, to ensure the exercise of the right to development." And, on December 4, 1986 the General Assembly formally endorsed the Declaration on the Right to Development (UNGA resolution 41/128), its lengthy, somewhat contradictory text (including no less than 16 paragraphs in the preamble!) testifying to its complex, controversial nature.[65]

Development can be linked to Shue's stimulating analysis of basic rights — to subsistence, security, and liberty. Such rights, he asserts, "are the rational basis for justified demands . . . enjoyment of them is essential to the enjoyment of all other rights."[66] All persons must have the right to physical security; there must be social guarantees of food necessary for survival; effective channels for political participation must exist. Governments, organizations, and other persons have, Shue argues, three correlative duties: to *avoid* depriving, to *protect* from deprivation, and to *aid* the deprived.[67] Systematic (as contrasted with accidental) deprivation is morally wrong. All three rights and correlative duties must be observed, not honored in the breach.

One can deduce from Shue the importance of democratization in enhancing effective participation. One can also deduce responsibility of wealthier countries to share their resources to aid the deprived. But the question is primarily political, not moral. Central to the UN debate over the right to development was whether it imposed a corresponding duty.[68] Many Western states argued it did not, and abstained or voted against the Declaration; most developing countries suggested that it did, particularly in light of other United Nations actions, and voted in favor. Despite the political posturing, there can be doubt of the importance of development to African proponents of human rights. Neglect of this concern would be a serious error. And, most assuredly, the proliferation of African NGOs focused on development underscores the need for it.

Let us sum up points raised thus far. The economic picture for Africa is dismal. Newly-launched efforts at democratization could risk foundering, because of negative trends in standards of living and levels of public confidence. The ouster or peaceful removal of many authoritarian regimes gave human rights NGOs greater political space in which to operate. They faced, and continue to face, difficult choices among strategies. No wonder, then, that their objectives and tactics have to adapt to changing circumstances.

Strategies for NGOs: Other Approaches

The six approaches I have just discussed — education, empowerment, and enforcement, based on documentation, democratization, and development — may be mnemonically easy; they do not exhaust the list of NGO functions. Laurie Wiseberg has provided nine.[69] Specifically, she focuses upon information gathering, evaluation, and dissemination; advocacy to stop abuses; legal aid, scientific expertise, and humanitarian assistance; lobbying national and international authorities; legislation to incorporate or develop human rights standards; education, conscientization, and empowerment; delivery of services; and keeping open the political system.

In the broadest sense, human rights NGOs concern themselves primarily with *protection* of individuals, or groups of individuals joined by a common characteristic. They seek — often passionately — to respond to abuses, committed almost invariably by governments against their citizens. Victims are highlighted by many human rights NGOs. Amnesty International (AI), the giant among these groups, has always placed individuals at the center of its successful strategy. AI groups adopt "prisoners of conscience," persons imprisoned for peacefully exercising their basic human rights. Amnesty group meetings invariably include time to write government authorities, requesting that this jailed Tibetan monk, that incarcerated Nigerian journalist, this interned Guatemalan advocate of indigenous peoples, etc., be released. The pressure inherent in thousands of letters petitioning for the release of a prisoner can be tremendous, indeed irresistible by all but the most repressive regimes. It is not the only means AI uses for helping imprisoned human rights activists, however. Amnesty runs an "Urgent Action" appeal, designed to bring rapid pressure on behalf of human rights advocates potentially liable to torture or extra-judicial killing, and a "Legal Support Network," intended to mobilize *pro bono* efforts by lawyers. SOS/Torture, an international network dedicated to eradicating torture, deluges governments with faxes, telegrams, and letters, urging humane treatment of persons presumed to be in danger of torture, and mobilizing public opinion for their protection.[70] AI, SOS/Torture, and many other NGOs seek *publicly* to pressure political authorities (both governments and armed opposition groups). They thus bring into the public arena the enforcement of the standards most governments have pledged to maintain through their constitutions and laws. Protection is ten/tenths of the law — and the ultimate goal of human rights work.

Underlying NGOs' protection of individuals is *information gathering, evaluation, and dissemination*. To mix metaphors, information is both blood and power. Blood, in the sense of the life-sustaining pulsation; power, in the sense of ability to change governments' policies and actions. To be credible, human rights NGOs must obtain and disseminate accurate details about the abuses they seek to correct. The effectiveness of NGOs is conditioned on how others perceive their performance in discovering and publicizing human rights abuses. "Without accurate and timely information, there can be no rational and effective NGO policies on human rights."[71] No wonder, then, that documented reporting of abuses ranks high among many human rights NGOs' priorities.

Advocacy to stop abuses draws on activists' legal skills. The information gathered must be processed, then used in the courts or political systems. Human rights need not rest on the involvement of highly trained lawyers, however. Training African paralegals — a kind of "barefoot lawyers" if you will — has become a major objective of the International Commission of Jurists (ICJ) and several nationally-based NGOs. Paralegals can spread knowledge of legal procedure to the grassroots and help develop foundations for civil society. Programs of paralegal training have succeeded in India and the Philippines, bringing understanding at the village level of how court systems work and of how to resolve conflicts in a variety of ways. According to ICJ's former Legal Officer for Africa, its programs welcome retired teachers, nurses, trade unionists, and other persons respected in their villages, who are trained to help in conflict resolution and in referring matters to legal settlement when appropriate. Their success in teaching others about human rights by using examples familiar to rural dwellers assists in the long run in creating a "human rights culture."[72]

Greater awareness of the legal system is not the only part of advocacy. A wide range of advocacy activities exists — public education, consciousness raising, enlisting other interest groups, constituency building — all intended to speak for those who cannot speak.[73] Examples could be multiplied here; they will not be, but can be found on subsequent pages.

Legal aid, scientific expertise, and humanitarian assistance utilize the skills of NGO activists in ways that improve daily life. By providing free legal assistance, for example, Namibia's Legal Assistance Centre has indirectly bolstered commitment to the rule of law. Forensic scientists have uncovered gruesome truths about earlier slaughters, raising the likelihood of prosecuting the perpetrators. In Ethiopia, Argentinian medical specialists were hired by the Special Prosecutor's Office (largely funded by SIDA, the Swedish International Development Agency) to examine human remains prior to trials, in which this evidence was an important part of the brief. Disasters such as civil war, famine, drought, and forced resettlement have also opened new challenges and opportunities for African human rights NGOs. Several have become part of intricate networks of humanitarian relief, usually in partnership with INGOs (e.g., Oxfam, Redda Barnen [Save the Children]), with UN specialized agencies (e.g., UNFP [United Nations Food Programme], UNHCR [United Nations High Commission for Refugees], or UNOSOM II [United Nations Operations in Somalia]), or with donor governments (e.g., the United States, the European Union). The ICRC (International Committee of the Red Cross) continues to exercise special responsibilities in humanitarian work.[74] Relief work may well be linked to development activities, as discussed earlier. External financing provides NGOs a margin of security vis-à-vis their governments. However, individual governments may want these resources. Accordingly, relief operations raise complex political issues for governments, NGOs, INGOs, and IGOs (inter-governmental organizations). So long as officials view NGOs as potential adversaries rather than partners in civil society, tensions will surface.

Lobbying, Wiseberg aptly notes, "is the essence of the democratic process."[75] This activity carries risks for NGOs, for they can be accused of becoming politicized. Yet, as Wiseberg also comments, "the human rights struggle is clearly a political struggle."[76] Human rights NGOs have learned how to obtain media attention, in the process often winning public relations battles with governments. On the other hand, the costs of publishing and distributing reports, and of pressing national authorities for reform, far outstrip NGOs' resources. Many live on the edge of extinction. Almost all African human rights NGOs derive most of their budgets from external sources, notably from developed Western states. Imagine, then, the political complexity: organizations sustained largely by foreign funds pressure governments for new policies — no wonder accusations of external interference are raised by critical regimes! I shall return to this matter in the concluding chapter.

Pressing for legislation incorporating human rights standards follows logically. If a nation's constitution includes explicit guarantees of rights, for example, legal remedies can be sought for violations. If laws are redrafted to reflect international norms, the result in most African states would be a higher threshold for protecting human rights. Hence, among the most significant developments in Africa's 1990s wave of democratization were constitutional redrafting (as in Ethiopia) and ratification of international human rights treaties. NGOs have marched in the front ranks of these changes, pressing for new treaties, urging implementation of existing ones, and using major political transitions to incorporate human rights norms into national laws and constitutions.

With *education, conscientization, and empowerment,* NGOs attempt to win hearts and minds, as well as to protect physical security. Several widespread attitudes in Africa — for example, the belief not only in a gender-based division of labor, but in a gender-based distinction of rights — can only be changed by long-term, patient learning. "Civic education," for example, provides people with limited experience of democracy some understanding of its rudiments. Empowerment, as suggested earlier in this chapter, mobilizes individuals and groups to fight for their rights. Only by knowing them, however, can one attempt to increase them. Outreach through education figures in the action agenda of every African human rights NGO.

Building solidarity among the oppressed, and legitimizing local concerns, are necessary but risky political steps for human rights NGOs. They must make clear that individual victims are not alone in their suffering, or that issues in particular countries are not going to be overlooked by others in the international community. Popular mobilization, as suggested above, challenges governments. Reaction, even retribution, can assail those wanting empowerment. African heads of state — like many Presidents everywhere — have thin skins. Accordingly, I am tempted to suggest, frail, nascent African human rights NGOs face major risks by taking on their governments directly in the national political arena, unless they have established links with other organizations, domestic or foreign. It stands to reason that they have greater chances for success by drawing on the support of more than the immediate sufferers. The importance of networking is another matter to which I shall return in the conclusion.

Delivery of services tends to require cooperation with the state, rather than pressure or opposition to it. The massive humanitarian relief delivered to Ethiopia during famine periods, for example, depended on close links between the government and relief and human rights organizations. Relationships were never easy, especially as civil war raged and food became a political tool. Some NGOs expanded dramatically, in the process diluting their quality and diminishing their commitment to human rights monitoring (if they ever saw that as one of their objectives). In order to remain in the good graces of even repressive governments so that urgently needed food could be distributed, most NGOs active in Ethiopian relief remained silent about the policies that helped bring about the disasters. Criticizing the Derg, the director of the major relief coordinating group believed, would have severely jeopardized the relief effort.[77] As long as humanitarian relief and services are necessary, this problem of remaining silent so as not to jeopardize access to victims, which requires cooperation with governments versus making negative comments on ill-conceived official policies, will remain.

Finally, African human rights NGOs seek to *open, or keep open, the political systems of their countries.* This task is far from easy. African human rights NGOs tend to be small, lightly funded, and concentrated in capital cities; hence, they must leverage their strength. They are frequently accused by critics of accepting foreign funds for nefarious purposes, and are depicted as representing the interests of narrow, self-interested groups. Keeping the political system open is thus a cardinal objective. Governments must be held accountable for their actions. The information gathering and lobbying already discussed thus are aimed toward political openness. Democratization seems a must.

As should be readily apparent, cooperation among human rights NGOs is essential for success. That is the theory; the reality is often different.

In general, growing networks among African human rights NGOs mark the 1990s. Thanks to the ICJ workshops, as discussed earlier, scores of them have learned about each other and explored common interests. Contacts make a real impact on operations. On the other hand, squabbles over direction, emphasis, areas of responsibility and the like have often divided NGOs.

Contacts require technological capacity as well as personal time. An NGO's most precious possession may be its fax machine, purchased with a small grant from a foreign foundation or government, enabling it to link up quickly with other groups. (Naturally, I presuppose that a telephone line can be procured, and that it remains in service. These are tall orders in many African countries.) The telecommunications revolution, especially fax connections, has transformed human rights activities in

Africa.[78] Most significant, issues or pleas for support can be sent globally (assuming, of course, that telephone connections are not cut), drawing attention from international NGOs. But how much impact will such efforts at networking likely have? We must turn to this issue in concluding this chapter.

How Effective Can African Human Rights NGOs Be?

An unpleasant but unavoidable fact marks African human rights NGOs. The overwhelming majority of them are limited in membership, restricted in funding, uneven in their impact. They operate in harsh social and political climates. The roots of civil society remain shallow through most of Africa. Governments pay little heed to NGO criticisms, and subject NGO leaders to various forms of pressure. The ability of most NGOs to change government behavior is limited. Do these observations mean human groups south of the Sahara are doomed to impotence for the foreseeable future?

Explanations of their weakness abound. Let me cite two, to introduce ideas that subsequent chapters will elaborate. According to Bratton, writing in the late 1980s, government oppression played the major role:

In practice, NGOs that specialize in human rights advocacy have been slow to gain access to, and take root in, Africa. The explanation rests with the sensitivity of African governments to the barest hint of negative international publicity about the management of domestic dissent.[79]

He goes on to comment, "In sum, the very existence of NGOs is a test of a government's stance of a basic issue of national governance: how to balance central political control with autonomy for civil organizations. . . . Therefore, the amount of space allowed to NGOs in any given country is determined first and foremost by political considerations, rather than by any calculation of the contribution of NGOs to economic and social development."[80] To Bratton, then, government opposition lies at the root of the perceived weakness of human rights NGOs.

Quite a different idea was advanced by Scoble earlier in the decade. He put the blame on social structure rather than government pressure:

The pervasive high salience of ethnic identity [in tropical Africa] operates both positively and negatively to inhibit the formation of secondary associations, especially overt human rights organizations.[81]

Thus, while Bratton concentrated on the pressures from above, and in particular on the concerns of governments, Scoble focused on the underlying social structure. Which is the greater obstacle: inherent social structure, or current national policies? Should emphasis rest on the state or on the society? There are no compelling grounds, at least at this point in our study, to favor one approach over the other. In all likelihood, both provide partial understanding. Only by examining civil society and specific NGOs in particular countries can a clearer response emerge.

My generation remembers well the raspy voice of Jack Webb: "The facts, ma'am, just the facts." What played well for "Dragnet" does not apply as adequately to comparative politics. Case studies to broaden knowledge (in addition to deepening understanding of a particular phenomenon or situation) need themselves to be conceived comparatively. The scholar's task is to gather information *in a fashion that can be used for arriving at broader observations.* I wish to try to draw general conclusions about the ability of NGOs to improve the protection of human rights in contemporary Africa. This involves assessing the strength of individual organizations, and reasons for the nature and type of government responses to NGO lobbying or pressure. To guide this research, I have used the following hypotheses about the strengths of African human rights NGOs as jumping-off points:

1. *Financial resources.* Severe budget constraints affect all human rights NGOs based in Africa, making them heavily dependent on grants from (primarily) North American and northern European governments and foundations. This relationship has led to some negotiation of goals and strategies between African leaders and their external funders. As a result, civil and political rights linked to democratization have been emphasized. Far less stress has been laid on economic and social rights linked to development, and practically no attention has been given to group rights for sub-national groups, unless these are defined by gender or occupation.

2. *Popular backing/membership.* To the extent that African human rights NGOs concentrate on civil and procedural rights involving extensive reliance on court systems, they draw their main support from urban, educated, and legally-aware individuals. A different situation can be presumed to prevail among NGOs that focus on economic and social issues. To the extent the latter concentrate on subsistence rights and development, they draw support from more rural, less educated individuals. Success in gaining government action is far more likely with urban-based, middle-class backing than with rural, lower-class support.

3. *Societal diversity.* African human rights NGOs are profoundly affected by ethnic animosities within societies, the strength of which varies inversely with the political significance of their main supporters. Human rights may be most threatened for members of ethnic

minorities who, for historical and cultural reasons, are scapegoated under conditions of national trauma. Thus, while it is generally assumed that "horizontal" associations are needed to strengthen civil society, "vertical" associations in fact also play an important role. A society based on pluralism of political and/or economic convictions may find compromise easier than a society marked by pluralism based on exclusive ethnic or religious identities.[82]

4. *Political space.* A major change of political regime can rapidly open the political space necessary for human rights NGOs to press their agenda on a national basis. Absent such a shift, NGOs will cluster their activities in areas of immediate class or ethnic group concerns, treaty obligations, or availability of financial support, each of which provides a degree of political space.

I derived these propositions for research while seated in my Buffalo office, based on reading and brief contact with several African human rights NGOs at meetings of the African Commission on Human and Peoples' Rights. Do they stand up to empirical investigation? The pages that follow will probe their validity. These hypotheses conclude the necessary background — the context of human rights in the four African countries, found in Chapter 1; the functions of NGOs in civil society in Chapter 2. It is time now to dig into the heart of this book: seeing how several domestic and international human rights groups have sought to improve political, social, and economic situations in one of the globe's least-studied areas.

Notes

1. See, among others, James S. Wunsch and Dele Olowu, *The Failure of the Centralized State* (Boulder, CO: Westview, 1990).

2. See, for example, Thomas Hodgkin's classic work, *Nationalism in Colonial Africa* (New York: New York University Press, 1957), or the equally noted study by James Coleman, *Nigeria: Background to Nationalism* (Berkeley and Los Angeles: University of California Press, 1958).

3. See, as examples, James S. Coleman and Carl G. Rosberg, Jr., eds., *Political Parties and National Integration in Tropical Africa* (Berkeley and Los Angeles: University of California Press, 1964); Aristide R. Zolberg, *Creating Political Order: The Party-States of West Africa* (Chicago: Rand McNally, 1966).

4. In this genre, see Robin Luckham, *The Nigerian Military: A Sociological Analysis of Authority and Revolt 1960–67* (Cambridge: Cambridge University Press, 1971) and Claude E. Welch, Jr., ed., *Soldier and State in Africa* (Evanston, IL: Northwestern University Press, 1970).

5. Recent articles include Adigun Agbaje, "In Search of Building Blocks: The State, Civil Society, Voluntary Action, and Grassroot Development in Africa," *Africa Quarterly* 30, 3–4 (1990), 24–40; Michael Bratton, "Beyond the State: Civil

Society and Association Life in Africa," *World Politics* 41, 3 (1989), 407–30; Naomi Chazan, "Africa's Democratic Challenge: Strengthening the State and Civil Society," *World Policy Journal* 9 (1992), 279–308; René Lemarchand, "Uncivil States and Civil Societies: How Illusion Became Reality," *Journal of Modern African Studies* 30, 2 (June 1992), 177–92; Peter Lewis, "Political Transition and the Dilemma of Civil Society in Africa," *Journal of International Affairs* 27 (1992), 31–54; and Dwayne Woods, "Civil Society in Europe and Africa: Limiting State Power through a Public Sphere," *African Studies Review* 35, 2 (September 1992), 77–100. An excellent chapter is Crawford Young, "In Search of Civil Society," in John W. Harbeson, Donald Rothchild, and Naomi Chazan, eds., *Civil Society and the State in Africa* (Boulder, CO: Lynne Rienner, 1994), pp. 33–50.

6. Alfred Stepan, *Rethinking Military Politics: Brazil and the Southern Cone* (Princeton, NJ: Princeton University Press, 1988), 3–4; quoted in Michael Bratton, "Beyond the State: Civil Society and Associational Life in Africa," 417.

7. Michael Bratton, "Civil Society and Political Transitions in Africa," 56.

8. John R. Heilbrunn, "The Social Origins of National Conferences: A Comparison of Benin and Togo," *Journal of Modern African Studies* 31 (1993), 298.

9. Quoted in Michael Clough, *Free at Last? U.S. Policy Toward Africa and the End of the Cold War* (New York: Council on Foreign Relations, 1992), p. 55.

10. Morten Kjaerum, "The Contributions of Voluntary Organisations to the Development of Democratic Governance," in Ann McKinstry Micou and Birgit Lindsnaes, eds., *The Role of Voluntary Organisations in Emerging Democracies: Experience and Strategies in Eastern and Central Europe and in South Africa* (New York and Copenhagen: Institute of International Education and Danish Centre for Human Rights, 1993), p. 13.

11. Laurie S. Wiseberg, "Defending Human Rights Defenders: The Importance of Freedom of Association for Human Rights NGOs" (Montreal: International Centre for Human Rights and Democratic Development, 1993), pp. 4–6.

12. As Stosic comments, the precise date of formation cannot be determined, for at their inceptions, NGOs "were so insignificant that no one took account." By the middle of the 19th century, however, NGO development started to occur. Borko D. Stosic, *Les organisations non-gouvernementales et les Nations Unies* (Geneva: Librarie Droz, 1964), p. 21. As White wrote over 60 years ago, "it was not until the second half of the nineteenth century that, impelled by forces released by the industrial revolution, the modern movement toward international organization began to gather impetus. . . . The earliest INGO's are to be found mainly in humanitarian and religious fields." Lyman Cromwell White, *The Structure of Private International Organization* (Philadelphia: George S. Ferguson, 1933), p. 4; cited in Stosic, *Les organisations non-gouvernementales*, p. 22.

13. Bertil Dunér, *Human Rights Spearheads: NGOs in the UN*, cited in Laurie Wiseberg, "NGO Self-Examination is the Missing Link in ECOSOC Review," *Human Rights Tribune* 1 (1994), 11–12.

14. Kjaerum, "Contributions of Voluntary Organisations," pp. 15–16.

15. Yves Beigbeder, *The Role and Status of International Humanitarian Volunteers and Organizations: The Right and Duty to Humanitarian Assistance* (Dordrecht: Martinus Nijhoff, 1990), p. 80. Gorman offers a similar set of characteristics: a) NGOs are formed voluntarily by citizens [private]; b) they enjoy tax-exempt status; c) their purpose is philanthropic; d) they are engaged in overseas relief and development activities; e) at least a portion of funding is private and voluntary. Robert F. Gorman, ed., *Private Voluntary Organizations as Agents of Development* (Boulder, CO: Westview, 1984), p. 10.

16. Beigbeder, pp. 92–93.

17. For a thoughtful discussion about the cross pressures, see Michael Bratton, "The Politics of Government-NGO Relations in Africa," *World Development* 17 (1989), 569–87.

18. Bratton, "Beyond the State," p. 425.

19. For figures on growth in numbers of NGOs up to the early 1960s, see Stosic, *Les ONGs et les Nations Unies*, pp. 21–33.

20. In 1980, 29 U.S.-based human rights NGOs focused on Africa, 23 of them on southern Africa; in 1982, there were 44 Western-Europe based human rights NGOs focused on Africa, 25 of them on southern Africa. Scoble deemed them weak: women's organizations concentrated on women in development, several religious groups were "weak, sectarian, and only tangentially involved" in human rights issues, PEN affiliates were "small and weak, working primarily to defend the occupational interests of writers," etc. Harry M. Scoble, "Human Rights Non-Governmental Organizations in Black Africa: Their Problems and Prospects in the Wake of the Banjul Charter," in Claude E. Welch, Jr. and Ronald I. Meltzer, eds., *Human Rights and Development in Africa* (Albany: State University of New York Press, 1984), pp. 183–84.

21. Human Rights Internet, *A Listing of Organizations Concerned with Human Rights and Social Justice Worldwide, Human Rights Internet Reporter* 15 (1994). The geographic index, for example, covers 67 pages.

22. "The Independent Study Into an Enabling Environment for NGOs: Summary of Issues and Recommendations " (Johannesburg: Development Resources Centre, 1993), p. 12. Some 20,000 of these are estimated to be developmental in nature. The study also estimated that each NGO employed an average of 35 persons, thus accounting for close to two million non-profit sector employees! My sense is that this definition is too loose, hence inflating the figures; nonetheless, the magnitude and importance of the NGO community must not be underestimated.

23. National Planning Commission table, reproduced in Susan Brown, "Assessment of Popular Participation in the Formulation and Implementation of Development Policies and Programmes: A Case Study of Namibia" (Windhoek: Namibian Economic Policy Research Unit [NEPRU], 1992), Appendix 2. This figure includes six umbrella NGO coordinating organizations, 36 national NGOs, 38 training and educational organizations, 18 church and church-related organizations, 18 women's associations, 15 environmental organizations, and 22 trade unions, leagues or business associations (ibid., pp. 5–6). Brown estimates that few have staffs larger than 10.

24. Robert L. Hovde, "Nongovernmental Organizations: Development and Advocacy in Changing Political Environments," unpublished paper prepared in 1992 for the Christian Relief and Development Association (CRDA). Hovde believes CRDA membership "encompasses most of the international private voluntary organizations working in Ethiopia, as well as a number of local nongovernmental organizations" (ibid., p. 5). Most are concerned with agricultural development and environmental issues; about 60 percent are international, 40 percent indigenous.

25. Jack Donnelly, "International Human Rights: A Regime Analysis," *International Organization* 40 (1986), 604–5. Also see David P. Forsythe, *The Internationalization of Human Rights* (Lexington, MA: Lexington Books, 1991), p. 57.

26. Asbjorn Eide, "The Sub-Commission," in Philip Alston, ed., *The United Nations and Human Rights: A Critical Appraisal* (Oxford: Clarendon Press, 1992), p. 259.

27. An excellent example comes from the interaction between DCI (Defense of Children International) and the drafters of the Convention on the Rights of the Child. For details, see Cynthia Price Cohen, "The Role of Non-Governmental Organizations in the Drafting of the Convention on the Rights of the Child," *Human Rights Quarterly* 12 (1990), 137–47.

28. Alston, "The Commission on Human Rights," in Alston, *The UN and Human Rights*, 203.

29. Micou and Lindsnaes, "The Role of Voluntary Organisations."

30. Stephen P. Marks, "The Complaint Procedure of the United Nations Educational, Scientific and Cultural Organization," in Hurst Hannum, ed., *Guide to International Human Rights Practice* (Philadelphia: University of Pennsylvania Press, 1992, 2nd edition), pp. 86–98; David Weissbrodt and Rose Farley, "The UNESCO Human Rights Procedure: An Evaluation," *Human Rights Quarterly* 16 (1994), 391–414.

31. Richard P. Claude, "Human Rights Education in the Philippines" (Manila: Kalikasan Press, 1991), pp. 22–24, 33. A shorter version appears in *Human Rights Quarterly* 13 (1991), 453–524.

32. Ibid., p. 40.

33. Ibid., pp. 43–44.

34. "Ethiopia in Transition: A Report on the Judiciary and the Legal Profession" (Washington, DC: International Human Rights Law Group, 1993).

35. Indeed, I had the privilege of observing a handful of Ethiopians, most of them associated with the Faculty of Law at Addis Ababa University, as they debated establishing an association of professionals to assist fellow citizens in November 1993. They faced a long, uphill task, for the idea of public interest law is only starting to appear in Ethiopia. There was no course in the law school on public interest law, and no significant requirement for pro bono work by members of the Bar. Most lawyers find employment with the government (the need for them is great). Further, the political risks of human rights work are high.

36. "Effective Implementation of International Instruments on Human Rights, Including Reporting Obligations Under International Instruments on Human Rights," UN Document A/44/668, 8 November 1989, p. 18. This statement, quoted from the preliminary report by the Special Rapporteur, Philip Alston, is repeated in the updated version of the report, UN Document A/CONF.157/PC/62/Add.11/Rev.1, 22 April 1993, p. 39. A far more critical view can be found in Anne F. Bayefsky, "Making the Human Rights Treaties Work," in Louis Henkin and John Lawrence Hargrove, eds., *Human Rights: An Agenda for the Next Century* (Washington, DC: American Society of International Law, 1993), pp. 229–95.

37. UN Document A/CONF.157/PC/62/Add.11/Rev.1, p. 21. By the end of the year, there was a total of 946 formal ratifications, divided as follows: ICESCR, 127; ICCPR, 125; first optional protocol, 75; second optional protocol, 19; CERD, 137; Apartheid, 100; CRC, 154; CEDAW, 128; CAT, 79. "Human Rights International Instruments, Chart of Ratifications as at 31 December 1993," UN Document ST/HR/4/Rev.9, p. 10.

38. Also very important is the incorporation of Charter obligations into the domestic legal frameworks. In Botswana, a case was decided in favor of plaintiffs because national law conflicted with the language of the African Charter, which formed part of domestic law. The judgment in the case in Botswana (Unity Dow v. Attorney General) is published in *Human Rights Quarterly* 13 (1991), 614–26; also see Lisa C. Stratton, "The Right to Have Rights: Gender Discrimination in Nationality Laws," *Minnesota Law Review* 77 (1992), 197–239.

39. Cindy A. Cohn, "The Early Harvest: Domestic Legal Changes Related to the Human Rights Committee and the Covenant on Civil and Political Rights," *Human Rights Quarterly* 13 (1991), 295–321.

40. Most treaty bodies meeting in Geneva seem to attract only two-three journalists to sessions; unless human rights problems have been highly publicized (usually by NGOs) and there is the prospect for a confrontation, the media take little interest. Although the press in Banjul does report on public sessions of the African Commission, other African newspapers stay away. One result is a vacuum of information about the treaty bodies' work. They remain obscure parts of the international human rights regime.

41. Laurie S. Wiseberg, "Human Rights Nongovernmental Organizations," in Richard Pierre Claude and Burns H. Weston, eds., *Human Rights in the World Community: Issues and Action* (Philadelphia: University of Pennsylvania Press, 1992, 2nd edition), 373.

42. John R. Heilbrunn, "The Social Origins of National Conferences: A Comparison of Benin and Togo," 277–99.

43. Carl Gewirtz, "Donors Tie Aid to Democracy," *International Herald-Tribune*, December 16, 1993.

44. In the four states examined in greater detail in this book, the following projects, illustrative of uses of the Democracy and Human Rights Fund, were funded in fiscal year 1993:

Ethiopia: $10,000 for Addis Ababa University Law School to purchase books for a human rights library; $20,000 also to the law school, to "establish a human rights curriculum . . . to sensitize law students about general human rights issues and international human rights law";

Namibia: $80,000 to the Ministry of Justice for community court justice training; $22,000 to the Legal Assistance Centre for a human rights TV film; $100,000 to NDI [U.S.-based National Democratic Institute] for local governance training;

Nigeria: $5,000 to the Nigerian Labour Congress for a library; $10,000 to the Civil Liberties Organisation to update its publication on prison conditions; $17,000 for the Legal Research and Resource Development Centre Legal Aid Clinic to provide free legal aid and services to women; $24,000 to the Constitutional Rights Project for an interactive seminar for law students on defending human rights cases;

Senegal: $25,000 to create a guide on women's marriage and divorce procedures, especially targeted to Muslim audiences; $22,500 for Senegalese jurists to write and print books that teach basic rights and recourse of citizens against illegal government acts.

45. See, as examples, National Democratic Institute for International Affairs and African-American Institute, *An Evaluation of the June 21, 1992 Elections in Ethiopia* (Washington, DC: NDI, 1992); National Democratic Institute for International Affairs, *International Delegation Report on the October 11, 1992 Presidential Election in Cameroon* (Washington, DC: NDI, 1992); National Democratic Institute for International Affairs, *The October 31, 1991 National Elections in Zambia* (Washington, DC: NDI, 1992); and National Election Monitoring Unit (NEMU), *The Multi-Party General Elections in Kenya 29 December, 1992* (Nairobi: NEMU, 1993).

46. In a speech read to the African Society, the Secretary General proclaimed, "Without a deep respect for human rights, efforts at development will be under-

mined by perpetual dissension and repeated conflict. Africa and the international community must search for new and more effective approaches to Africa's persistent developmental problems. Past approaches have not so far produced results commensurate with the effort." Quoted in *West Africa* (27 September–3 October 1993), 1729.

47. "Indivisible Human Rights: The Relationship of Political and Civil Rights to Survival, Subsistence and Poverty" (New York: Human Rights Watch, 1992).

48. Larry Diamond, "Promoting Democracy in Africa: U.S. and International Poicies in Transition," unpublished paper presented at the Fourth Annual East African-American Studies Colloquium, Kenya, July 19–23, 1993, p. 5.

49. David Williams and Tom Young, "Governance, the World Bank and Liberal Theory," *Political Studies* 42 (1994), 86.

50. Stephen P. Riley, "Political Adjustment or Domestic Pressure: Democratic Politics and Political Choice in Africa," *Third World Quarterly* 13, 3 (1992), 539.

51. Freedom House, *Freedom in the World* (New York: annual); figures respectively from *Freedom in the World 1989* (1990, p. 318); and *Freedom in the World 1992* (1993, p. 625).

52. *Africa Demos* 3, 1 (February 1993), 19.

53. Samuel Decalo, "The Process, Prospects, and Constraints of Democratization in Africa," *African Affairs* 91, 362 (1992), 7–35; Larry Diamond, "The Second Wind of Change," *Times Literary Supplement* 4709 (July 2, 1993), 43–46 and "Promoting Democracy," *Foreign Policy* 87 (summer 1992), 25–46; Sahr J. Kpundeh and Stephen P. Riley, "Political Choice and the New Democratic Politics in Africa," *Round Table* 323 (1992), 263–72; Mahmood Mamdami, "Africa: Democratic Theory and Democratic Struggles," *Dissent* 39 (1992), 312–18; Samuel Nolotshungu, "Africa in a World of Democracies: Interpretation and Retrieval," *Journal of Commonwealth and Comparative Political Studies* 30 (1992), 316–64.

54. Larry Diamond, Juan J. Linz, and Seymour Martin Lipset, eds., *Democracy in Developing Countries: Africa* (Boulder, CO: Lynne Rienner, 1988).

55. ECA Document E/ECA/CM.16/11. Note the following proposals for monitoring popular participation (paragraphs 24, 29, 30):

1. We proclaim the urgent necessity to involve the people in monitoring popular participation on the basis of agreed indicators and we propose the use of the following indicators, which are not necessarily exhaustive, for measuring the progress in implementation of the recommendations of the Charter. . . .
2. Freedom of association, especially political association, and presence of democratic institutions, such as political parties, trade unions, people's grassroot organizations and professional associations, and the guarantee of constitutional rights.
3. Representation of the people and their organizations in national bodies.
4. The rule of law and social and economic justice, including equitable distribution of income and the creation of full employment opportunities. . . .
7. Number and scope of grassroots organizations with effective participation in development activities, producers and consumers co-operatives and community projects. . . .
History and experience both teach that this world never works in compartments. The forces of freedom and democracy are contagious. Inevitably, and irresistibly, popular participation will have a vital role to play on the continent of Africa, and play that role we will.
It is manifestly unacceptable that development and transformation can pro-

ceed without the full participation of the people. It is manifestly unacceptable that the people and their organizations be excluded from the decision-making process. It is manifestly unacceptable that popular participation be seen as anything less than the centerpiece in the struggle to achieve economic and social justice for all.

56. In Namibia, for example, the Constitution entrenches civil and political rights in Chapter 3; no derogation or suspension of specified fundamental rights or freedoms is permitted. By contrast, Chapter 11 sets forth "principles of state policy" (including promotion of welfare of the people, foreign relations, asylum, principles of economic order, foreign investments, and sovereign control over natural resources) that "shall not of and by themselves be legally enforceable by any Court, but shall nevertheless guide the Government in making and applying laws to give effect to the fundamental objectives of the said principles."

57. Nor is affluence a certain receipe for ensuring satisfactory distribution of economic goods and services.

58. Summarized in *West Africa* (27 September–3 October 1993), 1719.

59. Cited in Diamond, "The Second Wind of Change," p. 43.

60. World Bank, *Poverty: World Development Report 1990* (New York: Oxford University Press, 1990), p. 10, figure 1.1. Real income 1980 dollars were used as the unit of measurement.

61. Cited in Diamond, "Second Wind of Change," p. 43.

62. United Nations Development Programme, *Human Development Report 1993* (New York: Oxford University Press, 1993), 136–37.

63. See Kéba Mbaye, "Le droit au développement comme un droit de l'homme," *Revue internationale des droits de l'homme* 2–3 (1972), 504–35.

64. "The International Dimensions of the Right to Development as a Human Right in Relation with Other Human Rights Based on International Cooperation, Including the Right to Peace, Taking into Account the Requirements of the New International Economic Order and Fundamental Needs," UN Document E/CN.4/1334, 2 January 1979. Also see Mbaye's paper to a 1978 UNESCO conference, published as UNESCO Document SS-78/CONF.630/8, 16 July 1979.

65. As Mbaye himself subsequently wrote, "This declaration is manifestly the result of successive compromises which finally make the internal coherence of the text debatable." Kéba Mbaye, *Les droits de l'homme en Afrique* (Paris: Pedone, 1992), p. 197; author's translation.

66. Henry Shue, *Basic Rights: Subsistence, Affluence and U.S. Foreign Policy* (Princeton, NJ: Princeton University Press, 1980), p. 80.

67. Ibid., p. 52.

68. For a vigorous negative response, see Jack Donnelly, "The 'Right to Development': How Not to Link Human Rights and Development," in Claude E. Welch, Jr. and Ronald I. Meltzer, eds., *Human Rights and Development in Africa* (Albany: State University of New York Press, 1984), pp. 261–83.

69. Laurie S. Wiseberg, "The Role of Non-Governmental Organizations," in *Put Our World to Rights — Towards a Commonwealth Human Rights Policy,* republished in Richard Pierre Claude and Burns H. Weston, eds., *Human Rights in the World Community: Issues and Action* (Philadelphia: University of Pennsylvania Press, 1992, 2nd edition), pp. 372–82. One should note, however, that she has more recently focused on two as "absolutely indispensable": information gathering, evaluation and dissemination; and keeping the political process open or creating political

space for democratic forces. Wiseberg, "Defending Human Rights Defenders," pp. 5–6.

70. For an analysis of the effectiveness of Amnesty International, HURIDOCS, the International Service for Human Rights and SOS/Torture in the context of Southeast Asia, see *International Human Rights Organisations: The Meaning of Their Work for Local Organizations with Case Studies from the Philippines, Indonesia and Sri Lanka* (The Hague: NOVIB, 1992).

71. Scoble, "Human Rights Non-Governmental Organizations in Black Africa," 177, 178. In her extension of the work she and her late husband carried out, Wiseberg deemed information gathering "one of the most important functions . . ." (Wiseberg, "The Role of NGOs," p. 373); I prefer the earlier wording.

72. Interview with Philip Amoah, ICJ Legal Officer for Africa, Geneva, September 16, 1993.

73. Scoble, "Human Rights NGOs in Black Africa," p. 178.

74. Valuable discussion of the ICRC can be found in David P. Forsythe, *The Internationalization of Human Rights*, 143–69; also see his earlier *Humanitarian Politics: The International Committee of the Red Cross* (Baltimore: Johns Hopkins University Press, 1977).

75. Wiseberg, "The Role of NGOs," p. 375.

76. Ibid.

77. Interview with Brother Gus O'Keefe, Addis Ababa, November 18, 1993.

78. Electronic mail is not nearly as important, because of the limited computer installations and restricted access to information highways such as Telnet. Considering that airmail letters commonly take three to four weeks to travel between African states, the value of faxes should be immediately apparent.

79. Bratton, "The Politics of Government-NGO Relations in Africa," p. 576.

80. Ibid.

81. Scoble, "Human Rights NGOs in Black Africa," p. 188.

82. The strategies for managing ethnic conflict outlined by Horowitz merit attention in this regard. Donald L. Horowitz, *Ethnic Groups in Conflict* (Berkeley and Los Angeles: University of California Press, 1985).

Part II
Using the Strategies

Chapter 3
Education and Long-Term Change: The Inter-African Committee on Traditional Practices

... for the moment at least, an educational campaign directed particularly at health professionals, school-girls, and patients in maternity clinics would be the most appropriate manner of beginning elimination of the custom. Legislation banning female genital operations might merely drive the operations underground...[1]

— Rhoda Howard

[Protection from female genital mutilation] cannot be done by talking or publishing articles or making movies and videos or holding conferences and meetings in the rest of the world. In the final analysis, this can only be done in Africa by a coordinated long-term and continuing effort to educate the people involved and to teach them on their own terms about health, about their own bodies and how reproduction functions: And then they will decide for themselves that these mutilations will stop. It is a long, hard and laborious process of education that is needed now, but I am afraid this is necessary and has to be done if we are serious about the goal — to eradicate female genital mutilation permanently so it will never and nowhere be practiced again.[2]

— Fran Hosken

A modest Geneva office across the street from the former GATT headquarters houses an NGO dedicated to changing several widespread, widely debated "traditional" African practices.

Since the mid-1980s, the Inter-African Committee on Traditional Practices Affecting the Health of Women and Children (IAC) has espoused a strategy of working from below, in order to eliminate a variety of harmful practices which start with, but are not confined to, female genital operations.[3] The IAC seeks deliberate change in social values. Its small, Switzerland- and Ethiopia-based international staff work in coordination with a variety of other NGOs, international agencies, and most important, national committees to coordinate educational and legislative efforts in Africa. They are dedicated to changing ideas about one of the most private matters imaginable: the functioning of women's reproductive systems and the shape of their external sexual organs. It is an area in which changing conceptions of human rights impinge directly on social mores.

The IAC emerged in part as a reaction against efforts, mounted largely by Western feminists and WHO specialists, to abolish all forms of female genital mutilation (FGM) without delay.[4] These practices were (and continue to be) found largely in a band of countries across the Sahel, from Senegal to Somalia. Two million girls (in most cases, the operation is done at or before puberty) undergo genital operations annually. According to one careful estimate, prepared for the 1993 World Conference on Human Rights, 114,296,000 females in Africa had been subjected to them.[5] There is thus no question about the ubiquity and significance of FGM. What is more interesting is the evolution of the issue as it became a perceived abuse of human rights: mooted initially in the late 1970s by a handful of persons in developed countries; debated widely during the 1980s in terms of "tradition" and "cultural relativism"; by the early 1990s, taken up by Africans as a legitimate target for national legislation. The path, however, was neither easy nor straightforward. For example, calling the operations "genital mutilation" rather than "circumcision" involved a significant change in consciousness. Female genital mutilation as a human rights question moved from concern among a small group of critics mostly outside Africa, to action among increasing numbers of Africans wanting change. But there were counter-currents. Debate and resolutions from various international fora in the mid-1970s engendered (and continue to receive) counter-criticisms in Africa. How could—and indeed, even how should—practices that are widespread and prized by many be changed? Would they be altered most efficaciously by external moral and humanitarian pressure, coming essentially from developed countries? Or would the most effective impetus come from within the affected area, with the key leadership and initiative from Africans?

As will be shown in this chapter, the answer was overwhelmingly the latter. The strategy chosen to combat female genital mutilation and other harmful traditional practices has focused on education, or, to use a term more common in the West, consciousness-raising. The Inter-African Committee (henceforth the IAC) and other groups involved with women's rights sensitized persons who considered "female circumcision" an aspect of culture beyond the usual reach of the state or definition of human rights and succeeded relatively rapidly. No longer is FGM a taboo subject for discussion or government action in Africa, due in large part to the Committee's efforts. From an issue espoused by a handful of Western feminists, genital operations have become targets of widespread discussion and increasing governmental action.

Central to the IAC's *modus operandi* has been education along the lines proposed in the headnote. The Inter-African Committee follows the first E of our triad of education, empowerment, and enforcement. Information campaigns aimed largely at health professionals, government officials, media specialists, and opinion leaders (especially in rural areas, where harmful traditional practices are widespread) constitute the IAC's most important avenue. Traditional birth attendants (TBAs) are fundamental targets for the IAC's educational efforts. The Inter-African Committee does not seek directly to empower groups as major actors in national politics, nor to lobby for laws that lack a foundation of popular support (although national legislation is a clear goal, to be sought within individual states once the necessary educational campaign has been mounted). Efforts to democratize seem somewhat tangential to the IAC's purposes, although documentation of its work is essential, and successful attempts at economic development might well facilitate the Committee's campaign. The IAC represents the quintessence of "promotion" of human rights. It seeks to lay the attitudinal foundation necessary for further change. The IAC works largely behind the scenes in its consciousness-raising.

Women's Rights and Human Rights

Female genital operations and other harmful traditional practices must be viewed against a dual backdrop: first, in light of the growing body of international human rights law that emphasizes non-discrimination between men and women and provides for affirmative action steps for women who have been disadvantaged; second, in the perspective of long-standing patterns of sexual differentiation, rooted in African values, that give priority to males.

Let us begin with international documents. The drafters of the United Nations Charter and the Universal Declaration of Human Rights sought to combat inequality among individuals. They were sensitive to the effects of language. Rather than use "he" or "man" as generic nouns to refer to both genders, they instead used terms such as "persons" or "men and women."[6] The UN Charter refers to the "dignity and worth of the human person" and to the "equal rights of men and women"; the UDHR, though it speaks of a spirit of "brotherhood" in individuals' actions, emphasizes the "equal and inalienable rights of all members of the human family." Non-discrimination figures prominently in both documents. The UDHR rejects discrimination "of any kind, such as race, colour, *sex,* language, religion, political or other opinion, national or social origin, property, birth or other status" (Article 1; italics added), adding to the UN Charter's list of race, sex, language, or religion (Article 55).

Translating gender-neutral preambles or statements of principle into meaningful governmental actions has proven far more complex, however. The conditions of women's lives throughout most of the developing world, and particularly in tropical Africa, have not improved significantly in recent years despite global treaties. That the United Nations endorsed the Convention on the Political Rights of Women (entered into force 1952) and adopted both the Declaration and then the Convention on the Elimination of All Forms of Discrimination Against Women (1967; 1979) manifested the inadequacy of non-discrimination clauses as a sole avenue of social change. More than legislation from above, dependent on the good will of governments for implementation, is needed. Where deep-rooted social attitudes interact with gross economic, social, and political inequalities, as is true throughout Africa, human wrongs rather than human rights result.

Part of the problem lies in Africa's macroeconomic position, which continues to erode, and to which reference was made in the preceding chapter.[7] Africa's position on world markets slipped seriously during the late 1980s and early 1990s. In the 1960–65 period, of a total income for developing countries of $801 billion, Africa accounted for 12 percent; by 1988–89, when the figure had grown to $3 trillion, Africa's share had shrunk to 7 percent.[8] (Figures calculated in real income 1980 dollars.) Conditionalities imposed by the International Monetary Fund and the World Bank, requisite to further assistance from them and most developed countries, reduced public payrolls and introduced greater market freedoms. They did not, however, reverse the slide toward greater marginalization of the continent as a whole in the global economy, and of particular groups within African societies. Without question, almost all residents of sub-Saharan Africa were worse off economically in the early 1990s than a decade or two earlier.[9] Poverty now marks more than three-quarters of the residents of sub-Saharan Africa. A 1990 World Bank report observed that 120 million Africans (30 percent of the region's population) live in extreme poverty, and another 180 million (47 percent) live in poverty. Just over half (56 percent) of children receive full primary education, compared with 83 percent for developing countries as a whole.[10] The United Nations Development Program, comparing sub-Saharan Africa with the world as a whole in 1993, found an average life expectancy of 51.8 years (versus 64.7 years globally), barely a quarter of the population with access to sanitation, an adult literacy rate of 47 percent, and a gross national product per capita of $490, less than one eighth the global figure.[11]

These macro indicators of limited development are compounded for women. Irrespective of their location, women historically did not and presently do not enjoy rights equal to men. Take, for example, Amartya Sen's calculation that 100 million women in developing countries are "missing," having died prematurely from gender bias.[12] The 1992 *World Development Report* found no country (of the 33 for which data were available) in which the "human development index" for females was equal to that for males. In developing countries generally, women work between

12 and 18 hours daily, while men work 8 to 12 hours; in Africa as a whole, women grow 80 percent of the household food.[13]

Hence what is certainly an uneven situation in developed countries is, in developing countries, undoubtedly a bad one. It is worst in Africa. Women south of the Sahara (especially in rural areas) suffer by comparison with their sisters in most other parts of the world. Cultural barriers interact with low levels of economic development. As just noted, recent years have witnessed serious declines in living standards through most of Africa, women and children bearing the brunt of the social cost. A few additional examples and figures will help. Marked disparities exist between the sexes in access to education, notably at secondary and tertiary levels. Life expectancies of 50 years, and infant mortality rates of 196 per thousand, contrast with the corresponding global averages of 62 years and 121 per thousand.[14] In Kenya women receive a mere 58 percent of men's shares.[15] According to a recent report on Rwanda, women are "often severely disadvantaged."[16] (This was a basic theme of the 1994 Cairo summit conference on women and social development.) Literacy rates for females are 61 percent those of males, for example. Urban dwellers have significantly greater access to clean water, lower infant mortality rates, and far less likelihood of living in impoverished conditions. Poor families tend to be large, racked by hunger, often unable to send children (especially girls) to school, short of assets, and required to spend about 70 percent of income for food. "Within the household the distribution of consumption often favors males and income-earning adults . . . a larger proportion of women's than of men's income tends to be spent on household nutrition and basic welfare . . . raising women's incomes is a good way to reach children as well as to strengthen women's status and bargaining power within the household."[17] Governments fail to reach the rural poor. Agricultural extension programs are usually geared to men, despite women's major role in farming. Legal systems remain skewed against women, vesting ownership exclusively in their husbands. As Howard correctly observes, "[African] women as a group suffer more from poverty than [African] men as a group, a direct result of their sexual status."[18] All these exist despite provisions in most African constitutions avowing equal treatment for all.

Clearly, then, formal legal norms conflict in Africa with socioeconomic and cultural realities. These problems have not passed unnoticed, if they have not necessarily been resolved. Non-discrimination on the basis of sex has become entrenched in international human rights law and the legal systems of most African states. Within almost all African societies, however, differential standards for males and females, based on both custom and law, continue to apply. These norms will not change rapidly. Systemic discrimination against women is the rule. How then can greater gender equality be achieved? The issue for discussion here involves the deliberate transformation of social mores and domestic law through international channels. The Inter-African Committee has sought to implant a desire for change at the grassroots, in the face of significant cultural inertia and limited interest by many governments.

Establishing the IAC: A Brief History

Moving an issue from periphery to center requires persistence and strong leadership. In discussing international attention to female genital mutilation (FGM), the names of Berhane Ras-Work and Fran Hosken always arise. The energy and persistence of these two advocates, despite their differing styles, have continued to focus international attention on methodologies of change. The importance of dedicated, energetic leadership is underscored in this case, similar to the other NGOs examined in this book.

In many respects, the opening salvos of the debate over the best approach to women's rights, and in particular to abolishing female genital mutilation, came with the 1979 WHO regional seminar, held in Khartoum, and with the 1980 UN Conference on Women, held in Copenhagen.[19] Some Western feminists, many from NGO backgrounds, squared off with government representatives unfamiliar with and unsympathetic to the lingo of women's liberation. While the latter were ready to defend the autonomy and integrity of their respective cultures, the former were poised to attack many of its basic values. Several persons attending the Copenhagen conference aimed their volleys at "female circumcision." It was brought to their attention in large part by Hosken, a forthright American crusader for women's rights who was well-informed about a subject previously of interest to only a few anthropologists. Her efforts were instrumental in achieving global awareness of the issue; however, they also led to acrimony over the most suitable way to approach it.

Hosken established the Women's International Network (WIN) in the mid-1970s to chronicle abuses against women and put NGOs into touch with each other. In many respects, WIN was the mother of other NGOs that focus on the rights issues confronted by more than half of humanity.[20] WIN's uncompromising stand on female genital mutilation reflected Hosken's own impatience with male-biased cultural mores and legal systems. Immediate action was required. Women from all around the world should unite on behalf of their abused African sisters. It was an approach, depending on one's perspective, either imposing galling western norms on other settings, or taking long-overdue action against a publicly-unrecognized abuse on which global action was necessary.

A strategy of frontal assault characterized the 1979 WHO seminar.[21] Its

call for rapid abolition of FGM evoked an African reaction. Some participants were castigated for cultural insensitivity, which could exacerbate
rather than alleviate the problem. To be effective in changing indigenous
values and practices, it was argued, leadership should come from within
Africa, not from outside it. Similar confrontations occurred within other
UN bodies, usually between Western-based spokespersons and NGOs
espousing rapid action by international fiat, and African governments
urging slower change from below. Notably absent were African women
themselves, a lacuna that was not to change until 1984 with the IAC's
establishment. Let us quickly review this history.

The 1980 world conference on women appealed to African governments and women's organizations to seek a solution. Many Geneva- and
New York-based agencies became involved in the widening debate over
genital operations. NGOs started to coordinate their activity, consulting
regularly about combatting harmful traditional practices and pressuring
UN bodies. The Working Group on Slavery of the UN Commission on
Human Rights considered FGM for the first time in 1981, and recommended further study the following year. In August 1983, the UN Sub-
Commission on the Prevention of Discrimination and the Protection of
Minorities appointed Mrs. Halima Embarek Warzazi (Morocco) to study
female genital mutilation.[22] The issue, obviously, was politically charged.
The Commission on Human Rights (composed, one should recall, of
government representatives rather than experts on the issues) broadened its scope into a working group, under the Sub-Commission, to analyze traditional practices affecting the health of women and children.[23]
The crucial step in terms of NGO involvement came a few months later.
In February 1984, an NGO-inspired seminar at Dakar, organized with the
assistance of the government of Senegal, UNFPA (United Nations Fund
for Population Activities), UNICEF, and WHO, led directly to the formation of the Inter-African Committee. Twenty African countries were represented by 100 delegates and observers. They became a nucleus for
change. The IAC was to coordinate national and international efforts to
abolish FGM. For the first time, as Nigerian attendee Dr. Irene Thomas
commented, women from Africa spoke for their own interests.[24] The
focus broadened, too, to include a whole host of harmful traditional
practices that impact seriously on the health of women and children.
Only a comprehensive plan of action implemented within individual
states would suffice.

Meanwhile, the UN's bureaucratic wheels continued to turn. Hosken
maintained her strong pressure. Three editions of *The Hosken Report* appeared in quick succession in the early 1980s. *WIN News* chronicled Hosken's tireless efforts, primarily to American and Western European audiences, to ensure development and health assistance was used to combat

genital mutilation.[25] Within the UN system, Mrs. Warzazi submitted a series of reports from her working group. Her 1986 report referred to several harmful traditional practices, including genital mutilation, facial scarification, nutritional taboos, early marriage, traditional birth practices, and preferential treatment for male children.[26] Mrs. Warzazi asked governments, UN agencies, and NGOs for their observations, but (not surprisingly) received few responses.[27] Governments were, in a word, unwilling to discuss what they considered a private matter. But in her final report (1991), Mrs. Warzazi noted a dramatic change of attitude. She concluded 1) that "noticeable progress" had been made in public awareness about the harmful effects of FGM, nutritional taboos, and practices related to delivery, 2) that more governments were "demonstrating willingness" to tackle harmful practices, and 3) that the IAC's efforts "have succeeded in breaking the taboo about harmful traditional practices through education and information campaigns."[28] How did the Inter-African Committee succeed in this complex task? What lessons can be drawn from its activities?

Implementing the IAC's Plan of Action

The IAC has been led for most of its history by Berhane Ras-Work, a quiet, persuasive advocate for women's rights. She became associated with the Inter-African Committee in 1984. Mrs. Ras-Work's own sensitivity to female genital operations came not during her youth in Ethiopia, but through Western television. She and her husband (an international civil servant) had moved to Geneva in 1970. A TV program on genital mutilation shocked her, as much for its patronizing tone as for its information. Nonetheless, it "started her thinking" about the most suitable approach to adopt.[29] Working from below to break the culture of silence that surrounded FGM, Ras-Work and the IAC took crucial steps during the 1980s and 1990s in consciousness-raising. Their task now is broadening from education toward enforcement, in which the national affiliates of the IAC take the lead in pressing both public education and governmental enforcement.

The IAC periodically examines its priorities for action. Their evolution, from the IAC's founding seminar in Dakar February 1984 to the regional conferences held in Addis Ababa in April 1987, November 1990, and April 1994, demonstrates increasing sophistication.[30] Thus, while the 1984 seminar examined only three broad objectives, the 1987 regional conference elaborated an extensive plan of action, to be implemented within ten years, involving both short- and long-term strategies. The 1994 triennial meeting took stock of progress, not breaking major new ground. Eradication of a whole range of harmful traditional practices before the millenium: this was and remains the Committee's goal.

Harmful practices fall into four categories: childhood marriage and early pregnancy; female genital mutilation; nutritional taboos; child spacing and delivery practices. Changing each involves an assault on deeply-rooted beliefs, well-entrenched interests, or both. Marriage and procreation are transcendent values for women in Africa. Expectations for them differ significantly from what is proclaimed by current Western values and human rights treaties. For example, the UDHR, the International Covenants, the Convention on the Elimination of All Forms of Discrimination Against Women, and other documents assert free choice for *individuals* to marry and establish families and to determine their size. By contrast, marriages in Africa (especially in rural areas) are arranged, polygamy socially accepted, a dowry ("bridewealth") expected from the husbands-to-be, and high fertility encouraged. Unmarried or childless adult females confront many social disadvantages. Widows face potential dispossession by their late husbands' blood relatives. Genital operations are perceived (among other things) as guaranteeing virginity, as marking entrance into adult life, as ensuring cleanliness, and as enhancing the ability to bear children. Many people have economic stakes in the system. Traditional birth attendants (TBAs) earn their livings not only by assisting at parturition but also by performing the various types of female circumcision. Male dominance suffuses the system; respect for the past sustains it. Women have little leverage with which to protest — indeed, older women defend "tradition" the most strongly.

The Inter-African Committee's strategies for change focus on education, as already noted. The plan of action speaks repeatedly of disseminating information, providing courses at all levels of schooling, creating awareness of adverse practices, mass mobilization through training, and outreach programs. There is a definite sequence. Only after open discussion of culturally sensitive matters would the IAC press for legislative changes. For example, the minimum age for marriage should be raised to 18, the IAC has urged, but in countries where such legislation exists, as in Nigeria, it is far more often ignored than enforced.[31] No law can exist in a social vacuum or stand against strong public opinion. The ground must be prepared for social change; political change will come in due course.

The greatest problem for the Inter-African Committee exists not in its overall goals, but in their necessarily highly decentralized implementation. As in almost any human rights area, the state level is far more important than the international level. The battles for change must be fought country by country. Educational programs must be tailored to the needs of particular societies. National legislation is necessary to raise minimum ages for marriage, once the requisite social consciousness has been achieved. Domestic actions are required to bring family life or sex education into curricula. But an office of a few women based in Geneva cannot wage the struggle in Addis Ababa, Bamako, or Cairo. Only a number of locally-based and -staffed groups, widely distributed through-out the continent, can hope to succeed.

As one would expect, marked differences exist among the 24 (as of mid-1994) national IAC affiliates. Sections were established first in Dji-bouti, Egypt, Gambia, Ghana, Liberia, Mali, Nigeria, Senegal, Sierra Leone, Sudan, and Togo.[32] By 1994, they had been joined (at least in theory) by national committees in thirteen others.[33] The committees cast their nets widely to win allies. Among the most important are traditional birth attendants, religious leaders, traditional rulers, professional bodies, and associations of market women. Not, in other words, all persons who are shakers-and-movers of national legislation. But once having awak-ened public awareness and won allies, so the strategy runs, the individ-ual sections would seek new laws, redirected government spending, and revised policies in many sectors. Even First Ladies could be asked for support!

Like the other NGOs studied in this book, tough economic realities affect what the IAC can do. Financial and operational constraints limit the extent to which the IAC in Geneva can support national chapters, through which the bulk of work is supposed to be carried out. Seed money, not long-term operational support, can be provided to units in Africa; they must develop their own fund-raising capabilities, however. Fund-raising absorbs a great deal of time, for no endowment or relatively sure annual allocation exists. Even with an extremely modestly paid staff, expenses are high. NGOs based in Geneva face one of the highest costs-of-living in the world. The triennial regional conferences and the peri-odic workshops and seminars cost a great deal, given travel costs within Africa. Even a budget hovering close to $2,000,000 per year comes no-where close to the need.[34] Hence the IAC's international initiatives are necessarily and deliberately collaborative. National sections must fend for themselves in many respects, although the Geneva office can furnish important educational materials—for example, slides of anatomical models, videotapes in English or French, or publications.

The IAC works to a significant extent in the rarefied world of IGOs, inter-governmental organizations. IGOs are composed of governments, largely staffed by males, and far better attuned to the needs of urban elites than to voiceless rural women most likely to suffer from harmful traditional practices. Organizational obstacles are more apparent than the advantages. Some of the IAC's partners—including WHO, the Economic Commission for Africa and UNICEF—are multi-purpose, multi-nation organizations whose concern for harmful traditional practices is overshadowed by more pressing economic or political matters. Three treaty bodies—CEDAW (Committee on the Elimination of All Forms of Discrimination Against Women), the Committee on the Rights of the Child, and the African Commission on Human and Peoples' Rights—seem to stand in a good position to facilitate the IAC's goals. However, their powers are essentially limited by the treaties' language, the capacity of the secretariats and commissioners, and the quality of reports from States Parties.[35] Governments confronting other claims for resources find it simple to spurn requests for material aid. In fact, most financial support comes from Western foundations and governments, and religious, women's and quasi-governmental groups focused on women's and children's issues. First World entities are vital to the IAC's functioning through their fiscal and policy support. For Mrs. Ras-Work and other IAC activists, accordingly, the quest for funds is a never-ending one.

A Case in Point: IAC in Nigeria

But it is in Africa rather than Switzerland that the major actions of the IAC occur. Geneva coordinates and facilitates; committees in individual countries implement and influence. Both levels must be effective for the long-term eradication of female genital mutilation and other harmful traditional practices.

One of the most successful IAC national groups is located in Nigeria. The ways it has dealt with education, strategic alliances with other NGOs, and pressures on successive Nigerian governments at the federal and state levels illustrate the problems of moving from broad goals that are internationally espoused, to specific goals that must be nationally legislated and locally implemented. Knowledge must be built from below, using the skills, insights, and influence of respected community leaders. Programs must be mounted that bring awareness of modern medical practices, though not in ways that might evoke a strong negative reaction. And, most likely first rather than last, effective leadership must be provided. Here one must recognize the extraordinary efforts of Dr. Irene Modupeola Thomas, gynecologist par excellence, whose determination and flair for organization have made the Nigerian section of the IAC a model for others.

Her quiet demeanor belies a spirit of indominable dedication. Any person meeting her would be impressed. Her commitment is deep-rooted and long-standing. Dr. Thomas (now well into her mid-70s) decided by age 11 that she would become a physician. Suffering, especially that of women and children, concerned her greatly. But advanced medical studies were not the usual path for young Yoruba women in the 1930s, even for daughters of relatively westernized parents in the effervescent Lagos area. Dr. Thomas's grit showed in secondary school, for the science and math courses requisite for admission to medical school could be followed only at a boys' school.[36] After eight years in family business, she entered the medical school of the University of Durham, England, in July 1944.

Shocking! Too mild a term, perhaps, for the psychological trauma Dr. Thomas experienced shortly after her return to Nigeria, now equipped with her MD degree. She was practising gynecology at the Massey Street Maternity Hospital, Lagos. One day, she came face to face with a 26-year old woman who was 26 weeks pregnant and had just been subjected to "circumcision" by excision of the clitoris and part of the labia minora. The operation had been blotched. The young woman was bleeding to death. "It was really touch and go. I asked, 'Why did you allow them to traumatize you?' Tears streaming down her face, she said, 'I couldn't do anything.' " The mother-to-be came from an ethnic group where female genital operations were not customary; her husband's mother insisted that the child could not be born without prior excision of the pregnant woman; the husband would not oppose his mother. Dr. Thomas felt, "This must never go on"; her male colleages said, "You will get used to it."[37] In reality, Dr. Thomas has never been reconciled to FGM, though her wisdom has grown in decades of combatting ignorance within Nigerian society, especially among women who are illiterate and far removed from modern medical treatment.

Genital operations are widespread in Nigeria, and in most countries of the Sahel. Sociologically, these operations form a central part in joining children to their age groups and gender identification, and in preparing them for eventual parental responsibilities. Male circumcision (with a high but not fully measured risk of tetanus from unsterilized knives) can be found in all Islamic areas and in most societies with Christian or traditional religious practices. Female circumcision affects between 50 and 95 percent of all women in Nigeria. Given the poor sanitary conditions, infections were and are common. Dr. Thomas's indignation emerged in her measured, scientific words at the 1984 Dakar conference, at which she presented her findings. "I was just waiting for an outlet to put in my fireworks," she said a decade later.[38]

I have already noted that women's health issues became prominent in the West through emphasis on "circumcision." But this is only part of a series of problems. Harmful traditional practices cover a wide gamut, as identified in Mrs. Warzazi's 1986 report mentioned earlier. In Africanizing the "circumcision" issue, African members of the IAC deliberately broadened the scope of their efforts. Health could be endangered by a wide variety of practices, highlighted in the 1987 IAC plan of action. All these problems could be (and still are) found in Nigeria. Marriage between 12 and 15 years of age (a normal occurrence in rural areas, particularly in the north) often means pregnancies before the child-bride has physically developed sufficiently. Birthing is difficult. To speed delivery, traditional birth attendants will sometimes slice deeply to widen the birth canal, without anesthetic or antiseptic, leading to severe complications.[39] The great majority of deliveries take place in villages, with no prenatal advice or perinatal care available.[40] Nutritional taboos limit pregnant women's caloric and vitamin intakes. Scarification risks infections. A simplistic halt to female genital mutilation would not work without simultaneously attacking a gamut of other practices and beliefs. Knowledge remains essential.

Dr. Thomas is graying and well into her 70s. She knows that miracles will not occur overnight. She continues to travel around Nigeria, each trip covering the best part of six weeks. Progress is slow, but not painfully so. She sees indicators of progress. Being illiterate or village bound does not destroy one's thirst for learning. Indeed, by showing that maternal and infant mortality rates drop as a result of IAC efforts, public support grows for altering various harmful traditional practices. As elsewhere in the world, parents seek to improve their children's chances of survival. Practices can and do change. Let me illustrate with an example from an Annang-inhabited area of southeastern Nigeria. Births there usually take place in villages. Annang women have gone to the nearest clinic or hospital only in cases of severe complications, frequently the result of botched deliveries by traditional birth attendants. Hence, progress depended on upgrading the TBAs' skills — an effort undertaken by the IAC Nigeria section. The figures are startling: thirty maternal deaths in three years prior to TBA training; fifteen deaths in the three years immediately afterwards; a mere four deaths in the following four years.[41] Knowledge was cumulative.

Programs in Nigeria encouraged or directed by the IAC have blended old and new. The attendees are qualified nurses and traditional birth attendants (who are, perhaps surprisingly, mostly male in the southeastern and western states). The long-term goal is to have at least one trainer of traditional birth attendants in each local government area, to carry on the training of more unskilled TBAs as they are identified. Distinguished patrons, such as the wife of the state's military governor or local elders, grace IAC training efforts with their presence. Program length varies. Three day programs are used to sensitize policy makers, professionals. and community members (market women, school children, and teachers) to harmful practices. Two weeks of training and information campaigns train the trainers who work directly with traditional birth attendants. Those with leadership qualities are identified for further schooling as supervisors. The IAC gives out certificates, both for prominent display on living room walls and, from an administrative standpoint, to ensure the registration of trained TBAs at their local maternity centers, to create a cordial relationship between trainers and trainees, and to develop a smooth-working referral system. The quality of perinatal care improves. Dr. Thomas and her colleagues derive immense satisfaction.

The Nigerian committee is probably the most successful of the 24 national committees. Others slumber in inactivity, at some times the result of severe internal conflicts (Somalia and Liberia are two obvious examples), at other times the consequence of poor leadership. It is difficult to dynamize groups in Africa from a base in Geneva. For that reason, the IAC started to shift most program activities (other than financial control and major liaison with donors and the international community) to Addis Ababa in mid-1994. How the changes are implemented belong in another study. The scorecard for the IAC's first decade seems impressive, given the obstacles of incomprehension and opposition it confronted when it started.

The activities of the IAC in Nigeria and other settings is truly "grassroots" work. It is not glamorous, exciting, or political. Some results can be dramatic, such as the Annang figures just cited, but much of the work will not bear fruit for several years. Total eradication of female genital mutilation by the year 2000 — the IAC's public goal — will likely not occur by that time, although the more severe forms of FGM are being practiced less widely. The practice is too deeply rooted to be excised quickly. A new generation of educated men and women must become influential within rural communities, where various harmful traditional practices remain widespread. So long as appropriate behavior continues to be defined by persons steeped in beliefs that are hallowed by misty traditions, and so long as females are culturally barred from positions of leadership, abuses to women's health will continue.

IAC programs try to avoid "politics," with the exception of seeing influential patrons for programs. "First ladies" are particularly prized, with the wives of the presidents of Burkina Faso, Ghana, and Guinea receiving star billing at the April 1994 IAC meeting in Addis Ababa. Persons of more limited prestige are sought for their knowledge of *local* conditions and community standing. Attitude change begins at the grassroots. "Outsiders" may be respected for their knowledge and social status; but their visits are invariably brief, and their long-term impact often limited. Hence village "influentials" are the persons to and through whom many programs are addressed. Can they translate their impact at the village level into change in regional or national settings? Experience to date suggests that professionals, notably doctors, trained midwives, and nurses, can link local concerns about health to policy makers. However, they often lack the political inclination to press for major policy changes. There will come a time when IAC strategy must seek allies for legislation — that is, when popular attitudes have shifted. That day is coming. Education about human rights can lead toward their implementation through legislation and legal enforcement.

The low level of scientific knowledge about reproduction, particularly in rural areas, compounds the problem of effecting rapid change. Until individuals are aware of the impact of harmful traditional practices on fertility and mortality, and until they are reasonably convinced that change means improvement, they are likely to cling to time-honored practices. Understanding precedes action. Among the IAC's most successful teaching devices are slides of plaster casts of female sexual organs, graphically showing the effects of different types of genital mutilation and consequences for giving birth.[42] Research is encouraged, to prove the harmful effects of FGM. A recent study in Sierra Leone involving 392 women found nearly twice the incidence of stillbirths or neonatal deaths among circumcised women compared with non-circumcised mothers.[43] FGM threatens maternal and child survival, contrary to what "tradition" teaches. Herein lies a basis for change. The strategic choice is significant. Throughout Africa, fertility is prized, and children honored. Hence, in indicating how child-bearing ability may be enhanced (through avoiding child marriage and genital mutilation, and by reexamining nutritional taboos), the IAC utilizes a long-standing value in favor of change. Sensitivity to language is also important. For example, IAC seminars at the village level discuss "spacing" births more openly than contraception. What could be considered Western or feminist language is generally avoided.

Ultimately, one could argue, economic improvement coupled with political change can best remove the fetters of outmoded practices and raise the status of women in Africa. True enough. Emphasis on education can go only so far in changing practices. Shifts in attitudes must be complemented by lessened barriers of poverty. The grim figures recounted at the start of this chapter should be recalled. But the economic advantage of individuals can be addressed. One of the most important targets for IAC work are traditional birth attendants, already featured in this chapter. They need alternative sources of income, as the money they earn from genital operations dries up. Greater use of birth spacing may result, over time, from development and urbanization. Families living on the margin of survival in rural areas see children as economic assets; families in urban areas face different economic conditions, in which children are more burdens than aids. And, as democratization facilitates greater governmental responsiveness to public opinion, one would hope for legislation (such as minimum age for marriage) that would be respected. But public opinion itself must be prepared. Changes in popular attitudes should come first—and that will take time. Some evidence from Nigeria has been cited. But because of vigorous leadership, Nigeria stands well ahead of most African countries. More leaders at the national level like Irene Thomas will be needed.

Is an approach from below "better" than an attempt to legislate from above? In the West, women's rights are often considered best approached through non-discrimination in constitutions and human rights treaties. In much of Africa, such an approach faces extraordinary cultural obstacles, this chapter has argued. Females confront greater problems than do males, from the time of their birth through their entire lives. Different and subordinate gender roles exist. Persons' responsibilities and rights derive not from their being humans *qua* humans, but from their being men or women. Equality between the sexes is viewed, especially in rural areas, as a biological and cultural impossibility.

The educational work of the Inter-African Committee is aimed at largely voiceless people. Rural African women of child-bearing age are unlikely to have gone beyond primary school (if they attend at all); they have little economic security; they are expected to be subordinate to their husbands and attentive to their offspring; they labor longer and for less reward than do their spouses. In political and economic terms, they seem marginal to those who exercise power. Yet they have rights, which in theory African governments enforce.

Have the efforts of the IAC increased human rights' awareness in sub-Saharan Africa? The answer, emphatically, is yes. Genital operations, formerly veiled in secrecy and condoned as an integral part of culture, have become subjects for general discussion. The most persuasive testimonial comes from the person largely responsible for the debate in the first place. As Fran Hosken recently wrote, "There has been a major change in attitude in Africa under the leadership of African women. . . . [E]verything has changed. At last it is possible to talk about female genital mutilation without getting a blank stare or being attacked as racist, as I have been so many times."[44] Ms. Hosken participated in the 1994 Addis Ababa conference of the IAC and was applauded for her contribution. Strong advocacy from a dedicated Westerner, transformed into effective long-term strategy by well-informed Africans, had transformed public opinion. Severe forms of female genital operations are diminishing in Africa.

Much remains to be done, however, with respect to other rights for women. Additional strategies may be necessary. Human rights are taken, not given. They require mobilization, based on information and education. Evidence seems to come from the material surveyed above. Laws against childhood marriage exist in several countries, but are often honored in the breach rather than the observance. Legislatures of many states, Kenya being a noteworthy example, have sidetracked bills advancing women's rights (although in 1982 President Daniel arap Moi banned clitoridectomies, after the deaths of 14 young girls who had undergone the operation). The legislature of one Nigerian state voted down a bill proposing a ban on female circumcision.[45] Public pressure and awareness appear to have been insufficient to get either laws or enforcement throughout large parts of the continent. Male-dominated African parliaments seem to take little interest in women's rights.

Hence, I conclude, echoing Berhane Ras-Work, Irene Thomas, Fran Hosken, Rhoda Howard and others, that change comes with small steps, taken from below. *Festina lente*— make haste slowly— makes sense in combatting harmful traditional practices, at least at this point. Basic knowledge about reproduction and the harmful effects of diverse practices must become widespread. Educational campaigns can be encouraged from above. Meaningful change can occur as a result of special courses and growing public enlightenment. Progress will be uneven, given the decentralized nature of national committees' work. But progress is being made, and will continue. At some point, education helps to empower women and to facilitate enforcement of equal rights.

Notes

1. Rhoda E. Howard, *Human Rights in Commonwealth Africa* (Totowa, NJ: Rowman & Littlefield, 1986), p. 205.

2. Fran Hosken, *The Hosken Report: Genital and Sexual Mutilation of Females* (Lexington, MA: Women's International Network, 1994, 4th edition), p. 376.

3. Howard finds the terms "female circumcision" and "female genital mutilation" misleading. The former term analogizes similarity between procedures carried out on boys and girls when the surgery is usually far more drastic for girls; the latter term suggests an intention to harm. Howard, *Human Rights in Commonwealth Africa*, p. 203. Four types of procedures can be differentiated. From least to most severe, they include 1) "ritualistic circumcision," with simple nicking of the clitoris by a sharp instrument, 2) "sunna," with removal of the outer layer of skin over the clitoris, 3) clitoridectomy, with complete excision of the organ and possibly parts of the labia minora, and 4) infibulation, with removal of virtually all external genitilia. Alison T. Slack, "Female Circumcision: A Critical Appraisal," *Human Rights Quarterly* 10 (1988), 441. A somewhat different classification has recently been advocated. Nahid Toubia, "Female Circumcision as a Public Health Issue," *New England Journal of Medicine* 331, 11 (September 15, 1994), 712.

4. Far and away the most prominent foe of female genital operations is Fran Hosken, an American journalist and crusader for women's rights. Her perspective is firmly rooted in the rhetoric and values of Western feminism, which do not play well in sub-Saharan Africa. Take, for example, these citations from the fourth edition of her famous book:

The contempt for the female of the species, which is the basic cause of the mutilations, discrimination and abuse by men must be challenged and dealt with everywhere at its source. . . . What are called "cultural traditions" in reality are practices that support the ritual abuse of women, systematically damaging women's health and strength to make sure of their subordination to men. . . . The politics of genital mutilation are first all the patriarchal politics of controlling production and reproduction of the wholly-owned female labor force — the primary resources of male power and wealth.

Hosken, *Hosken Report*, pp. 9, 16, 315.
Typical of negative responses would be the following:

The furore in the US over female circumcision, where it has taken on the prominence of a *cause celèbre*, is hardly surprising. There is always something or other which American women with their generally anti-men and extreme feminist attitude, feel bound to take up on behalf of women world-wide, in much the same way as their government sees itself as the world's policeman . . . The patronising and maternalistic attitude is what many of us find totally unacceptable.

Marilynne Charles, "An Open Wound," *West Africa* (27 June–3 July 1994), 1138.
    5. Nahid Toubia, *Female Genital Mutilation: A Call for Global Action* (New York: Women, Ink., 1993), p. 25. About two-thirds come from five countries: Nigeria (50 percent of women estimated as "circumcized," hence 30,625,000); Ethiopia and Eritrea (90 percent; 23,940,000); Egypt (50 percent; 13,625,000); and northern Sudan (89 percent; 9,220,400). WHO estimates between 85 and 114 million.
    6. The linguistic relativity issue remains joined in French, where *droits de l'homme* has not been superseded by (for example) *droits humains* (which is used to refer to rights under humanitarian law) or *droits de la personne*; in Canada, the term *droits personnels* is occasionally used.
    7. The body of this and the following three paragraphs come from my article, "Human Rights and African Women: A Comparison of Protection Under Two Major Treaties," *Human Rights Quarterly* 15 (1993), 549–74.
    8. *Poverty: World Development Report 1990* (New York: Oxford University Press for the World Bank, 1990), p. 10.
    9. For example, the third periodic report submitted by Rwanda indicated that real GDP (Gross Domestic Product) per inhabitant had fallen 4.3 percent in 1987, a further 7.1 percent in 1988, and 10 percent in 1989! UN Document CEDAW/C/RWA/3*, 25 February 1991.
    10. *World Development Report 1990*, p. 29, Table 2.1.
    11. *Human Development Report 1993*, p. 139.
    12. Cited in Jodi L. Jacobson, *Gender Bias: Roadblock to Sustainable Development* (Washington, DC: Worldwatch Institute, Paper 110), p. 19.
    13. Ibid., p. 15.
    14. World Bank, *Poverty*, p. 29. Somewhat different figures come from the UN Development Program: life expectancy at birth for women from sub-Saharan Africa of 53.6 years, compared with the world average of 67.3 years. *Human Development Report 1993*, p. 151.
    15. Cited in ibid., p. 11.
    16. UN Document CEDAW/C/RWA/3*, p. 31.
    17. Ibid. For concrete steps to combat these differences, see Chapter 9 and the work of TOSTAN in Senegal.

18. Howard, *Human Rights in Commonwealth Africa*, p. 189.

19. I hasten to add these were not the first examples of UN interest. In 1952, the Commission on Human Rights studied human rights in Trust and Non-Self-Governing Territories, noting some practices impaired the health and dignity of women. In 1958, ECOSOC invited WHO to examine "the persistence of customs which subject girls to ritual operations." The WHO Executive Board aptly noted that study of the medical aspects "could not be undertaken in isolation but must be related to the cultural and socio-economic background of the countries concerned." And, in 1975, the World Health Assembly gave particular attention to traditional practices and their effects on the health of women and children. A working group was established in 1977. *United Nations Action in the Field of Human Rights* (New York: United Nations, 1988), pp. 148–49.

20. Examples of such NGOs are IWRAW and the Women's Action Project of Human Rights Watch. Working with international treaty bodies has become the province of IWRAW, the International Women's Rights Action Watch, established in Minneapolis by Arvonne Fraser (whose husband, as a member of the House of Representatives in the mid-1970s, led the Congressional effort to incorporate human rights standards into major American legislation); Human Rights Watch established its women's rights project in 1990.

21. The final report of the Khartoum seminar was published as UN Document EM.SEM.T.PR.AFR.HTH.WM/44; the original is World Health Organization, Regional Office for the Eastern Mediterranean, "Traditional practices affecting the health of women and children: Female circumcision, childhood marriage, nutritional taboos, etc.: Report of a Seminar, Khartoum, 10–15 February 1979" (WHO/EMRO Technical Publication No. 2, 1979).

22. Resolution 1983/1, 31 August 1983. The resolution also named Mr. M.Y. Mudawi as an expert, but he apparently did not participate in the study.

23. Resolution 1984/48 of 13 March 1984, subsequently endorsed by ECOSOC (Resolution 1984/34 of 24 May 1984).

24. Interview with Dr. Irene Modupeola Thomas, Lagos, February 23, 1994.

25. For details of her activities, see *Hosken Report*, esp. pp. 351–53, 359, 372 and elsewhere.

26. UN Document E/CN.4/1986/42.

27. See preliminary report, UN Document E/CN.4/Sub.2/1989/42 and Add. 1; and the final report, UN Document E/CN.4/Sub.2/1991/6, 5 July 1991.

28. UN Document E/CN.4/Sub.2/1991/6, p. 36.

29. Interview with Berhane Ras-Work, Geneva, Janury 19, 1994.

30. For reports, see "Rapport du séminaire sur les pratiques traditionalles ayant effect sur la santé des femmes et des enfants en Afrique" (1984) and "Report on the Regional Seminar on Traditional Practices Affecting the Health of Women and Children in Africa" (1987, 1990, 1994), all published by the Inter-African Committee in Geneva.

31. As IAC program officer Dr. Tamunosa Okiwelu commented at the 1994 Addis Ababa meeting, early marriage is common: 44 percent of African women get married before age 15, thus putting both mother and baby at risk.

32. *Newsletter*, #1, August 1985.

33. Including Benin, Burkina Faso, Cameroon, Chad, Côte d'Ivoire, Ethiopia, Guinea, Guiné-Bissau, Kenya, Mauritania, Niger, Tanzania, and Uganda.

34. The proposed IAC budget from May 1994 to December 1996 is divided into four segments: program for national committees; networking and advocacy; education; and administration and operation. The national committees, responsible

for programs for training courses, would absorb nearly two-thirds of the proposed 1995 budget of $1,887,264. Each would be responsible for a program for traditional birth attendants, another for trainers. The 1994 triennial conference cost just over $315,000, with support of $20,000 or more from a wide variety of largely Western sources (e.g., Norwegian Agency for Development Cooperation, USAID, Population Action USA, Redda Barnen Sweden, the Government of the Netherlands, the Canadian Embassy in Addis Ababa/CIDA, and the World Bank).

35. For further details on CEDAW and the African Commission, see Welch, "Human Rights and African Women." One should note that the Convention on the Rights of the Child includes a direct obligation on ratifying governments: "States Parties shall take all effective and appropriate measures with a view to abolishing traditional practices prejudicial to the health of children" (Article 24, 3).

36. Dr. Thomas had been offered a scholarship in 1934 to enter the medical assistants' course at Queen's College, but turned it down to become a full-time sixth form student at King's College—where her four elder brothers had all received their education. Advanced medical training was not available in Nigeria until the late 1940s, with the establishment of the University College of Ibadan and subsequently the University College Teaching Hospital.

37. Interview with Dr. Irene Thomas, Lagos, February 23, 1994.

38. Ibid.

39. The chief problem is known widely in Nigeria as VVF, vesico-vaginal fistula. The misdirected knife (or the sudden move of the pain-wracked woman) cuts between the cervix and the bladder or rectum. The result is continuous discharge of bodily wastes through the vagina, generating unpleasant odors and often leading to divorce. VVF repairs constitute a major gynecological specialization in Nigeria, with one hospital in Lagos devoted to it. A special hospital in Addis Ababa also repairs these fistulas.

40. In studies done in Nigerian local government areas, several interesting findings emerged. For example, 90 percent of traditional birth attendants in part of Ogun State were male, who were patronized by all pregnant women in the area. Nutritional taboos meant many highly nourishing foods were not eaten—for example, milk was considered in this area to make the child too large for delivery, and oranges were believed to cause bulging membranes. Sixty to 75 percent of women give birth in villages, attended by TBAs or midwives with no prior study of anatomy or physiology. Figures from reports published in *Your Task* (annual publication of the Nigerian IAC chapter, n.d.), I, 2.

41. Table, *Your Task*, 23.

42. Analogously, Fran Hosken devoted a great deal of effort to publishing and distributing booklets about childbirth, showing the harmful consequences of FGM.

43. Olayinka A. Koso-Thomas and Mabel E. Willoughby, "Report on Traditional Practices and their Influence on the Choice of Contraceptives among Women in Sierra Leone" (Geneva: WHO and IAC, 1994), 26. There were other contrasts between the groups: 10.3 percent of the "circumcised" women surveyed had lost three or more children through still-births or neonatal deaths, compared with 2.2 percent for the non-circumcised group; initial intercourse was painful for 86.1 percent versus 51.9 percent; prolonged labor had marked 29.4 percent and 17.3 percent respectively (Ibid., 26, 29, 51).

44. *Hosken Report*, pp. 1, 3.

45. Interview with Dr. Irene Thomas, Lagos, February 23, 1994.

Chapter 4
Empowerment and Group Rights: Ogoni, Oromo, and Casamançais Claims for Autonomy

1. All peoples have the right of self-determination. By virtue of that right they freely determine their political status and freely pursue their economic, social and cultural development.
2. All peoples may, for their own ends, freely dispose of their natural wealth and resources without prejudice to any obligations arising out of international economic cooperation, based upon the principle of mutual benefit, and international law. In no case may a people be deprived of its own means of subsistence.
3. The States Parties to the present Covenant . . . shall promote the realization of the right of self-determination, and shall respect that right, in conformity with the provisions of the Charter of the United Nations.
— Article 1, International Covenants

All peoples shall have the right to existence. They shall have the unquestionable and inalienable right to self-determination. They shall freely determine their political status and shall pursue their economic and social development according to the policy they have freely chosen.
— Article 20, 1, African Charter on Human and Peoples' Rights

States enjoying full sovereignty and independence, and possessed of a government effectively representing the whole of their population, shall be considered to be conducting themselves in conformity with the principle of equal rights and self-determination of peoples as regards that population. Nothing in the foregoing paragraphs shall be construed as authorizing any action which would impair, totally or in part, the territorial integrity, or political unity, of such States.
— "Declaration on Principles of International Law concerning Friendly Relations and Co-operation among States in accordance with the United Nations Charter" (1970)

What constitutes a "people"? No one can say with precision. In an era of strong group feelings, where "nationalism" stands as a paramount value, the precise boundaries of a "nation" remain under debate. Should each "people" or "nation" enjoy a right to sovereign independence? How do and should political borders interact with cultural boundaries? Can a multi-ethnic or multi-national state survive in the face of conflicting group claims for power? These questions — of paramount importance at the start of this century — raced to the forefront of international consciousness in the early 1990s. The rapid collapse of the Soviet Union and Yugoslavia, and ethnically-based civil wars simmering in such widely separated countries as Sri Lanka and Rwanda, demonstrated the durablity of ethnic awareness as bases for political tension.

No surprise. Just as democratization and empowerment unleash opportunities for *individuals* to press their claims, so they open up the chance for *groups* to demand greater recognition and power. And therein lies an issue that continues to loom large throughout Africa. It started before independence, but accelerated later. Despite broadly-based anticolonial fronts, dissension lurked just below the surface. Once "home rule" was achieved, the issue of "who shall rule at home" dominated politics. Recently-won self-government seemed threatened by splintering from within. Authoritarianism, in retrospect, seemed better at driving ethnic pluralism underground than at creating a solid sense of national unity.

African leaders have long been concerned with the potential for fragmentation along ethnic lines. With rare exceptions, sub-Saharan states are conglomerations of groups, thrown together by the vagaries of colonial boundaries.[1] States preceded nations. In essence, "Nigeria" came into being long before a substantial number of its residents felt themselves to be "Nigerians." They felt themselves far more likely to be members of the Igbo, Tiv, or Hausa peoples than citizens of the Nigerian nation.[2] *Punch* once satirized the sitution: the first panel of its cartoon showed Africa unmarked by boundaries, the second with borders drawn as a result of colonialism, the third a continent with many times the number of boundaries, the final a heap of dust. The inevitable result of Balkanization, the cartoonist realized, was a fragmented, powerless set of mini-states, tangential to much of global politics and economics.

Many early African politicians pressed for unity in the face of division. While Senegal's Senghor advocated federation and railed against "micronationalism," Ghana's Nkrumah pressed for political unification of newly-independent African states.[3] Their failures have been documented elsewhere, and need not detain us here.[4] Although fear of destabilization based on ethnicity did not result in a "United States of Africa," it did result in creation of the Organization of African Unity, pledged to maintain the inherited status quo. The OAU has, from its inception, taken strong stands against revising borders or dividing states, in order to accommodate "sub-national" claims.[5] Among its principles are preservation of unity within inherited frontiers, "unreserved condemnation" of plotting against sister states, and respect for sovereign equality.

"Self-determination" lies at the heart of the matter. *Who* constitutes a people? *What* economic and political rights can they claim? *How* can they achieve self-determination? Is it a once-and-for-all-time act? Should "external" self-determination, with the achievement of independence, preclude later "internal" self-determination, through secession? There is an enormous literature on self-determination.[6] However, a skeptic might assert, the basic issues remain no clearer now than when the new post–World War I boundaries of Europe and the treaties to protect minorities stranded in other states were negotiated.

In terms of human rights, self-determination occupies a singular position. It stands first in the two International Covenants, as quoted in this chapter's headnote. The common Article 1 was inserted into the ICCPR and ICESCR in large part as a result of pressure from Third World countries. Determined to end the scourge of externally-imposed colonialism, which touched deep political nerves, they pressed the UN General Assembly to adopt the Declaration on the Granting of Independence to Colonial Countries and Peoples.[7] Its gist later appeared as Article 1 of the Covenants. The political effect has been nicely summarized by Donnelly:

> In practice, then, the internationally recognized right to self-determination, despite its seeming breadth, has been treated as an extremely narrow right. States' fears of secession and governments' fears of revolution have combined to restrict the right to self-determination to little more than a right to sovereignty for those states (and colonies) that currently exist. Given that the right to self-determination emerged as part of the struggle against Western imperialism, this is not surprising.[8]

What would be the likely result, were groups *within* existing independent states to claim that they enjoyed the right to self-determination, and hence to separate political status? They can expect sharp opposition, indeed probably forcible repression, from governments. Feeling their sovereignty under threat, governments treat claims for self-determination (which may in reality be requests for a fairer share of the political and economic pie) as demands for unacceptable secession. The weak basis for national unity in multi-ethnic societies encourages leaders to turn to coercion rather than to compromise. They could point to the "once-and-for-all-time" nature of self-determination: disaffected communities must work within the confines of their own political systems, not create a sovereign new one. One of the most telling examples comes from the African Charter on Human and Peoples' Rights. Individuals have the duty "to preserve and strengthen the national independence and the territorial integrity of [their] country" (Article 29, 5).

There is a basis, however, for considering rights of groups within international human rights law, even though well short of political autonomy. Let us look at Article 27 of the ICCPR:

In those States in which ethnic, religious or linguistic minorities exist, persons belonging to such minorities shall not be denied the right, in community with the other members of their group, to enjoy their own culture, to profess and practice their own religion, or to use their own language.

The framers of the Covenant believed that its non-discrimination clauses would suffice in most cases. All persons would be treated equally; *ergo*, claims could be resolved through democratic, legal means. Individualism coupled to the rule of law would prove adequate. In reality, where ethnic or other social divisions are deep-rooted, respect for the minority is less likely than tyranny of the majority. Respect for the identity of the community — in other words, for some form of group rights — is essential.[9]

Thus, in dealing with empowerment and group rights in this chapter, we are focusing on one of the trickiest, most emotional issues in both contemporary Africa and current human rights debates. Ethnic groups seeking to empower themselves collide with the desire of states to maintain centralized control. Even modest claims for a share of administrative responsibility can touch a hot button in the capital. Pluralism, far from being viewed as an essential building-block and a safeguard for competitive democracy, is perceived as a weapon of potential destruction. And, in the polished corridors of Geneva and New York, the legal interpretation of self-determination and the place of the individual versus the group in human rights remain items of serious disagreement. Rather than attempt to resolve these matters at this point, it is appropriate to turn to three ongoing ethnically-based movements. MOSOP of Nigeria, the OLF of Ethiopia, and the MFDC of Senegal epitomize the conflicts inherent when sub-national groups seek greater political and economic clout, and use the language of human rights to do so.

Are these three groups NGOs, as I have used the term elsewhere in this book? They do operate (echoing Schmitter's definition, quoted early in Chapter 2) between primary units of society and ruling collective institutions. On the other hand, they emphasize the collective identity of specific groups, and are willing to use violence. They seek political power, particularly the OLF. All started obscurely, as cultural movements within groups that felt marginalized. They have become, or are becoming, political movements. Their strategies of empowerment and struggle evolved in politically and socially repressive settings. Civil society was particularly weak in Ethiopia; not surprisingly, the Oromo Liberation Front has transformed itself over time into a resistance movement. It has not functioned, at least recently, primarily as either a classic political party or a non-governmental organization. Analogous tendencies can be found in MOSOP and the MFDC. Hence, empowerment as a strategy tests the boundaries of the concept of a human rights NGO. This is a lesson found both in this chapter and in Chapter 8, where we examine democratization. Human rights NGOs can remain pristine, in a sense, by focusing on education, enforcement, documentation, and (more arguably) development. When they concentrate on empowerment and democratization, human rights NGOs may cross an indistinct boundary into political activism of a different sort.

MOSOP (Movement for the Survival of the Ogoni People)

The Ogoni live atop some of the richest real estate in Africa. Rivers State of Nigeria houses a substantial part of the country's oil industry. Petroleum has been the cash source that keeps Nigeria semi-solvent. Well over 90 percent of its foreign exchange earnings come from oil royalties and sales. Export taxes provide the lion's share of national revenues. The funds accrue directly to the federal government, which then metes out shares to Nigeria's 30 states and nearly 600 local governments. And, as should be expected, the allocation of the revenues received by Lagos (or stuck to the fingers of greedy politicians) has long stirred hot political debates. Should inhabitants of major mineral- or export crop-producing areas receive a high proportion, based on the principle of derivation? Or should the funds be allocated on the basis of population and need, in order to foster broader national development? Ought special steps to be taken to reserve jobs for villagers where industries are located, or should positions be filled on other criteria? If environmental damage occurs, who takes responsibility? to whom or what would compensation be provided?

From one point of view, Ogoni demands arise from the accident of their location. Nigeria as a whole has received billions of dollars from oil — most of which seems to have disappeared into the national economy and/or private hands without satisfactory accounting and without perceptible benefit to most Nigerians, and particularly to the areas of origin. Few petrodollars have flowed back to the Ogoni area, with the exception of investment in capital-intensive wells, pipelines, and refineries. Few Ogoni benefit from jobs, development, or amenities in the oil industry. Instead, they suffer serious environmental degradation that has polluted fishing streams and fresh water sources, poisoned land through spills and blow-outs, and created an atmosphere fouled by decades of flaring natural gas. All the environmental costs, few of the economic rewards: this has become a widespread view among the Ogoni.

From another perspective, Ogoni demands reflect a long-standing emphasis on local autonomy in Africa. The distant state cannot be trusted to understand or act effectively on grass-roots priorities. Indeed, government may be more predator than servant, an agent of exploitation rather than protection. Because the public sector appears to reward the private interests of those who control it, persons outside the privileged inner circles turn to kinship networks and emphasize personal ties. Ogoni actions, in short, are nothing new. Colonial rule created government machinery distant from the people, something both to be defended against and to be pressed for resources; only through ethnic links could balance be obtained. As Ekeh has stressed in a seminal work, the "two publics" in Africa respond to different issues.[10] The result is a curious paradox, in which venality is bemoaned in general terms and confidence in government in general remains low, but specific funds and jobs for local areas are avidly sought.

Ogoni demands illustrate the interplay of politics, economics, and ethnicity. Political and socio-economic change do not necessarily directly diminish ethnic awareness and identity; they may in fact provoke it. As Young has written, "cultural collectivities are not simply disembodied primordial givens, but contingent patterns of solidarity whose activation depends on the organization and mobilization of consciousness on the one hand, and the intrusion of the political process in the form of perceived domination, competition, threats or advantages, on the other."[11] There is a kind of yin-yang principle: a latent sense of identity can be crystallized as a result of political pressures. Once articulated, claims of ethnic discrimination in an economic zero-sum game (or worse, as in Nigeria for much of its recent history, a declining-sum game) take on a life of their own, complicating the building of national unity. Rights of the group have been denied.

In claiming the right to a greater financial share, Ogoni leaders challenge the fundamental principles of centralized government. Control of revenue is the basis of political power in Nigeria. And, in speaking in terms of rights for a people, they unconsciously echo demands by earlier African leaders for redrawing political borders.[12] No wonder that on May 5, 1993, the Babangida administration ordained the Treason and Treasonable Offenses Decree, under which the death penalty could be imposed for advocacy of "ethnic autonomy."

Nigeria's ethnic complexity was briefly noted in Chapter 1. In broad terms, the role of "minorities" — groups other than the Fulani, Hausa, Igbo, and Yoruba — have increased their political clout. The clearest measure comes in the multiplication of states: from four regions in the mid-1960s, to a dozen states later in the decade, to 19 in the mid-1970s, to 30 in 1995. Nigeria has seemingly come closer to the path sketched by early nationalist leader Obafemi Awolowo, who favored building a central political system upwards from ethnic communities.[13] The reality is quite different. Power and resources flow downward. The federal government's stranglehold over revenue allocation has already been noted; this is complemented, naturally, by supreme political power, exercised for more than two-thirds of Nigeria's history by the armed forces and almost always by a leader from the north.[14] Regional dominance at the center has its parallel at the state level. Despite numerous divisions of the three regions with which Nigeria was endowed at independence, none can claim homogeneity. Each state has a dominant community and several subordinate groups. In the former Eastern Region, the Igbo held control and the Ijaws constituted a restive minority; in Rivers State, the Ijaw hold the pre-eminent position, the Ogoni are one of the State's minority groups. The capital, Port Harcourt, is essentially a city of Igbo and Ijaw. The 500,000 Ogoni[15] (to use the figure claimed by MOSOP, the Movement for the Survival of Ogoni People) live in the Niger River delta, where roads barely exist and most travel is via boat, or, for important oil company officials, by helicopter.

The Ogoni movement, though based on culture, sprang in reality from politics, intensified by the paradox of oil riches amid environmental squalor.

Ogoni solidarity initially drew upon a sense of grievance engendered in the Nigerian civil war (1967–70). During this, many non-Igbo groups of the "Republic of Biafra" felt discriminated against. Although the oil-producing area around the Ogoni was taken by Nigerian forces by early 1968, concern about "outside" dominance could not be quelled. A "supreme cultural organization" of the Ogoni called KAGOTE was established at the war's end, based on the elite (traditional rulers, high government functionaries). It in turn gave birth to MOSOP, which continued to be directed by members of the political upper crust. (To assume that ethnicity is primarily the province of the less educated in Africa is mistaken. "Detribalization" does not automatically result from greater education, job mobility, or other measures of "modernization." Leadership of ethnically-based movements has become a major avenue for aspirant leaders.) Claims based on rights emerged. In 1990, MOSOP drafted an Ogoni "bill of rights," which asserted that oil revenues should not be transferred away from their regions of origin — and which, if implemented, would mean a tremendous windfall for almost all parts of Rivers State.

Ogoni identification and militantcy have been pressed most vigorously by the well-known author Ken Saro-Wiwa. Catapulted into international prominence through his novels, dramas, and children's books, he became politically incensed by the wheelings and dealings of the Babangida government. Chosen as Publicity Secretary, Saro-Wiwa soon became MOSOP's president and symbol of the movement. He turned his pen and prominence to the plight of his people. His critiques of the Nigerian political system became increasingly strident.[16] Arguing that the Nigerian federal system under the military became essentially unitary, with oil resources transferred from the Niger delta area to areas the government favored, Saro-Wiwa did not mince his words:

The extinction of the ethnic groups in this [delta] area appears to have become policy. . . . The present structure of Nigeria spells the death-knell of the Ogoni and other delta minorities and their environment. Solving none of our traditional problems, it merely intensifies the murderous struggle for power at the centre by the majority ethnic groups and is an invitation to chaos.

What we require is a loose federation or a confederation of egalitarian ethnic interdependence. The federating ethnic groups should hold a National Conference now to resolve the basis of their union and install an interim government in which the military will have no role.[17]

These were risky words indeed, when backed by actions that struck directly against the pulsating heart of the oil industry.

Ogoni complaints were focused on Shell, as well as Nigeria's military government. It was an astute choice: the London-based firm had not endeared itself to people of the Niger River Delta who suffered environmental degradation but did not enjoy either jobs or significantly better facilities. MOSOP claimed Shell had taken away $30 billion from "Ogoni-land" since 1958, where a cursory look "shows an immeasurable level of poverty, squalor, underdevelopment and complete absence of basic social amenities such as electricity, pipe-borne water, hospitals, roads, and recreational facilities."[18] To quote from another MOSOP publication,

In the 35 years, Shell have [sic] operated with such total disregard of the environment that the Ogoni people have come to the conclusion that the company is waging an ecological war on them. . . . The response of Shell has been to appeal to the rulers of Nigeria for whom oil means a lot of money in private pockets and in the public purse. Together, the two have mounted a campaign of intimidation and terrorism against the Ogoni people and its leaders.[19]

Published complaints turned to public protests. MOSOP put on pressure, both in Nigeria and through international human rights bodies. It encouraged deliberate confrontation with Shell. In turn, faced with what it considered a significant threat, the Nigerian government responded with police and military units.

In the early 1990s, MOSOP adopted increasingly militant action, claiming neither government nor Shell officials were responding to their complaints. It staged a large protest march January 4, 1993. MOSOP claimed 300,000 participated — an unrealistically high estimate, but nonetheless an important event. A war of words escalated, with pollution a major topic. Shell alleged that 50–60 percent of oil spills in 1992 and 1993 were caused by sabotage[20]; MOSOP argued that Shell used outdated equipment liable to metal fatigue.[21] Confrontation became inevitable as positions hardened. In April 1993, crops planted along a planned pipeline route were uprooted, increasing tension. Nigerian soldiers guarding the construction workers opened fire. Eleven persons were wounded, one killed. The construction firm suspended its operations.[22] Saro-Wiwa was detained a few weeks later, his passport impounded when he attempted to leave Nigeria for the World Conference on Human Rights. Amnesty International and other international human rights NGOs, alerted by MOSOP, sent out appeals for Saro-Wiwa's release, because of his heart condition. (Further indication of the importance of networking to enhance the impact of human rights NGOs.) Significant additional military units were moved into the Ogoni area in late June. Saro-Wiwa was charged on six counts July 13, 1993, including sedition and unlawful assembly.[23]

The war of nerves — and increasingly of confrontation — continued to escalate. It took on not only an aura of opposition to Shell, but naked ethnic conflict allegedly egged on by Rivers State leaders. Several Ogoni villages were sacked between July and September 1993 by members of the Andoni group (though MOSOP vigorously protested that the sackings were not communal clashes). The death toll was high, even if below the 1000 claimed by MOSOP. Nigerian troops enforced an uneasy peace, while peace-making efforts began. The National Council on Inter-Governmental Relations convened a conference in early October; it claimed that "all parties" accepted an immediate resolution, that the military's presence "has noticeably enhanced the process of peace and restoration of law and order within both communities," that "there were NO outstanding issues" between Ogoni and Andoni, and that violent activities are "vehemently condemned." Significantly, Saro-Wiwa did not sign the final communiqué.[24] Also of note, distinguished Nigerian political scientist Claude Ake, who had tried to mediate earlier, who chaired the "peace conference," and who was respected by all sides, publicly expressed misgivings about the shotgun "solution." In an open letter to the Governor of Rivers State, he criticized the "hasty and dangerous judgment" that no conflicts existed between the two groups. "I worry that this Peace Agreement so hastily made and proclaimed may promise more normalcy than what actually exists especially considering its brave commitments to ensuring safe passage."[25] At best, an armed tacit truce existed at the end of 1993, Shell's expansion plans on hold, Ogoni grievances unsatisfied, and many parts of the Nigerian political establishment strongly antagonistic to Saro-Wiwa and MOSOP.

What made the Bori Road confrontation and Saro-Wiwa's detention more than minor historical blips was the publicity they received around the world. MOSOP has taken its case effectively to international human rights groups. UNPO, the Holland-based NGO known as the Unrepresented Nations and Peoples Organization, has distributed Ogoni documents widely. Also showing an interest in Ogoni matters is the International Federation for the Rights of Ethnic, Linguistic, Religious and Other Minorities, based in New York. Amnesty International, as already observed, sent out an action alert on Saro-Wiwa, calling him a prisoner of conscience.[26] In summer 1993, MOSOP members attended the Vienna World Conference on Human Rights and the Geneva meetings of CERD (Committee on Racial Discrimination) and the UN Sub-Commission on the Prevention of Discrimination and Protection of Minorities. Their material was widely circulated, and the Nigerian government called upon to respond.[27]

In all likelihood, the Ogoni are far from the most disadvantaged group in Nigeria. However, given the millions (and perhaps billions) of oil dollars that have been siphoned off into private hands over decades, and given the visible and audible[28] negative impact of petroleum production, anger and frustration are understandable. But the Ogonis have gained international attention for their cause. By taking the Ogoni case to other NGOs and to UN human rights bodies, MOSOP has achieved a high level of recognition. It is a lesson sure to be followed elsewhere in Africa. Indeed, though individual NGOs may be small and weak, they need not be isolated. A chorus of voices can be raised globally literally within hours, thanks to fax, telephone and E-mail connections. NGO networking provided the Ogoni a global platform on which to parade their grievances and depict the heavy-handed responses of Shell and the Nigerian government.

The simmering debate over the annulled Presidential elections, discussed in Chapter 1, overshadowed the Ogoni crisis. But there were important parallels reflecting profound distrust about the ability of the government to act in an effective, disinterested fashion. They showed the close connection among ethnic and regional grievances, economic disparities as spurs to political action, the negative impact of restrictions on NGO and political party activity, and the crippling effects of Babangida's and his flunkies' attempts to retain their grip on power. Indeed, dramas similar to the Ogoni confrontation were (and are being) played out all through Nigeria. So long as human rights remain imperfectly implemented and the political system stays unresponsive to popular pressures for change, confrontations between "The Authorities" and "The People" will recur. That it took a seemingly ethnic form through MOSOP was neither coincidental nor determinative. For, so long as governments are perceived as remote, unresponsive, and dominated by "others," collective organization based on common culture will, in multiethnic settings, remain a widespread response.

OLF (Oromo Liberation Front)

On the surface, the situation of the Oromos in Ethiopia appears strikingly different from that of the Ogoni in Nigeria. While the Ogoni represent a small minority in Nigeria, the Oromos constitute a substantial plurality in Ethiopia, and possibly as much as half the population.[29] The Ogoni seek representation in new Nigerian institutions based on equality of ethnic groups and revenue based on the geographic location of the country's oil supplies; the Oromos demand political power, based on demographic facts, but have no special resource claims. While the Ogoni feel impoverished in the midst of billions of dollars of oil annually produced, the Oromos are even more impoverished in the midst of a poor country.

Rhetorically, the two governments take different stands on ethnicity. Ethiopia under the Charter of the Transitional Government emphasizes ethnic identity as a paramount political organizing principle; Nigeria under the 1979 Constitution stresses "federal character" but eschews "tribalism." "Federal character" means that individuals' ethnicity was not asked in the 1992 census; the same year, the reorganization of Ethiopian government meant the establishment of ethnically-based regions.[30] Whereas Ogoni concerns were quickly and effectively flashed around the world through NGO networks, Oromo complaints remained mostly confined to Ethiopia and attracted little international sympathy. While the Oromos fought vigorously against the Mengistu regime in the lengthy, bloody civil war, the Ogoni lack the inclination, arms and numbers to undertake much more than village-level protests. Ken Saro-Wiwa's name enjoys a certain amount of global recognition; Oromo leaders are unknown outside Ethiopia.

These differences, I would argue, should not obscure the similarities. Claims by the Ogoni and Oromos (as well as the Diola of the Casamance, the subject of attention later in this chapter) reflect a continuing reality of politics in sub-Saharan Africa. Societies are vigorously pluralistic, based on ethnicity. Cut-throat competition for economic and political power encourages persons to turn to the primordial sentiment of kinship. By stigmatizing the outsider and exalting the insider, the ambitious can create powerful movements.

The Oromos (formerly called Gallas, now considered a derisory term) have functioned since the late 19th century within an Amhara-dominated system. Prior to that time, the Oromos were themselves vigorously expanding and incorporating other groups. Their cradleland was likely southern Ethiopia. In the words of a leading Oromo historian, "there is no such thing as a 'pure' Oromo tribe derived from a single founding father . . . the history of the Oromo people is . . . a story of fusion and interaction by which all tribes and groups had altered and been transformed constantly."[31] Early in the 16th century, increased population and possibly the introduction of the saddled horse resulted in major expansion by the Oromos. They collided with the Amhara who, in turn, imposed further drastic changes. Many Oromos adopted sedentary agriculture; widespread conversion to Christianity or Islam had strong impact. But the most marked effect came through the establishment of Amhara dominance. "The vast majority of the Oromos came to see the Amhara and the state they represented as colonialists, bent on exploiting them and stripping them of their culture."[32] Or, as another specialist expressed, "After centuries of self-sufficient independence, the different Oromo peoples were conquered by Shoa [the center of the historic Amhara kingdom] during the last two decades of the last century. . . . The Oromos were colonized; many were sold into slavery, others were reduced to near serfdom, and much of their land was expropriated."[33]

Amhara dominance over Ethiopia, established by war, was maintained by cooptation. As Clapham emphasized, "Although Ethiopia has continuously formed a multiethnic political system, participation in national political life normally required assimilation to the cultural values of the Amharic core: the Amharic language, Orthodox Christianity, and a capacity to operate within the structures and assumptions of court administration."[34] Due to the "plasticity" of Amhara identity, individuals of Oromo background could achieve high rank. Again to quote Clapham,

Being Amhara is much more a matter of how one behaves than of who one's parents were; and without this capacity for assimilating other peoples into a core culture which can be regarded as national, and not the exclusive property of a particular group of people, the Ethiopian state would probably have been unable to sustain itself in the first place. At the same time, it is precisely because Ethiopia has this core identity, associated with one people but also claiming a special national status, that it suffers from much more intense problems of national identity and integration than other African states . . . under the guise of the "nationalities" questions, [subordination of one's own original affiliation] has presented the revolutionary regime with its single most intractable problem.[35]

Ethiopia is, in reality, a multiethnic state with a dominant core. Baxter aptly commented, "The almost unbroken and absolute political domination and cultural dominance of the Amhara has resulted in the public presentation of Ethiopia as a state with a much more unitary culture than, in fact, it has."[36] Ethnic origins had little importance *if* individuals adopted the cultural values identified with Amhara culture. Intermarriage and forcible conversion to Christianity affected the landowning class.[37] At the top of the socio-political hierarchy, assimilation occurred. But for the largely peasant population, the experience was quite different. Under Emperor Haile Selassie, Orominya could not be used in schools, courts, or government offices. The regime feared a possible up-surge of Islam and of the Oromos. Its chosen path was to emphasize Amhara cultural values. The central government consistently combatted peasant rebellion and dissension by increased central control and re-duced local autonomy.[38]

It is important to note, however, that the opportunity for self-determi-nation declared in the Charter of the Transitional Government of Ethi-opia did not spring full-blown from the brow of Meles Zenawi. We must probe briefly into the roots of "nationalities."

The collapse of the imperial regime in 1974 unleashed a period of great turbulence.[39] A complex struggle erupted between segments of the armed forces and civilian political movements, the most active of them inspired by Marxist beliefs. Non-Amharic leaders were prominent. Incip-ient senses of class struggle and ethnic identity surfaced. These divergent currents were linked by common interest in revolutionary change. Mei-son (the Amharic term for All-Ethiopian Socialist Union) drew heavily from Oromos, the EPRP (Ethiopian People's Revolutionary Party) from Tigreans. Their common framework of thought meant, in Clapham's judgment, that

they could reach agreement on two broad themes. The first was that the repres-sion of nationalities within imperial Ethiopia could be ascribed to the class basis of the regime, and that the removal of class exploitation, most obviously repre-sented by land alienation in the south, was therefore the essential prerequisite for a solution to the problem. . . . The second was that "nationalities" should be recognised and accorded a right to "self-determination" and an equal place in the Ethiopian state. It was assumed that the removal of class oppression would make this second stage unproblematic. Where they differed was over the issue of whether "self-determination" should include a specific right to secession.[40]

When the Derg announced its program in April 1976, total break-up of the multiethnic state was far from its objective. Nationalities would be accorded "full right to self-government," with regional autonomy "to determine the contents of its political, economic, and social life, use its own language and elect its own leaders and administrators to head its internal organs."[41] Internal autonomy under a national government: this was the extent, at least rhetorically, to which the Derg would go. On the other hand, the Oromo Liberation Front, founded in 1973, advocated establishment of the independent Democratic Republic of Oromia.[42] The OLF sought to build national consciousness as prelude to political action. It was to emerge in 1976, as Meison was decimated and, more im-portant, as the lingering remnants of Haile Selassie's regime collapsed, as the leading advocate of Oromo autonomy. The OLF's demands pressed to the extreme the self-determination the Derg purportedly favored.

In reality, the Derg never decentralized. Amhara dominance continued.[43] The statements quoted in the paragraph above were penned when Mengistu and his allies in the military were linked to Meison. This tactical allliance collapsed in mid-1977, when the Somali invasion and Meison's defeat by the EPRP in bloody street battles in Addis Ababa shifted the political balance. The Derg pursued rigidly centralizing policies. "Nationalities" remained rhetorical flourishes, trotted out on such occasions as establishment of the Nationalities Institute in 1983 and the appointment of the Constitutional Drafting Commission in 1986.[44] The original policy (1975–77) of appointment of regional administrators from within the regions themselves was abandoned. Tensions grew. And, long before the Derg had consolidated its power in the capital, its control over parts of the countryside was being contested.

Those interested in the history of the civil war should look elsewhere; my interest here lies in its impact on the Oromos. Conflict intensified the sense of Oromo identity. In a sense, this was thrust upon them. Baxter asserts, "Simply, national consciousness has been forced on [the] Oromo as a people and as individuals."[45] The struggle against the Derg gave members of this numerous but decentralized group a stronger sense of cohesion. Oromos continued to feel excluded.[46] Their quest for greater autonomy was enhanced. Empowerment through self-determination: the Oromos would achieve stronger identity. But how strong was this sentiment? How far could this take them and the OLF? The answers remain unclear in part because struggle among Oromos has been almost as significant as Oromo resistance against others.

Rhetorical commitment to "nationalities," we have already noted, marked the strident political competition of the mid-1970s. Oromos dominated Meison, which in turn enjoyed considerable influence in Addis Ababa and the surrounding region. Geography was on their side. Not only do Oromos constitute the most numerous ethnic group in Ethiopia; they can be found in almost all its parts, and dominate from Walega, Shoa, and Haraghe southwards.[47] But numbers alone do not make a nation. Identity must be consciously built, especially in a state like Ethiopia where upwardly mobile people could gain power and prestige by submerging themselves into the receptive core identity. Efforts at evoking Oromo consciousness were fitful, and really did not start to take off until the anti-Derg struggle began in earnest. A document, *The Oromo: Voices against Tyranny*, circulated secretly in Addis Ababa in 1971. The OLF started its armed struggle in the tumultuous year of 1974.[48] Constructing an Oromo sense of unity for the struggle against the Derg was considerably complicated by the regime's land reform in the south, which won it considerable support, and by differences between Christians and Muslims. A "politically coherent" Oromo identity proved difficult to develop — and, as a consequence, so did an effective organization.

The OLF was very much a junior partner in the war against the Derg. The TPLF (Tigrean People's Liberation Movement) formed the core. TPLF leaders sought power within Ethiopia, not separation from it. They favored an end to centralized Amhara dominance, rather than break-up of the Ethiopian state of which they had historically formed a core. Their quest for self-determination stopped at establishing a revised political system for Ethiopia; it did not extend to severing its major constituent parts, with the exception of Eritrea. The TPLF pressed its case for territorial rather than ethnic autonomy. In short, the TPLF wanted to maximize regional autonomy, not to balkanize the entire country. Its willingness to accept the secession of Eritrea following a referendum earned them the emnity of many Amhara nationalists.

The lengthy civil war ravaged much of Eritrea and Tigre. Significant parts of the Oromo-inhabited areas were lightly touched. Government levies of men and money were deeply resented. But conflict did not surge across the entire Oromo section in a manner that could have galvanized an even sharper sense of ethnic identity. Indeed, sectional differences marked the Oromo's ambiguous struggle to determine their own future. They had no clear territorial basis; for, although Oromos lived in twelve of Ethiopia's former administrative regions, they formed a majority in only one. Religion divided rather than united them, with many southern Oromos prominent in the Orthodox church, and with large numbers of northern Oromos Muslim.[49] Within the Ethiopian state itself, some Oromos occupied prominent positions, while others rejected its basic organization. Finally, no person with the presence of Ken Saro-Wiwa or Father Senghor (whom we shall meet shortly when discussing the Diola of Senegal) emerged as spokesman for the OLF. Empowerment, to repeat, meant reorganization within Ethiopia (and, in particular, resolution of land issues); for some Oromos, but not all, empowerment would lead to secession and independence.

Why did the 1992 Ethiopian election precipitate a brief civil war between the OLF and the TPLF? Did this stem from a belated but nonetheless important upsurge of ethnic solidarity? Did it presage a stronger Oromo identity? I believe the answers to both are affirmative. Campaigning and balloting were held under unsettled conditions. Distrust was rampant. In keeping with the coalition nature of the struggle against Mengistu and his cronies, each entity was responsible for organizing in its major areas. The OLF had considerably less organizational strength than the TPLF. As junior partner in the anti-Derg struggle, the OLF chafed at the restrictions it perceived. The TPLF appealed openly for votes throughout the country, obviously including areas in which Oromos were in a majority. It moved to set up junior compliant partners within the EPRDF. The OLF lacked the cohesiveness the TPLF had built through

years of struggle. Feeling potentially excluded from the emerging constellation of power, the OLF became increasingly hostile to the entire
electoral process. Bad blood between the OLF and TPLF was accentuated by pell-mell mobilization of voters. A crude OLF trick resulted in the
expulsion of the head of one of the international observer teams.[50] A few
days before the formal balloting, the OLF withdrew from the election.
Fighting erupted; the better-organized, better-armed TPLF quickly interned and disarmed about 18,000 OLF fighters. The OLF thus emerged
from the mid-1992 electoral process with neither significant representation in the Council nor a credible military presence.

One should not conclude, however, that the struggle for empowerment has ended. Oromo efforts for autonomy are likely to increase. On
the other hand, they will meet greater resistance from the center. The
Transitional Government (TGE) made good on certain provisions of the
Charter. Eritrea seceded peacefully, the TGE having encouraged a peaceful plebiscite, in which well over 99 percent of the area's inhabitants voted
for independence. But self-determination in the sense of full territorial
separation halted there. An autonomous "Oromia" was not created, although internal boundaries were redrawn. A huge new administrative
region surrounding Addis Ababa was created, in which Orominya has become the language of local administration, education, and justice. Installation of the new government was hardly proceeding smoothly when I
carried out field work in November 1993, however. Amharas were com-
plaining about the "chauvinism" Oromos were starting to illustrate —
forgetting, I am tempted to add, that many of them may have been guilty
of the same trait at earlier points.

Will the episodic Oromo question for a clearer identity be "solved" by
geographic and political juggling? It seems likely that the Orominya-
speaking region could foster, for the first time, a sense that Oromos are
truly central to Ethiopia's identity. Addis Ababa (a region unto itself)
looks like an Amhara island in an Oromo sea. If the twelve regions and
two cities with regional status indeed come to enjoy significant political
and economic powers, the currently diffuse sense of Oromo nationhood
could coalesce and increase, and thus further strain the country's fragile
unity. What has been ethnic identity could turn into national identity.[51]
Ethiopia's mosaic of power would become even more complex ethnically.
At the current time, Tigreans control the central government. Many
Amharas feel embittered by their marginalization after centuries of
power. The Oromo grope for a role. The future will, I believe, see a
crystallization of a sharper sense of Oromo unity, which will conflict with
the Tigrean-Amhara core. The potential for greater conflict is inherent
in the system.

Indeed, the continued political uncertainty in Ethiopia accentuates the ambiguous position of the Oromos. The OLF joined with several other opposition groups in December 1993 to create the Council of Alternative Forces for Peace and Democracy (CAFPDE). This coalition calls for upholding the rights of political prisoners, fair treatment of the opposition, and — a sticking point for many OLF members — the unity of Ethiopia. As one of the best-informed observers of the political scene has written,

> The Oromo remain a rather fractured people, however, and difficult to organize for political action. Nor is the OLF in a position to give significant leadership to the opposition movement. This is particularly true because the OLF remains at odds with other parties in the opposition over the issue of Ethiopian unity ... The opposition is consequently weak (although it is getting stronger) and fragmented (although it is becoming more united). It is also increasingly frustrated and desperate, knowing that it must rally its forces and make its case with due haste.[52]

But, to conclude this section, was there any realistic alternative to regionalizing Ethiopia, yet stopping short of full independence for sections other than Eritrea? The struggle against the Derg was mounted by groups defined on territorial and ethnic foundations. These groups deeply resented the Derg's maladministration, directed from the center. Achieving much greater provincial autonomy was a crucial goal. The Marxist-style language about "nationalities" encouraged belief that strokes of the cartographer's pen and prose from the constitution-drafter's word processor would resolve Ethiopia's long-standing tension between center and periphery. The "solution" was thus implicit in the definition of the "problem." The complex question, I would argue, lies not in how Ethiopia decentralizes some powers to the regions, but in how Oromo leaders (and persons from other ethnic groups) utilize the system. Might Ethiopia come to resemble India, in which states enjoy their own languages and a fair degree of autonomy, while the center maintains a core political and cultural identity? Or might Ethiopia fragment as did the Soviet Union, the internal boundaries and the rhetoric of self-determination combining in a process of collapse? Much will depend on how (and whether) the OLF becomes a coherent political force. My bet is that, consistent with centuries of Ethiopian history, the Oromos will remain politically and religiously divided, lukewarm supporters of the central government of a country whose multiethnic nature has been made even more apparent by years of struggle. Regionalization, in short, need not be the first step on the slippery slope of disintegration. But this preliminary assessment could well prove incorrect. The largely Tigrean leaders of the EPRDF could crystallize further ethnic solidarity among their opponents, particularly by imposing harsh central rule.

The Oromos argued that their numbers should give them greater political power; the Ogoni claimed that the wealth beneath their soil should give them economic benefits and equality with other ethnic groups. What about a group that lacked both large population and a strong potential economic basis? The history of the simmering Casamance rebellion gives us a third angle on the problems of self-determination and empowerment as collective human rights.

MDFC (Mouvement Démocratique des Forces Casamançais)

The boundaries of African countries were often drawn in historically amusing ways. Imagine, if you will, a treaty transferring part of one state's shadowy claim to territory to another, based on a promise of fishing rights in codfish-rich banks. Such a swap resulted in the accretion of the Casamance (an area roughly the size of Belgium) to Senegal. The treaty of May 13, 1886, between France (ruler of most lands between the Senegal and Gambia rivers) and Portugal (claimant between the Casamance and Sherbro rivers) was far from atypical. In those days of colonial aggrandisement, exchanges of territory among European powers were common. Unforeseen consequences occasionally arose. Among them, over a century later, was an unexpected yet easily-foretold uprising. For the dispute within the Casamance has its roots firmly planted in the culture of the Diola (sometimes transliterated Jola), the largest ethnic group in southern Senegal.[53]

A quick look at a rainfall or vegetation map of Senegal will show the ecological basis of social difference. The great majority of the country—and of the English-speaking enclave of The Gambia, which nearly splits Senegal—lies in the Sahel zone. Less than 500 millimeters of rain annually (concentrated in the two-month rainy season) result in an open landscape, broken only by baobab trees thrusting their gaunt, leafless limbs skyward, and by herds of humped zebu cattle or short-haired goats grazing through the thorny scrub. One can drive for hours north or east from the Senegalese coastline, the flat countryside becoming progressively drier. Go south from Dakar, and little changes as well. It is nearly impossible to tell where Senegal ends and The Gambia begins, unless the customs officers are unusually busy. But continue further south, once having taken the ferry across the bridgeless Gambia River, and the vegetation changes. The dry, lightly-treed surroundings known to the Wolof, Toucouleur, Peuhl, or Serere of other parts of Senegal and The Gambia shift to the dense growth of the south, the flat land of the Diola.[54] The Casamance marks the start of the dense forest that used to stretch several thousand miles from southern Senegal to northern Angola (with a brief interruption through Ghana and Togo). This is a different world indeed from the wide-open spaces further inland and to the north. With annual rainfall at Zinguinchor of 1535 mm per year, the setting is verdant. It is also flat. No point is more than 60 meters above sea level; the Casamance river itself barely moves, falling only seven centimeters per kilometer (just over four inches per mile).[55] Diked fields green with rice shoots have replaced the shifting bush fallow cultivation of peanuts, sorghum, and millet characteristic of northern Senegal and The Gambia.

This environmental boundary is also a cultural frontier. The Diola have resisted to a large extent the "Wolofization" and Islamization of Senegal.[56] As a consequence, they have become further marginalized. As two critics of government policy observed, "This marginalization is not an historic accident but stems from political choice; it is accentuated by the fact that the Casamance is a region with difficult access."[57]

If the Casamance region was added to the French Empire in a little-noticed episode of colonial mapmaking, one might also argue that the Gambia region was kept from it by other oddities of imperial rule. The British had traded for slaves and natural products along the Gambia river for centuries before French military officers started to push the *tricouleur* inland from the coastal villages of Dakar and Saint-Louis. Efforts to trade English claims for, say, a French-ruled, sugar-producing Caribbean island failed.[58] The Casamance thus suffered from multiple separation from the main body of Senegal: isolation imposed by the Gambian enclave; differentiation based on vegetation and lifestyle; resistance to the trends of Wolofization and Islamization.

The contrast, to be certain, should not be overplayed. Separatist sentiment in the Casamance did not spring from simple geographic or cultural determinism. The contrasts I have just highlighted for Senegal are certainly no greater than the contrasts between the Nigerian coast to the south and the boundary with Niger to the north, or between the arid northern heights of Tigre and the verdant forests of southern Ethiopia. The great majority of African countries are multiethnic. To a significant extent, their frontiers cut across ecological zones. But what geography may propose, culture, economics and politics may dispose. Also underlying the distinctiveness of the Casamance were important land-control and administrative matters. The storm signals were flying well before scores died in December 1983, the official start of the uprising, but by no means the first event in it.

The first contacts of Casamance peoples with Europeans came through slavery, carried out by Portuguese. According to one source, the name of the region's major town, Zinguinchor, came from the Portuguese sentence "I came, they wept."[59] The chequered history of "pacification" has been well documented elsewhere.[60] France's self-styled "civilizing mission" ran into unexpected obstacles. The area's restiveness, dense vegetation, remoteness and limited economic development interacted during the colonial period to produce a sleepy, underdeveloped region. The administration of Senegal seems to have shot first, thought second. As French anthropologist Christian Saglio wrote, "The history of the lower Casamance since 1866 has been marked by an unbelievable number of revolts, punitive expeditions and treaties, each village demanding a special agreement."[61] There were already problems aplenty from forcible requisitions of rice and livestock, from tax raids, and from forced labor to build roads. Levies of troops to fight in the trenches of World War I were particularly resented. Casamance was an area, in short, where the usual colonial formulas for ruling brought not peace, but intensified regional and ethnic grievances. Governor-General Joost van Vollenhoven said, in 1917,

We are not the masters of the Casamance; we are only tolerated there. . . . The Casamance must not be a type of wart in the colony, of which it should be the jewel.[62]

Not until well after World War I was the "fierce resistance" of the Diola ended.[63] A brief uprising occurred in 1940. Alinsitowe Diatta, a Diola chambermaid then working in Dakar, was (like Joan of Arc) "told by voices" that she must return to her people and urge them to stop cultivating peanuts and paying taxes. The colonial administration reacted strongly, burning her native village and exiling her to arid Timbuktoo. She thus joined the growing Diola pantheon of resistance heroes.[64] Resentment continued to simmer during the colonial period. Even the general political ferment after World War II did not obscure Casamance concerns. On March 4, 1949, Ibou Diallo, Emile Badiane (both *instituteurs*), and 121 others signed the manifesto of the Mouvement Démocratique des Forces Casamançais (MFDC), asking for the right to elect local representatives. The MFDC did not figure prominently in the run-up to independence, however. The region, and in particular the Diolas, remained on the margins. The government made no significant adaptation of policies.

Regional grievances came to a boil within a few years of independence, however. As just noted, the centralizing formulas of the French were maintained. The powerful Ministry of the Interior appointed regional governors and district prefects. Members of the National Assembly, drawn from the ruling Parti Socialiste, did not have constituencies from which they were chosen, but were elected as part of a single national list. Practically no Diola entered the inner circles of the ruling party. Proclamation of the *domaine nationale* in land removed the traditional powers of local communities over allocation. Administrative functionaries seem to have profited especially. An increasing number of non-Diola people moved into the Casamance. Charcoal burners plied their trade, chopping down parts of sacred forests. Peanut growers occupied choice land. With their Muslim beliefs and different agricultural styles, these settlers were resented.[65] They gained dominant positions in commerce and fishing. "Solutions" were sought by tinkering with bureaucratic structures.[66] As would the Ogoni, the Diolas came to believe that other groups were profiting from what had been their patrimony.[67]

The MFDC surfaced in late 1982. In the vivid words of the Dutch anthropologist van der Klei, rumors rapidly circulated on Christmas Eve that there would be a major demonstration against the Senegalese regime in Zinguinchor:

> The morning of the following day [December 26, 1982], an impressive procession entered the city from the west side . . . Some men carried bottles of palm wine; apparently, they had already consumed copiously. Almost all the men carried amulets and several adorned themselves with palm branches, "like the warriors of yesteryear," as our informants told us. At the head of the procession, someone carried a large white flag. Others held up placards with the inscription "Free Casamance." Women were present in great numbers, especially in the front rows; they also carried amulets, as well as calabashes (Diola symbols of fertility). Attributes like palm wine, the "camouflage" of warriors and the calabashes clearly indicated it was a Diola affair. . . .
> The tail of the procession reached the chief administrative building on the central place. Just in front of it, the police had barred the route, but the throng overturned the barriers. Some shots rang out—the police should have aimed low, in the legs—but that didn't suffice to stop the crowd. Finally, some men succeeded in lowering the Senegalese flag in front of the building to raise their own flag, with general acclamation. Some chaotic skirmishes followed, but finally the police withdrew to their precinct. The Senegalese flag was lowered in front of other government offices. According to some informants, even one policeman was killed; among the marchers there were some wounded. After the "defeat" of the police—scarcely two hours after the entry of the procession into the city— the participants [*manifestants*], boasting of their success but in good order, headed back out of town.
> Our section of town remained agitated all day. But the atmosphere wasn't really tender, rather excited and joyous. . . . Everywhere pamphlets of the "Mouvement des forces démocratiques de la Casamance" were distributed . . . the pamphlets called for the immediate independence of the Casamance.[68]

This festive mood dissipated as the regime marshalled its own forces. Meetings continued in the sacred woods around Zinguinchor. The authorities were concerned, but had little idea how to counter the autonomist tendencies effectively. On December 6, 1983, a group of 15 police entered a sacred wooded area near Zinguinchor to break up a meeting of presumed separatists. "For the Diola, this was an unthinkable action: only the initiated persons of the village could enter that sacred place."[69] Three gendarmes were hacked to death, four others wounded; several persons were injured in reaction. A wave of arrests followed. Court sentences were handed down December 14 against presumed separatists on the grounds they had compromised the security of the state. Four days later, an unexpected fury erupted as Senegalese security forces faced off against villagers. At least 24 persons were killed (including four police and seven gendarmes); some estimates ran as high as 100 deaths. It was the worst outbreak of violence in the history of independent Senegal. But it was certainly not unprecedented. To quote Saglio,

The events of Zinguinchor are not surprising. In effect, there is a continuous thread between conquests and resistance in the Casamance: whether it be the Portuguese, the Mandingoes, the French or the Senegalese administration, the same scenario always recurs: law against custom, an imported, imposed and incomprehensible law, which menaces breaking the equilibrium and harmony created by custom. When the administration wants to impose a centralizing, authoritarian system of values by force, custom, which is ordinarily flexible and empirical, shrivels up and becomes dangerously reactionary.

In the Casamance, it is never an armed people or an organized party that confronts the adversary, but simple village communities that spontaneously react when they feel themselves attacked at the heart of their traditions and style of life.[70]

Geschiere and van der Klei, by contrast, stress the coherence and larger vision shown in the MFDC pamphlets. In their view, the problem revolved around resentment of the entire Casamance against the colonization and exploitation of "the North," often simply designated as Senegal.[71] There was clear evidence of coordination and advance preparation. In other words, the antipathies utilized by the MFDC were, in effect, creating a clearer sense of Diola unity.

The Diola were highly decentralized in their traditional forms of governance. In keeping with the thickly forested nature of their homeland, where communication was far harder than in the savannahs of the north, decisions were made by the elders on a village-by-village basis. Caste or hierarchy, well known elsewhere in Senegal, did not figure in Diola society. Islam and various brotherhoods were important among northern Diola, not among those living south of the Casamance River. The decentralized nature of Diola society both facilitated the emergence of the resistance, and complicated its resolution. The MFDC proved prone to factionalism, "northern" and "southern" sections emerging. Life "in the bush" reduced the opportunities for coordination. On the other hand, geography facilitated resistance. Arms, food, medicine, and other supplies could be readily smuggled across the borders of Guinée-Bissau or The Gambia.[72] The *maquisards* of the MFDC thus profited from physical and social conditions that kept alive the spirit of rebellion. They licked their wounds, trained, and established forest hide-outs. They did not undertake any offensives; nor, for their part, did Senegalese security forces try to crush them. For the remainder of the 1980s, an uneasy quasi-truce existed.

Why did this simmering dispute erupt again in the early 1990s? A likely reason lies in sudden intensification of national security concerns. Senegal confronted enormous, unexpected political challenges from its neighbors. A mini-war broke out with Mauritania in 1989 over control of disputed borderlands. Relations with The Gambia were exacerbated by break-up of the modest confederation the two countries had formed. Frontier incidents with Guinea-Bissau added to the complications. The Senegalese government became edg, and more authoritarian. Incidents between the police, gendarmes or soldiers, and members of the public multiplied.

The MFDC also picked up its own level of anti-regime and anti-"northern" actions. (It is customary in the Casamance to say that if one is traveling to Dakar he or she is "going to Senegal"; persons from outside the region are referred to as "northerners" in a derogatory fashion, almost in the way Latin Americans refer to "gringos.") Violence escalated. On September 1, 1992, gunfire erupted in the village of Kaguit, seven kilometers from the border with Guinée-Bissau; its 2,000 inhabitants fled, not wishing to be trapped between the Senegalese military and MFDC *maquisards*.[73] Some of the killings were ethnic in nature, directed against non-Diola. For example, 31 Senegalese from other groups were murdered in the fishing village of Cap Skirring in October 1992, adjacent to one of the country's major resort areas.[74] In turn, security forces (army and gendarmerie) shelled several villages. Approximately 15,000 persons fled from the Casamance, 80 percent of them to Guinée-Bissau.[75] The elections of early 1993 resulted in further violence. On February 21 alone, the day of the hotly-disputed presidential balloting, 24 persons who defied MFDC threats in order to vote were killed. More than 200 died in military sweeps through the region.[76] A cycle of violence and counter-violence had emerged. The economy of the region was skidding downhill, with the shocks to the tourist industry and agriculture. Could it be solved?

The Casamance region is now (mid-1994) under a cease-fire. It is partial. Abbé Augustin Diamacoune Senghor signed on behalf of his wing of the MFDC on May 31, 1991; others remain unreconciled. Arms have not been collected, nor have guerrilla fighters given any major promises of arranging a truce. Sporadic behind-the-scenes negotiations continue. As the chief negotiator for the government explained to me, immediate results were not to be expected, for a substantial gulf of mistrust had to be bridged.[77] But the level of tension has dropped. Tourists have started to return to the lovely beaches, meaning a small dip in the staggering unemployment rate. It is perhaps the one bit of positive news, from the Diola perspective. "Northern" administrators (primarily Wolof and Serere) continue to hold leading positions. Resentment over land remains high. Since the enactment in 1964 of the law on "national domain," the government has enjoyed extensive powers of land redistribution, as previously noted. Increasing settlement by "northerners," in the judgment of well-informed observers, has reinforced Diola fear that all their lands may be forfeit. The sacred groves help maintain consciousness of the opposition between strangers and those native to the region.[78]

The "Casamance problem" remains chronic, if not necessarily immediately acute.[79] I suspect the French administrators of the early twentieth century had the best idea. They favored restructuring the administration. Their appeals fell on deaf ears, for they contradicted the basic centralizing presuppositions of French colonial administration. Bureaucratic maneuvering and political second thoughts seem to have stalled a 1992 initiative on regionalization. President Abdouf Diouf called in April 1992 for a division of power. Instead of a regional council that could only "request," an elected regional assembly with major role in planning, education, health and the like would be established.[80] No serious effort at implementation had occurred two years later. Useful political steps foundered on inertia. Fine idea; poor follow through.

The sense of Diola grievance will not be assuaged by a few small political concessions; nor can it be eradicated by escalation of force. The dense forest provides excellent shelter for the bush fighters. The sacred groves offer traditional means of communication. Paradoxically, the forest both unites and divides. The decentralization of Diola society, combined with the pressures of combat, mean that Diola fighting groups often work in isolation. A cease-fire signed with one leader may well be — and indeed has been — ignored by others. Endemic factionalism within the MFDC, as already observed, perpetuates conflict. Its followers' diffuse sense of grievance against "Senegal" and its largely Wolof inhabitants cannot be readily assuaged. Long-term, patient efforts at dialogue are necessary. The sense of marginalization, implanted over decades, must be reversed. Greater decentralization of power must form part of these attempts. Although this cuts against the grain of Senegalese administrative philosophy and the sweep of the country's history, it must be carried out.

The government of Senegal should take note of the sweeping administrative reorganization of Ethiopia, and even of the provincial and state governments respectively of Namibia and Nigeria. A serious political vacuum exists in Senegal (and, for that matter, in practically all African states *d'expression française)*. Elected governments exist at the national level, and in large towns. There are few intermediary elected bodies. At the regional and district levels, power rests with appointed administrators. Why not consider decentralization of some powers and a larger popular role? This idea has been bruited about in Senegal for several years, but talk has yet to lead to serious consideration. The Franco-Senegalese tradition of Jacobin centralization remains strong. But with a measure of provincial autonomy, regional grievances could well diminish.[81] They seem likely to grow with the country's economic travails.

The organizations I have examined in this chapter differ in many respects from the other NGOs analyzed in this book. They became involved in violence; sought major political restructuring; focused on collective grievances; and were highly selective in their use of human rights norms. MOSOP, the OLF, and the MFDC were (and remain) dedicated to a certain type of empowerment. They want to redraw the maps of their countries and reshape basic economic and political parameters. These movements challenged the sovereign control of the Ethiopian, Nigerian, and Senegalese governments, and as such, were liable to strong repression. They engaged in overt political struggles, not being content (as are classic human rights NGOs) to limit their challenges to governmental power to published documents, petitions, or other pressures through established channels. They utilized "traditional" symbols and means of communication together with modern means of resistance. Their sense of unity was defined in large part by resentment against exploitation by "outsiders" — even though these "outsiders" were citizens of the same countries.

In advocating some type of self-determination, MOSOP, the OLF, and the MFDC seemed to their critics to be engaged in a zero-sum struggle. What they wanted, so it appeared, the national administration would have to surrender. In reality, however, another approach existed. It might be possible to arrive at a mutual accommodation, through dividing or decentralizing power. Having responsive levels of administration closer to the people can help resolve some basic issues. The failure of centralized state structures in Africa had become manifest by the early 1990s. Does this mean that decentralized structures will be put in place? Can greater measures of democratization provide a solution? The task will be difficult, for it involves cutting against decades or more of practice. The attempt should be made, nonetheless. Until then, the question of who constitute a "people" will remain a salient, divisive political issue through most of tropical Africa. Self-determination was achieved at the level of the state as a whole; it remains incomplete at the level of ethnic groups.

Notes

1. Even supposedly homogeneous African societies are characterized by potentially serious divisions. The exacerbation of clan identification and conflict in Somalia — long touted by African specialists as a model pastoral democracy, relatively free from destructive internal rivalry based on group identification — stands as a case in point.

2. However, the sense of ethnic unity may also be a product of enclosure within a colonial state. As the highly respected Africanist Thomas Hodgkin argued several years ago, the concept of being "Yoruba" may be no older than that of being "Nigerian." Thomas Hodgkin, *Nigerian Perspectives: An Historical Anthology* (London: Oxford University Press, 1960), pp. 2–3.

3. Léopold Sédar Senghor, *Nation et voie africaine du socialisme* (Paris: Présence Africaine, 1961); Kwame Nkrumah, *Africa Must Unite* (London: Heinemann, 1963).

4. For Senghor's policies, see William J. Foltz, *From French West Africa to the Mali Federation* (New Haven, CT: Yale University Press, 1965) and Gil Dugué, *Vers les Etats-Unis d'Afrique* (Dakar: Editions Lettres Africaines, 1960); for Nkrumah's policies, see W. Scott Thompson, *Ghana's Foreign Policy, 1957–1966* (Princeton, NJ: Princeton University Press, 1969) and Claude E. Welch, Jr., *Dream of Unity: Pan-Africanism and Political Unification in West Africa* (Ithaca, NY: Cornell University Press, 1966), esp. pp. 292–335.

5. Eritrea's reestablishment was seen as a necessary exception: it had existed prior to 1950 as a political entity distinct from Ethiopia (despite the many cultural and economic links between them); its people had struggled for decades for independence following the territory's incorporation into Ethiopia; a referendum organized with substantial international involvement showed an overwhelming majority favoring independence; the Meles government conceded in advance that it would accept the referendum's results. No such favorable constellation of factors marked Biafra's or Katanga's earlier efforts to secede; indeed, the crisis over Katanga figured prominently in the formation of the OAU.

6. Yonah Alexander and Robert A. Friedlander, eds., *Self-Determination: National, Regional and Global Dimensions* (Boulder, CO: Westview, 1980); S. James Anaya, "The Capacity of International Law to Advance Ethnic or Nationality Rights Claims," *Iowa Law Review* 75 (1990), 837–73; Lee H. Buchheit, *Secession: The Legitimacy of Self-Determination* (New Haven, CT: Yale University Press, 1978); Aurelio Cristescu, *The Right to Self-Determination: Historical and Current Developments on the Basis of United Nations Instruments* (New York: United Nations, 1981); Héctor Gros Espiell, *The Right to Self-Determination: Implementation of United Nations Resolutions* (New York: United Nations, 1980); Hurst Hannum, *Autonomy, Sovereignty, and Self-Determination: The Accommodation of Conflicting Rights* (Philadelphia: University of Pennsylvania Press, 1990); David B. Knight and Maureen Davies, *Self-Determination: An Interdisciplinary Annotated Bibliography* (New York: Garland, 1987); Yilma Makonnen, *International Law and the New States of Africa: A Study of the International Legal Problems of State Succession in the Newly Independent States of Eastern Africa* (Paris: UNESCO, 1983); Robert McCorquodale, "Self-Determination Beyond the Colonial Context and Its Potential Impact on Africa," *African Journal of International and Comparative Law* 4 (1992), 592–608; Ved Nanda, "Self-Determination Under International Law: Validity of Claims to Secede," *Case Western Reserve Journal of International Law* 13 (1981), 257–80; Benjamin Neuberger, *National Self-Determination in Postcolonial Africa* (Boulder, CO: Lynne Rienner, 1986);

Michla Pomerance, *Self-Determination in Law and Practice: The New Doctrine in the United Nations* (The Hague: Nijhoff, 1982); Christopher D. Quaye, *Liberation Struggles in International Law* (Philadelphia: Temple University Press, 1991); Dov Ronen, *The Quest for Self-Determination* (New Haven, CT: Yale University Press, 1979); U.O. Umozurike, *Self-Determination in International Law* (Hamden, CT: Archon, 1972); Heather A. Wilson, *International Law and the Use of Force by National Liberation Movements* (Oxford: Clarendon Press, 1988).

7. UN General Assembly Resolution 1514 (XV), 14 December 1960. Significantly, paragraph 6 of the declares, "Any attempt aimed at the partial or total disruption of the national unity and the territorial integrity of a country is incompatible with the purposes and principles of the Charter of the United Nations." No doubt the on-going Katanga crisis stirred the concern of delegate as they voted.

8. Jack Donnelly, *Universal Human Rights in Theory and Practice* (Ithaca, NY: Cornell University Press, 1989), p. 148.

9. An especially interesting essay in this regard is Michael McDonald, "Should Community Have Rights? Reflections of Liberal Individualism," in Abdullahi Ahmed An-Na'im, ed., *Human Rights in Cross-Cultural Perspectives: A Quest for Consensus* (Philadelphia: University of Pennsylvania Press, 1992), pp. 133–61.

10. Peter Ekeh, "Colonialism and the Two Publics in Africa," *Comparative Studies in Society and History* 17, 1 (January 1975), 91–112.

11. Crawford Young, "The Temple of Ethnicity," *World Politics* 35, 4 (July 1983), p. 659; also see, by the same author, *The Politics of Ethnic Pluralism* (Madison: University of Wisconsin Press, 1976).

12. Three examples should suffice. In the mid-1950s, as economic development boomed in Côte d'Ivoire, Ivoirien politicians increasingly bridled about the amount spent in Senegal and in other parts of the federation of French West Africa. As Berg and Morgenthau convincingly demonstrated, the "balkanization" of the federation reflected financial interests of the better-off: Eliot Berg, "The Economic Basis of Political Choice in French West Africa," *American Political Science Review* 54 (1960), 391–405; Ruth Schachter Morgenthau, *Political Parties in French-Speaking West Africa* (Oxford: Clarendon Press, 1964). The attempt by Katanga to secede from the former Belgian Congo similarly reflected the rich region's desire to keep its revenue close at home: Jules Gérard-Libois, *Katanga Secession* (Madison: University of Wisconsin Press, 1966); Catherine Hoskyn, *The Congo Since Independence, January 1960–December 1961* (London: Oxford University Press, 1965). Finally, the attempt to create an independent Republic of Biafra was based in part on income from oil produced in the Niger Delta, a large part of which was included in the former Eastern Region of Nigeria: John de St. Jorre, *The Brothers' War: Biafra and Nigeria* (Boston: Houghton Mifflin, 1972). The disastrous consequences of Katanga's attempted secession weighed heavily on African leaders as they established the Organization of African Unity, whose strong stand in favor of inherited boundaries and against secession has already been noted.

13. Obafemi Awolowo, *Path to Nigerian Freedom* (London: Faber, 1947, republished 1966).

14. With the exception of Obasanjo's period of head of state, northerners have headed the federal governmentfor no less than 29 of the first 33 years of independence. See the chapter dealing with the 1993 Nigerian presidential election — one independent observers considered generally fair and honest, but aborted by President Babangida.

15. Population statistics are political dynamite in Nigeria. The number of in-

habitants of an area essentially determine how much revenue will be allocated from federal sources; their ethnic identity provides a significant guide to their political leanings. The Nigerian government has attempted to depoliticize the census, and in particular to end inflated claims of population size. By national policy, persons' ethnicity is not asked. Origin by state has been used in filling government positions, in order to reflect the "federal character" of the country. Such an approach does not solve grievances felt by minorities *within* individual states, who see quotas filled by the states' dominant minorities. In addition, aggrieved groups such as the Ogoni have claimed an inflated number of indigenes and hence inadequate representation. I have no doubt that ethnic skewing exists in Nigeria and that many groups are underrepresented on a percentage basis, if certain figures are to be believed. Thus, it should not be surprising that Ogoni point to their limited number in senior positions, while critics suggest they are overrepresented. As of September 1993, there were two Ogoni as Cabinet Commissioners (out of seven), two directors-general out of twenty-nine; of the three federal commissioners from the state, two were Ogoni, according to figures compiled by Bardian Lekara of Bori Polytechnic.

16. See *On a Darkling Plain: An Account of the Nigerian Civil War* (London: Saros, 1991); *Nigeria, The Brink of Disaster* (London: Saros, 1991), *Similia: Essays on Anomic Nigeria* (London: Saros 1991) and *Genocide in Nigeria: The Ogoni Tragedy* (London: Saros, 1992).

17. Ken Saro-Wiwa, "Reaching for the Roots," *West Africa* (16–22 December 1991), 2102.

18. *Ogoni Review* I, 5 (September 1993), p. 1.

19. "Briefing Note on Ogoniland and the Ogoni People of Nigeria," ca. October 1993.

20. Letter from E. W. Nickson (Shell public relations officer) to *The Ecologist*, 15 October 1993.

21. "Briefing Note," p. 1.

22. In a letter 3 May 1993 sent to the general manager of Shell in Port Harcourt, the divisional manager of the construction firm noted,

We are currently unable to work on the remain 5Km section in the Bomu area due to unprovoked hostile acts on our work-force and equipment by the entire community. This Security threat [sic] has already put our Personnel at considerable risk and we are not prepared to endure such further aggressions.

Letter from J. K. Tillery, Divisional Manager, Willbros West Africa, Inc., to J. R. Udofia, Shell Petroleum Development Company, 3rd May 1993. An attached "Review of Events" gives the following account of the shooting of April 30:

The machines commenced in the morning and continued work. At 10.00 am the WWAI site team contacted the Choba Base and reported that a large crowd of villagers had gathered on the Right of Way. Fortunately there was a Military presence to control the situation and to offer protection to the workers and equipment. The tension developed to a level where there was real danger to personnel, and the Army were drawn into a confrontation by the hostile Villagers.

And, continuing the company's chronicle, a public relations effort was "intensifed." However,

No-one from the community turned up at the meeting [to discuss grievances and pay token compensations] and a delegation was sent to the village to investigate the problem but there was no response from the villagers.

Within the hour the villagers launched a full confrontation against the workplace and personnel in the form of a massed demonstration along the Bori Road. The Crowd forced the crew down the Bori Road and the retreat was controlled by the Army. Due to the opposition, and to ensure that we continued to operate within the SPDC [Shell] guidelines for such situations, we were forced to withdraw from the area where upon the villagers set about vandalizing the equipment that had been left on the site. There was extensive damage caused ranging from sabotage and theft of parts that could be removed to malicious damage such as filling the fuel and cooling systems with sand so as to permanently damage the mechanics. (Ibid; capitalization as in original)

23. He was not charged under the new Treason and Treasonable Offenses Decree, which came into force May 5, but rather under the criminal code of Eastern Nigeria, which did not include the death penalty. Among the six charges were unlawful assembly, conferring with seditious intent, and circulating such seditious publications as a pamphlet, "1993 Presidential Elections: Why Ogoni Must not Vote," the "Ogoni National Anthem," and the "Ogoni National Flag."

24. "Joint Resolution by the Ogoni and Andoni Communities, Rivers State Government, the Rivers State Peace Conference Committee and the National Council on Inter-Governmental Relations (NCIR) Abuja in the Matter of the Ogoni/Andoni Disturbances," typescript, October 6, 1993.

25. Letter of October 19, 1993, from Professor Claude Ake to Chief Rufus Ada George, Executive Governor of Rivers State. This document, and several of those cited in footnotes above, are reproduced in "Ogoni Background Material November 1993" (The Hague: UNPO [Unrepresented Nations and Peoples Organization]).

26. AI Index AFR 44/07/93, 20 July 1993 (London: Amnesty International, 1993).

27. I attended the CERD hearing August 10, 1993, during which several references were made to the Ogoni, obviously on the basis of MOSOP and other NGO material. As should be expected, the senior Nigerian representative downplayed the gravity of the situation. Interestingly, a senior African member of the Committee, concerned by the amount of attention given to a matter that didn't figure in the official report submitted by Nigeria, responded with a lengthy personal statement, criticizing "political" intrusions into CERD's work. This stands as a sharp reminder that members of UN human rights treaty bodies do not unreservedly welcome, support, or utilize NGO input.

28. The high-pitched shriek of flaring natural gas cuts through the delta air at many points. Had this valuable resource been tied better into national development (as in generating electricity), Nigeria's economic doldrums might not be so deep.

29. Although census figures by ethnic group were not available at time of writing, I see no reason to question the estimate of Baxter, who says the Oromo are "almost certainly . . . the largest ethnic group in Ethiopia and make up somewhere between a third and a half of its population." Paul Baxter, "The Problem *of* the Oromo, or the Problem *for* the Oromo," in I. M. Lewis, ed., *Nationalism and Self-Determination in the Horn of Africa* (London: Ithaca Press, 1983), p. 135.

30. As I write this paragraph, Nigerians are debating how to ensure diversity in their proposed constitutional conference. Three elected representatives per state, plus several nominees, appears likely. In other words, those who constitute the majority in each state are likely to hold the upper hand.

31. Mohammed Hassen, *The Oromo of Ethiopia: A History 1570–1860* (Cambridge: Cambridge University Press, 1990), p. 4; quoted in P. T. W. Baxter, "The Creation and Constitution of Oromo Nationality," in Katsuyoshi Fukai and John Markakis, eds., *Ethnicity and Conflict in the Horn of Africa* (London: James Currey, 1994), p. 177.

32. Edmund J. Keller, *Revolutionary Ethiopia: From Empire to People's Republic* (Bloomington: Indiana University Press, 1988), p. 160. Keller goes on to comment, "The destruction of Oromo culture [under Haile Selassie] . . . was systematic. . . . The majority of the Oromo were viewed as mere subjects . . . . Oromo areas were the backbone of the Ethiopian economy" (ibid., pp. 160–61).

33. Baxter, "Creation and Constitution of Oromo Nationality," p. 169.

34. Christopher Clapham, *Transformation and Continuity in Revolutionary Ethiopia* (Cambridge: Cambridge University Press, 1988), p. 21. Also see Donald N. Levine, *Greater Ethiopia: The Evolution of a Multiethnic Society* (Chicago: University of Chicago Press, 1974).

35. Clapham, *Transformation and Continuity*, pp. 24–25.

36. Baxter, "The Problem *of* the Oromo, or the Problem *for* the Oromo," p. 130.

37. Patrick Gilkes, *The Dying Lion: Feudalism and Modernization in Ethiopia* (London: Julian Friedmann, 1975), pp. 204–5.

38. Baxter, "Creation and Constitution of Oromo Nationality," p. 170.

39. For details, see Keller, *Revolutionary Ethiopia*; Marina and David Ottaway, *Ethiopia: Empire in Revolution* (New York: Africana, 1978); and John Markakis and Nega Ayele, *Class and Revolution in Ethiopia* (Nottingham: Spokesman, 1978). However, for the Oromos, there were important antecedents of struggle, detailed in Gilkes. Among the major events were the Azebo/Raya revolt of 1928, the 1936 Wollega movement in which Oromo leaders petitioned for their area to be placed under British rule as a prelude to self-government, and the Bale rebellion of 1963–70. Gilkes, *The Dying Lion*, pp. 206–14.

40. Clapham, *Transformation and Continuity*, p. 198.

41. Ibid., p. 199; spelling error corrected.

42. Keller, *Revolutionary Ethiopia*, p. 163. The OLF was dedicated to the "total liberation of the entire Oromo nation from Ethiopian colonialism."

43. Baxter quotes the following figures of Amhara dominance from *STORM: Somali, Tigray and Oromo Resistance Monitor*: 109 Amharas among the 123 members of COPWE (the Commission to Organize the Party of the Working People of Ethiopia), six of the seven executive committee members, and 13 of the 14 chief administrators of regions.

44. The narrow scope for the Nationalities Institute can be gleaned from its purposes: it was to help "resolve minor contradictions among nationalities" on the principle that "chauvinism and narrow nationalism must be eliminated." Clapham, *Transformation and Continuity*, p. 200.

45. Baxter, "Creation and Constitution of Oromo Nationality," p. 170.

46. Perhaps most tellingly, the Politbureau of the Workers' Party of Ethiopia consisted exclusively of Amharas and Tigreans, although the Oromo are the most numerous ethnic group in Ethiopia. Keller, *Revolutionary Ethiopia*, p. 238.

47. Clapham, *Transformation and Continuity*, p. 216.

48. Ibid., p. 216.

49. Ibid., p. 218.

50. Respected UCLA professor Edmund Keller, former President of the African Studies Association and author of a standard work on revolutionary Ethiopia from which I have already quoted extensively, publicly urged Oromo to vote. His remarks were recorded, then altered and broadcast by OLF supporters. As a result of the changes, it seemed as though Keller was appealing directly for support for the OLF, not generally for participation in the electoral process. This hoax caused considerable embarrassment; it also revealed the political naiveté of OLF leaders.

51. Anthony D. Smith, *The Ethnic Origins of Nations* (Oxford: Blackwell, 1986). Indeed, Baxter's work seems to point in this direction. In his most recent publication, he examines "four aspects of pan-Oromo ethnicity which could ease the creation of an Oromo national identity": common language; widely shared and deeply felt symbols and values; the ease of incorporation into Oromo culture; and permeable clan structures. "Creation and Constitution of Oromo Nationality," p. 174.

52. Robert L. Hovde, "Democracy and Governance in Ethiopia: A Survey of Institutions, Issues, and Initiatives in the Transitional Period," unpublished paper presented at the XIIth International Conference of Ethiopian Studies, September 5–10, 1994 (East Lansing: Michigan State University), pp. 20, 22.

53. The Casamance population is about one-seventh that of Senegal as a whole. Of this, the Diola account for roughly one-third (219,742 of 911,829). The other main ethnic groups of the region are the Peul (104,522) and Mandingo (107,209). Mamadou Diallo, *Le Sénégal* (Paris: EDICEF, n.d.), p. 132.

54. Wolofs dominate, with 43.7 percent of Senegal's population; Pulaar speakers (Peuhl and Toucouleur) account for 23.2 percent; Serère come third, with 14.8 percent; the Diola, with 373,960 members counted in the 1988 census, are thus the fourth largest group. Figures from Abdourahmane Konaté, *Le problème casamançais: mythe ou réalité?* (Dakar: n.p., 1993), p. 75. The Zinguichor region (Basse Casamance) included 398,680 persons (5.7 percent of Senegal's population), and the Kolda region (the upper Casamance) 606,790 (8.8 percent) (ibid., p. 74). Just over 60 percent of the Zinguinchor region population were Diola. Ibid., p. 73. Linares, observing that the Diola (Jola) constitute between six and eight percent of the Senegalese population, provides a figure of 260,000 to 340,000. Olga F. Linares, *Power, Prayer and Production: The Jola of Casamance* (Cambridge: Cambridge University Press, 1992), p. 5.

55. Christian Roche, *Histoire de la Casamance: Conquête et résistance 1850–1920* (Paris: Karthala, 1985), pp. 15, 18.

56. Donal Cruise O'Brien, "Langue et nationalité au Sénégal: l'enjeu politique de la wolofisation," *Année africaine* (Paris: Pedone, 1979), 319–35; cited in Momar Coumba Diop and Mamadou Diouf, *Le Sénégal sous Abdou Diouf: Etat et société* (Paris: Karthala, 1990), p. 46.

57. Diop and Diouf, *Le Sénégal sous Abdou Diouf*, p. 47.

58. Historical efforts at territorial swaps are summarized in Claude E. Welch, Jr., *Dream of Unity: Pan-Africanism and Political Unification in West Africa* pp. 250–91; greater detail can be found in the sources cited therein, and in Boubacar Barry, *La Sénégambie du XVe au XIXe siècle: Traite negrière, Islam et conquête coloniale* (Paris: L'Harmattan, 1988).

59. Christian Saglio, *Casamance* (Paris: L'Harmattan, 1984), p. 7.

60. Roche, *Histoire de la Casamance: Conquête et résistance*.

61. Saglio, *Casamance*, pp. 10–11; author's translation.

62. Saglio, *Casamance*, p. 10.

63. Dominique Darbon, *L'Administration et le paysan en Casamance* (Paris: Pedone, 1988), p. 182.

64. Another was Djînabo Bodji, or Bigolo ("elephant"). He was killed by French troops in May 1906, and quickly became the focus of popular legend. (His name is emblazoned on the lycée of Zinguinchor.) According to Saglio, Diola women fled to the sacred forest for a week, then emerged wearing black wraparound skirts. They entered the city and stood in front of the regional administrator's office. "After stopping, silent and menacing in front of the Gouvernance, the youngest of them stepped aside to allow their elders, completely naked, to pass through. This nudity was simultaneously a curse and a forecast of death. One of the administrator's daughters died that night, carried off by a mysterious, thunderbolt disease" (ibid., p. 18; author's translation). Of such events legends are born, and rebellion can be justified. For a far more detailed exposition of rural rebellion, see Claude E. Welch, Jr., *Anatomy of Rebellion* (Albany: State University of New York Press, 1980).

65. The role of religion is complex and much-debated. Perhaps most important is the fact that indigenous, Christian, and Muslim beliefs all played important roles. A detailed analysis can be found in Jacqueline Trincaz, *Colonisations et religions en Afrique Noire: L'exemple du Zinguinchor* (Paris: Harmattan, 1981).

66. As Diop and Diouf note, "accent was always put on narrowly-conceived solutions (*solutions politiciennes*), [such as] division of the region [or] better representation of Casamance leaders in the government, and not on political and economic solutions destined to slow the process of marginalization of the Casamance peoples." *Le Sénégal après Abdou Diouf,* p. 49; author's translation.

67. Interview with Marcel Bassene, Dakar, March 8, 1994. Bassene, a deputy from the opposition PDS, has served as an *interlocuteur valable* between the Senegalese Government and MFDC factions; his business card carries the impressive title, "Députe chargé de mission à la Présidence de la République coordonnateur de la paix en Casamance." In the apt words of Linares, "Underlying all the unrest is a persistent contradiction. The Jola feel at once neglected by the central government and 'colonised' by the *nordistes*. . . . The Jola must be made to feel that they partake of power, that they are in control of their own destiny." Linares, *Power, Prayer and Production,* p. 222.

68. Peter Geschieri and Jos Van der Klei, "La relation état-paysans et ses ambivalences: modes populaires d'action politique chez les Maka (Cameroun) et les Diola (Casamance)," in Emmanuel Terray, ed., *L'Etat contemporain en Afrique* (Paris: Harmattan, 1987), pp. 315–16. Author's translation.

69. Ibid., p. 318.

70. Saglio, *Casamance*, p. 23. For details on social structure, see Louis-Vincent Thomas, *Les Diola: essai d'analyse fonctionnelle sur une population de Basse-Casamance* (Dakar: Institut Français de l'Afrique Noire, 1959). Some idea of the acephalous nature of Diola society can be gained from its linguistic and political diversity: ten dialects, several of which verge on mutual unintelligibility, four independent languages, more than 500 separate and largely independent communities. Linares, *Power, Prayer and Production,* pp. 5–6.

71. Geschiere and van der Klei, "La relation état-paysans," p. 320.

72. Interview, Marcel Bassene, March 8, 1994.

73. "Rapport sur les événements de Kaguit, Casamance, Senegal" (Dakar: Rencontre Africaine pour la defense des droits de l'homme [RADDHO], 1992).

74. This and other incidents resulted in the virtually complete shutdown of a

large part of Senegal's tourist industry during winter 1992. The industry had just started to recover in late winter 1994 when I carried out field work; most facilities were operating at half capacity, and guests were advised not to travel off the main roads and to remain in the hotels at night.

75. *Country Reports . . . 1992*, p. 217.

76. Body counts are, however, liable to much uncertainty. In the 1993 report on human rights practices, the State Department observed that Senegalese troops "reportedly killed 80 MFDC rebels and took no prisoners during a March battle" (*Country Reports . . . 1993*, p. 239). Well-informed observers raised their eyebrows, for despite their high degree of professional training, Senegalese officers are prone to expend lots of ammunition at great distance from their targets. Tons of ordnance may only have ripped the palm trees to shreds.

77. Interview with Marcel Bassene, March 8, 1994.

78. Geschiere and van der Klei, "La rélation état-paysans," 326.

79. According to Darbon, "This general incapacity of communication [between the hierarchical colonial and the Senegalese state and anti-state Diola societies] results from the lack of common points of reference capable of regulating relations between structured, hierarchical and personalized organizations on the one hand, and, on the other hand, of fluctuating, individualized, individualistic and egalitarian structures." D. Darbon, "Le culturalisme bas-Casamançais," *Politique Africaine* 14 (1984), 127. Author's translation. Darbon is thus far more dismissive than Geschiere and van der Klei of MFDC organizing ability and of the emergence of a sense of Diola unity (especially around Zinguinchor) in the face of "northern" threats.

80. Konaté, *Le problème casamançais*, p. 58.

81. I am not as confident, however, about a reduction in ethnic grievances. The Diolas harbor resentments not only against "northerners," but against other Casamançais, notably the Mandingos. A "solution" that focused on tribe rather than region might exacerbate tensions.

Chapter 5
Enforcement by Reports and Complaints: The African Commission and the ICJ

The process of satisfying a State's international reporting obligations should be seen as an occasion for achieving a variety of objectives. Ideally, it will be considered to be an integral part of a continuing process designed to promote and enhance respect for human rights rather than as an isolated event absorbing precious bureaucratic resources solely to satisfy the requirements of an international treaty. In other words, the process should be treated as an opportunity rather than a chore or formality. It is an opportunity to reaffirm a government's commitment to respect the human rights of its own citizens and to reassert that commitment in the domestic political forum. It is an opportunity for domestic stock-taking and for the adoption of measures to remedy any shortcomings which have been identified. And it is an opportunity to proclaim to the international community that the government concerned is serious about its international commitments.[1]

— Philip Alston

Preparing this chapter awakened long-dormant memories. As noted in the Introduction, my first major research on human rights in Africa, at both undergraduate and graduate levels, relied heavily on governments' reports regarding treaty obligations. For Namibia, on which my baccalaureate thesis was based, material submitted to the League of Nations Permanent Mandates Commission by South Africa, and post-1945 studies prepared under United Nations auspices, provided the scholarly grist. For Cameroon and Togo, on which my doctoral dissertation focused in part, French and British government reports, in addition to Visiting Mission and other UN Trusteeship Council material, gave me the essential background information. No question: these documents were as dry, dusty, and unreadable as might be imagined. To be sure, the bureaucratic prose national and international civil servants employ rarely sparkles. Far more often, it conceals disagreements or delicate situations under a fog of dense verbiage. The diplomatic ritual seems to require a special, convoluted vocabulary that can, nonetheless, have a major long-term impact.[2] "Organs" (such as a "treaty body") are "seized," the approved wording would run, meaning in reality that a specially designated group had been informed of a particular situation. A few hours' reading such reports can cause eyes to roll, pen to falter, good prose to weaken.

How closely related are official documents to actual conditions? Reporting may seem far removed from the "real world" of NGOs' activism. NGOs' concern with protecting aggrieved individuals or groups mandates immediate appeals, not leisurely composed, discussed, and perused studies. *Protection* of human rights forms (for most NGOs) their ultimate rationale. They work, in large part, to save individual victims from bodily abuse, social discrimination, political retribution, or similar indignities. *Promotion* of human rights does involve a more leisurely pace, entailing changing attitudes over extended periods of time. Promotion provides the raison d'être of such significant entities as the African Commission on Human and Peoples' Rights or the UN Commission on Human Rights. These groups customarily operate on the basis of studies prepared by special rapporteurs or (as is the subject of this chapter) documents prepared by governments, discussing conditions in their countries.

The process of submitting and examining reports fits within a seamless web of standard-setting, promotion, implementation, and protection of human rights.[3] Reports from ratifying countries (in the official jargon, "States Parties") lie at the heart of the African Commission's work.[4] Its activities are paralleled, in crucial respects, by respected INGOs (international NGOs) such as Amnesty International or the International Commission of Jurists, both of which will figure in succeeding pages. What is examined in this chapter is an essential linchpin between national and international levels, and between the enunciation and propagation of human rights concepts (standard setting and promotion) and the actual protection of individuals or groups.

Philip Alston, from whom the opening quotation was taken, has contributed significantly to improving the process of reporting. As a scholar, he has published and edited perceptive critiques. As a rapporteur for, and later Chair of, a major UN human rights treaty body, he has pressed for more effective utilization of reports, ensuing discussion ("meaningful dialogue," he hopes), and subsequent follow-up. He and others like him have attempted to make the task of compiling and presenting reports more than a "diplomatic chore."[5] They appear to have enjoyed scant success. At the point, reports do not form a significant part of the African human rights scene. Most states—including, I am sorry to say, a significant majority of African countries—follow the route of "the least possible expenditure of diplomatic staff resources, with little involvement on the part of those in the government who are actually concerned with the rights in question, and with no involvement at all of the broader range of social partners in the community,"[6] including NGOs. The result, Alston continues, "is an all too often sterile reporting system that yields few, if any, genuine insights."[7] The question raised in this chapter is whether this system can be coaxed into productivity.

My experience in the early 1960s with League of Nations and United Nations documents made me nod my head in vigorous agreement when I first read this statement. Reporting represented little more than a ritualistic system, so it appeared. States paid lip service and little more. The reporting process linked bureaucrats, diplomats, and "experts" in what seemed to represent the maximum level of international supervision to which Western states could be pushed in the first half of this century, and newly-independent African countries for much of the remainder. The experience of the African Commission on Human and Peoples' Rights, which relies heavily on reports from ratifying countries, illustrates the chief lesson. Ritualistic ratification by governments leads to inadequate reports or to none whatsoever. Unless NGOs press vigorously, in cooperation with the African Commission or similar treaty bodies, the reports that are produced and the discussion that ensues within the Commission will have scant impact within individual states.

What has led to reporting systems for human rights treaty bodies, as suggested in the headnote? What effects have they had in enforcement? How have they affected African governments? What benefits have resulted to African human rights NGOs and the individuals or groups for whom they speak? Has the African Commission on Human and Peoples' Rights, which has examined reports from a fraction of the ratifying countries, established the basis for constructive dialogue? To what extent have African human rights NGOs contributed to and benefited from the reporting process? Can this process ensure protection of human rights? Answering these questions is essential to fuller insight. This chapter sketches the background to systems of reporting, the impact of NGOs on human rights within various reporting systems of the United Nations, and specific steps taken by the African Commission and the International Commission of Jurists. In the pages that follow, the fundamental question remains: Can and do reports by states lead to better protection of human rights in Africa?

Reporting in Global Perspective

The end of the "war to end all wars" gave substantial impetus to the belief that some aspects of states' actions were subject to international review.

World War I enhanced the concept that peace required greater openness by governments. In part, the push came from Wilsonian concern about secret diplomacy, which many believed had encouraged the conflict. With "open covenants openly arrived at," states would become more responsible to the international community as a whole for their actions. In part, the impetus for openness reflected a recognition that national and international matters could not be readily disentangled. However, given the importance of sovereignty, only a voluntary system could be established. States would have to concur in advance as to how they could be bound. A modest system of international supervision based on reporting was one outcome of this hardly-equal contest between international disclosure and national sovereignty.

Three specific means of international supervision, two of them involving reporting, flowed from the various treaties ending the War: 1) creation of the League of Nations, and in particular the Permanent Mandates Commission, once conflicting territorial claims had been settled; 2) establishment of the International Labour Organization (ILO) as a path-breaking grouping of governments and representatives of workers and employers; and 3) signing a series of treaties between the major victorious powers and several central European states governing treatment of minorities within the latter's boundaries.

The Permanent Mandates Commission (PMC) emerged from the swirl of post-World War I colonial claims. Two of the defeated Central Powers (Germany and the Ottoman Empire) possessed territories coveted by the victors. Territorial ambitions, such as South Africa's desire for German-ruled Southwest Africa, or Japan's claims to German-controlled treaty ports in China, had to be satisfied. British and French military officers and colonial officials sought to convert their military triumphs in the Middle East and Africa into political hegemony. Wilson and his supporters wanted international accountability, however, not merely an extension of colonial hegemony. Secret pacts, such as the notorious Sykes-Picot agreement on Ottoman territories in the Middle East, complicated the equation. After a great deal of diplomatic maneuvering not crucial to this analysis, the result was a very modest system of supervision under the League of Nations. The former German colonies of Kamerun and Togo were split between the British and French empires; the overwhelming majority of German East Africa became the British-administered territory of Tanganyika, while Belgium ruled the densely-inhabited mountain kingdoms of Ruanda and Urundi; Southwest Africa was administered as an integral part of the Union of South Africa.

Though modest, international supervision was not non-existent. The respective administering powers were obligated to submit reports, focused largely on economic and social conditions. These documents were examined by the nine-member PMC. "Human rights" as a term does not appear in the voluminous documentation of this Commission; the term was not then in wide usage. The League of Nations gave NGOs no legal status, although its creation gave them "great moral support."[8] On the other hand, the PMC examined many issues (such as slave-like practices) central to human rights and the concerns of non-governmental organizations. It posed questions, based on the mandate agreements and regular reports, to which administering powers had to respond. The PMC's expertise proved important in establishing its credibility; many Commissioners, such as Sir Frederick Lugard (in many respects, the creator of Nigeria in terms of its current boundaries) had extensive experience in colonial government. The Commission benefited as well from analyses prepared by the Mandates section of the League secretariat. Although its twice-yearly sessions were held in private, detailed summaries were published quickly. The PMC received and utilized information from NGOs.[9] And, perhaps most important, the pattern set by the PMC provided the post-World War II foundation not only for the new UN Trusteeship Council and agreements, but also for the "declaration on non-self-governing territories" incorporated directly into the UN Charter.[10] At least in selected parts of Africa, the principle of accountability, based on periodic reports and on the interests of the population, became established. The colonizing power was responsible (at least in theory) to the global community.[11]

The International Labour Organization also utilized reports extensively as a means of enforcement. Since its inception in 1919, the ILO has drafted more than 170 conventions, which ratifying states are obligated both to put into effect and to provide information annually on their implementation. The special attention given ILO reports provides a system of reporting and examining worthy of wider knowledge and emulation. Within the ILO, a 20-member Committee of Experts and an inclusive tripartitite Committee (composed of representatives of governments, employees, and employers) discuss the reports in detail at the annual conference. Success can be attributed to "extensive assistance provided to Committees by a large number of highly trained secretariat officials . . . the technical examination of reports selected in a manner which minimizes political influence, a subsequent examination by a body more sensitive to political issues and also more capable of bringing political pressure to bear in a public manner, and by making the examination an integral part of the annual political meeting of the Organization."[12] As Leary points out, crucial parts of the ILO system have not been carried over into the reporting systems used by various UN human rights treaty bodies and the African Commission on Human and Peoples' Rights, however. This is, in a word, unfortunate, because of the careful monitoring provided by the ILO secretariat and the combination of technical and political decision making.

The third part of this historical background had far less impact than the Mandates/Trusteeship systems and the ILO. Effective international supervision of European minorities never really came into effect after World War I, despite the good intentions of many statesmen. The minorities treaties were based on noble intentions, yet led to insignificant results. They were signed, as noted above, with the victorious countries rather than with the League of Nations or a specialized body as the enforcement agents. This meant that not much was accomplished as a direct result. The allies had little desire to look into the internal affairs of other states. Not until well into the 1960s, with the activities of both the UN Sub-Commission on the Prevention of Discrimination and the Protection of Minorities, and the Committee on the Elimination of Racial Discrimination (CERD), did the UN turn on a global basis to similar issues.

I do not wish to overstate the direct results of these three developments, either on the great majority of tropical Africa, or on the role of non-governmental organizations. NGOs took no direct role in establishing the PMC and ILO, and had limited impact on them for much of their history. The Permanent Mandates Commission supervised only five colonial territories in tropical Africa[13]; ILO conventions had minor effects, due to special exceptions made for colonial territories. No significant human rights NGOs were headquartered in tropical Africa during this period (roughly 1919 to 1945). Various Europe-based entities, such as the Anti-Slavery Society (since renamed Anti-Slavery International), did pressure and inform the Permanent Mandates Commission, which could receive communications. They could not observe the Commission's discussions, however, nor provide direct rejoinders to government reports. Without an extensive process of public disclosure or visiting missions, the PMC worked in a relative vacuum, dependent on the administering authorities for most of its information.

With the birth of the United Nations, many practices of the erstwhile League of Nations were carried over and modified in light of the new UN Charter. The Charter, it should be recalled, upheld "respect for human rights and fundamental freedoms" as one of its basic objectives. And (so the optimistic reasoning ran), the guarantees of Article 1 of the Charter would ensure each United Nations member state would treat all persons "without distinction as to race, sex, language, or religion." The new Economic and Social Council was authorized to "make suitable arrangements for consultation with non-governmental organizations" in the area of human rights. Hence, the door was opened — slightly. The ILO started to function as a UN specialized agency — in reality, making little difference in the well-established reporting system summarized above, since the ILO had functioned essentially independent of the League of Nations. Far greater changes came in the Mandates system, which was transformed into the Trusteeship system. Many of its former Middle Eastern charges received independence. Political goals became far clearer. According to Article 76 of the Charter, the so-called trust territories should show "progressive development towards self-government or independence as may be appropriate to the particular circumstances of each territory and its peoples and the freely expressed wishes of the people concerned." Discussions within the Trusteeship Council and General Assembly and, in particular, sending visiting missions, had marked effects on the pace of political change. Indigenous organizations took root in such areas as Cameroon, Tanganyika, and Togo, pressing the administering powers for serious political advance.[14] The demand for self-determination through the Trusteeship system constituted the first major effort by Africans to use the United Nations directly as a vehicle for human rights. Even more significant, Article 73 entailed political progress for all colonial possessions, not just the Trust Territories treated in Article 76.

But how could the United Nations—an organization of governments—be certain that member states would in fact honor their obligations?

Threats to international peace and security could be dealt with by the Security Council, wherever they might occur. But hopefully such threats would be rare. Most UN goals would be carried out by member states, which would "fulfill in good faith the obligations assumed by them" through the Charter. However, the United Nations was precluded (by Article 2,7) from intervening "in matters which are essentially within the domestic jurisdiction of any state." As we shall see subsequently, a similar concern for sovereignty marked the Organization of African Unity and impacted directly on its creation, the African Commission on Human and Peoples' Rights. It took years of patient effort before human rights was accepted as a matter beyond the narrow jurisdiction of a particular country.

In the UN system, reports provided an important basis for international awareness. States agreed to provide information on how they would meet their responsibilities. In the ponderous prose of Article 64 of the UN Charter, the Economic and Social Council "may make arrangements with the Members of the United Nations . . . to obtain reports on the steps taken to give effect to its own recommendations and to recommendations falling within its competence made by the General Assembly." In 1950, France proposed that governments report annually on how they had "promoted respect for, and the progress of, human rights in the preceding year."[15] The Commission on Human Rights adopted this idea, and thus began what all observers considered a highly unsatisfactory system: fewer than half the United Nations members submitted reports.[16] Three developments were necessary for reporting to take on renewed life: activism by UN treaty bodies focused on specific rights; studies by Western governments (notably the United States) on individual countries; and pressure from NGOs. Since these processes have been documented elsewhere, there is little reason to examine them in detail.[17]

Several detailed treaties based on the UDHR's general standards have since been drafted and ratified. Most rely on reports from States Parties "on legislative, judicial or other measures taken" to implement specific provisions. Useful guides and critical assessments have been published.[18] With the exception of the Human Rights Committee, however, fulllength monographs of treaty bodies have yet to appear.[19] No doubt fascinating material exists for those willing to pore through the summary records, interview surviving committee members, and consult with NGOs. The scholarly harvest awaits reaping.

The African Commission and Limits to Reporting's Effectiveness

There are several ways to examine reporting as a means of promoting and protecting human rights. One can look first at the treaty itself and the guidelines issued by the supervising body. How strong and detailed are their clauses? Are the obligations of states clear? Do they reflect standards of achievement beyond those established in their constitutions and legal systems? In other words, must the ratifying states enhance their levels of human rights performance as a direct result of their ratifications? Beyond these matters of wording, one can examine, secondly, the reports submitted. Are the reports detailed, responsive to the treaty and reporting guidelines, and accurate? Do they only present governments in the best possible light, carefully omitting potentially embarrassing matters, or are they relatively candid in recognizing problems? Were the reports written following consultation with relevant NGOs and independent specialists, or were they produced in an essentially closed universe of government officials? Third, one can consider the depth and quality of the examination given to reports by the treaty body concerned. How many hours are devoted to discussion? How detailed and wide-ranging are the questions posed — and the responses provided? Are NGOs able not only to attend the discussion, but also to provide information to members of the treaty body? Are the experts themselves well-informed, independent individuals? Finally, one can analyze the follow-through on reports and other communications. Do staff members of the treaty body efficiently process documents? Are Commissioners (or whatever they may be called) able to utilize staff expertise? Do they have access to documentation other than that provided by governments in their reports?

Strong criticisms of the African Commission have been leveled in all four areas. Judged against the other regional documents and bodies — in Europe and the Americas — Africa appears weak. In fairness, however, one must also note the absence of a regional human rights body for Asia, home of half the world's population,[20] the Middle East, and the Pacific Ocean countries. That Africa has a continent-wide human rights treaty body is no insignificant feat.

Problems with the African Charter

The African Charter of Human and Peoples' Rights is, by contemporary international standards, a weak document. Examples will make this clear. Some critics assail the Charter on legal grounds. For example, there is no explicit prohibition of forced labor (although Article 5 does bar "all forms of exploitation and degradation of man . . ."). No mention is made of secret balloting, merely that representatives shall be "freely chosen . . . in accordance with the law" (Art. 11). The procedural safeguards for legal recourse in Article 7 are weak.[21] Although freedom of conscience and free practice of religion are "guaranteed," according to Article 8, there is a kicker: "No one may, *subject to law and order*, be submitted to measures restricting the exercise of these freedoms" (italics added).[22] Many articles are weakened by "clawback" clauses, which limit their specific application from the beginning. Unlike derogation clauses, which permit suspension of previously granted rights only under specific conditions, clawback clauses restrict rights in all respects and under wideranging conditions, for example by making them subject to undefined reasons and conditions.[23] As Gittleman has written,

the African Charter is woefully deficient with regard to the right to liberty. As that right is subject to national law, the Charter is incapable of supplying even a scintilla of external restraint upon a government's power to create laws contrary to the spirit of the rights granted . . . an individual is given no greater protection than she or he would have under domestic law. Even if such protection is adequate in most situations, the Charter does not exist to cover most situations; its purpose is to deter the occasional abuses a government imposes upon its citizens.[24]

On the other hand, some of the phrases criticized by Gittleman can be found in other international human rights documents. Article 6 of the African Charter reads, in part, "No one may be deprived of his freedom except for reasons and conditions previously laid down by law"; Article 9 of the International Covenant on Civil and Political Rights states, "No one shall be deprived of his liberty except on such grounds and in accordance with such procedures as are established by law."

Further objections have come from inclusion rather than exclusion.

More than any other major human rights document, the African Charter imposes duties on individuals.[25] Note the potentially chilling effect of the following obligations, all included in Article 29:

The individual shall also have the duty . . .
3. Not to compromise the security of the State whose national or resident he is;
4. To preserve and strengthen social and national solidarity, particularly when the latter is threatened;
5. To preserve and strengthen the national independence and the territorial integrity of his country and to contribute to its defense in accordance with the law. . . .

Once again, however, one should compare words with deeds. The African Charter's emphasis on duties can be attributed to its drafters' desire for a distinctly African character. In reality, as of mid-1994, there was no evidence of duties having any practical impact on states' actions, states' reports, or the activities of the African Commission. Nor had there been significant discussion of the "third generation" rights included in the Charter.

Criticism has been leveled against the African Charter for the place accorded traditional values that, though accepted within society, may be harmful to individuals. Article 17,3 requires the state to promote and protect "morals and traditional values recognized by the community." What are governments' responsibilities if these values themselves have negative effects? We looked at the issue of female circumcision earlier in this book, for this issue acutely juxtaposes universal standards to the right to integrity of the body versus cultural relativism. But, once again, we should recognize that the drafters were concerned with "positive" African values. I believe the negative effects of this article have been overstated. Although they did not define these, the drafting history of the Charter shows no sympathy on their part for protecting practices or values perceived as backward, on grounds of tradition. Given the speed with which the African Charter was drafted and passed,[26] lacunae of this sort are understandable.

Why do these and similar limitations appear in the African Charter? One ready explanation comes from the conditions and timing of its preparation. The Charter was drafted on behalf of the Organization of African Unity by persons sympathetic to governments' desires (perhaps interpreted as necessities and preconditions), and desirous of including African values. The OAU itself was far more concerned early in its history with ensuring stability for newly independent countries and self-determination for remaining colonial areas, than with protection of human rights within its member states. Clement Nwankwo, an eminent Nigerian human rights advocate, has put the situation well:

Founded in 1963 amidst the wave of decolonization that was then sweeping Africa, the Organization of African Unity (OAU) was brought into existence by newly independent states concerned above all with safeguarding their own sovereignty and territory integrity and opposing the remaining presence of colonialism on the African continent . . . Aside from denunciations of colonialism and apartheid, the OAU gave little attention to matters touching on human rights and democracy. Not surprisingly, the nondemocratic regimes that predominated in Africa preferred this arrangement: they had created the OAU not to champion human rights, but to help preserve regional stability and shield against foreign intervention. . . .

Hobbled by severe limitations and replete with contradictions, the Charter has not been able to ameliorate the serious problem of human rights abuses in Africa. But perhaps it was never intended to in the first place . . . the Charter that emerged from this climate was aimed more at creating an impression of liberalism than at curbing human rights abuses in Africa, most of which were being perpetrated by the very governments that signed the instrument.[27]

The weaknesses evident in defining rights in the Charter are echoed in arrangements made for the African Commission on Human and Peoples' Rights. The Commission operates within a more restricted set of parameters than almost any other human rights treaty body. But it has also been criticized — somewhat too harshly, in my estimation — because of its members' relatively low profile, various teething pains in establishing the Commission, and limitations within the Charter. Each should be examined.

The African Charter makes clear that the Commission plays a minor role in enforcement. Although "measures of safeguard" fall under the Commission, it is subordinated to the OAU's Assembly of Heads of State and Government (AHG), and has an ambiguous relationship with the OAU Secretariat. Real power in the OAU rests with African Presidents, who assemble annually for their summit session — two to three days, usually, of bonhomie and resolution-passing. Admittedly, considerable prior work is carried out by the Council of Ministers, composed of the African equivalents of the Secretary of State. They meet twice per year, one session devoted primarily to budget and administrative matters, one session to preparing the AHG summit; however, the Council of Ministers has no direct human rights role in terms of the African Charter. The Council and the Assembly are explicitly political bodies, based on states. It is naturally in the interest of those assembled to turn a blind eye to events within member countries. A *noli me tangere* attitude has generally pervaded the OAU. The Organization regularly condemned human rights abuses, particularly the absence of self-determination for non-members on the African continent (notably, of course, South Africa), but remained silent in the face of abuses within member states. Nwankwo's criticism, quoted a few paragraphs ago, is true at its core. The OAU tended, in its critics' eyes, to become a club of presidents, dedicated to self-preservation, unwilling save in rare cases to concern itself with domestic issues. "Non-interference in internal matters" became a cardinal point of OAU practice. This attitude was then reflected in the African Charter on Human and Peoples' Rights, and in particular in its Secretariat, to which we shall return later in the chapter.

On the other hand, should the OAU shake off a bit of its state-centric, status-quo orientation, it could take greater interest in human rights within individual states. An energetic Secretary-General could inspire greater action and energize the lethargic OAU bureaucracy; an active set of Chairmen could set a tone of greater OAU interest. (The Chairmanship changes annually, with the selection of the president whose country hosts the annual conference of heads of state.) In reality, the most likely avenue of change will come from the Commission itself, whose responsibilities and activities we must now examine.

The Charter is clear on the subordinate position of the African Commission. As a group of part-time experts, it is subject to decisions made by the Presidents who attend the annual summit. The OAU Assembly elects all eleven members of the African Commission by secret ballot from persons nominated by states.[28] More important, "All measures" taken by the Commission in fulfilling its mandate "shall remain confidential until such a time as the Assembly of Heads of State and Government shall otherwise decide" (Art. 50, 1), although the Chairman of the Commission may publish reports on its activities after these have been "considered" by the OAU Assembly. (Here, let it be noted parenthetically, the Commission could be more active in disseminating information about its work, a question to which we shall return.) As might be expected, the Commission's published reports have been anodyne summaries, noting that meetings were held or communications discussed, with little if any indication of their substance. Should the African Commission learn through communications of "special cases which reveal the existence of a series of serious or massive violations of human and peoples' rights," the Commission shall "draw the attention of the Assembly . . . to these special cases"; the Assembly, in turn, may request an "in-depth study . . . and make a factual report, accompanied by its findings and recommendations" (Art. 58, 1 and 2). The African Commission, in short, has no direct powers of enforcement[29]; it must rely on essentially voluntary action by heads of government who may themselves have condoned or even encouraged human rights abuses. No continent-wide court of human rights exists, despite the examples of the European and American courts, and despite the "Law of Lagos" of the International Commission of Jurists, discussed later in this chapter. No wonder the second Chairman of the Commission wrote,

The enforcement mechanism is unsatisfactory. In the absence of a court and effective measures for a breach, the Charter may well be a paper tiger except for effective public opinion that may be whipped up against the offender . . . The Commission will have to develop its practice beyond the narrow confines of the express words of the Charter.[30]

The strictures of confidentiality have been vigorously criticized by NGOs, and privately questioned by Commission members; these concerns have succeeded. Over time, as will be discussed shortly, the Commission has opened more and more of its proceedings to observation by NGOs. Further, the Commission has carved out somewhat greater autonomy than the African Charter seems formally to permit. For example, it successfully claimed the power to examine reports. We shall turn shortly to the depth of this examination.

What about the backgrounds and interests of those selected to serve on the African Commission? The Charter prescribes that they be "chosen from amongst African personalities of the highest reputation, known for their high morality, integrity, impartiality, and competence in matters of human and peoples' rights, particular consideration being given to persons having legal competence . . . [they] shall serve in their personal capacity" (Art. 31). Throughout its brief history—for the first members could not be elected until July 1987, shortly before the African Charter went formally into effect—individuals on government payrolls have predominated.[31] Such should not be surprising: African lawyers are absorbed, with few exceptions, into government service as bureaucrats, judges, or even ambassadors, or into academic life (there are, with the exception of Egypt, essentially no private universities in OAU member states)[32]. Two of the three Commission chairs have been law professors; the other chair was trained as a lawyer and diplomat, had chaired the UN Committee on Economic, Social and Cultural Rights, and had remarkable fluency in Arabic, English, and French, enabling him to play a crucial bridge role within the Commission.

The Commission is, obviously, a small group. Few academics and NGO members have attended its sessions and published about its activities. Thanks to support from the US Institute of Peace and a Fulbright grant, I attended three Commission sessions and interviewed several of its members. I respect the thoughtfulness the Commissioners bring to their tasks, the frustrations they feel when this work is impeded by inefficiency or disregard, their concern for bolstering the Commission's public image and its private effectiveness. They work long hours for relatively modest honoraria (at least at levels common in developed countries); they recognize the negative image of human rights in Africa around the world; they want to encourage states to meet their constitutional and treaty obligations; they seek to promote constructive dialogue with governments, in a spirit of reason. The Commission's members are, on the whole, persons dedicated to strengthening legal systems. They are reformers, not revolutionaries. They tend far more toward accommodation than confrontation. They sketched a relatively ambitious program early in the Commission's history,[33] and have made progress I consider significant, in light of its resource and personnel problems.

But ineluctable facts remain: the African Commission on Human and Peoples' Rights lacks the range and clarity of human rights as defined in major UN human rights treaties as well as in regional agreements such as the European Convention on Human Rights and the American Convention on Human Rights; no court exists through which additional steps could be pursued; the Commission must formally depend on moral suasion and the OAU Assembly for action, since the Charter has no clause obligating States Parties to implement even Assembly decisions; the Assembly has proven itself unwilling to criticize events and actions within member states; the Commission is only beginning (as of late 1993) to make public statements; the OAU has been hamstrung by financial issues, and the Commission has had to turn to other, primarily UN and European, sources of support for many activities; the independence of a substantial proportion of Commission members from governments has come into question. In an ideal and non-political world, these fetters on human rights enforcement through the African Commission might not exist, but they do. The question, then, is how successfully they have been countered. Part of the answer lies in the (non)-cooperation of OAU member states.

Problems with Reports

To meet their obligations under the African Charter on Human and Peoples' Rights, ratifying states agree to provide periodic reports. Article 62 mandates each country to "undertake to submit every two years . . . a report on the legislative and other measures taken with a view to giving effect to the rights and freedoms guaranteed by the present Charter." There were no precise statements about who would receive and consider such documents, or about the Commission's role. The Charter's drafters were fully aware of the general international practice by which groups of experts—as the African Commission was to be—examined states' reports, questioned their representatives directly, and drew on various sources of information for their work. They were also aware of the efforts made by the UN Commission on Human Rights, a group composed of states, to utilize reports. A clear choice between independent specialists and explicitly political officers might have aroused debate within the OAU. Hence, I am tempted to conclude, the framers left the matter deliberately vague, lest the chances for the Charter's ratification be jeopardized. They did not preclude the possibility, in other words, that the Assembly of Heads of State and Government might be the main body concerned with reports—a sure recipe for neglect.

Shortly after its establishment, the Commission moved to fill this lacuna in the Charter. In October 1988 it adopted guidelines for periodic reports—then waited two and a half years before the first were ready for discussion. As I have written elsewhere, most states have not taken their obligation to report seriously.[34] Initial reports were to provide the constitutional, legislative, and general context for the rights defined in the African Charter. Subsequent reports, supposedly submitted every two years, would discuss changes in this framework, and give more details on the human rights situation, problems incurred, and the like. The quality of reports sent to the African Commission has been highly variable.[35] Almost all the documents submitted have been brief and lacking supporting documentation. Although Commissioners are too diplomatic to criticize states publicly, they nonetheless express concern privately about the slow pace of receipt, the uninformative nature of much documentation, repeated problems with informing states about the dates when their reports are scheduled for discussion, participation of relatively uninformed representatives (often the nearest ambassador of the reporting country is pressed into service, having little prior knowledge of the report's contents or the Commission's role), and the non-attendance of states when scheduled for consideration. The Commission has regularly urged the OAU summit to adopt resolutions calling for speedy preparation of detailed reports, with limited impact as of mid-1994.

Let me take the case of Nigeria, a country that appears elsewhere in this book in its flip-flop efforts to democratize. As Africa's most populous state, Nigeria has sought international recognition of its importance. Its brief flirt with petroleum-based affluence in the late 1970s and early 1980s gave it financial clout; indeed, a Nigerian Trust Fund was established to loan surplus petrodollars to other African countries. Nigeria took the major initiative in creating ECOWAS (the Economic Community of West African States) in 1976, in convening a 1990 conference in its capital Abuja to strengthen African economic and political unity, and in providing the bulk of military support for ECOMOG, the ECOWAS Military Observer Group that played a frustrating role trying to reestablish peace in war-torn Liberia. All these examples suggest a country eager to exert leadership. However, its record relative to international human rights has been (to use an overly kind term) spotty. Nigeria hosted the ninth session of the Africa Commission, in April 1991. Members (at least those who attended; for the first time in the Commission's history, a quorum could not be mustered) were treated to a lavish dinner hosted by

President Ibrahim Babangida. But no report on Nigeria was provided, other than a letter of transmittal from the Nigerian High Commission in The Gambia, stapled to the table of contents of the (partially suspended) constitution! Professor Umozurike, the Chair of the African Commission, was deeply embarrassed by his government's cavalier neglect of the reporting obligation — apparently the result of bureaucratic inertia and uncertainty as to where responsibility rested. He made numerous private appeals to the Ministry of Foreign Affairs and the Ministry of Justice to settle their turf battles and get the work done. Discussion of Nigeria was rescheduled at the eleventh session (Banjul, October 1992). Nigeria failed to appear. The same occurred at the twelfthth session (Banjul, April 1993). Not until the thirteenth session (Addis Ababa, December 1993) was a 14-page report ready, on the table for discussion, and an official representative in place.[36]

Even with this checkered record, Nigeria was in a small minority of countries that have met their treaty obligation. Only 15 states had submitted reports as of early 1994, meaning 35 ratifying states had yet to respond to the numerous invitations of the Commission and the resolutions of the OAU Assembly to submit their initial documents. A minimal report is doubtless better than none at all, for it provides the Commission and attending NGOs the opportunity for at least some public discussion. Total disregard seems to be a deliberate snub of the entire process. It cannot be explained away by lack of resources or lack of knowledge. The pleas of the OAU (and of UN treaty bodies) can be readily ignored by governments scornful of human rights.

But how effective can examination of state-prepared reports be? Don't potentially self-serving submissions by governments need to be balanced by other sources of information? Given the strictures of confidentiality, how can the Commission most effectively utilize communications sent directly to it about alleged abuses of rights? What about documentation prepared and submitted by NGOs?

Problems in Examining Reports and Communications

The African Commission has benefitted from a steep learning curve with respect to their primary official source of information: the reports from States Parties. Due in large part to emerging informal links with NGOs, which have provided additional input (both written and by personal appearance), Commissioners' analyses have become far more pointed and informed. Communications sent directly to the Commission also give its members grist for questions, although the impact of communications (which are considered confidential) cannot be ascertained directly.

The first round of examining reports, as Gaer observed, was disappointing.[37] An average of 45 minutes was devoted to discussion, with brief, overlapping remarks by Commissioners and limited use of additional sources of information. Once again, the experiences of the African Commission paralleled those of other treaty bodies. A troubling question early in the history of CERD, for example, was whether *any* body of information other than government reports could be used.[38] This issue has been now laid to rest. Commissioners in whatever human rights monitoring entity can utilize three major sources: 1) official reports, which are examined in public sessions, with questions directed at government officials flown in for the occasion; 2) communications, which are discussed in private sessions, overwhelmingly involve charges against governments, and may lead in flagrant and multiple cases to public criticism; and 3) other information, which individual Commissioners receive or seek out, to broaden their knowledge of particular countries or situations. It stands to reason that the greater the amount of information available through all these sources, the more detailed questioning could become.

There exists, as well, an immeasurable personality factor. Commissioners naturally bridle at any suggestion that they do not question government representatives with sufficient vigor. Though they pose their queries in the convoluted, delicate language of diplomacy, they know their personal and institutional credibility rests on effective use of information. Commissioners who act under the watchful eyes of NGO representatives must walk a narrow path between undue deference to governments, which would entail general acceptance of reports and at most gentle inquiries of the representatives, and wholesale acceptance of NGO criticisms, which some Commissioners believe could poison the "constructive dialogue" the process promotes. When the African Charter's reporting process began, I believe, many Commissioners were neither convinced of the value of NGO-provided information, nor comfortable in appearing critical of governments. They had little direct experience with reports and NGOs alike. A baseline of expectations had to be established, communicated to governments and NGOs, and used in the public questioning. By the eleventh session, the Commission turned a corner.[39] Stung by criticism about shallow, uncritical acceptance of states' reports, and increasingly aware of the interest of NGOs and various funding bodies, Commissioners became far more vigorous in their questioning. They started to refer publicly to information received from other sources — including memoranda pressed upon them in hotel corridors by NGO representatives. Pointed, knowledgeable questions would, after all, both enhance constructive dialogue with states and respond to comments from NGOs. Some members of the African Commission who earlier regarded NGOs as less-than-desirable critics began to refer to them as partners. Hence, in addition to the affinity for governments all Commissioners felt upon their election, many soon developed a sensitivity toward, and tacit links to, NGOs. The evolution was fascinating to observe! Familiarity bred not contempt, but acceptance. The psychological effects of having public sessions and consistent attenders strengthened the African Commission's handling of reports. As record-keeping improves, and summaries or transcripts of these examinations become available, the quality of the "constructive dialogue" should increase further.[40]

I have already mentioned, but not yet discussed, communications to the African Commission. Examination of them falls outside the limelight of public sessions. They receive only elliptical references in official reports. Communications have yet to play a leading role in the human rights dramas of contemporary Africa, at least insofar as the African Commission is concerned. No single case arising from a communication was referred by the Commission to the Assembly through the sixth (1993) activity report, even though this report mentioned specific cases dealt with by the Commission, and was adopted by the Assembly of Heads of State and Government without change.[41] On the other hand, complaints submitted by individuals, or, more likely, by NGOs on behalf of affected persons or groups, will undoubtedly grow in importance.

The input of NGOs relative to governments grows immensely in the case of petitions sent to the Commission. While government-generated reports deal with general situations in broad-brush terms — laws of general applicability, national statistics — communications often focus on individual cases — persons imprisoned for their beliefs or actions, for whom some NGO or associate appeals for assistance.

The African Charter differentiates between communications from states and "other communications." There is little surprising in the provisions for either. State Parties, to use the legal term, may complain against others for breaching Charter provisions. The OAU Secretary-General and the Chairman of the African Commission are supposed to be informed. Alternatively, the communication can be sent directly to the Commission, which can deal with it. After obtaining "all the information it deems necessary and after having tried all appropriate means to reach an amicable solution" (Art. 51), the Commission would prepare a report. A great deal of verbiage for minimal results: in Africa as in other settings, these state-versus-state procedures are never invoked. Simply put, governments are far more likely to use bilateral or other existing OAU channels in case of disputes than the slow, uncharted process of complaint. Other communications "relating to human and peoples' rights" — in other words, arising from individuals — may be considered by the Commission *if* several conditions are met. Article 56 sets forth a lengthy but not unusual string of requirements. Communications must include the name(s) of the complainant(s), be compatible with the OAU Charter or African Charter, not be written in "disparaging or insulting language directed against the State concerned," not be based exclusively on news media sources, be sent after local remedies have been exhausted,[42] be submitted within reasonable time, and not deal with cases previously settled under UN or OAU principles. The Commission decides by majority vote on admissibility (Art. 55).

In the view of Amnesty International, the African Commission should seek to strengthen its independence. AI was among the first NGOs to be granted observer status by the Commission; its representative has attended almost all sessions, spoken on specific issues, and sent numerous communications directly to the Commission's secretariat. Shortly before the 1993 OAU summit meeting, Amnesty International urged three specific reforms of the African Charter through a special protocol. First, Article 58 would be amended to permit the Commission to carry out studies a) in *any* case where there are reasonable grounds to believe the Charter has been violated, not only if there were "serious and massive violations" and b) without the prior necessity for approval by the OAU Assembly of Heads of State and Government. Second, the Commission should publish its annual report after it has been considered by the Assembly, rather than assume the Assembly could preclude publication. With respect to communications, AI also urged that the Commission change its practice to conform with other human rights treaty bodies, in which all matters would be published except a) names of authors wanting confidentiality, b) actual deliberations on pending communications, and c) particular cases where justice is better served by confidentiality.[43] Improvements in the Commission's Rules of Procedure could also streamline the Commission's effectiveness without the hassle of drafting and ratifying a special protocol.[44]

Considering the scale of human rights violations in Africa, one would expect the Commission to receive a flood of petitions, letters and the like. There has been no spate. Indeed, at least as of early 1994 there has been only a trickle. The Commission has, further, found itself stonewalled by states unwilling to accept Commission involvement in what they deem domestic matters. Commission members nevertheless decided, at their twelfth session, to go ahead with consideration of communications, giving states an additional deadline of two months, as most governments did not reply to Commission initiatives. Take the following statistics regarding actions taken at the thirteenth session (29 March–7 April 1993). A mere 14 new communications (an average of barely two per month) were officially received. The members dealt with 46: three were declared inadmissible, five declared admissible (three from named individuals; all dealt with English-speaking countries), 13 led to requests for further information from the states concerned, eight resulted in requests for further information from the complainants, eight were "closed," while five and three dealt respectively with Sudan and Rwanda.[45] At the fourteenth session (December 1993), the Commission spent most of its time in private session, to make up for previous delays. It dealt with no less than 60 communications, only seven of which were new. The numbers are orders of magnitude smaller than those received by the (Inter-)American and European Commissions on Human Rights. At the 15th session (April 1994), the Commission reconsidered 70 of the total 134 communications submitted so far.[46] At the 16th session (October 1994), the Commission considered a mere eight new communications plus 54 old ones; of these, nine were decided on the merits, five were declared admissible and seven inadmissible, eight were deferred pending receipt of additional information, seven required notifications be sent to governments for comments, one (!) was closed, thirteen were not dealt with due to time constraints, and no fewer than eleven required missions to the state concerned.[47]

Human rights are most abused in civil wars or widespread ethnic violence. Enforcement of personal security takes on the greatest seriousness under these circumstances. Ideally, such conflicts should not break out; realistically, they should be mitigated. The Organization of African Unity ought to take a role in encouraging peace. However, it is not well-structured to take on these roles.[48] Disputes within member states present the OAU with profound dilemmas. The organization deplores interference in domestic matters, and supports constituted authority. It has historically shied away from involvement, unless disputes have spilled across borders, aroused international concern, and/or threatened the intra-African harmony the organization promotes. Faced with intractable conflicts, the OAU has temporized and turned to personal solutions. An elaborate Commission on Mediation, Arbitration and Conciliation was created early in the Organization's history, but never functioned; instead, the OAU has utilized presidential missions, hoping that small groups of senior statesmen can somehow achieve peace.[49] These efforts had a mixed record. The "African Mechanism Apparatus for Preventing, Managing and Resolving African Crises" established late in 1993 under the OAU Summit Bureau represents the most recent attempt. Somalia and Liberia, in both of which military peace-keepers were frustrated in bringing peace, underscored the importance of earlier, "political" solution. Burundi provided the first test case for the "Mechanism."

Personalized diplomacy, possibly reflecting African respect for age, certainly mirroring centralization of leadership, has been widespread. The African Commission has followed a similar trajectory. The Commission's increasingly favored *modus operandi* involves negotiating visits by

Commissioners "in order to discuss with competent authorities [the] allegations contained in the communications"; such requests were made after the thirteenth session to Chad, Mauritania, Nigeria, and Togo, for example. The record is not encouraging; previous pleas for cooperation have gone unanswered. For example, faced with numerous serious allegations about human rights violations in Rwanda and Sudan, the Commission first referred the matter to the OAU Chair, then (apparently in the face of OAU inaction) decided in October 1992 to seek approval from the two governments for visits by two Commissioners. Silence greeted the requests, and the Commission had to decide whether to ask the OAU Assembly of Heads of State and Government to take the next step, namely making a factual report, accompanied by findings and recommendations. Since the Assembly meets but once a year, prospects for speedy action appear dim, even for emergency situations. But problems of personal visits do not stem solely from OAU or government inaction. Members of the Commission could not visit Mauritania, to which they had been invited in late 1993, because of a lack of resources.

The case of Malawi political dissidents Orton and Vera Chirwa exemplifies the Commission's ineffectiveness — and the inability of other groups — in the face of determined government resistance. The Chirwas were distinguished lawyers and brave individuals. Orton Chirwa, the first African lawyer in Malawi, served in the early 1960s as his country's Minister of Justice; his wife was the first Malawian woman to become a lawyer. Both left their country for neighboring Zambia in 1964, and founded the Malawi Freedom Movement (MAFREMO) to oppose the dictatorial rule of president-for-life Kamuzu Banda. They were allegedly abducted from Zambia by Malawian security agents in 1981, brought before a traditional court, denied access to legal counsel or the right to call witnesses, and sentenced to death on charges of treason. (The sentences were subsequently commuted to life imprisonment.) The convictions and harsh conditions of the Chirwas' imprisonment aroused international outrage. Numerous NGOs and governments took notice.[50] Several communications on the Chirwas' behalf were sent to the African Commission, which, following its usual procedure, asked the Malawi government for further information, then for a visit by Commission members. Silence greeted these queries. It was a case of growing frustration for Commission members, some of whom knew the Chirwas personally. Orton Chirwa died in prison October 20, 1992, after eleven years in prison; ironically, the African Commission was meeting that very day, debating *in camera* what further steps to take. Justice delayed was justice denied for Orton and Vera Chirwa (even though she was eventually released). I seriously doubt that the African Commission could have made any difference. Far more powerful international pleading from governments and NGOs could not sway the Banda regime. But the unfortunate outcome gave the Commission the impetus for greater vigor. The specific mention given the Chirwa case in the final communiqué of the twelfth session marked a first for the Commission. Henceforth, it would pursue communications about individuals with more dispatch and an enhanced sense of urgency. Pursue, that is, as far as its administrative capacity permitted.

Problems in Implementing Commission Actions

Thus far, I have concentrated on the eleven persons who compose the African Commission, and made passing reference to those who attend its biennial sessions. But who takes responsibility for ensuring the part-time Commissioners are effectively serviced? or that official and private communications are properly received and handled?

For much of the Commission's history, these questions would have been sarcastically answered, "No one." Problems with the Secretariat reveal a fundamental truth about human rights at the global or regional level. Effectiveness has several components: statutory, resource, personality. Thus far, I have focused primarily on the formal powers of the Commission as shown by the Charter and revealed in Commission discussions. It is time to look at the level of human interaction, notably at the roles played by the Secretariat and by successive Chairs.

Institutions are shaped by individuals, especially at their beginning. The African Commission was poorly served by its administrative officers in its first several years, close observers agree. Communications have been misplaced, necessary paperwork not completed, mandates ignored, opportunities for additional funding let slip. Tensions between Commmissioners and the Secretariat erupted publicly in the twelfth session (Banjul, October 1992). Among the bill of particulars:

- Commissioners were not adequately informed of developments in the Secretariat;
- no summary reports or minutes were prepared on a timely basis, lack of funding being cited as a major reason;
- files were misplaced and documents not translated into the Commission's three working languages;
- provisional agendas and meeting dates were not established with sufficient advance notice;
- communications were not followed up speedily or effectively;
- offers of funding from non-OAU sources were neglected;
- directives by the Commission's Chairman were not implemented;
- et cetera, et cetera . . .

These shortcomings within the Commission's office were exacerbated by the Secretary's insistence that he reported to OAU headquarters in Addis

Ababa rather than to the Chair of the Commission, and by the OAU's severe funding problems. (In reality, however, the Commission has never, to my knowledge, exhausted the funds it was allocated from the OAU, or provided directly by primarily Northern donors. Members of the Commission expressed amazement when I publicly cited their budget at the April 1994 ICJ workshop.)[51] The OAU has itself led a hand-to-mouth existence. States have been lax in paying their dues. New demands on the Organization, such as civil wars, have stretched its capacities well beyond reason. The OAU did not provide the Commission with a legal officer until mid-1992; frustrated by internal problems, he left in summer 1993 for another job. The Commission would have no documentalist were it not for non-OAU funds. Until the African Commission has an adequately staffed and funded Secretariat, responsive to its members' needs, the Commission will remain severely impeded in its effectiveness.

This sorry list above presents a clear contrast to the staff work given to United Nations and especially to ILO conventions.[52] Despite severe financial problems and the heavy burden carried by Centre for Human Rights and other Geneva- and New York-based UN offices, human rights treaty bodies are serviced: summary minutes are prepared, documents and sessions translated, materials circulated in relative abundance. The European and Inter-American Commissions and Courts receive significant support. In terms of staff, the Inter-American Commission has seven professional employees, the European Commission no less than 40.[53] The far greater financial resources of Western Europe and the Western Hemisphere make higher levels of support possible. Arguably, however, this disparity is because political will for international assessment of human rights is greater in Europe and the Americas than in Africa, the result in turn of longer experiences with democracy and the rule of law.

This chapter has been grim reading. It has focused on a small, weak institution whose mandate and support are limited. The African Commission draws its duties from a toothless Charter; it suffers from serious staff and resource deficiencies; it cannot yet count on lengthy, positive experience with reports to strengthen the process itself; communications to the Commission have rarely been used to protect the rights of specific individuals. All these points are true. Nonetheless, the ACHPR is starting to make a serious contribution to protecting as well as to promoting human rights in Africa. It has been helped by the active involvement of NGOs, which are obviously interested in strengthening human rights and the rule of law throughout Africa. No NGO has been more significant than the International Commission of Jurists. Its work on behalf of the African Commission merits attention at this point.

The ICJ and the Creation and Improvement of the African Commission

The Geneva-based International Commission of Jurists (ICJ) has provided the best-informed consistent NGO pressure on the African Commission and its reporting mechanism to enhance efficiency and input. Indeed, were it not for the efforts of ICJ General Secretary Adama Dieng, the African Charter on Human and Peoples' Rights might still be languishing in the limbo of unratified treaties. It is nearly impossible to underestimate the ICJ's role in bringing both the Charter and the Commission to life.

The ICJ was born as a Cold War tool, funded in part by covertly-channeled CIA funds. It followed an essentially American set of priorities in its early years, then expanded and became less politically partial. Under the leadership of Sean MacBride (winner of both the Nobel and Lenin peace prizes, respectively in 1974 and 1976), the ICJ made strengthening international law and institutions a top priority. Revelations about the CIA's financial support proved nearly fatal, however, and the concluding years of MacBride's leadership (1963–70) were, as Tolley stresses, more times of "damage control." The ICJ was rescued by Niall Macdermot, who redirected it toward campaigns for economic and political justice, as Tolley has well described.[54] I shall concentrate in this section specifically on the ICJ's efforts 1) to encourage establishment of the rule of law generally in developing countries, 2) to bring the African Charter on Human and Peoples' Rights into force and its Commission into effective operation, and 3) to rally African human rights NGOs to utilize the African Commission as a channel for pressure.

The ICJ occupies well-appointed quarters in suburban Geneva. Secretary-General Dieng presides over a relatively small multinational staff, in which Africa is well-represented. Dieng and the program coordinator hail from Senegal. Most of their work takes place in the rarefied atmosphere of Geneva. The United Nations' European headquarters, with its Centre for Human Rights, is a few minutes drive away across the wealthy, international-organization-studded section of Grand Saconnex. An uninformed observer might underestimate the impact of the ICJ on significant aspects of human rights in Africa. More than any other organization, it has pressed on a global basis for respect for the rule of law, an essential underpinning of human rights. The ICJ's 1993 receipt of the United Nations human rights award testified to its highly-regarded efforts.

The ICJ measures its output in publications (its *Review* and *Newsletter*, reports on violations and on the independence of judges and lawyers in specific countries, studies of various rights [e.g., impunity], seminar conclusions), in testimony to UN bodies such as the Sub-Commission on the Elimination of Discrimination and the Protection of Minorities, and in training programs (such as for paralegals). Its views on the rule of law and the role of lawyers have been defined in the alliterative Act of Athens (1956), the Declaration of Delhi (1959), the Law of Lagos (1961), and the Resolution of Rio (1962). Thus, much like the UN Commission on Human Rights in its initial years, the International Commission of Jurists sought at the outset to set standards. As "liberal idealists for the rule of law," in Tolley's phrase, the ICJ proselytizes as vigorously as its small central staff permits. It seeks to enhance the work of similarly-inclined NGOs, through networks of legal and human rights specialists.

The "Law of Lagos" provides a convenient starting point for the Commission's impact on Africa. One hundred ninety four participants, from 23 African countries and many others, assembled in Nigeria's capital January 3–7, 1961, under the chairmanship of a distinguished Indian jurist.[55] They extended the rule of law—defined in the Declaration of Delhi as "adherence to institutions and procedures, not always identical, but broadly similar, which experience and tradition . . . have shown to be essential to protect the individual from arbitrary government and to enable him to enjoy the dignity of man" — to all countries, independent or colonial. In order to bring the Universal Declaration on Human Rights into effect, they invited study of an African Convention on Human Rights, and creation of a continent-wide court.[56] These recommendations on an African treaty would not bear fruit for many years. Their success could be attributed to the efforts of Dieng, the ICJ's Secretary-General since 1990, and before that legal officer for Africa.[57]

Adama Dieng belongs to a group of noteworthy Senegalese who, as noted in Chapter 1, rose to prominent human rights positions by the early 1990s: Pierre Sané, head of Amnesty International[58]; Ibrahima Fall, Assistant Secretary-General of the United Nations responsible for the Centre for Human Rights; Jacques Diouf, head of FAO (Food and Agriculture Organization); Lamity Kama, UN special rapporteur on arbitrary detention; El Hadji Ibrahima Guissé, co-special rapporteur for the Sub-Commission on impunity; Bacre Waly Ndiaye, special rapporteur on extra-judicial, summary or arbitrary executions. Many, and especially Dieng, had been inspired by the noted Senegalese jurist Kéba Mbaye. To understand human rights in Africa, including the ICJ and the African Commission, one must give attention to Judge Mbaye.

More than any other person, Kéba Mbaye merits the title, "Father of Human Rights in Africa." International specialists know Mbaye most for his emphasis on the "right to development." (His contributions to the 1986 United Nations declaration on the right to development are discussed in Chapter 9.) Mbaye's distinguished international career became a model for younger jurists; his personal contacts inspired many Senegalese directly. In the late 1970s, he chaired the UN Commission on Human Rights and served concurrently as President of the International Commission of Jurists. Mbaye inspired much of the text of the African Charter on Human and Peoples' Rights, chairing the group of experts who elaborated the first draft. Not surprisingly, the International Commission of Jurists supported publication of Mbaye's book, *Les Droits de l'Homme en Afrique*,[59] to which Adama Dieng contributed a foreword in the form of a "homage . . . for this most precious gift" given the ICJ on its 30th anniversary. Mbaye crowned his legal career with appointment to the International Court of Justice, on which he was serving as this book was written. Surely a distinguished career.

In essence, three steps had to be taken. First, a treaty faithful to international human rights standards but also sensitive to African needs had to be drafted.[60] Approval by the OAU and ratification by states would come second. Third, the verbiage of the treaty would have to be translated into effective action. In all, the ICJ took a leading role, its role giving impetus to actions of the UN Commission on Human Rights. Kéba Mbaye was active in both entities.

In March 1977, the UN Commission adopted a Nigerian draft resolution (co-sponsored by Benin, the Philippines, Senegal, Tanzania, and Zaire) calling on the UN to urge regional organizations such as the Organization of African Unity to adopt regional human rights conventions. A UN study group was established, which received documentation from the Council of Europe and the Organization of American States, but not the OAU. It expressed general agreement that member states and regional organizations should take the initiative, rather than the UN. In March 1978, the Commission adopted another Nigerian resolution, requesting the UN Secretary-General both to transmit the report to member states and regional organizations, and to organize suitable regional seminars.[61] Events started to speed up. Meanwhile, the ICJ convened a colloquium in Dakar in 1977 whose report was widely distributed and used by the UN in its later Cairo and Monrovia meetings devoted to discussing a draft treaty. In what it later called the "decisive step,"[62] the ICJ called together 40 African lawyers from French-speaking countries in Dakar in 1978.[63] Four members of this group lobbied ten French-speaking heads of state to support such a treaty.[64] Mbaye persuaded President Senghor of Senegal to introduce a resolution in 1979, calling on the OAU to convene African experts to prepare a draft human rights treaty. By mid-1981, the experts had finished their draft, having drawn heavily from proposals prepared by Mbaye, who in fact served as rapporteur of the drafting committee.

Mbaye took pride in introducing what he called "positive African cultural values" in the Charter: the preponderant role of the family, morale, community.[65] In Africa, Mbaye wrote,

rights are not conceived as a type of sword placed in the hands of an individual to let him defend himself against the group. [Rights] are considered instead as a group of rules protecting the community, of which the individual is part.[66]

This conception of African distinctiveness remains a continuing issue in the promotion and protection of human rights within the OAU.

Adoption of the African Charter on Human and Peoples' Rights took place at the 1981 OAU summit in a "hasty and secretive manner."[67] Little fanfare accompanied the Assembly's action. Some observers felt the OAU wanted to preclude future criticism for its failure to condemn the human rights abuses of dictators such as Idi Amin, Jean-Bedel Bokassa, or Macias Nguema. Cynical public relations move or not, the Charter could take on a life of its own only were it ratified, but that took place slowly. Twenty-six OAU members had to deposit instruments of ratification before the African Charter could come into effect. The initial pace was languorous. One state ratified in 1981, five each in 1982 and 1983, two in 1985. The ICJ decided on a dramatic step. It convened a meeting in Nairobi in December 1985 aimed at securing the additional eleven needed ratifications. Not until Dieng engaged in proselytizing missions following this important ICJ meeting did the pace quicken. No less than fourteen countries completed action in 1986, with the Charter's official date of entry into force October 21, 1986. Other states followed suit, with five ratifications in 1987 and 1989, one each in 1990 and 1991, and six in 1992; only Eritrea, Ethiopia, Seychelles, South Africa, and Swaziland remained outside the fold by early 1994.[68] The ICJ also worked on procedures to implement the Charter, with six of the eleven jurists it assembled in June 1987 subsequently elected to the Commission, and with all but two of the ICJ's recommendations being adopted as rules of procedure.[69]

The most important recent ICJ contribution to human rights in Africa has come through encouraging NGOs' awareness of each other and of the Commission. The process started in October 1991, with the first three-day, pre-session workshops for African and international human rights NGOs. (The idea, as should be expected, had a longer history. Wolfgang Benedek, an international law professor from Austria, and Adama Dieng recommended in 1987 that such sessions be held.) Such efforts came naturally to the ICJ. For more than 30 of its 40 years, it had worked toward an effective, Africa-wide body focused on human rights. For the ICJ, bringing together grassroots organizations and increasing the flow of communications to the African Commission were tasks happily undertaken. Thanks to financial assistance from Canada, Germany, and Sweden, the workshops could be held; support from the African

Commission itself (which officially co-sponsors the events) and the African Centre for Democracy and Human Rights Studies in Banjul have spread some of the administrative burden. An average of 50 participants from human rights NGOs have attended each workshop. They have received basic briefings on the African Commission's work, with some Commissioners happy to provide information. Each ICJ workshop has focused on particular themes: women's rights; the right to development; fair trial; a protocol establishing an African Court of Human Rights. Each has concluded with a set of resolutions exhorting the African Commission or the parent OAU to take specific steps, such as increasing funding, improving Commission procedures, preparing guidelines, or clarifying the Charter and Rules of Procedure.

The ICJ-run workshops aim at facilitating independent activity by NGOs. Each attending NGO is encouraged to reach out directly to the African Commission. Professor Benedek prepared a booklet in both French and English entitled "How to Address a Communication to the African Commission," which explains the nuts and bolts of the ACHPR's procedure on communications. The ICJ would like to see NGOs consulted in the preparation of country's reports, active in documenting human rights issues independently, and willing to pressure the African Commission for action. In other words, the workshops ideally would both empower African human rights NGOs and strengthen the African Commission. All would gain by greater knowledge and cooperation, so it appears. The ICJ thus took on an undisputed (though not tension-free) role as the leading international NGO focused on networking among African human rights NGOs. Its steps to build awareness of the Commission and to facilitate links among NGOs have paid off. When the resolutions of the workshops are published (the Danish human rights center has allocated funds), their importance will become even more apparent.

Should we conclude, in light of such progress, that the African Commission's channels for both formal state reports and NGO communications may yet effectively protect human rights in Africa?

The depth, detail, and objectivity of a country's report speak volumes about its commitment to human rights. Non-performance by many African governments in reporting parallels their abuses against citizens. Some of the worse human rights offenders have been the least likely to provide information, despite their ratification of treaties requiring regular reports. A few examples should suffice. Zaire submitted its initial report under the International Covenant on Civil and Political Rights nine years late, despite ten reminders and numerous direct contacts with government officials.[70] Although almost all African countries have ratified the International Convention on the Elimination of All Forms of Racial Discrimination, only a handful have taken the treaty's obligations seriously. Swaziland had, for example, received 24 reminders for its report, originally due in 1976, Sierra Leone 23, Liberia 20.[71]

Reporting serves many functions for ratifying countries and treaty bodies. The Committee on Economic, Social and Cultural Rights, in its first General Comment, identified seven major objectives of reporting: 1) ensure comprehensive initial review of national legislation, administrative rules and procedures and practices; 2) ensure ratifying states monitor the actual situation on a regular basis; 3) provide a basis for elaborating clearly stated, carefully targeted policies; 4) facilitate public scrutiny of government policies and encourage involvement of sectors of society; 5) provide a basis for evaluating progress made toward meeting Covenant obligations; 6) enable ratifying states to develop better understanding of problems and shortcomings in their efforts; and, 7) facilitate exchange of information among states and develop better understanding of common problems.[72] Similar advantages exist for NGOs. A reporting process, *if properly done*, facilitates dialogues not only between the international monitoring body and the government, but also between human rights NGOs and the ratifying state.

"Properly done," of course, can be said far more easily than it can be practiced. Tension inevitably exists between NGOs and governments. The checkered histories recounted throughout this book underscore the point. By their very nature,[73] most non-governmental organizations focus on official abuses. They publicize shortcomings of those in power. Distrust, even outright hostility, mark relations between governments and human rights NGOs. Rapid establishment of cooperation should not be expected. As a minimum, however, NGOs should be involved in reviewing official reports when they are sent to international human rights monitoring bodies. NGOs should have an opportunity to present rejoinders or supplements to these bodies. Ideally, they should also take part in gathering information and evaluating the effectiveness of government policies.

Namibia has manifested the most open policy. The government has relied heavily on NGOs, international agencies, and consultants in drafting reports due under international human rights treaties, and in developing strategies for national action. Two examples should suffice. Preparation of the first report to CEDAW (Committee on the Elimination of Discrimination Against Women) was a top priority, for which both external and Namibian government funding has been obtained.[74] The action program for children, published in December 1991, drew heavily on NGO expertise.[75] Namibia's first report due under the Convention on the Rights of the Child was prepared by Diane Hubbard, an independent consultant, with financial assistance from UNICEF.[76] The Department of Women Affairs (housed in the Office of the President) worked with a UNICEF consultant on a "national communication strategy in support of the UN Convention on elimination of all forms of discrimination against women." Such cooperation — essential given the limits of funding and expertise — exists, I believe, largely because of a fortunate constellation of factors. The Namibian government takes pride in its human rights record. Relatively generous external funding has been provided for workshops and consultants. Cooperation and trust between SWAPO and several human rights groups dates to the liberation struggle, as discussed in the following chapter on legal aid.

The reporting obligation, in other words, can bring together governments and NGOs. The story is quite different with respect to communications, however, since they usually point to official abuses of power. Any cooperation shown in reports, born of necessity or of policy, will not be found in communications. When NGOs inform the African Commission (or, for that matter, any international human rights body) of breaches of treaty obligations, the challenge to governmental authority is clear. Promotion of human rights can be facilitated by government-NGO links; protection of human rights entails tensions. The African Commission's high degree of confidentiality is an understandable response, although excessive in the view of close observers, including myself.[77]

Without question, the functioning, expertise, and recognition of the African Commission has been enhanced by the ICJ workshops. The presence of NGOs has stiffened the resolve of Commissioners to probe more deeply into states' reports. NGO-provided information has improved the reporting system in furnishing additional details. The ICJ booklet on how to address communications to the African Commission is certain to increase their volume. African human rights NGOs have gained greater knowledge of others' needs, objectives, and commonalities. Fledgling groups have thus been drawn into an Africa-wide network. The desire of the ICJ to broaden its impact has interacted with the needs of the African Commission and African human rights NGOs to themselves engage in constructive dialogue. In the process, both reporting and communications as means of human rights enforcement have been strengthened. Much remains to be done, without question. The groundwork for substantial expansion had come into existence by early 1994, however.

Notes

1. Philip Alston, "The Purposes of Reporting," in *Manual on Human Rights Reporting* (Geneva: United Nations Centre for Human Rights, 1991), pp. 13–14.
2. For fascinating commentaries on UN prose, see Iain Guest, *Behind the Disap-*

pearances: Argentina's Dirty War Against Human Rights and the United Nations (Philadelphia: University of Pennsylvania Press, 1990). The following paragraph is illustrative of his striking insights:

Critics of the United Nations often underestimate the importance of reports. In the U.N., the written word has less immediate impact than a verbal protest, but carries more weight. Unlike one of Gabriel Martínez's searing insults [Martínez was the representative in Geneva of the Argentinian military junta], the pain starts as a dull ache. It then grows as the report is translated into several official languages; presented before the Human Rights Commission, ECOSOC, and the General Assembly; used by journalists who are too lazy to attend meetings; sent to 157 different governments; lodged in filing cabinets; and scanned by diligent researchers at the International Commission of Jurists and Amnesty International. Here is something solid and tangible that can be used, reused, and thumbed through hundreds of times. It is, potentially, a formidable weapon. (p. 231)

3. David P. Forsythe, *The Internationalization of Human Rights* (Lexington, MA: Lexington Books, 1991), pp. 56–57.

4. It could be argued that investigation of complaints submitted by individuals should constitute the bulk of the African Commission's work. Indeed, a substantial portion of its twice yearly sessions are devoted to private meetings focused on these "communications," in the official language of the African Charter, states' responses to them, and possible Commission action. These processes are veiled from the public eye. I have accordingly opted to concentrate on public aspects of the Commission's work, and in particular on its responses to states' reports. That these reports are often lacking in detail and potentially misleading in direction are discussed both in this chapter and in Chapter 7, which focuses on NGOs' contributions in documenting human rights problems.

5. Alston, *The United Nations and Human Rights: A Critical Evaluation* (Oxford: Clarendon Press, 1992), p. 491.

6. Ibid.

7. Ibid.

8. Borko D. Stosic, *Les organisations non-gouvernementales et les Nations Unies* (Geneva: Librarie Droz, 1964), pp. 30–31.

9. "Without any particular plan to do so, the [Permanent Mandates] commission gradually came to function as a kind of center for the organization and transmission of information about colonial administration. The information came from the mandatory powers and from the Mandates section of the Secretariat, but it also came from the many private groups that were interested in education, mission work, transportation, arms limitation, disease control, suppression of the slave trade, and the like." Dorothy V. Jones, "The League of Nations Experiment in International Protection," *Ethics and International Affairs* 8 (1994), 82–83.

10. Even the possibility of independence was foreseen in the mid-1920s. For example, at the sixth session of the Permanent Mandates Commission, Lugard commented that Southwest Africa could not be incorporated into South Africa unless the territory gained self-government and the League of Nations consented to surrender of the mandate. Permanent Mandates Commission, *Minutes* (Geneva: League of Nations, 1925; document C.386.M.132.1925.VI), p. 59.

11. Article 73 of the United Nations Charter calls on all colonizing powers

a. to ensure, with due respect for the culture of the peoples concerned, their political, economic, social and educational advancement, their just treatment, and their protection against abuses;

b. to develop self-government, to take due account of the political aspirations of the peoples, and to assist them in the progressive development of their free political institutions, according to the particular circumstances of each territory and its peoples and their varying stages of advancement; . . .

e. to transmit regularly to the Secretary-General for information purposes . . . statistical and other information of a technical nature relating to economic, social, and educational conditions in the territories for which they are respectively responsible . . .

12. Virginia A. Leary, "Lessons from the Experience of the International Labour Organisation," in Alston, ed., *The United Nations and Human Rights,* p. 596.

13. Of the four former German colonies, Togo and Kamerun were divided, the British-ruled sections being incorporated respectively into the Gold Coast and Nigeria, the French-ruled parts (which were larger) being governed as distinct entities in loose association respectively with French West Africa and French Equatorial Africa; Ruanda-Urundi was split from Tanganyika and placed under Belgian rule; the mandate agreement for Southwest Africa permitted the Union of South Africa to govern it as an "integral part" of its territory.

14. For detailed analysis about Cameroon and Togo, see Claude E. Welch, Jr., *Dream of Unity: Pan-Africanism and Political Unification in West Africa* (Ithaca, NY: Cornell University Press, 1966), esp. pp. 37–249.

15. CHR, *Report of the Sixth Session,* UN Document E/1681 (1950), paragraph 47, cited in Howard Tolley, Jr. *The U.N. Commission on Human Rights* (Boulder, CO: Westview, 1987), p. 36.

16. Tolley, *The U.N. Commission on Human Rights,* p. 87.

17. For historical details, see, inter alia, Sandra Colliver, "International Reporting Procedures," in Hurst Hannum, ed., *Guide to International Human Rights Practice* (Philadelphia: University of Pennsylvania Press, 1992, 2nd edition), pp. 173–91, and David P. Forsythe, *Human Rights and World Politics* (Lincoln: University of Nebraska Press, 1989, 2nd edition revised), pp. 47–50.

18. Alston, *The United Nations and Human Rights;* Hannum, *Guide to International Human Rights Practice;* United Nations Centre for Human Rights and UNITAR, *Manual on Human Rights Reporting* (New York: United Nations, 1991).

19. Dominic W. McGoldrick, *The Human Rights Committee: Its Role in the Development of the International Covenant on Civil and Political Rights* (Oxford: Clarendon Press, 1991).

20. Reasons for the reluctance of Asian governments to establish a regional treaty body are explored in Virginia Leary, "The Asian Region and the International Human Rights Movement," in Claude E. Welch, Jr. and Virginia Leary, eds., *Asian Perspectives on Human Rights* (Boulder, CO: Westview, 1990), pp. 13–27.

21. Participants in the ICJ workshop prior to the eleventh session prepared a detailed set of suggestions for strengthening the protections of Article 7, and a resolution on fair trial. To my knowledge, however, no major steps had been taken by the time of writing to amend the Charter, which in any event would be a complex, cumbersome process. As Benedek points out (personal communication, 18 January 1994), the Commission has elaborated its interpretation of Article 7, although the strengthening is not to the full satisfaction of NGOs.

22. *Ordre publique,* the term used in French versions of the African Charter and in other international human treaties, has quite different connotations than the English-language term "law and order," which is marked with political overtones. Perhaps closer to the intention of drafters is Article 18, 3 of the ICCPR, which, in speaking of freedom of thought, conscience and religion, indicates this "may be subject only to such limitations as are prescribed by law and are necessary to protect public safety, order, health, or morals or the fundamental rights and freedoms of others." I am indebted to Wolfgang Benedek for this point.

23. Richard Gittleman, "The Banjul Charter on Human and Peoples' Rights: A Legal Analysis," in Claude E. Welch, Jr. and Ronald I. Meltzer, eds., *Human Rights and Development in Africa* (Albany: State University of New York Press, 1984), p. 158.

24. Ibid., p. 159.

25. As Robertson observed, "the States concerned wished to put forward a distinctive conception of human rights in which civil and political rights were seen to be counter-balanced by duties of social solidarity, just as they are complemented by economic and social rights and supplemented by peoples' rights." A. H. Robertson and J. G. Merrills, *Human Rights in the World* (Manchester: Manchester University Press, 1989), p. 216. Duties in the African Charter are being examined by Julia Harrington of Harvard Law School.

26. Relative to other major international human rights documents, the African Charter had a brief drafting history (less than 30 days). It aroused no discussion at the meeting of the Organization of African Unity, being adopted at midnight of the final day, without formal recorded vote. Fatsah Ouguergouz, *La Charte Africaine des Droits de l'Homme et des Peuples: Historique, portée juridique et contribution à la protection des droits de l'homme en Afrique* (Paris: Presses Universitaires de France for the Institut Universitaire de Hautes Etudes Internationales, 1993), p. 64. Also see B. G. Ramcharan, "The Travaux Préparatoires of the African Commission on Human Rights," *Human Rights Law Journal* 13, 7–8 (1992), 307–14.

27. Clement Nwankwo, "The OAU and Human Rights," *Journal of Democracy* 4 (1992), 50–51. Indeed, non-intervention in domestic matters remains a cardinal principle of the OAU. Its collective silence in the face of ethnic massacres in Burundi in 1972, or the excesses of the Idi Amin regime in Uganda later in the decade, were noted by scholars at the time. But it should be noted that the United Nations itself was similarly quiet. See, for example, Leo Kuper, *Genocide: Its Political Use in the Twentieth Century* (New Haven, CT: Yale University Press, 1981), pp. 161–85, or Claude E. Welch, Jr., "The OAU and International Recognition: Lessons from Uganda," in Yassin El-Ayouty, ed., *The Organization of African Unity After Ten Years* (New York: Praeger, 1975), pp. 103–17.

28. Of course, it is general practice for international human rights treaties that *ratifying* countries — States Parties — elect members of the relevant committee of experts. Until the great majority of OAU members had ratified the African Charter, selection of Commissioners by the Assembly may have seemed anomalous; with the nearly-universal ratification reached by 1990, this concern disappeared.

29. There should be no surprise here, as the same situation obtains for the European and American Commissions. Enforcement depends on states. But a significant difference exists in terms of *prior* agreement by States Parties. Under the European Convention, reports on alleged violations and petitions prepared by the Commission must be considered by the Committee of Ministers, which decides, by a two-thirds majority, whether there has been a violation. Following this, "the High Contracting Party must take the measures required by the deci-

sion of the Committee of Ministers . . . The High Contracting Parties undertake to regard as binding any decision which the Committee of Ministers may take . . ." (European Convention, Art. 32,2,4). No such mandatory language appears in the African Charter.

30. U.O. Umozurike, "The Protection of Human Rights under the Banjul (African) Charter on Human and Peoples' Rights," *African Journal of International Law* 1 (1988), 83.

31. The original members included lawyers from The Gambia, Libya, and Zambia, a former foreign minister and assistant to the President of Mali, an Egyptian ambassador, the Minister of the Interior of Congo, a former foreign minister of Uganda, judges from Tanzania, Botswana, and Senegal, and a history professor from Gabon. All were male. As of October 1993, five of the "founding fathers" remained in service. The Commission included:

Name	Nationality	Yr elected	Profession
Atau-Koffi Amega	Togolese	1993	ex-judge
Ibrahim Badawi El-Sheikh (chair, 1991–93)	Egyptian	1987	diplomat
Alioune Blondin Bèye	Malian	1987	UN diplomat
Emmanuel Victor Oware Dankwa	Ghanaian	1993	professor
Vera Valentina de Mello Duarte-Martins	Cape Verdean	1993	judge
Sourahata Baboucar Semega Janneh	Gambian	1987	lawyer
Robert Habesh Kisanga	Tanzanian	1987	judge
Youssoupha N'Diaye	Senegalese	1987	government lawyer
Isaac Nguéma (chair, 1987–89, 1993–)	Gabonese	1987	professor
Mohammed Hatem Ben Salem	Tunisian	1992	lawyer
U. Oji Umozurike (chair, 1989–91)	Nigerian	1989	professor

An informal principle of geographical distribution established when the Commission was founded has been honored in the breach rather than the observance. A majority of its members currently hail from West Africa, only one each from eastern and central Africa, none from southern Africa. Mrs. Duarte-Martins is the first and only woman.

32. According to Donald Ekong (Secretary General of Association of African Universities), 10 of Africa's 51 states have no university whatsoever; 27 have one; seven states have two; only seven have more than two. *West Africa* (13–19 December 1993), 2248.

33. The "Programme of Action" adopted in February 1988 included three types of activities: research and information; quasi-legislative; cooperation. It appears in *Human Rights Law Journal* 9 (1988), 352, and in Claude E. Welch, Jr., "The African Commission on Human and Peoples' Rights: A Five-Year Report and Assessment," *Human Rights Quarterly* 14 (1992), 50–51.

34. The problem is an endemic one. Frankly, many states lack the commitment, resources, and expertise to prepare the timely, detailed reports treaty bodies wish to receive. Late, unduly brief reports have characterized all the UN human rights treaty bodies. In its first two general comments, for example, the Human Rights Committee (responsible for monitoring reports submitted under the Interna-

tional Covenant on Civil and Political Rights) bemoaned the delays encountered and the fact, despite guidelines, that many remained "so brief and general that they do not satisfy the reporting obligations" (General Comment 2, 1981; reproduced in "Compilation of General Comments and General Recommendations Adopted by Human Rights Treaty Bodies," UN Doc. HRI/GEN/1, 4 September 1992, 2). A decade earlier, CERD (the Committee on the Elimination of Racial Discrimination) had also pointed to deficiencies in reports (see especially General Recommendations I, II, IV, V and VI; ibid., 55–58).

35. For commentary, see Felice D. Gaer, "First Fruits: Reporting by States under the African Charter of Human and Peoples' Rights," *Netherlands Quarterly of Human Rights* 10 (1992), 29–42. Her observations were based largely on the ninth and tenth sessions of the Commission, which can be kindly described as learning experiences. Far more care now goes into the Commissioners' questioning, a highly positive development for reporting.

36. The Government of Nigeria appears to have been in near-complete disarray in preparing and presenting its report. Much the same could be said of the Commission's secretariat itself. The Nigerian representative who appeared in the Addis meeting had not been informed of the proper dates of the session; most of the report was written in Banjul, partly with the help of NGOs, which also prepared a counterreport, sharply critical of the government's annulment of the June 1993 elections. Additional details appear in Chapter 8.

37. Gaer, "First Fruits."

38. In the dry words of Partsch, "The interpretation of this provision [that CERD make recommendations "based on the examination of the reports and information received from the States Parties"] has caused significant Committee debate. Some members have sought to construe the article narrowly and have argued that CERD could make suggestions to a State Party *solely* on the basis of information submitted by that State. . . . Eventually, the Committee decided that Article 9(2) permits it to consider any official documents of the reporting State. . . . The Committee will not examine information obtained from the mass media or from non-governmental organizations." Karl Joseph Partsch, "The Committee on the Elimination of Racial Discrimination," in Alston, ed., *The United Nations and Human Rights*, pp. 351–52. Not until late 1991 did CERD start to utilize NGO material. Interestingly, the senior African member of the Committee, George Lamptey (Ghana), has been a vocal opponent of NGO input.

39. Claude E. Welch, Jr., "Breaking New Ground," *West Africa* (9–15 November 1992), 1920.

40. For example, the Danish Center for Human Rights arranged for tape recording and transcribing (although not necessarily releasing to the public) those parts of the 13th and 14th sessions devoted to states' reports.

41. The famous—or infamous—Annex XI to this report gave detailed information about communications submitted to the Commission, including names. Whether the result of clerical error or not, this one-time glimpse into the inner workings of the private process intrigued observers of the Commission's work.

42. There is an exception: ". . . unless it is obvious that this procedure is unduly prolonged." Given delays in African courts, such a clause allows for a potentially more flexible process than under the European Convention or the Optional Protocol of the ICCPR.

43. "Amnesty International's observations on possible reform of the African Charter on Human and Peoples' Rights" (London: Amnesty International, June 1993; IOR 63/03/93). The report aptly concludes,

None of these proposed changes in the African Charter will effectively promote and protect human rights in Africa unless the states parties demonstrate the political will to implement the guarantees in this treaty in national law and practice, to submit timely and comprehensive periodic reports, to cooperate with the African Commission in its examinations of communications under Article 55 and to provide the African Commission with the financial and other resources it needs. (Ibid., p. 5)

44. To take one example, Commissioners decided at the twelfth session to amend the rules, so that the substance of communications would be sent promptly to the state concerned for comment; if no reply were received within 90 days, the Commission would then decide whether the communication was admissible on the basis of all information available. The state would then have two months to submit information on the merits of the case. Were there no response, the Commission would then decide what steps to take. The Commissioners also decided that consideration of states' reports should not be indefinitely deferred if official delegations did not arrive. However, this decision was not utilized at the fifteenth session, to which both Benin and Cape Verde failed to send spokespersons, and the delegation from Mozambique was incomplete.

45. Annex XI, "Confidential Information on Communications other than those of Member States," attached to "Sixth Annual Activity Report of the African Commission on Human and Peoples' Rights for 1992–1993," Organization of African Unity document AHG/191 (XXIX), 28–30 June 1993. The annex states that 41 communications were dealt with, seemingly a typographical error.

46. Gerd Oberleitner and Claude E. Welch, Jr., "15th Session of the African Commission on Human and Peoples' Rights," *Netherlands Quarterly of Human Rights* 12, 3 (1994), 333.

47. Astrid Danielsen and Gerd Oberleitner, "16th Session of the African Commission on Human and Peoples' Rights," *Netherlands Quarterly of Human Rights*, in press.

48. For these reasons, OAU Secretary-General Salim Salim proposed, and the OAU Council approved, creation of the "African Mechanism Apparatus for Preventing, Managing and Resolving African Crises." It is to be funded with five percent of the OAU's budget, provided this is not less than $1 million, through a special OAU Peace Fund. *West Africa* (29 November–5 December 1993), 2171.

49. I. William Zartman, *Ripe for Resolution? Conflict and Intervention in Africa* (New York: Oxford University Press, 1989, updated edition).

50. See, as examples, the Department of State *Country Reports*, Amnesty International annual reports, "Malawi: Ignoring Calls for Change" (New York: Lawyers Committee for Human Rights, 1992), or "Where Silence Rules" (New York: Africa Watch, 1990).

51. Lest I be accused of digging into secret matters, I learned of the Commission's budget from a report written by Commissioner Nguéma for the World Conference on Human Rights and circulated at Vienna. Annual allocations from the OAU were as follows: 1988–89, $150,000; 1989–90, $742,163; 1990–91, $520,736; 1991–92, $467,980; 1992–93, $501,881. Isaac Nguéma, "Contribution relative à la Commission africaine des droits de l'homme et des peuples," UN Doc. A/CONF.157/PC/62/Add.2, p. 3.

52. Leary, "Lessons from the Experience of the ILO."

53. Wolfgang Benedek, personal communication.

54. Howard B. Tolley, Jr., *Global Advocates for Human Rights: The International Commission of Jurists* (Philadelphia: University of Pennsylvania Press, 1994).

55. International Commission of Jurists, *African Conference on the Rule of Law: A Report on the Proceedings* (Geneva: ICJ, 1961).

56. In reality, reference to the proposed Convention and Court occurred in an unplanned fashion. No hint of either was made in the carefully prepared prospectus for discussion, nor in the extensive papers presented by African jurists to the three committees into which participants at the meeting were divided. The afternoon of January 5, as the committees were discussing draft final reports and resolutions, François Amorin of Togo offhandedly suggested (in the committee devoted to human rights and government security, the legislature executive and judiciary) that the final declaration take note of an African Convention on Human Rights, to be approved by the various governments. He presented a resolution, in French, the following morning, which was accepted in principle; however, it came too late to be included in the report of Committee I, and appears only in the final resolution completed after the meetings concluded. For details, see *African Conference on the Rule of Law*, 110–13. The relevant paragraph in the "Law of Lagos" reads

4. That in order to give full effect to the Universal Declaration of Human Rights of 1948, this Conference invites the African Governments to study the possibility of adopting an African Convention of Human Rights in such a manner that the Conclusions of this Conference will be safeguarded by the creation of a court of appropriate jurisdiction and that recourse thereto be made available for all persons under the jurisdiction of the signatory States.

Pursuing this resolution did not become a priority agenda for the ICJ until Kéba Mbaye's presidency, 1977–85. During the 1970s and 1980s, 11 Africans were elected to the Commission: Godfrey L. Binaisa of Uganda (1971), Keba Mbaye of Senegal (1972), Boutros Boutros-Ghali of Egypt (1973), Alphonse Boni of Côte d'Ivoire and Kwamena Bentsi-Enchill of Ghana (1974), Taslim O. Elias of Nigeria (1976), François-Xavier Mbouyom of Cameroon (1979), Amos Wako of Kenya and Rahsoomer Lallah of Mauritius (1981), Juma Reginal Sawaya Mawalla of Tanzania (1982), and Kofi Kumado of Ghana (1988). Tolley, *Global Advocates for Human Rights*, table, pp. 158–60.

57. For a biography of Dieng, see "The Passionate Advocate," *West Africa* (10–16 May 1993), 769, and Tolley, *Global Advocates for Human Rights*, pp. 180–84. Dieng's major contact with Mbaye came in the late 1970s, when Mbaye served as President of the Supreme Court of Senegal, with Dieng as Registrar and personal assistant. The two men cooperated in Mbaye's draft of the African Charter. Dieng completed several research projects on racism as a UNESCO consultant, served as a legal columnist in Dakar, earned a diploma at the Hague Academy of International Law, and taught journalists at the Institut Internationale des Droits de l'Homme in Strasbourg. He became legal officer for Africa at the ICJ in 1982, rising to executive secretary in October 1989 and secretary-general a year later.

58. Born in Dakar in 1948, Sané came from a family of Casamance origin; his father cut his political teeth as a trade union organizer; his uncle (whom Pierre regarded as his godfather) became a militant in the opposition political party PRA-Senegal; his mother, one of the first female head teachers in Senegal, became involved in the women's movement. Sané's pre-Amnesty work included accountancy, development, and advanced degrees from the London School of Economics and Carleton University (Ottawa). For details, see "Accounting for Human Rights," *West Africa* (20–26 December 1993), 2289.

59. Paris: Pedone, 1992.

60. For details of the drafting history, see Edward Kannyo, "The Banjul Charter on Human and Peoples' Rights: Genesis and Political Background," in Claude E. Welch, Jr. and Ronald I. Meltzer, eds., *Human Rights and Development in Africa* pp. 128–51; Kéba Mbaye, *Les Droits de l'Homme en Afrique* (Paris: Pedone, 1992); Philip Kunig, Wolfgang Benedek, and Costa Ricky Mahalu, *Regional Protection of Human Rights by International Law: The Emerging African System* (Baden-Baden: Nomos, 1985); and Fatsah Ouguergouz, *La Charte africaine des droits de l'homme et des peuples: Une approche juridique de droits de l'homme entre tradition et modernité*, pp. 46–64.

61. For details, see Kannyo, "The Banjul Charter on Human and Peoples' Rights," pp. 138–39 and Mbaye, *Droits de l'Homme*, p. 145.

62. International Commission of Jurists, *ICJ Report on Activities 1986–1988* (Geneva: ICJ, 1989), p. 3.

63. For details, see "Le Développement et les Droits de l'Homme: Rapport d'un colloque africain francophone à Dakar," special issue of the *Revue Sénégalaise de Droit*, 1979.

64. As Mbaye wrote, "This committee made several trips to French-speaking countries carefully chosen on the basis of the presumed interest of their presidents for human rights and their influence within the OAU. Its members explained to the heads of state and political authorities of these countries that it was necessary and urgent that Africa be equipped with a commission on human rights . . . their efforts were not in vain." Mbaye, *Droits de l'Homme*, p. 149 (author's translation). The main visitor was, of course, Adama Dieng.

65. Mbaye, *Droits de l'Homme*, p. 162.

66. Ibid., p. 163.

67. Amnesty International, "Amnesty International's observations on possible reform," 5. To be specific, President Jawara of The Gambia pressed at midnight of the last day for final adoption of the African Charter, which was accepted without debate or even a formal vote. Cited in Ouguergouz, *La Charte africaine*, p. 64.

68. Calculated from Annex I, AHG/191 (XXIX).

69. *ICJ Report of Activities 1986–1988*, p. 4.

70. Torkel Opsahl, "The Human Rights Committee," in Alston, ed., *The United Nations and Human Rights*, p. 398.

71. Draft report of the Committee on the Elimination of Racial Discrimination to the General Assembly at its Forty-Eight Session, CERD/C/43/CRP.1/Add.2, p. 4. No fewer than 328 reports from 109 States Parties had not been received by the opening of its August 1993 meeting.

72. Summarized in Alston, "The Committee on Economic, Social and Cultural Rights," p. 492.

73. This presumes independence. GONGOs ("governmental NGOs") and QUANGOs ("quasi NGOs") cannot be overlooked. Often created or encouraged by governments to soften criticism, such bodies complicate the judgment of NGO effectiveness.

74. UNIFEM allocated 60,000 Namibian dollars for a literature review to establish a baseline, and to prepare the first report to CEDAW; UNIFEM also pledged 45,000 dollars for research on discriminatory laws. On a more cautious note, the program as a whole will require significant external support, still being lined up. Contributions from UNIFEM and UNICEF of 150,000 dollars, and Namibian government pledges of 182,900 dollars, cover only a fraction of the proposed 668,300 dollar program. Government of Namibia, Department of Women Affairs, "National Communication Strategy in Support of the UN Convention on Elimi-

nation of All Forms of Discrimination Against Women 1993–1995" (Windhoek & Capital Press, 1993), pp. 35–37.

75. Republic of Namibia, *National Programme of Action for the Children of Namibia* (Windhoek: Capital Press, 1991).

76. "A Commitment to Our Children: Namibia's Country Report Under the United Nations Convention on the Rights of the Child" (Windhoek & Capital Press, 1992). Ms. Hubbard, a Harvard Law School graduate, has worked extensively on human rights matters, through the Legal Assistance Centre directed by her husband, Andrew Corbett (see following chapter for details about the LAC).

77. The ICJ suggested one avenue at the workshop preceding the thirteenth session (April 1993). Whenever an NGO filed a petition or communication with the African Commission, it would send a copy to the Central Register of Complaints, maintained by the ICJ in Geneva. To the surprise and disappointment of ICJ officers, no complaints generated by an African human rights NGO had been received by January 1994.

Chapter 6
Building the Rule of Law:
Legal Aid and Enforcement in
Namibia and Nigeria

1. All persons shall be equal before the courts and tribunals. In the determination of any criminal charge against him, or of his rights and obligations in a suit at law, everyone shall be entitled to a fair and public hearing by a competent, independent and impartial tribunal established by law. . . .
3. In the determination of any criminal charge against him, everyone shall be entitled to the following minimum guarantees, in full equality: . . .
(d) . . . to have legal assistance assigned to him, in any case where the interests of justice so require, and without payment by him in any such case if he does not have sufficient means to pay for it.
— International Covenant on Civil and Political Rights, Article 14

Every individual shall have the right to have his cause heard. This comprises . . . (c) the right to defence, including the right to be defended by counsel of his choice.
— African Charter on Human and Peoples' Rights, Article 7, 1

Skeptics about the effectiveness of international human rights treaties usually focus on issues of enforcement. Even though states ratify high-sounding treaties, they often lack the ability, resources and above all, the political will to enforce their provisions. The limited success of the African Commission in getting compliance provides an immediate example. Without remedy, critics argue, human rights in reality do not meaningfully exist.

Such positivist concerns remain today a fundamental issue for human rights in Africa, and indeed throughout the world. If adequate redress cannot be provided, so the argument runs, isn't the entire superstructure of law undermined? Do countries that ratify treaties calling for goals well beyond what the popular culture supports, or what the economic system can provide, contradict their desired goal? Shouldn't there be a reasonable link between proclaimed willingness to implement, and ability to do so? The "rule of law," to use a noble phrase, may rest upon what the system can realistically deliver, not upon what it may promise.

Effective enforcement thus depends upon prior establishment of a framework of laws, a system of civil and criminal justice, and an overarching constitutional framework in terms of written documents. I would argue that enforcement rests as well on a facilitating democratic human rights culture, *based on the principle of equal application of non-discriminatory laws.* Enforcement of the laws occurs in authoritarian states, but 1) the laws themselves may be blatantly discriminatory, 2) application may be arbitrary and capricious, 3) no consistent philosophy of human rights may guide the making of law, and 4) limits on the power of the people to bring about changes in laws may exist.

What about settings in which a legal framework, judicial system, and other appurtenances exist — yet the law enforced is discriminatory? What if the law itself makes distinctions that fly in the face of basic human rights principles? What if significant distinctions among individuals based on their race, gender, religion, or social status are written into the civil and criminal codes? Do human rights exist in such settings? Certainly not in the sense of equal protection for all.

Apartheid used a legal framework to enforce discrimination based on race. South Africa's panoply of racially based legislation, given mighty impetus by the 1948 electoral victory of the National Party, used legal formulas in a thoroughly discriminatory way. Buttresssed by an ideology of racial superiority, apartheid principles determined the application of the laws throughout the republic. The same was true for Namibia, administered as an integral part of South Africa from 1915 until shortly before its independence.

The enforcement of human rights in Namibia, with which this chapter begins, has followed a curious, twisting path. In order to use law as an instrument to *defend* human rights, it was first necessary to transform the fundamental foundations of the law that existed. Nothing short of a legal and political revolution was required.

One can look at Namibia's revolution macroscopically, as in the liberation of the entire country from South African rule and apartheid legislation. One can also look at revolution through a more detailed microscope, concentrating on individuals and groups that struggled for change. Only when they had succeeded in shifting the basic principles of law to enforcement based on *equality among individuals,* rather than enforcement dependent on *separation among groups,* could human rights take constitutional form in Namibia. Not until a handful of lawyers decided to challenge apartheid through the courts and in the political arena by forming the Legal Assistance Centre of Namibia (LAC) did indigent victims of government actions have recourse to legal solutions. By working both to change the law and to work within its constraints, the LAC helped revolutionize the enforcement of human rights. By all accounts, it performed outstanding service to Namibia in its final years of South African rule, and in the era of independence. The LAC continues to be regarded as the most important human rights NGO in Namibia.

What it teaches about creating the rule of law provides lessons for the entire African continent.

In the following section, the macroview is given. We will start with a necessary but complex, compressed history of Namibia as an object of international diplomacy (expanding what was presented in Chapter 1), and then examine the coercion used by South Africa to maintain its power and by SWAPO to assert its own. In the following section, we will shift to the microview, and concentrate on the Legal Assistance Centre before and after Namibia's independence.

Toward Namibian Independence: Diplomatic and Military Maneuvers

Battles to transform Namibia were staged on several fronts. Within the United Nations, pressure had been exerted on South Africa from the early 1950s to treat the one-time mandated territory as separate, and to move it speedily toward independence. (Recall the discussion in Chapter 1 about the establishment of the League of Nations and the fate of former German and Ottoman territories.) South Africa had claimed that the demise of the League ended its obligations, meaning that "South West Africa" was unquestionably an integral part of its territory, hence (under the doctrine of domestic sovereignty) immune to the United Nations' claims. Critics argued that international responsibility continued despite the transition from League to UN, that apartheid was repugnant to the UN's basic principles, and that accordingly domestic sovereignty could not be invoked to defend racially discriminatory laws.

The long, frustrating process of establishing international accountability in the face of South African intransigence lasted decades. It involved 1) debates in the UN General Assembly and its Fourth (Trusteeship) Committee, in which petitioners appeared in growing numbers, 2) opinions from the International Court of Justice, and 3) resolutions from the Security Council. Let us compress a great deal of history and thousands of hours of debate into a few paragraphs.

Following the collapse of the League of Nations and the creation of the United Nations, the government of South Africa moved vigorously to end international supervision and to continue to govern "Southwest" as the country's fifth province. The newly installed National Party government amended the constitution in 1949, removing all references to the mandate and allowing whites direct representation in the South African parliament. On the request of the General Assembly, the International Court of Justice issued its first advisory ruling in 1950, asserting (somewhat contradictorily) that the mandate remained in force despite the extinction of the League and the Permanent Mandates Commission, that

South Africa had no obligation to conclude a trusteeship agreement with the UN, but that South Africa had no right unilaterally to change the mandated territory's status. In 1953, the General Assembly resolved to supervise the mandate, despite lack of South African cooperation, by means of a special committee; oral petitioners started to appear before the committee, an action blessed in another International Court advisory opinion. A Good Offices Committee created in 1956 failed to reach agreement on negotiations.

Among the turning points of the complex history, the July 1966 ruling by the International Court of Justice stands out prominently. Liberia and Ethiopia (both members of the former League of Nations) decided in 1960 to challenge South Africa's rule, using the binding powers of the International Court. In a stunning, unexpected decision six years after the suit was originally filed, the Court dismissed the suit by a single vote without ruling on its merits. This galvanized the General Assembly into action. By resolution 2145, it revoked the mandate; a year later, it established the United Nations Council for Southwest Africa, to administer the territory. (These were words without immediate practical impact. Since South Africa held de facto control, the Council focused its activities in New York and in Lusaka, Zambia, where the UN Institute on Namibia was located.) The Security Council concurred and, resorting once again to the International Court, asked for an advisory opinion on the legal consequences of South Africa's continued presence. On June 21, 1970, in a landmark decision, the Court declared this presence illegal. A powerful opinion by Judge Tanaka, frequently cited in casebooks, showed how apartheid violated customary international law.

All the legal maneuverings in The Hague and New York had little direct impact on conditions within Namibia, however. Apartheid legislation was applied throughout the area, resulting, for example, in the displacement of thousands of people from their homes and resettlement in squalid townships. The South African government sought a so-called internal solution, though it took care never to close the door completely on working with the United Nations. (For example, Secretary General Kurt Waldheim visited Namibia in March 1972, and sent a special representative a few months later. South African Prime Minister John Vorster even asserted in early 1975 that the peoples [in keeping with apartheid's presumptions of distinctive cultures, South African leaders always used the plural in referring to the inhabitants of Namibia] would determine their own political constitutional future, even with an option of independence.) Efforts were hence directed from Pretoria to create an administration that would obtain UN blessing without changing the real balance of power. On September 1, 1975, constitutional discussions began, leading in just under a year to establishment of an "interim government" that (at least in South Africa's eyes) could lead to independence for "SWA/Namibia."

The situation was a non-starter, in the eyes of the great majority of United Nations members. Early in 1976, the Security Council unanimously called on South Africa, by resolution 385, to take steps to transfer power to the people of the territory. South Africa appeared intent on reaching a solution favorable to its interests. On the other hand, some prospect for peaceful resolution based on constitutional progress existed. Western pressure on South Africa intensified, notably from the five members of the so-called contact group (Canada, France, the Federal Republic of Germany, the United Kingdom, and the United States). Would the United Nations accept the internal solution South Africa had pressed for, based on the combination of Tribal Authorities and white-only legislators who would constitute an "interim government"? Or would the UN press for a more sweeping solution? Between the whites-only referendum of May 18, 1977 (called to approve a three-tier system of government and independence), and June 10, 1977, South Africa shifted course. It agreed to suspend plans to establish an "interim government," agreed to appoint an administrator to work with the United Nations for elections, and accepted the contact group as mediators. SWAPO, somewhat reluctantly, concurred. By late summer 1978, it appeared as though success was at hand. A tentative date for independence was set for December 31, 1978. By means of resolution 435, adopted September 29, 1978, the Security Council established UNTAG (United Nations Transition Assistance Group) to help with the transfer of power to the people of Namibia. All seemed in order for a peaceful independence.

Then the carefully constructed diplomatic edifice collapsed. Secretary-General Waldheim's proposals for progress were accepted by the United Nations and SWAPO, but rejected by South Africa. SWAPO boycotted a whites-only December 1978 election organized by South Africa, which the General Assembly later declared null and void. So-called "proximity talks" in New York in March 1979 broke down, although a subsequent meeting in Geneva worked for a demilitarized zone along the Namibia-Angola border. Meanwhile, South Africa encouraged the self-styled National Assembly, under DTA (Democratic Turnhalle Alliance) leader Dirk Mudge, to act as a quasi-government. Based on a constitution (called AG8) adopted in April 1980, the "first tier" government controlled the budget, civil service, police, and military (the South West Africa Territorial Force, SWATF, which combatted SWAPO actively), while "second-tier" governments ruled over ethnically-defined homelands. There the situation essentially rested for several years, caught in the toils of international politics.

The United States role was especially important in the prolonged negotiations that followed. With the shift from Carter to Reagan, American policy changed. "Constructive engagement" and "linkage" between Cuban withdrawal from Angola and South African disengagement from Namibia became the new watchwords. Several years more were to elapse before the diplomatic game ended. The most noteworthy constitutional step came when the contact group set forth a series of principles in mid-1982.[1]

There were thus political, military, diplomatic, and legal dimensions in the evolution to Namibia's independence. The history of SWAPO involved guerrilla struggle against South Africa, political conflict with the internal government, and growing contacts with the international community. In its efforts, SWAPO used the language of human rights—first and foremost in terms of self-determination, increasingly of constitutional guarantees of human rights—as a major goal.

The war South Africa waged to maintain its grip on "Southwest" entailed draconian laws and counterinsurgency operations that disrupted— and ended—the lives of thousands. As already noted, the South African-sponsored administration established separate military and police units (SWATF, the South West African Territorial Force, and SWAPOL, the South West African police). Command rested firmly in South African hands. Security units (notably the infamous *Koevoet* ["crowbar"]) operated essentially without restraint. They launched attacks across international frontiers, occupying southern Angola in search of SWAPO base camps, and often located military installations adjacent to schools. They instituted harsh restrictions on civil liberties. The counter-insurgency strategy of South Africa meant using supposedly unbeatable armed might to cow the populace.[2]

At the same time, however, the administration in Windhoek realized its precarious position vis-a-vis public opinion, both domestic and international. The South African government could not hope to maintain long-term control of Namibia unless it attached a veneer of human rights and political sensitivity to its actions. It tried to win recognition as a benign ruler, with scant success. Internal elections were organized without SWAPO participation, as already noted, and an administration dominated by the DTA established. The DTA used a strategem of legal reform, viewed by cynics as a smokescreen, yet in the longer run an important contribution to Namibia's constitutional framework. Institutions separate in theory from South Africa were established for the renamed "South West Africa/Namibia." In 1982, South Africa accepted the contact group's principles concerning a proposed constituent assembly and constitution. These principles proposed the establishment of an overarching legal framework binding the legislative arm, and thus departing totally from the basic South African conception of parliamentary sovereignty.[3] A bill of rights, in other words, was contained in the implementing legislation, even though what had been supposedly granted was immediately restricted by the so-called "Protection of Fundamental Rights Act."[4] The world's stress on constitutional principles and human rights was thus reluctantly conceded by South Africa. The question to human rights activists within Namibia was whether promises of change could be translated into reality.

Founding the Legal Assistance Centre

The story of the Legal Assistance Centre begins, though it doesn't end, with individuals. Of the persons who made possible a climate for strengthening human rights through enforcement, none was more significant than the LAC's founder, Advocate David Smuts.

Smuts is a mild yet intense man. Quick in his movements, ever polite in his demeanor, this balding, bespectacled, soft-spoken lawyer scarcely resembles a revolutionary. Yet his protracted battle within the legal system of Namibia prepared the way for a post-independence respect for the rule of law — once the law, that is, could be administered in a non-discriminatory fashion. To grasp the full picture of the transformation, let us look first at the decolonization of Namibia by political and military means, then turn to the legal actions in which the LAC was central.

Thoughts of challenging the government's basic legal framework were far from Smuts' mind in 1980 when, fresh from his undergraduate and legal studies at the tranquil Stellenbosch campus in South Africa, he took on his first human rights litigation. No other firm in Windhoek — indeed, in the entire province of Southwest Africa — was willing to risk trying such cases. The plaintiffs were usually poor Blacks, unable to provide the upfront fee required for legal consultation. The likelihood of success in court was small, for the Roman-Dutch legal heritage of South Africa gave great discretion to the state. The presumption of innocence was a weak slogan at best. Most magistrates and judges, themselves all white at that time, shared the mindset that made apartheid possible. Legislation such as the Terrorism Act gave the police sweeping powers of arrest, detention, banning, and the like that were nearly impossible to challenge in court. Martial law applied in much of the north. Open combat raged along the Angolan border, lending credence to the South African government's claim of an aggressive "Communist onslaught." The system, in brief, was rigged against effective legal challenge from below. It was not totally immune, however, as Smuts was to discover.

Two years into his legal practice in Windhoek, Smuts took a break and went overseas for further study. While at Harvard, where he completed his LL.M. in 1983, he came into close contact with American civil rights lawyers. They were employing legal strategies Smuts felt merited being used in Namibian courts. "Public interest law" could be tried in Namibia. Near-by successes by advocates in South Africa also caught his attention. The Legal Resources Centre in Johannesburg had already established a significant record in defending victims of the apartheid system. Its pioneering actions provided an additional inspiration and model. Struggling for human rights in pre-independence Namibia through the legal system involved immense frustration and numerous setbacks for Smuts and the few other lawyers in willing to try to defend SWAPO members or supporters accused under the wide range of apartheid legislation. But they learned quickly. Use the law in more assertive ways; challenge the government directly; attack the basic principles of discriminatory statutes; seek test cases that might set precedents for overturning a whole series of laws: these were points he learned.

Much of the 1980s yielded meager results. Applications for relief were dismissed, suits rejected. Not until 1985 did Smuts win a court decision. And this and later victories could do little more than provide relief to a handful of plaintiffs, unless the decisions could be cited as precedents. The legal system could not carry the entire burden by itself. Namibia as a whole lacked major institutions of civil society, laws founded on equal protection, a government that reflected the will of the majority, and a military that sought the hearts and minds of the people. Especially in the north, the chief center of half the population and most SWAPO support, human rights work was nearly impossible. Martial law, poor communications, widespread intimidation, and inherent bias in the system made any advocate's task nearly impossible.

In 1986, Smuts started to think seriously about establishing a human rights center in northern Namibia. There, the ravages of battle and official abuses of human rights were most common. He realized that change would require active cooperation from churches. It was necessary, but not simple. Namibian values have long been influenced by Christian teachings; "render unto Caesar" statements were common. Major denominations (particularly Evangelical Lutherans, from Finnish and Rhenish roots; also Anglicans and Catholics) had to be persuaded to take political stands against a government armed with immense powers, and to which they had traditionally deferred. Some churches feared their property would be destroyed. Others were concerned about treading into political waters when their tasks should be spiritual. The growing intensity of the war, the increasing support for SWAPO, and personal commitment to change persuaded church leaders they needed to take further steps. In 1987, Bishops Haushiku (Roman Catholic), Dumeni (Evangelical-Lutheran) and Kauluma (Anglican) joined in a suit to free detainees held several years without trial. This was to be the key legal action brought by the Legal Assistance Centre. Once this suit succeeded, the logjam was broken. Churches became active partners in the effort. They brought victims to get legal aid, spread information, and lent their great legitimacy to the effort. Through the Council of Churches of Namibia (CCN), the denominations encouraged additional cases. Enforcement of human rights through law, even if major biases existed in it, would help Namibia in its struggle for independence. Once self-government was won, moreover, the law could be reformed and legal aid continued as a means of further change.

Three reasons led to the founding and funding of the Legal Assistance Centre. First, the sheer volume of human rights work in the north required full-time personnel (paralegals as well as lawyers and advocates); there was far too much work for an individual to handle. Second, a potential major benefactor was ready to offer support. The Ford Foundation recognized the need in Namibia for an organization analogous to the Legal Resources Centre it was already supporting in South Africa, and sent Geoff Budlander (as of mid-1993 the national director of the Legal Resources Centre) as consultant to carry out a feasibility study. He concluded that a comparable office should be set up and that Smuts (were he willing) should head it. Smuts initially demurred, wanting a Black to do so; in his words, "lots of persuasion was necessary."[5] Sufficient funding then had to be arranged. It took a full year to get donors' help to set up an office in the north. The need was urgent. As Smuts wrote subsequently,

At the commencement of [the LAC's] activities in July 1988, northern Namibia had been subjected to more than ten years of guerrilla war and with it, human rights abuses on a large scale, which included mass detentions, deaths, disappearances and the destruction of property. . . . The need for the centre was made all the more pressing by virtue of the fact that, as at the time of its inception . . . there [were] no full time practising lawyers based in the far northern region of Namibia where more than half of the Namibian population lives.[6]

The Legal Assistance Centre thus came into being through a conjunction of obvious need, Smuts's dedication, and external financial support. It drew its inspiration from many analogous groups. Privately-funded American civil rights lawyers had long brought test cases on behalf of Blacks and other disadvantaged persons. Closer to home, as already mentioned, was the South African Legal Resources Centre, established in 1978 and supported (in part) by private bodies, diplomatic missions, and NGOs.[7] Workable models thus existed. All depended on the good will of individuals and largely external sponsorship. The LAC would take the cases of indigent clients that were "in the public interest in which the outcome may have an impact on the rights of a group of people rather than cases which merely benefit an individual."[8] It would not — and could not, for a variety of reasons — charge its clients fees. Financial support from within southern Africa was unlikely, given the political climate; external funds were essential.

Dramatic shifts were occurring on the political landscape as the LAC took shape. While the South African military tried to win the war, the South African government attempted to deal with its political repercussions, domestic and international. As already noted, the so-called "Interim Administration" was paraded before the world as the legitimate government of "SWA/Namibia." This unusual entity dated from 1978, when the "tribal homelands" became "self-governing" as a result of a decree (Proclamation AG8 of 1978). So-called "second-tier authorities" were established to administer the affairs of the territory's ethnic groups — Baster, Caprivi, Coloured, Damara, Herero, Kaoko, Kavango, Nama, Owambo, Tswana, and White. The "first tier" supposedly watched over national matters; in reality, it did not stray far from South African preferences. Most notably, however, the "Interim Government" hesitantly adopted some human rights language and steps in its transparent but futile bid for legitimacy.

"I wanted to show the entirely empty commitment to human rights that the Interim Government was making," Smuts later stressed.[9] (Indeed, calling a bill that restricted the interim Bill of Rights the "Protection of Fundamental Human Rights Act" testified to the hypocrisy of the situation.) It was not the only prong in his attack. Given the nature of the legal system, little relief could be expected without much broader societal transformation. The supporting institutions of a race-neutral civil society had to be created as a counterpoise to the "separate cattle pens"[10] into which the population had been segregated. As long as students, trade unionists, mass media, and the like were divided by ethnicity rather than united by nationality or interest, the numerically small but economically and politically dominant whites could hang on to control.

By no stretch of the imagination was it easy to establish the Legal Assistance Centre. For example, finding suitable accommodations in the poorly developed, strife-torn north proved difficult. The LAC did not want to be linked with the suspect territorial administration, which offered it space, nor did it want to endanger churches by using their facilities. Hence, special quarters had to be built, designed to withstand shelling and to provide security for files. A lawyer's flat was erected adjacent to the record room for additional protection. Staffing was also a problem. Trained legal talent in Namibia was scarce. Hence the northern office, based in the town of Ongwediva (and three advice offices opened near Tsumeb in the central northern region, near Walvis Bay, and in Rundu in the northeast) were staffed by paralegals, instructed by Windhoek-based lawyers. Cases involving advice only could be resolved by paralegals; cases involving potential litigation were referred to attorneys based at the LAC in Windhoek. Smuts travelled frequently to Ongwediva, a distance of more than 700 kilometers, sometimes twice a week, to coordinate the work.

As should be expected, the majority of the Centre's early work came from the war-torn north. Close to 500 cases were handled by the office at Ongwediva in its first year of operation, about 75 percent of which involved human rights abuses by security forces (assault, rape and detention of civilians); approximately 260 civil claims for damages were brought in Namibian courts.[11] Labor cases accounted for most of the remainder of the Centre's load. Unfair dismissals, under- or non-payment of wages, workmen's compensation claims, and even constitutional issues fell into this category.[12] The result was an entity

largely limited during this period to the use of law as a means of redress within the structure of repressive apartheid laws. The sheer quantity and urgency of these matters led the lawyers employed at the Legal Assistance Centre to become largely a 'reaction unit' at times rather than a force capable organizing the law in a more creative manner.[13]

Funds from foreign governments, NGOs and foreign churches were necessary, as shown in Table 3. One should note the absence of contributions from within southern Africa itself. The Legal Assistance Centre was, and remains, almost entirely dependent on overseas grants for its continued functioning. In the absence of an endowment, and in the socio-economic and political context of the region, annual grants from external donors will continue to be critical. Some are already reducing their commitments, or converting them more into project than institutional support. The problems inherent in such changes in donors' priorities will be examined later in this book.

A few other persons shared this vision of a Namibia freed from South African control, rid of the incubus of apartheid that had so affected the society. Smuts, in short, was fighting a lonely but not a single battle. One of his major allies, and for the past several years one of the most important figures in Namibia's politics, was Gwen Lister, another young white liberal, also educated in Cape Province of South Africa. Lister, with her University of Cape Town BA in political philosophy, started work as a journalist in 1974 with the Windhoek *Advertiser*. Her increasingly critical comments about the government's actions resulted in a warning from the paper's proprietor Dirk Mudge (himself already active on the political stage, and later to become head of the DTA) that she "tone things down." Lister complied by resigning and starting her own weekly newspaper, the Windhoek *Observer*. Its tart comments on the government's

TABLE 3: Income, Legal Assistance Trust of Namibia (donations, in Rand)[14]

	1990	1989
Australian Government		10,741
Canadian Government		30,000
Church of Norway	49,850	250,748
Church of Sweden	195,600	166,200
Danchurchaid	149,344	155,597
Ford Foundation	269,375	473,875
Interfund		120,612
Lawyers Committee USA (Roderick MacArthur Foundation)	54,269	48,114
Oxfam		30,000
Norwegian Government		723
World University Service	70,984	
Total	789,422	1,286,610

policies resulted in its banning in 1984, an action she successfully challenged in court. But Lister was a marked woman. Once again, she was instructed to write more discreetly; once again, she resigned, this time taking several other staff members with her, to establish another new publication.

Smuts and Lister recognized the fundamental significance of independent media for Namibia to advance politically. Freedom of the press had not marked South West Africa, as a segment of South Africa; it would have to be established for meaningful human rights to exist in an independent Namibia.[15] They spent a year lining up funds for an independent newspaper. Thanks to European Community[16] money and other resources, *The Namibian* started publication in 1985. Unlike other newspapers, it documented the war in the north, growing discontent among students, and pressures on the majority Black population in detail and perspective unmatched by the essentially White-oriented newspapers of the time. Smuts continued to provide legal advice — of which plenty was needed, given the web of laws South Africa had enacted to muzzle dissidence. Smuts and Lister had entered dangerous waters. Both received death threats and were ostracized by other whites. Lister, several months pregnant, was detained in June 1988 for publishing details of proposed emergency legislation and refusing to name the person who leaked the information. She knew the risk. The Official Secrets Act, Smuts had warned her, would inevitably result in her detention, possible prosecution, and likely banning of the paper.[17] Offices of *The Namibian* were firebombed in October 1988 by a right-wing White group. Journalism in war-torn Namibia was clearly a hazardous profession; establishment of an independent press did not occur without resistance from those in control.

In addition to free media, civil society requires freedom of association.

(Though this term is applied most frequently to the right to establish and join trade unions, under various ILO Conventions, it appears in both International Covenants — indicating the interdependence of so-called first and second generation rights.) The laws of Namibia, at least in the period of South African rule, severely impeded workers' right to organize and strike. Smuts accordingly advised labor activists on how to establish unions. He further encouraged students to organize. Both NUNW, the National Union of Namibian Workers, and NANSO, the Namibian National Student Organization, brought new elements to the political scene. General strikes and school boycotts were unknown until the late 1980s; they then became domestic weapons in the struggle to end apartheid. By bringing Windhoek to a near standstill, and by marching through its streets, the NUNW and NANSO manifested the wide popular support for SWAPO and independence. The Legal Assistance Centre stood ready to help their members in case of arrest or detention. These organizations, joined by the Council of Churches, worked together in the end-game before independence.

Human Rights Enforcement Under Namibia's Constitution

The Legal Assistance Centre has faced new challenges since independence. The struggle for dignity and equality has taken a different form since Namibia's new constitution was debated and ratified by the elected Constituent Assembly.

The Namibian constitution is, with respect to human rights, probably the world's most detailed and strongest constitution. Chapter 3 — "Fundamental Human Rights and Freedoms" — prescribes a series of rights enforceable through Namibian courts. Having a constitution with a precise bill of rights which all parts of the government must uphold naturally shifted the focus for Namibian NGOs. They no longer had to struggle to achieve self-determination and end the severe restrictions of South African rule; they could work through "their" government. No question: groups like the Legal Assistance Centre and the Council of Churches in Namibia had supported SWAPO in the struggle for independence; the new SWAPO regime was morally and politically obliged to act on NGOs' human rights concerns. The law was changing, and with it the nature of enforcement as an NGO strategy.

The Namibian constitution is a human rights dream. More than any other constitution in Africa, at least as of early 1994, it protects human rights in detail. There are more than words. Other African countries have documents with similar noble sentiments; but many lack the will to enforce.

The Namibian constitution facilitates judicial remedies for strongly-protected human rights. As Article 5 indicates, fundamental rights and freedoms "shall be respected and upheld by the Executive, Legislature and Judiciary and all organs of the Government and its agencies and, where applicable to them, by all natural and legal persons in Namibia." The constitution has become a touchstone of national pride. Ministers look to it as the foundation for a "new culture of human rights."[18] Members of the National Assembly carry and refer to copies during debates. *Abacus*, a weekly newsletter for high school students, privately published under the auspices of the Educational Publications Trust of Namibia, carries easy-to-understand summaries of constitutional provisions. Promotion efforts are widespread. NGOs such as the Namibian Institute of Democracy have translated the constitution into local languages and distributed the pamphlets widely. The strategy of human rights enforcement can work in Namibia because of its constitutional foundation and its support by leading sectors of society.

Chapter 3 of Namibia's constitution covers a wide sweep of human rights: protection of life and liberty, respect for human dignity, equality, privacy, property, political activity, administrative justice, the family and culture, prohibition of slavery and forced labor, safeguards in arrest, detention, and fair trial, freedom of movement, and more appear in it. Specific rights are guaranteed to all persons in freedom of speech, expression, thought, conscience and belief, religious practice, association, peaceful assembly, movement, residence, and occupation. Chapter 3 cannot be weakened by ordinary means. The legislature, executive, and government agencies "shall not take any action which abolishes or abridges the fundamental rights and freedoms conferred by this Chapter." (Article 25; Article 131 restates the prohibition, and entrenches the fundamental rights and freedoms). The drafters of Namibia's constitution wanted to create a legal instrument that *enforced the rule of law based on explicit rights.* Constitutional rights could be restricted only by laws "necessary in a democratic society and . . . required in the interests of the sovereignty and integrity of Namibia, national security, public order, decency or morality, or in relation to contempt of court, defamation, or incitement at offense." Persons who believed their rights were infringed or threatened could seek remedy through the courts or the Ombudsman, and could receive monetary compensation for the damage they suffered.

This ringing language was shaped from many sources. One was the 1982 statement of fundamental principles, accepted unanimously as a basis of discussion when the Constituent Assembly met. This came as a surprise, since SWAPO (which had won 41 of the 72 seats) had refused to endorse the statement during the electoral campaign. Some provisions were politically distasteful to SWAPO, such as provisions that property could not be repossessed by the post-colonial government, that civil servants would not lose their jobs because of change in the regime, and that the final version of the constitution would require a two-thirds rather than simple majority. As one witness wrote,

It came as a complete surprise, therefore, when SWAPO's Foreign Secretary Theo-Ben Gurirab rose at the end of the first day's sitting of the Constituent Assembly and proposed that the house should accept the 1982 Principles for inclusion in the Constitution. For a moment there was stunned silence, then members on all sides of the house erupted into a round of applause, and the motion was carried unanimously.[19]

A spirit of compromise was thereby engendered. Most matters were ironed out by consensus behind closed doors, through a steering committee of 21 members assisted by three legal advisers.[20] Within two months, the draft was ready for consideration in public by the full Constituent Assembly.

The varied international backgrounds of SWAPO members and the midwife role of the United Nations also enhanced the prominence of human rights in the constitution. Probably more than any other country in the modern world, Namibia owed its existence to successful international pressure for self-determination. UNTAG, the UN Institute for Namibia in Zambia, and regular General Assembly debates manifested the UN's multiple roles. Many political refugees and exiles had been educated outside Africa, notably in Scandanavia, eastern Europe, Cuba, and the United States. Their experiences overseas (including the collapse of European communism) coincided with rising global consciousness of human rights.

But a nobly-worded constitution cannot ensure adequate protection of human rights. NGOs will remain essential. But for NGOs in Namibia, the task is complicated by the country's poverty, certain "traditional" assumptions and practices, and skeletons in the government's closet.

Even the most far-reaching constitution can remain a dead letter if there is reluctance to test its meaning in court. Have the LAC and other Namibian lawyers used the constitution aggressively enough to litigate for rights? Human rights cases have declined dramatically since independence. Assaults by security force members dropped from 24 percent of cases in 1989–90 to three percent in 1990–91.[21] By mid-1993 human rights cases accounted for no more than 10 percent of the work of the LAC and its affiliated advice offices.[22] Now that a reasonably effective framework for the rule of law has been established, its significance for the lives of ordinary citizens must become part of popular culture. Legal proceedings will continue to play an important part, nonetheless. The current LAC director vigorously rejects charges of indifference to human rights issues. Two important examples are rulings in cases supported by the LAC, in one of which judges deemed corporal punishment in schools as cruel, inhuman, and degrading treatment (Article 8,2,b), and the other of which required police to bring accused persons before a court within 48 hours, regardless of distance or convenience factors.[23]

But a culture of silence continues to veil the fate of a few hundred detainees held prior to independence by SWAPO and the SWATF. The delicacy and potentially embarrassing nature of the issue are obvious. Most of those in SWAPO hands, it has been presumed, were executed for alleged collaboration with the South African enemy. Most victims came from non-Owambo groups, and many had more extensive education than the guerrilla fighters. Calls for accountability have come and gone in Namibia, with occasional promises of government action followed by silence. The matter was raised pointedly during the 1989 campaign for the Constituent Assembly by the so-called Parents' Committee, and was not convincingly rebutted by SWAPO. Many observers believed the opposition DTA used the issue in a successful effort to block SWAPO from gaining the two-thirds majority in the Constituent Assembly necessary to bring major changes in the draft constitution. The Parents' Committee, DTA, and other groups gained an international audience in late 1992, when Africa Watch published a highly detailed report entitled "Waiting for Accountability." It chronicled gross abuses of human rights, largely in SWAPO-run detention camps. Critics argued that a government priding itself on its commitment to human rights should make every possible effort to get to the bottom of the issue. Smuts (by 1992 back in private practice) joined critics of the government's silence:

> Reconciliation is premised upon the notion of forgiveness. . . . The policy of national reconciliation cannot, if honestly applied, form a justification for precluding thorough investigation of past abuses. Ultimately, this policy cannot succeed unless it is based upon an acknowledgement and assessment of the past. . . . The principle which should should be clearly applied by the government is that anyone who has committed gross human rights abuses is simply unfit to hold a position of authority. . . . Without an acknowledgement and knowledge of past abuses and addressing them in a principled manner, the elaborate steps taken in the constitution to prevent their recurrence are undermined.[24]

And, in neighboring South Africa, the ANC (African National Congress) made history as a liberation movement when, prior to the nation's first racially non-restricted elections, it admitted responsibility for deaths in detention of several hundred persons.[25]

The greatest obstacle to enforcement as a strategy in Namibia—and indeed in most countries of Africa—arises from the limits to government action inherent in limited economic development. The Namibian Constitution itself reinforces these limits. As elsewhere in Africa, constitutions set the framework with which rights are recognized and enforced domestically. They proclaim the protected liberties, indicate how international treaty obligations fit with domestic law,[26] and provide the basis for enforcement, through establishing security and judicial systems. Constitutions are — at least in theory — documents that merit special respect. Crafted for more than the passing moment, they express the ultimate ideals of the political system. At the same time, however, they should not (it is argued) proclaim unrealizable goals. Constitutions that far outstrip governments' ability to "deliver" risk increasing public cynicism. Better not to cast disrepute on the supreme law of the land, so this argument runs, by placing in it what likely cannot be accomplished.

There are no direct guarantees in the Namibian constitution of basic economic rights: to at least survival levels of food, shelter, and preventive health care, and to opportunities for work. Are these pie-in-the-sky expectations for poor countries such as Namibia? Does the constitution's emphasis on a detailed series of largely "first generation" rights neglect economic matters that deeply concern the Namibian people? Should and can the ultimate legal framework attempt to guarantee certain minima?

This question has long vexed constitution drafters. The 1922 constitution of newly-independent Ireland differentiated immediately enforceable political goals from broader economic strategies, as did the 1947 constitution of India and the 1979 constitution of Nigeria. Economic matters appear in the Namibian Constitution, among the "Principles of State Policy" (Chapter 11). The warning is clear: such matters "shall not of and by themselves be legally enforceable in any Court, but shall nevertheless guide the Government in making and applying laws to give effect to the fundamental objectives of the said principles" (Article 101). Among the major aims in promoting the welfare of the people are

- legislation to ensure equality of opportunity for women (in addition to affirmative action measures to overcome "the fact that women in Namibia have traditionally suffered special discrimination . . ." [Article 23, 2]);
- labor legislation to ensure "that citizens are not forced by economic necessity to enter vocations unsuited to their age and strength";
- membership of the ILO (International Labour Organization) and, "where possible," adherence to its Conventions and Recommendations;
- "fair and reasonable" access to public services;
- regular and adequate pensions for senior citizens;
- social benefits and amenities for the unemployed, incapacitated, indi-

gent, and disadvantaged "as are determined by Parliament to be just and affordable with due regard to the resources of the State";

- a legal system that promotes equal opportunity by providing free legal aid in defined cases;
- payment to workers of "a living wage adequate for the maintenance of a decent standard of living";
- achievement of "an acceptable level of nutrition and standard of living of the Namibian people";
- encouragement of the populace through education and organizations "to influence Government policy by debating its decisions"; and
- "maintenance of ecosystems, essential ecological processes, and biological diversity of Namibia and utilization of living natural resources on a sustainable basis for the benefit of all Namibians, both present and future."

I hope you are as impressed by this list as I was. Constitutional non-enforceability notwithstanding, the fact remains that government acts and actions can be judged by the people against these high aspirations. Despite its caveats, the Namibian constitution sets a steep task for the government. These goals never will be completely achieved. Since the economic base is weak — as assuredly is the case in Namibia, as through essentially all of Africa — all aspirations for social welfare cannot be met. The question remains whether the government may have opened itself up to charges of hypocrisy or inadequacy. Several persons I interviewed in Namibia expressed the view that the goals were far too high and hence risked bringing the entire government and constitution into disrepute. Major steps in economic development are essential. Without significantly more resources available to it, the government of Namibia can promise its citizens jam tomorrow, but never give enough jam today. Land reform is essential for development and justice for Namibians; yet there must be just compensation, with little assurance acquisition and redistribution of extensive white-owned ranching and agricultural operations could satisfy the land hunger of Owambo peasants.

What functions, then, will the Legal Assistance Centre fulfill in coming years? Its role since independence has changed in significant ways. As already noted, human rights abuses have dropped from three-quarters to one-tenth of the case work. Yet problems remain, and the LAC continues to pursue impact litigation, focusing on the constitution and abuse of power. It is becoming increasingly involved in advocacy and research, and third, has stressed education and training. A paragraph or two on each is in order.

Somewhat to its surprise, the LAC has not been deluged since independence by clients wanting to litigate constitutional matters. The courts remain arcane, distant, possibly fearsome entities to most Namibians. Further, and in my belief more important, the SWAPO government has maintained a broad basis of popular support. Taking it to task or to court runs counter to the public grain. Criticism, especially of President Sam Nujoma, is seen as inappropriate.[27] Those in power can still rest to a significant extent on their laurels: SWAPO ended South African rule; it can thus bring justice to all. Government spokespersons periodically convene NGOs for discussions about reform. Legislation is promised; more important, it is often enacted. The limited number of human rights and constitutional cases pursued by the LAC thus reflect two facts, in its director's view: lack of understanding among Namibian lawyers and the populace as a whole about working within a constitutional democracy; and decisions to pursue broad-based reform through the legislature rather than address piecemeal constitutional violations in the courts.[28]

If laws are to be reformed, the nature of change must be delineated. Advocacy and research are essential. The Namibian government itself has sought advice; external development agencies have commissioned research by persons linked to the LAC.[29] The range covered is impressive: children's and women's rights; gender equality; the land question; labor conditions and workers' compensation laws; accountability for the police force; the constitutionality of civil imprisonment for debts; small cooperative development. The LAC and independent researchers in Namibia have become partners in legal reform. Future enforcement of laws should benefit from the involvement of NGOs in their drafting. However, whether effective consultation will occur prior to legislative consideration remains an item of concern.[30]

Third, the LAC has sought (along with other Namibian groups) to train paralegals. The newly-established Faculty of Law at the University of Namibia will take a role also. The need is urgent. Namibia resembles other African countries in the dearth of indigenous lawyers, particularly women. (About five percent of the lawyers in private practice are Black; fewer than ten percent are women.[31]) Historically, the LAC and CCN (Council of Churches in Namibia) placed paralegals in the "front line" of human rights work. They advised potential clients on strategy (including whether courts could likely satisfy their claims), took statements, gathered evidence, and prepared the essential groundwork for litigation. In short, paralegals made the judicial system accessible to the people at a level impossible with attorneys alone. Serious efforts at training paralegals and using them as major contacts with aggrieved individuals are needed in Namibia and elsewhere in Africa, to make enforcement a viable strategy for protecting human rights.

Legal Assistance, Enforcement, NGO Consultation, and the Rule of Law

As noted earlier in this chapter, Namibia's Legal Assistance Centre was modeled on South Africa's Legal Resources Centre (LRC). Brief comparisons of their activities with the Kituo cha Sheria of Kenya are potentially useful for assessing implementation as a human rights NGO strategy throughout the continent.

The LRC stands alone in Africa in terms of size. In 1992, it employed 119 persons, including 42 lawyers, spread across six regional offices and a national office. The vast majority of the LRC's budget came from non-South African sources (7,018,448 rand from overseas, 1,203,447 rand from within). Germany provided 24 percent, the United States 18 percent, the United Kingdom 14 percent, other Western countries 17 percent, local sources 12 percent, and investment 14 percent. About 3,000 new case files were opened in 1992, while close to 22,000 requests for assistance were handled by advice, negotiation, or referral.[32] Even these resources fall far short of the desired goals of spreading positive experience of a legal culture through a transformed South Africa, however.

Kituo cha Sheria (Swahili for legal help) operates in Kenya on a far more modest scale, though with no less impressive objectives. Kituo started its operation in 1973. Known then as the Kituo Cha Mashauri, it was a purely volunteer organization of lawyers and law students; not until 1985 did it employ its first lawyer.[33] (By contrast, the Legal Resources Centre, with Ford Foundation and other funding, had a full-time core staff from its inception in 1978.) Kituo, the LRC, and the Namibian Legal Assistance Centre proclaim the same goals: protecting rights through providing legal services for those unable to afford them; promoting rights through community outreach, publications, research, and training programs; helping create a culture of the rule of law, in which the law itself is fairly administered; advising the government on establishing nondiscriminatory rights; and, ultimately, lobbying for democratic, responsive government.

The majority of people in Africa have had unpleasant, confusing contact with the legal system. Consider the following problems. Arbitrary arrests; police corruption; court proceedings conducted in Western languages unknown to most; disjunctures between what traditionally had been accepted in village dispute resolution and what can be used before magistrates: all these affect how law is perceived. Enforcement of values little known in communities, through procedures and personnel distant from popular understanding, has serious limitations. Can the legal systems through which human rights are enforced in Africa be demystified? Will the work of the LAC, or of paralegals trained by the Nigerian Legal

Research and Resource Development Centre, establish the "rule of law"? It is appropriate at this point to see how a small number of Lagos lawyers have moved to expand access to law for poor people.

The LRRDC of Nigeria

"It was one of the loneliest days of my life," Tokunbo Ige observed. "There I was, in a bare office with a chair and table, but no telephone or files—and no clients." She had acted on personal conviction and hope more than on rational financial calculation. Instead of pursuing her law practice full time with the usual range of corporate and well-off individual clients, she had decided to enter the demanding world of human rights work. On May 2, 1990, Mrs. Ige became the heart, soul, brains, and for a while sole staff of an important Nigerian NGO.

The Nigerian Legal Research and Resources Development Centre (LRRDC) typifies the unusual dedication and risk-taking the founders of NGOs exhibit. They are willing to work long hours for limited pay and recognition, in a quest often belittled by their colleagues. Given the slight knowledge of human rights characteristic of much of contemporary Africa, these activists are regarded with more than a little skepticism, and occasionally with a great deal of distrust, by those in the political establishment. They scrounge for funds from numerous sources (often foreign, thus raising criticisms about their "independence"). They stitch together seed grants until they can establish a track record, then seek longer-term project funds, all the time running to stay in place. They try to spread their message to potentially interested groups, but find, once the value of their work becomes known, that their resources still fall far below what is required.

For Mrs. Ige, a clear and present need existed. Human rights were protected in Nigeria by the courts, despite ouster clauses and other restrictions. Access to the courts required legal advice, and hence a lawyer. Few in Nigeria could afford to hire a lawyer—and the overwhelming majority never committed a felony that might entitle them to free assistance. Economic circumstances meant, in her estimate, that perhaps one in a hundred of those who needed legal protection could afford to seek and receive it. Those who most needed assistance were hampered by the least knowledge and the lowest incomes. For example, poor women who had been raped or abandoned by their husbands realistically had no place to turn to in the formal legal system. Though they knew they had been wronged, they knew not how to right the situation. But until the victims became aware of possible solutions, they would remain on the margins. Had they lived in compact, relatively homogeneous villages, existing "traditional" systems of compensation could have been used.

But in the turbulent, multi-ethnic Lagos setting, few such "traditional" forms of protection could be found. Neither the "modern" nor the "customary" system of justice worked for such persons.

As should be obvious, enforcement as a strategy for human rights NGOs must be closely linked with education. Roughly speaking, two types of connections exist between enforcement and education. First, entities like the LRRDC focus on often illiterate, usually poor, undoubtedly marginalized persons with limited (if any) formal schooling. For them, human rights consist largely in finding ways to survive in the face of personal tragedy (divorce, loss of property following a spouse's death). These are the types of issue with which the Namibian Legal Assistance Centre now deals primarily, and for which the LRRDC would like to develop programs. Second, education can be aimed at enhancing knowledge about human rights for a highly educated, relatively affluent group, lawyers in particular, for whom enforcement is an essential part of their professional life. Members of this group may not have vivid personal experiences of social deprivation, but they do have skills essential for protecting human rights through the courts. Both aim toward the same overarching objective: developing a "culture" of human rights that links knowledge about issues to awareness of possible solutions. But the audiences they serve and the methods they employ differ significantly.

Tokunbo Ige, as already noted, chose to start along the first of these approaches. What led her to create the LRRDC? What issues has it confronted? What can be learned from its experiences for promotion and protection of human rights in Africa? How do her experiences differ from those of David Smuts and the Namibian LAC?

To establish the Legal Research and Resources Development Centre, Mrs. Ige needed knowledge, resources, and commitment—necessary, obviously, for the founder of any NGO. Her knowledge came partly from studying constitutional law at the University of Lagos in the mid-1980s and human rights law at the University of Essex, partly from an internship in London with Interights in 1989, and largely from her personal awareness of the needs of poor women in the urban area. There were few human rights NGOs in Nigeria in the late 1980s; the oldest such explicit organization, the CLO (Civil Liberties Organisation) was founded by young lawyer Clement Nwankwo in 1987; the indefatigable city lawyer Gani Fawehinmi was starting his one-man crusade to re-establish the rule of law.[34] The months with Interights accordingly gave Mrs. Ige a sense of what NGOs could accomplish. Resources came from her uncle, who furnished the bare but serviceable office in Yaba, far from being the most affluent section of Lagos. Commitment came — well, who knows? She says her work is "worth doing,"[35] for the wheels of justice barely turn for the persons the LRRDC seeks to reach. As already indicated, these were individuals lacking the knowledge and financial resources necessary to go to the courts.

The most visible, widespread evidence of the Centre's work comes through its series of pamphlets, published with support from USAID. Written in basic English, usually using question-and-answer formats, these booklets concentrate on legal problems an ordinary Nigerian is likely to confront in daily life: arrest, bail, custody of children, divorce and separation, landlord-tenant relations, maintenance, marriage, rape, search by police, women and the right of residency, and making a will.[36] These are important problems, but not ones on which "tradition" or daily experience may provide many insights. A lacuna of knowledge and manifest need made the series advisable. How can the "success" of these publications be measured? By, Mrs. Ige responded, reading the two to three responses that come in the mail per day, for at the back of each booklet is a brief questionnaire asking for comment and information. Should the series be translated into Hausa, Igbo, and Yoruba, presuming funding, the impact and distribution would further increase.

Publication must be buttressed by actual legal services. Here, the LRRDC has turned to training paralegals, as have human rights NGOs throughout the world. The LRRDC had, as of early 1994, prepared 43 young women and men to assist persons in the mid-western Nigerian city of Benin and in the southwestern town of Ijebu as assistants. The Lagos-area concentration of human rights organizations and legal aid efforts would thus be diminished. Awareness that "law" could be used on behalf of the underprivileged would gradually transform how Nigerians tend to view its workings. Further training efforts were planned for the far north-eastern city of Maiduguri, the important northern city of Kaduna, and the eastern city of Enugu. In other words, services would be available outside the capital, even if not yet in rural areas.

A third step came with establishment of a legal clinic in Lagos that would "take us back to more human ways of settling disputes." Issues highly important to individuals, but far from earth-shattering in their significance to civil liberties in Nigeria, are treated here. Rather than use the adversarial procedures familiar in Western-style courts, dispute settlement techniques are employed. In Mrs. Ige's view, a non-litigatory approach fits better with the needs and backgrounds of persons (largely poor urban women) who seek its services. The clinic's location near the Daleko market, in the poor Mushin section of Lagos, was carefully chosen. Nineteen paralegals, trained from members of the market community, serve individuals' needs.

To reach out effectively, a legal aid clinic or similar activity must be accessible. The sites of the LRRDC and of its clinic seem ideal in this respect. A hundred meters to the north of the Centre itself is the bustling

Yaba taxi park, thronged all hours of the day with persons buying and selling, pushing their ways into the overcrowded yellow cabs and *molues*, joining in the exuberance of Lagos urban life. A woman wanting advice from the Legal Research and Resources Development Centre need take only a few steps, go to the back of a building (navigating along a narrow open passage between the drip of an air conditioner and up a outside staircase) to the office. Help—in the form of a reference library and advisers—would be there. Or she could turn to the Daleko market group of paralegals, trained by the LRRDC, for advice. To make the "rule of law" more than a slogan, thus, requires attention to placement of legal aid clinics, to content of programs, to approach to potential clients. Access is thus much more than geography; it is a matter of tailoring programs to the specific needs of numerically large but politically insignificant citizens.

The experience of FIDA's (*Federación Internacional de Abogadas*, International Federation of Women Lawyers) clinic in Enugu, Nigeria, should also be noted. Its activities are intended to help bridge the gulf between written law and actual practice. "In most cases," Ms. Oby Nwankwo told a Columbia University symposium on public law in 1991, "women's rights in Nigeria are safeguarded in legal provisions, but in practice discriminatory administrative measures are put in place and women accept them because of their ignorance of the law."[37] Examples: a working husband can claim a tax deduction for his wife, but not a working wife for her unemployed husband; a married working mother must obtain a letter of consent from her husband should she seek deductions for her children; a woman cannot obtain a passport without her husband's permission. These petty harassments typify the far larger problem of serious gender inequalities, deeply rooted in African culture, to which reference was made in Chapter 3. As human rights advocates emphasize equality, they will encounter resistance from the zealous guardians of "tradition." Custom justifies many gender-specific actions against women. But so does, it is apparent, the administration of law.

Education of paralegals has (as of this writing) extended far more through English-speaking than French-speaking Africa. Typical is the listing in the International Commission of Jurists manual for training special legal assistants: eight of the 10 countries listed are Anglophone, and they account for 13 of the 15 programs.[38] This should be no surprise. Development within common law frameworks rests heavily on litigation and precedent. Change within code law frameworks depends largely on legislative initiative and administrative regulation. While students in the *Faculté du Droit* look toward careers as magistrates employed by the government, students in the Faculty of Law often expect to enter the private sector. Few from either group, unfortunately, think about public interest law, including human rights work. Bar associations have taken leading political roles in Ghana and Kenya; because of the nature of legal practice, they can be far more critical of regimes than can similar groups in Senegal or Togo, for example. They need also to be active in spreading knowledge of the law through popular groups.

"Law in the service of the people" may be a comforting slogan; it is a challenging ideal. "Equal application of the laws" is an equally problematic, difficult issue. Realizing both these goals throughout Africa will remain a challenge for decades to come. They require lawyers to move from the familiar confines of office or courtroom to public settings. They must practice law in ways pragmatically significant to the people. Hence, broad constitutional cases will pale in importance to access to treated water or decent sanitary facilities for urban slum dwellers. Socio-economic issues and matters of personal status (marriage, inheritance) stand highest in their immediate priorities. For city residents, the most useful legal service might be the "civil rights card," printed in Swahili by the Kituo cha Sheria, informing citizens of their rights when arrested, or Kituo's leaflet telling women about steps to take after being raped. For rural residents, the most useful legal service might involve settling land disputes, perhaps by conciliation or the work of paralegals short of actual litigation.

Legal aid remains confined to a few cities in Africa. The great majority who live in rural areas remain outside the direct reach of groups like the LAC, the LRRDC, or Kituo. Cases in the judicial system for which legal assistance is available involve a minute fraction of the potentially justiciable issues. On the other hand, some positive experience with law as a solution to issues bolsters its importance in emerging human rights cultures. The current geographic and social confines of legal aid pose problems, but not insuperable ones. Migration to urban areas is swelling their populations; and knowledge of what occurs there spreads throughout entire countries. Thus, although only few people may profit directly from specific legal aid services, the message goes out through "radio trottoir" to the wider community.

Perhaps the most fitting conclusion to this chapter comes from Andrew Corbett, whose observations about the Legal Assistance Centre apply throughout Africa:

The LAC is keenly aware that rights awareness should be fostered and that channels for effective assertion of rights should be opened up; nevertheless the actual practice of rights is the most meaningful way of educating the public about their content. It would also be wrong to rely too heavily on lawyers and legal institutions for the assertion of fundamental human rights. Laws and bills of rights can be extremely weak instruments to protect human rights, as it is not government or lawyers that create a human rights practice, but the people themselves. . . . People will only be prepared to actively defend human rights when an understanding has developed based on shared experience and an acknowledgement that these rights are for the protection of all.[39]

Notes

1. UN Document S/15287, letter from the five members of the Western contact group, 12 July 1982.

2. Richard Dale, "Melding War and Politics in Namibia: South Africa's Counterinsurgency Campaign, 1966–1989," *Armed Forces & Society* 20 (1993), 7–24.

3. Gerhard Erasmus, "The Namibian Constitution and the Application of International Law," *South African Yearbook of International Law* 15 (1989/90) (Cape Town: VerLoren van Themaat Centre for International Law, 1990), 81.

4. The Legal Assistance Centre persuaded the Namibian Supreme Court prior to independence that this Act should be set aside since it conflicted with the Bill of Rights contained in the Interim Government's empowering legislation. South Africa's utilization of human rights standards testifies to the importance of this dimension of the struggle for liberation.

5. Interview, Windhoek, October 22, 1993.

6. *Annual Report of the Legal Assistance Trust and the Human Rights Trust, 1 July 1989 to 30 June 1990* (Windhoek: Capital Press, 1990), p. 10.

7. The contributions of South Africa's LRC may well prove to have been as important to that country's political evolution as those of the Namibian LAC. In brief, it was founded as a non-profit entity in Johannesburg, aimed at encouraging belief in the value of law as an instrument of justice, through providing legal and educational services in the public interest. A decade after its founding, it had grown to six regional offices and a national office, a staff of 95 (including 33 lawyers), a new case load of 3,489 files, and a budget of 6.3 million South African rands. The 1989/90 case load for the LRC provides an interesting contrast to the LAC's case load. In South Africa, labor matters accounted for 33.3 percent of all cases, pensions and administrative law 16.5 percent, land and housing 13.5 percent, consumer matters 10 percent, and "other" (including human rights and state of emergency matters) 26.7 percent. Grants from overseas donors were more than four times the grants from within South Africa, the two largest contributions coming from the U.S. Office of Development Affairs and the Washington-based South African Legal Services and Legal Education Project. *Report of the Legal Resources Trust and the Legal Resources Centre, South Africa, for the Year Ended 31 March 1990* (Johannesburg: The Trust, 1990).

8. *Annual Report 1989–1990*, p. 11.

9. Interview, Windhoek, October 22, 1993.

10. David Lush, *Last Steps to Uhuru* (Windhoek: New Namibia Books, 1993), p. 19.

11. Andrew Corbett, "The Legal Assistance Centre in Transition," unpublished paper, p. 3.

12. *Annual Report 1989–1990*, p. 25.

13. Ibid., p. 17.

14. Ibid., appendix, p. 8. The report differentiatess between income and "donations," the latter including gifts from the Dutch agency NOVIB and Trocaire, totaling an additional nearly 270,000 rand.

15. Lister's accomplishments resulted in her 1992 receipt of the Press Freedom

Award from the Committee to Protect Journalists, the only woman among the five winners. She continues to crusade for freedom of the press, not confining her efforts to Namibia. She is the chief shaker and mover in the recently-established Media Institute of Southern Africa (MISA), dedicated to expanding media freedom and other rights in the region, upgrading the training of journalists, and ensuring that outsiders do not lose sight of the serious devastation wrought in Angola. Financial assistance from Scandanavian countriesas in many other human rights undertakings in Southern Africamade possible MISA's creation in 1993 and publication of its bimonthly newsletter.

16. These funds were terminated since shortly after independence, although the fiscal foundation of the newspaper was by no means secure. Promotion and protection of human rights requires an independent press — which, in the political and economic contexts of many African states, may necessitate external support for years to come.

17. Lush, *Last Steps to Uhuru*, p. 116.

18. Deputy Minister of Justice, Adv. R. V. Rukoro, cited in Raoul Wallenberg Institute Report No. 9, "Human Rights Workshop Namibia, 18–24 February 1991" (Lund: The Institute, 1991), p. 20; this example could be multiplied scores of times.

19. Lush, *Last Steps to Uhuru*, p. 264.

20. The advisers included Gerhard Erasmus (as of early 1993, Harry Oppenheimer Professor of Human Rights at the University of Stellenbosch) and Arthur Chaskalson (national director of the Legal Resources Centre of South Africa). Erasmus lived in Windhoek during the entire period, and worked late most evenings drafting legal language and proposing alternative approaches in areas of dispute. Interview with Professor Erasmus, Stellenbosch, October 27, 1993.

21. *Annual Report of the Legal Assistance Trust and the Human Rights Trust, 1 July 1990–30 June 1991*, p. 16.

22. Corbett, "LAC in Transition," p. 3.

23. Ibid., p. 4.

24. Dave Smuts, "Accounting for Violations in the Context of National Reconciliation," *Namibia Brief* 16 (March 1993), 12–13.

25. Nelson Mandela's proposal to acknowledge the deaths publicly, though hotly debated for six hours by senior ANC officials, was recognized as an appropriate step in reconciliation and openness. Interview with ANC legal adviser Asmal Kadar, Cape Town, October 26, 1993.

26. The most noteworthy aspect is whether a treaty, once ratified by a State Party, immediately becomes enforceable through the legal system ("self-executing") or requires additional enabling legislation ("non-self-executing"). Further, in ratifying a treaty, a State Party has the right to insist on restrictions in applicability (reservations), as well as indicate its interpretation of specific wording (declarations and understandings).

27. Herein lies a fundamental problem for the Namibian National Society for Human Rights (NSHR). Executive Director Phil Ya Nangoloh faxes regular complaints about government actions or inactions to the media, and prepares detailed reports on specific matters. However, his broad-brush indictments of SWAPO policies lack impact since they are perceived as inspired in part by political animus. (Ya Nangoloh himself was a detainee of SWAPO, and lost a brother in these camps.) Interviews, Windhoek, October 7–21, 1993. Major NSHR publications include: " 'Etopola', The Practice of Torture and Other Cruel, Inhuman or Degrading Treatment or Punishment in Present-Day Namibia" (Windhoek:

NSHR, April 1, 1993); "The Namibia Country Report on the Status of the UN Convention on the Rights of the Child: A Critical Analysis" (Windhoek: NSHR, 1992); and "Annual Human Rights Report for 1992" (Windhoek: NSHR, January 12, 1993).

28. Corbett, "LAC in Transition," p. 4. The most recent published annual report showed a clear shift toward cases involving social and economic rights. Of more than 300 files opened in 1990–91, nearly 80 percent fell into these categories, as shown below:

Dismissals and notice pay claims	49
Workmen's Compensation claims	15
Pension claims	11
Housing	3
Deaths and medical negligence	2
Assaults and harassment	1
Other labor matters	2
Deportation and refugee matters	0.5
Disappearance	0.5
Maintenance	0.5
Advice to community-based organizations	0.5
Other matters	14

"Annual Report 1990–91," p. 14.

29. For example, SIDA (Swedish International Development Agency) commissioned an analysis of gender; UNICEF and UNESCO underwrote costs for a study of the rights of the child; the Friedrich Ebert Stiftung assisted with a two-volume manual explaining the country's labor code.

30. Susan Brown, "Assessment of Popular Participation in the Formulation and Implementation of Development Policies and Programmes: A Case Study of Namibia" (Windhoek: Namibian Economic Policy Research Unit, 1992).

31. Corbett, "LAC in Transition," p. 4.

32. *Legal Resources Trust [and] Legal Resources Centre, Report for the Year Ended 31 March 1992* (Johannesburg), passim.

33. Gathii Irungu, "Twenty Years Caring for Justice," *Haki Mail* (quarterly journal of the Kituo Cha Sheria) 1, 1 (April 1993), 6.

34. Fawehinmi deserves a biographer. A man of immense energy, larger than life in physique and enthusiasm, he attributes his personal commitment to human rights to privilege (his father was a well-off timber merchant) suddenly interrupted by poverty. While studying law in London, his father (debt-ridden rather than affluent) died, cutting him off without a shilling. Finding work where he could, often as a hospital orderly, Fawehinmi completed his legal studies, returned to Nigeria, and built a lucrative practice. He prided himself on being the leading legal gadfly of the Babangida government, filing suits to challenge the "ouster clauses" whereby the constitution was suspended and courts were enjoined from enforcing basic rights. In one of the most noted cases, an application for habeas corpus, the judge ruled, reluctantly one must suppose, that Decrees 2 and 13 had removed the court's jurisdiction and that, "on the question of Civil Liberties, the law courts of Nigeria must as of now blow muted trumpets" (quoted in Clement Nwankwo, Dulue Mbochu, and Basil Ugochukwu, "Nigeria: The Limits of Justice" [Lagos: Constitutional Rights Project, 1993], p. 57.) Fawehinmi's ire against the regime was especially pronounced in its patent unwillingness to inves-

tigate the letter-bomb assassination of crusading journalist Dele Giwa. Fawehinmi brought suit so that, in the absence of effective investigation by the authorities, private prosecution of the alleged assassins—who, in Gani's view, were members of the national security agency (SSS)—could be undertaken. The effort succeeded, briefly; then the attorney general of Lagos state decided to prosecute directly. As one observer commented, the charge, "apparently deliberately carelessly drafted," was ultimately quashed on application by the accused (Akia Ibidapo-Obe, "Remedies for Breach of Fundamental Rights," in M. A. Ajomo and Bolaji Owasanoye, eds., *Individual Rights Under the 1989 Constitution* [Lagos: Nigerian Institute of Advanced Legal Studies, 1993], p. 132, n. 41). This suit also led to a counter-suit against Chief Fawehinmi by Colonel Alilu Akilu of the State Security Services for damages, which was still dragging on in early 1994. For some details, see Olisa Agbekoba, "The Role of Non-Governmental Organisations in the Development and Protection of Individual Rights," in ibid., pp. 148–49. With the April 1994 announcement that political activity would be permitted in Nigeria as of January 1995, Fawehinmi expressed interest in entering the fray directly. He spoke of establishing a radical party.

35. Inteviews with Tokunbo Ige, Lagos, February 17, 1994; Banjul, April 18, 1994.

36. In addition to these eight, the LRRDC had, as of February 1994, also published somewhat more complex booklets on the Nigerian court system and on the African Charter on Human and People's Rights. Mrs. Ige co-authored a booklet distributed and utilized in ICJ paralegal training sessions. Amy S. Tsanga and Olatokunbo Ige, *A Paralegal Trainer's Manual for Africa* (Geneva: International Commission of Jurists, 1994).

37. *Public Interest Law Around the World: Report of a Symposium Held at Columbia University in May, 1991 With Descriptions of Participating Legal Organizations From Twenty Countries* (New York: Columbia Human Rights Law Review and the NAACP-LDF, 1992), p. 112.

38. Tsanga and Ige, *Paralegal Trainer's Manual*, pp. 99–101.

39. Corbett, "LAC in Transition," p. 5.

Part III
Extending the Impact
of NGOs

Chapter 7
Documenting Human Rights Problems: Ethiopian, Namibian, and Nigerian Examples

> When the human rights treaties were first written, enforcement was intended
> largely to depend on a system of state reporting . . . The idea that governments
> will take the opportunity to present their internal human rights situation to
> international forums in self-critical or negative terms is illusory . . . it is quite
> clear that what was supposed to be the secondary role for international
> monitors has turned out to be the primary hope for the victims of human rights
> abuses.[1]
>
> —Anne Bayefsky

Recall the basic functions of NGOs discussed in Chapter 2. Laurie Wiseberg, perhaps the world's leading specialist on human rights NGOs, compressed their duties into two "absolutely indispensable" ones: information gathering, evaluation and dissemination; and keeping open the political system.[2] In the preceding chapters we have seen examples of both, tied to efforts for education, empowerment, and enforcement. It is now appropriate to concentrate on that most precious of NGO assets, information. How do they collect, analyze, and distribute documentation about human rights problems? What impact can such information have on various publics? Can NGO reports and the publicity given them cumulatively change governments' behavior? Can they work in developing a "human rights culture" within entire societies?

Thanks to NGOs, conspiracies of silence by human rights violators have become increasingly difficult to establish and maintain. Spotlights of international publicity are turned on problem areas. The issues vary, as earlier chapters have shown. Some matters are cultural. Long-concealed practices such as female genital mutilation have been forced into the open, often at the cost of much acrimony, and debates on future steps undertaken. At other times, the concerns are economic, as gaps between groups, regions, or the two genders grow. How to reduce inequalities stirs major discussion, based on information that is brought to public attention. Still other issues are political. Opponents of those who hold power in a given area (usually national governments, but sometimes resistance movements) are harassed or worse. For rectification, they turn to human rights groups for assistance. People systematically discriminated against can, with NGO help, utilize the media and international arenas for support. In short, those who suffer now have recourse, thanks not necessarily to their governments, but to private organizations.

This chapter argues that documentation of human rights violations goes a long way toward reducing many types of human rights abuses. NGOs play the paramount roles in uncovering and publicizing problems. State reports, as the quotation at the start of the chapter indicated, cynically are diplomats in another guise: sent abroad to lie for their country. This does not mean, however, that NGO reports are automatically accurate and bias-free. Private organizations, like governments, have points of view to express. NGOs are also constrained in terms of resources, and thus must scramble hard to get funds for investigation, documentation, and distribution of their findings. Compared to governments, almost all NGOs (and assuredly national human rights groups in Africa) are poor. They must make up for their material shortcomings through expertise, commitment, external revenue, and connections with wider activist networks. These are challenging, essential tasks.

Documentation and monitoring hence are central to protecting human rights. By careful, detailed, persistent, and appropriately circulated studies, and by special urgent appeals when needed, human rights groups can play David to governmental Goliaths. Or, to change the metaphor, they can prove the word-processor mightier than the Kalashnikov.

Issues in Documentation: For Whom? To What Ends?

With one notable exception, human rights NGOs seek to publish and publicize the results of their documentation.[3] They do not (save for tactical reasons) circulate their findings only to inner cliques or to government officials. What governments or powerful figures seek to conceal, NGOs attempt to publicize. The strategy is thus one of open disclosure. Public knowledge is power.

To Whom Is Monitoring Directed?

But, one must ask, knowledge of what? If ignorance about human rights is widespread, how effective can documentation efforts about abuses be? If governments are not responsive to NGO pressure internally, will public opinion from outside the country have more effect? Many choices of strategy must be made.

One major choice involves the balance between broad efforts to educate national audiences about issues, and focused attempts to influence specific decision-makers. Let us take, for example, establishing the rule of law. Recall the work of various legal aid groups discussed in Chapter 6: the Legal Assistance Centre of Namibia, the Legal Research and Resources Development Centre of Nigeria, Kituo cha Sheria of Kenya. Each sought to demystify "the law" through explanatory pamphlets in simple language, focused on issues of daily life. These showed how courts could be used by uneducated market women or the like, and how citizens could protect their rights through use of paralegals or on their own. This choice was deliberate. Such persons are often victims of the legal system because of their ignorance of how courts operate; consequently, there was little reason for them to have confidence in "the rule of law." Further, unless "the law" were demystified, constitutional safeguards would lack public support and understanding. In order to build public support, widespread educational efforts were and are necessary, what French speakers call *sensibilisation* or *vulgarisation.* To reach the largest number, emphasis may lie less on rectifying specific abuses than on building a wider awareness of the potentially beneficial side of the legal system.

But there was another, more elitist, prong to the LAC's actions, and those of similar groups advancing human rights through the judicial system. They brought test cases, argued on constitutional and arcane legal grounds, before bewigged judges or suited magistrates. In such instances, the fine points of the law, directed to a highly specific audience of important officials, were key. Experts talked to experts. Wider knowledge, and in particular awareness of the possibility that the legal system could be used to help ordinary people, was sought by the NGOs discussed in the preceding paragraphs; deeper knowledge, focused application, and in particular, making important judicial decisions and enforcing constitutional norms, were sought by these groups. The documentation utilized and distributed naturally differed. What is provided to possible victims and to their potential defenders will not be identical in these two types.

Should primary attention be given to specific persons — to individual victims of abuses — or to larger groups of potential sufferers who may themselves not have run afoul of the system? Should appeals be directed primarily to citizens of the specific country where the problems exist? Or should appeals be aimed outside the state, specifically at politically and economically powerful groups? African human rights NGOs have chosen a variety of paths.

Once again, the choices NGOs make are not either/or. Obviously, individual/group and national/international levels are linked. Human rights NGOs document specific cases, as well as general conditions; they appeal to global public opinion, in addition to domestic audiences. But there are noteworthy differences in style and attention. Individuals suffering gross abuses such as unjust imprisonment or torture must be released or relieved quickly; hence, NGOs focused on such matters of protection press for rapid action and may spend less time analyzing general conditions. They try to influence those with power, with speed a premium. Activism and immediate action are the objectives. As examples, recall how Amnesty International chapters bombard officials with pleas for release of prisoners of conscience, or how SOS/Torture tries to head off alleged torture through a torrent of faxes and telegrams. But some human rights issues are not amenable to such quick fixes for specific persons. Public opinion must be prepared in advance. The idea that violations are occurring must first become established in the popular mind. Female genital mutilation is a case in point. Awareness of the negative aspects of the practice had to be established and become a matter of open discussion, rather than a closely-held secret in rural settings, before legislation could be pressed for and other efforts at abolition made. As a result, the type of strategy dictates the nature of information sought and distributed. Documentation by the Inter-African Committee and its national chapters fits the strategy of education; SOS/Torture appeals, based on the information it collects, fall in the strategy of enforcement.

Different target groups have different data needs. The type of documentation sought and the audiences to which it is directed vary. Lopez conveniently contrasts the interests of three groups: activists, policy-makers, and scholars.[4] Members of each have their own concerns about victims, rankings of human rights, and consequent data needs. Table 4 summarizes his observations.

In deciding on whom to focus their reports and documentation efforts, NGOs generally try to reach as wide an audience as possible. Their leaders recognize that for tactical reasons they may choose to direct some to the media, as part of popular outreach; some might be aimed at government policy-makers (including judges), and hence be more restricted; some might not be distributed at all. But the overall strategy of open disclosure remains the preferred path. African human rights NGOs must obtain, confirm, and distribute their findings. But in so doing, they confront charges to their impartiality.

Answering Allegations of Bias

Whether NGOs follow primarily a domestic or primarily an international route in publicizing their findings, they are likely to be accused by opponents of anti-national or anti-governmental bias.

Most African human rights NGOs are nationally based. They document abuses within their own states. Most are broadly critical of their governments, and usually correctly so. But the politically powerful have their defenders and means of protection. NGOs' documentation may be

TABLE 4. Charting Different Agendas[5]

Concern	Activist	Scholar	Policy-maker
the victim	• wants to protect, help, release • focuses on victim, rulers and mid-level perpetrators	• asks why these victims • focuses on rulers as key targets of action	• asks what can we do about the situation of the victims
ranking of human rights	• there is no ranking within a set of specified rights[6]	• some types of gross violations of human rights (GVHR) clearly worse than others	• ranks some higher than others based on wider political criteria
data needs	• conditions of victims and the specific acts taken against them	• must address who was victimized, when, by whom, and why	• GVHR varies, can be compared with other available social and political indicators

castigated by critics as simple political opposition, rather than as serious efforts to correct problems. Reports can be brushed off as motivated by ill-will or narrow interests. Sometimes the critics have reason. NGO leaders may personally have collided with their governments and carry (or be presumed to carry) this animus into their work. Their efforts to investigate and publish arise from bitter experience, as well as personal commitment. Bias may creep in. Establishing and maintaining credibility are thus continuous tasks for human rights NGOs, for attacks are to be expected, deserved or not. These tasks are difficult.

Some examples may help. In Namibia, Phil Ya Nangolah heads the Namibian Society for Human Rights.[7] It is, essentially, a one-person operation. He and his organization (at least in late 1993) were barely surviving. (Its major grant, some 4000 Namibian dollars per month [about $1100], came from a conservative, Bavaria-based foundation.) I met him in a small, rather shabby office in downtown Windhoek. A certificate from the Strasbourg International Institute for Human Rights hung on the wall, along with posters for the 1993 Vienna World Conference on Human Rights and "Equality for Women by 2000." Newspapers on his desk were open to the "help wanted" section to supplement the Society's grant funds, for he had nearly reached the end of his personal resources. Books about police detention and international human rights treaties were piled high on his desk and a small near-by table. The telephone and fax machine (for no human rights NGO in Africa can operate effectively without these!) buzzed occasionally as we discussed the NSHR's origins and objectives and, in particular, his role in starting it.

Similar to that of many human rights advocates, Ya Nangolah's involvement came about largely through individual circumstances. He had (like all Namibians of his generation) become politically involved; however, over time, he developed serious reservations about SWAPO's commitment to preventing or correcting human rights abuses, and gradually moved into opposition to it. In 1968, when Ya Nangolah was in school, SWAPO guerrillas arrived in his home area. Tensions grew, as nationalists and defenders of the apartheid status quo vied for support. Families were divided. Ya Nangolah's father was accused of being a South African collaborator; Phil himself was accused of being a SWAPO terrorist. Ya Nangolah left Namibia for further education in 1974 (he was then in his mid-teens), travelling to Angola, Zaire (where he was jailed for two months as an alleged Rhodesian spy), and Zambia, where he attended a SWAPO school. After spending a year as a SWAPO guerrilla, he was arrested by party agents, according to him because of jealousy about his educational achievements. Deeper personal tragedy struck. His brother was executed by SWAPO members in 1977, allegedly for assisting the South Africans. The finger of suspicion pointed at Phil as well. Ya Nangolah was accused of selling SWAPO secrets to "imperial agents" in Finland. He resigned from SWAPO while studying in the United States, joined the splinter group SWAPO-D, which "understood problems of new arrivals," and subsequently dropped any political affiliations. In other words, as a political activist, Ya Nangolah had questioned how SWAPO conducted its business, and had publicly identified himself with an opposing group. He was and remains skeptical of the government's promises. "Thirty years without democracy means organizations like the Namibian Society for Human Rights are needed." "We have a wonderful constitution, but it doesn't help if it is not put into practice."

NSHR documentation is subjected to a great deal of criticism by SWAPO supporters, and occasionally by others less committed to the government. Ya Nangolah is assailed both for his continuing concern about SWAPO detainees who disappeared or were killed without subsequent accounting, and for his generally critical attitude toward the government. Most Namibians linked to SWAPO want to keep the books closed on the fate of these detainees. Some, like Ya Nangolah, Human Rights Watch/Africa, and David Smuts (see Chapters 1 and 6), believe that continued secrecy undermines SWAPO's credibility. Whatever the outcome may be, Ya Nangolah's understandable personal concerns about SWAPO accountability and his personal suffering affect how his organization's reports are perceived.[8] Yet these circumstances should not detract from the importance of his messages. Victims of the brutal war of national liberation should be accounted for; even the most solicitous of governments with respect to human rights has faults. The openness of Namibia is being tested by gadflies like Ya Nangolah.

A second example is furnished by EHRCO, the Ethiopian Human Rights Council. It is headed by a crusty retired professor of geography, Mesfin Wolde Mariam. He became a human rights activist as an extension of his research. Studying the 1958 Tigray famine "transformed my professional outlook. I saw horror that has stayed in my nightmares. . . . I always wanted to do something about it," he said during our first interview in November 1993.[9] In 1984, he published *Rural Vulnerability to Famine in Ethiopia 1958–77*, a technical study with important human rights overtones. As long as there is an exploitative government, he came to realize, Ethiopia will *always* suffer the danger of famine.[10] Widespread hunger, in his view, is not an issue of drought or overpopulation, but of national policy. He carried out similar research in 1986 in Welo and Northern Shoa, both areas seriously affected by food shortages under the Derg. *Suffering Under God's Environment*,[11] published in 1991, confirmed his earlier view. Ethiopia won't get rid of famine without a representative government, he discovered once again. Democracy, in turn, requires effective protection of human rights; effective protection, in turn, requires groups that monitor and publicize abuses.

Mesfin founded EHRCO in October 1991 to test the reality of the July 1991 transitional Charter (which, it should be recalled, stated, "individual human rights shall be respected fully, and without any limitation whatsoever"[12]). And, since that time, the Ethiopian Human Rights Council has been a thorn in the government's side, critical of many of its actions. To Mesfin and his colleagues, the 1991 overthrow of the dictatorial Mengistu regime was a step in the right direction. However, much more remains to be done. Indeed, in their view, the high hopes of the early months under President Meles Zenawi have proven incorrect. While proponents of the Transitional Government note that human rights conditions have improved since mid-1991, opponents point to the serious abuses that remain. Are there "hopeful signs of due process," as EHRCO commented in its second report (February 13, 1992), or has hope turned into "wishful thinking," as the third report (July 16, 1992) stated? The "contradiction between rhetoric and practice"[13] — alas, found in almost all states of the world — remains unresolved. The Ethiopian Human Rights Council publicizes information the EPRDF often considers misinformed or inflammatory; EHRCO believes the government must do a far better job in correcting human rights problems.

Antagonism between the Ethiopian government and the Ethiopian Human Rights Council is strong. Each EHRCO report includes details of complaints sent to it, which usually (but not always) have been confirmed by EHRCO staff. Property confiscated by the dominant party; persons dismissed from their positions; individuals detained unduly prior to trial; disappearances: all are grist for EHRCO reports. They are politically embarrassing, especially as the EPRDF government holds elections, installs a new constitution, and seeks foreign aid for reconstruction and development.

As should be expected, EHRCO reports receive both unofficial bad-mouthing and official critiques.[14] By assailing their accuracy and the probity of their authors, the EPRDF government and its supporters react in the typical fashion. Governments do not want national dirty linen laundered in public — especially if some allegations implicate their leading members. Wouldn't it be better to work quietly and directly with the government, rather than rush into print with complaints, they argue. In their view, behind-the-scenes consultation (the equivalent of "quiet diplomacy"?) is the best type of action. They assert that all reports of abuses are subject to suspicion. There must be political animus in highlighting problems, they suggest. According to human rights activists, since the message is not liked, the messenger unjustly bears the blame. But critics do have grounds for complaint. Some EHRCO allegations are incomplete or inaccurate (due, the organization claims, largely to the secrecy that shrouds wide areas of Ethiopian life and the difficulties of confirmation). But they are not automatically without substance.

One close observer of the Ethiopian NGO scene provided the following assessment:

> EHRCO is an extraordinarily important indigenous nongovernmental organization that is fast becoming an effective advocate for human rights in Ethiopia. It provides both a voice for the rule of law as well as an outlet for reporting the abuses of the TGE [Transitional Government of Ethiopia] and the opposition. Its effectiveness lay in its impartiality and commitment to a peaceful resolution of conflict, in its tenacity in pursuing leads and conducting preliminary investigations even if rudimentary in nature, and in its unflagging courage to report its findings regardless of the backlash it may experience.[15]

The barriers of mistrust between the Ethiopian Human Rights Council and the Ethiopian government typifies human rights NGO-government relations through most of Africa. Both are contesting for political space and popular attention. EHRCO faces the complex tasks of educating the Ethiopian public about the importance of human rights and validating its evidence of abuses; the regime faces the equally daunting problem of translating its verbal commitment to human rights into national policy. In order to do so, the government must deal with the issues raised by Mesfin and his colleagues. EHRCO documentation cannot be brushed off as self-interested, nor can it be dismissed despite occasional errors. No human rights NGO can expect 100 percent accuracy, though this is their objective.

Thus far, I have concentrated on national public opinion. But human rights is a matter of global concern. International public opinion, and in particular views in developed, aid-giving countries, is a chief target for NGO documentation. The open disclosure sought by human rights groups parallels the duties shouldered by governments and demanded by major donors. As argued in Chapter 5, many African governments have, by ratifying international treaties, become responsible for reporting officially about and correcting human rights problems. They must submit information to bodies of experts, and, through them, to world public opinion. NGOs are increasingly preparing and transmitting counter-reports to the treaty bodies through networks with Geneva or Banjul connections. African governments are also under other types of pressure to improve and publicize their human rights performance—which provides another obvious opening for NGOs. Donor countries increasingly attach conditions for economic assistance: no aid without better protection of human rights. Democratization and development (the subjects of the following two chapters) require steps by governments. How satisfactorily this performance has been in global terms can be answered in part by NGO documentation—especially, of course, if the results are made widely available through the media.

Reaching Out to the Media

The public aspects of NGO research must be stressed. Human rights NGOs do not carry out research simply for the sake of knowledge; they do so to get results. Their studies are intended to shape government policies and mould public opinion. To do so, they work via press, radio, and television. National and international NGOs share a common interest in gaining media attention. Informing and influencing popular perceptions are major goals of documentation. But which audiences are most important? which are most accessible?

Public opinion about human rights may be strongest in Western industrial states, to which NGOs (whether based in Africa or in the West) seek to appeal. Here is an area in which well-funded, readily accessible INGOs (international NGOs) based in Geneva, London, or New York have manifest advantages. Human rights organizations in Addis Ababa, Banjul, or even Cape Town cannot expect international (largely Western) publicity, unless their reports are picked up and trumpeted by other groups. As a result, networking is central to NGO documentation. African human rights groups push for continent-wide or regional exchanges of information. The ICJ-organized workshops provide a meeting ground. Similarly, international human rights NGOs establish links to Africa-based NGOs. Networking efforts have to date, in my opinion, had only limited success.

The human rights media scene continues to be dominated by INGOs, both because of their carefully-established contacts and, more important, the depth and frequency of their reports. Human Rights Watch/Africa, for example, cultivates links to national TV and radio networks, the New York *Times*, the Washington *Post*, the *New Yorker*, and the like; its studies of civil and political rights have built a reputation for accuracy. HRW/Africa's coverage of human rights is, however, far from continent-wide or issue-inclusive in scope. Though not the youngest of the Human Rights Watch family, it is among the smaller in terms of number of full-time researchers. Funding has been difficult to obtain, relative to HRW's success for analyses of Eastern Europe. Certain African countries have been emphasized, due to their size, susceptibility to American pressure, political significance, and range of human rights problems. Ethiopia, Kenya, Liberia, Nigeria, Rwanda, Somalia, South Africa, Sudan, and Zaire have received extensive HRW/Africa attention; Malawi, Mauritania, Zambia and Zimbabwe have also been the focus of more than one study.

For most of the organization's history, civil and political rights have received far greater attention than economic, social, and cultural rights. The specific mandate and "institutional culture" of Human Rights Watch as a whole emphasize the former. HRW's roots lie in long-standing American emphasis on "first generation" rights, in the civil liberties (and especially ACLU) background of Aryeh Neier, its first Director, in the organization's initial emphasis (in Helsinki Watch) on emigration of Soviet and other Eastern European Jews, in the interests of major donors, and in the belief that governmental leaders (or leaders of rebel movements) are largely responsible for abridging human rights. "Structural" abuses of human rights arising from poverty do not fall in Human Rights Watch's official mandate. The interdependence of rights is acknowledged, but somewhat reluctantly. Indeed, HRW's major study did not appear until September 1992. Entitled "Indivisible Human Rights: The Relationship of Political and Civil Rights to Survival, Subsistence and Poverty," it argued that many economic and cultural privations such as famine, land maldistribution, environmental degradation, and abuse of workers' rights, arise from political conditions. Democratic accountability, freedom of movement and residence, and freedom from arbitrary deprivation of livelihood would have mitigated the four issues studied.

The studies of Human Rights Watch/Africa have been carried out, almost without exception, by its own staff members. This provided, according to former HRW director Aryeh Neier, higher, more consistent quality.[16] Such a procedure had its down-side as well. An HRW specialist would arrive for a few weeks of field work, sometimes working closely with local human rights NGOs, sometimes acting independently. The reports are carefully edited in the New York headquarters prior to release. (That Human Rights Watch/Africa was based in London for several years, and later in Washington, complicated matters somewhat.) The only major exception to this general policy of using staff members for field research with only indirect reliance on local NGOs was HRW's release under its own imprint (both in the original French and in a later English translation) of the international commission's report on Rwanda.[17] Since one of the commission's members was Alison DesForges, chief researcher for earlier HRW/Africa reports on Rwanda, an internationally-respected specialist on that country, and an extremely active member of the HRW/Africa board member, the exception is quite understandable.

For Human Rights Watch as a whole, the issue of cultural relativism poses a minor problem; for Human Rights Watch/Africa, it is relatively significant. HRW does not focus on the full gamut of human rights as set out in the Universal Declaration of Human Rights, but concentrates, as just noted, on civil and political rights. In the view of some leaders of African human rights NGOs whom I interviewed in my field work, this narrow mandate weakened HRW's claim to speak on behalf of "global" or "universal" human rights, for it appeared to be pursuing a restricted set of rights, of interest primarily to American policy-makers. They also questioned HRW's strong stance against weakening its commitment to universal standards by recognizing even "weak" cultural relativism.[18] In their eyes, this focus should have resulted in greater sympathy for cultural relativism: you in the West emphasize civil and political rights; we in the south stress economic, social, and cultural rights. Caught in the middle was Abdullahi An-Na'im, Executive Director of Human Rights Watch/Africa between 1993 and 1995. He was deeply concerned, as a widely published scholar, with the ways in which human rights are interpreted in different cultures.

An-Na'im recognized that HRW/Africa must work cooperatively with African human rights NGOs to break what he calls a growing "human rights dependency." With such dependency, these organizations will not be effective in supporting in their own societies. A "human rights culture" must be developed, "committed to internationally recognized standards and capable of motivating a wider community to act in support of that shared commitment." Attention must be given to the "context and experience" of individual cultures. Human Rights Watch/Africa "needs to collaborate with competent and credible local human rights NGOs in collecting information, verifying and corroborating allegations of violations, planning and implementation of advocacy strategies, and so forth." Partnerships of this sort would represent a new direction, and to critics within HRW as a whole might undercut its civil and political rights emphasis, and its quality control through largely self-generated studies. An-Na'im insisted that HRW/Africa "critically evaluate the standards and operations of African NGOs, especially those with whom it might wish to collaborate."[19] Not an easy task! The questions An-Na'im raised are indeed fundamental. I hope this book provides partial answers to these questsions. Much more could, and should, be written about Human Rights Watch; I regret having to be so brief here.[20]

Note must be taken of other international NGOs with significant impact on human rights in Africa. Anti-Slavery International, widely recognized as the oldest continuously-existing international human rights NGO, issues regular reports that gain widespread attention. ASI can, from its London base, effectively spotlight such abuses as traditional slavery (still practiced in Mauritania despite four government pledges for abolition), bonded labor, oppression of women, exploitative child labor, and threats to indigenous peoples. Amnesty International takes great care in getting its myriad, carefully-researched publications (including urgent action appeals on behalf of individuals as well as longer-range studies focused on specific countries) to "makers and shapers" of public opinion. AI's London-based research staff of 200 is at this time probably larger than the combined professional staffs of all human rights organizations in tropical Africa; no less than 25 researchers work on Africa, 17 of them on sub-Saharan countries.[21] These international NGOs illustrate — they certainly do not exhaust — the links between research and the media. Credibility established over time, carefully nurtured global media contacts, ample research budgets (certainly relative to the levels achieved by tropical African human rights NGOs), greater detachment from local pressures: these are advantages national human rights groups cannot match. One consequence, explored in the conclusion of this chapter, is imbalance.

Nationally-based NGOs have major points in their favor, however. Most important, they are deeply and continuously involved in their own societies. They can respond more rapidly in cases of emergency than can regional or global NGOs; they can cultivate internal information sources over longer periods of time; they are sensitive to local problems and priorities. While access to international media is bound to be far more difficult for them, they can turn to the local press. The explosion in the number of private newspapers in Africa since the political opening of 1990 means government-directed publications no longer monopolize the market, though they continue to dominate in many countries. The Fourth Estate itself may gain readers by spotlighting human rights problems and by publicizing NGO documentation. Thus, a direct relationship exists between the "space" enjoyed by the press and by human rights

NGOs. Both are bound in symbiotic relationships. The deepening of civil society in Africa rests in part on analyses by human rights NGOs, brought to public attention by privately-owned media. The less the government's control of the press and other means of public communication, the more the publicity NGO documentation can receive.

The amount of public attention given to human rights abuses nationally and internationally also varies, as should be expected, with the nature of the problems. Widespread violence against innocent civilians will almost certainly get ample media exposure. The butcheries of Rwanda in the spring of 1994 received immediate global coverage; genocide is big news anywhere. The evidence compiled by UN Special Rapporteur René Degni-Ségui confirmed what television viewers around the world already recognized: hundreds of thousands of Tutsis and Hutus died in orchestrated slaughters. Most human rights documentation, fortunately, does not involve such gruesome events. It concentrates, instead, on what could be called finer points of the law and on less obvious abuses than mass murders. Nonetheless, they can add up to withering indictments of governmental and/or resistance group actions. But the more complex or the more politically sensitive this documentation becomes, the greater the problems of getting coverage turn out to be.

African human rights NGOs are bound to increase both their volume of research and their links to the media. These will not be simple, however. As relatively new, lightly-funded entities, most are inexperienced in preparing detailed reports. Their priorities have pressed them in a somewhat different direction. NGO leaders seek to resolve immediate problems. Most are, first and foremost, human rights activists. Immediate tasks — get that person released from detention, prevent the police from beating that suspect — take priority over long-term analysis. Although the need for research is recognized, the urgency of action is overriding to many. Research and publication are secondary priorities — that is, unless funds are directly attached. Hence, in addition to reaching out to media, African human rights NGOs must stretch out their hands to funding agencies, for their protection as well as their promotion activities.

Finding Support for Documentation

To a significant extent, major research by African human rights NGOs has resulted from external financial support. Grants from such entities as the Ford Foundation, the Norwegian Agency for Development Cooperation, the Danish Centre for Human Rights, or USAID have underwritten the costs of many of the studies cited in this book. NGO leaders recognize the funding realities: major funding must be found outside their countries.[22] Human rights activists have, of necessity, learned the games of grantsmanship to establish and maintain their organizations. As a consequence, donor priorities influence NGO strategies. Allocations are less difficult to obtain for specific projects than for general institutional support. For example, it is easier to find dollars to prepare a report on prison conditions than to obtain dollars for day-to-day activities. Hence, NGOs apply regularly for research funds since, as part of the overhead, the rent, telephone, and salary bills can be met.

Could domestic sources of funds be found for research? Yes, but only in very modest amounts. For the foreseeable future, research on human rights in most African countries will continue to be carried out largely by international NGOs; national NGOs will rely heavily on grants, most likely from Western sources, for their own research. In only a handful of countries — certainly South Africa; also Nigeria, Kenya, Ethiopia, Tunisia, and Egypt; perhaps Senegal and Zimbabwe — have national NGOs documented patterns of abuse on any consistent basis for more than a year or two. Seed money from outside is necessary to get the monitoring process started; continuing support is necessary to maintain it.

However, the difficulty of gaining local financial support must not be used as an excuse to avoid it. Fund-raising is an important means toward three goals: 1) creating greater domestic awareness of NGOs' goals; 2) enhancing knowledge about human rights abuses; and 3) providing citizens a sense of "ownership" for the NGOs that thereby become more responsible to them. Support from outside the country, experience has shown, makes many African human rights NGOs less democratic. They perceive themselves as more accountable to foreign funders than to their own constituencies.[23]

Other dangers exist. The priorities of external funders may diverge from the priorities and needs of domestic human rights NGOs. At worst, the agenda for action will reflect concerns that are important to the donor but relatively trivial in terms of national needs. The NGOs themselves can become distorted. Too great a dependency on a small number of grants, diffuseness as a result of pursuing too wide a variety of projects, priorities established more by what is fundable rather than what is urgent: all these issues mark some of the NGOs among the dozens I studied for this book. But the negative aspects should not be unduly emphasized. Documenting and publicizing human rights issues is a paramount task for NGOs. They can neither survive easily nor undertake significant research without international grants. Faddism exists, to be certain.[24] It should not (like charges of anti-government animus) detract from the importance of NGOs' monitoring efforts, however. External funding for documentation is a necessary feature of the current human rights scene. It is a fact, not a fatal weakness.

Training to Enhance Documentation

Documentation by African human rights NGOs depends on both international human rights standards and locally gathered information. Documentation is becoming more feasible for NGOs as training has improved. Before turning to case studies from Nigeria to see how specific organizations have used research to promote and protect human rights, it is appropriate to spend a few moments looking at efforts to improve the quality of documentation through coordinated programs. In brief, impetus and funds have come largely from Western sources; however, an increasing number of NGOs have developed their own expertise. The trend is clearly toward Africa-based expertise and training programs, even if financial support for them continues to flow largely from developed countries.

HURIDOCS is one of the scores of NGOs that populate Geneva. Funded largely by Norwegian and other Western sources, and chaired by an energetic Ghanaian law professor, HURIDOCS is unusual in the human rights community. Housed in a modest ground-floor former apartment down the slope from the main train station (though not as far as the costly, fashionable lake shore), HURIDOCS has a limited, intriguing mandate. Its acronym stands for Human Rights Information and Documentation Systems International. As this suggests, HURIDOCS both trains persons in the technical details of documentating international human rights standards, and seeks to establish a common foundation for documentation. It does not itself monitor or publicize abuses. Rather, it seeks to establish the technical foundation on which systematic monitoring will be possible.

HURIDOCS started programs in sub-Saharan Africa shortly after the "second independence" opened up new fields of action for human rights NGOs. It held workshops in Kinshasa, Zaire, September 1991; Banjul, The Gambia, August 1993; and Nairobi, Kenya, October 1994. Specialized training has been given as well to NGOs like the African Centre for Democracy and Human Rights Studies (Banjul), the Institute of Southern African Studies (Roma, Lesotho), the Civil Liberties Organisation (Lagos, Nigeria), and the Legal Resources Centre (Harare, Zimbabwe).

HURIDOCS also has developed what its leaders consider a globally valid standard format for reporting human rights violations. The massive pressures experienced in Sri Lanka, especially by Tamils, provided a test case; parts of the former Yugoslavia others. Since 1985, it has labored to refine the standard format.[25] No African human rights NGO has, at least as of mid-1994, utilized it for any length of time.[26] But computer software and hard-copy versions are ready for use. Might one envisage the day in which global electronic links flash details about human rights abuses around the world, making possible the apprehension and trial of systematic violators? Would the proposed African Court of Human Rights utilize information prepared in the HURIDOCS format? Systematic gathering of evidence for use in possible prosecution could dramatically shift the dynamics of human rights enforcement in Africa.

Technological advances, in particular computerization, have already started to revolutionize human rights documentation in parts of Africa. A noteworthy example comes from the Special Prosecutor's Office (SPO) in Ethiopia. Here, techniques previously utilized in El Salvador and currently employed for the War Crimes Tribunals for the former Yugoslavia and Rwanda are being applied. In all these areas, widespread killings of political opponents (mostly anti-government persons) or persons of a particular ethnicity occurred. Rarely, however, were written orders given, at least at senior levels of the government, for the massive slaughters. If paper trails do not exist, proving responsibility in a court of law is very difficult. Prosecution cases must be built on circumstantial evidence, based on meticulous combing of documents and cross-referencing — tasks possible only with the speed and data storage capacities of computers. How successful can this highly specialized documentation prove, in terms of outcomes?

The Special Prosecutor's Office in Ethiopia is not a human rights NGO. Nonetheless, its goals and *modus operandi* have direct relevance to NGO activity. It has documented systematic, gross violations of human rights. Rather than focusing on the small fry, relatively speaking — *kebelle* heads who signed death warrants — the SPO is trying (as of December 1994) senior Derg officials who allegedly instigated the policies. The task is mammoth, well beyond the scope of what Ethiopia could support were it not for major external assistance and computer capabilities.

The Transitional Government of Ethiopia established the Special Prosecutor's Office in August 1992, months behind schedule. It was to investigate close to 2,000 former Derg officials who were being detained at that point. (The number of detainees subsequently grew to more than 2,500, as additional evidence was unearthed.) The desire to build air-tight legal cases and prosecute the truly culpable ran headlong into a questionable practice: continued detention of the suspects, the great majority of whom were in fact unlikely to come to trial. Continued suspension of *habeas corpus* was one price of the quest for adequate documentation, the Special Prosecutor's Office claimed; monitoring groups such as Amnesty International became increasingly critical. An unrealistic timeframe, delayed and insufficient funding, the heritage of 17 years of repression, problems in working out a court strategy: all these impacted on the SPO's work.[27] Despite 200 persons working on data input in late 1993 (when 500 more were needed, given the magnitude of the task), the Special

Prosecutor's Office suffered from credibility. Were the human rights costs of holding roughly 2,500 persons (by January 1994) for more than two and a half years without trial greater than the benefits of the better-prepared trials that were to result? The dilemma was not an easy one to resolve.

HURIDOCS and the Ethiopian Special Prosecutor's Office highlight a crucial problem in human rights documentation. Dramatically different levels of technological development and financial support risk dividing rather than uniting human rights NGOs and other relevant organizations. Amnesty International or Human Rights Watch/Africa, both global in their concern, can summon up far more resources than can African human rights NGOs. The latter are valued sources of information, but because of their size, more limited experience, and other factors, they are not equal partners. First World and Third World human rights NGOs have similar goals; they do not necessarily have identical work styles; they certainly face different types of political pressures. Western NGOs have more experience with packaging information for the media, treaty bodies, or other audiences. African NGOs have greater opportunity for on-site, continuous investigation, quite likely a better "feel" for particular circumstances, and (often) less domestic suspicion about their serving external interests. Both need to cooperate in sharing information. Undue fascination with technological advances, or excessive concern about local particularities, can restrict the needed dialogue. NGOs must be able to communicate effectively with each other, given the importance of networking. Human rights documentation cannot be the preserve of any group.

To summarize the lessons of this chapter thus far: documentation provides an essential foundation for NGOs' efforts in education, empowerment, and enforcement. Clear, unbiased reporting on human rights issues is an essential objective. Human rights matters are ultimately tried more in the courts of public opinion than in courts of law; accordingly, sensitivity to cultural constraints is important. Without effective research and presentation, including a free press, the impact of human rights NGOs would be far lighter. Means for collecting and analyzing information are changing rapidly. Regular, detailed exchanges of ideas about gathering documentation are essential.

Documentation in Action: Nigerian Police and Prison Conditions

As has been shown throughout *Protecting Human Rights in Africa*, strong commitment by an individual or small group of persons helped get an NGO started. The early history of two Nigerian organizations, the Civil

Liberties Organisation (CLO) and the Constitutional Rights Project (CRP), was bound up with the interests of Clement Nwankwo. How he became involved should be of interest.

Nwankwo received his undergraduate degree at the University of Nigeria, Nsukka, in 1984, then after a year in law school spent his 12 months of required national service with the Legal Aid Council. He had extensive contact with persons in detention, and represented many in court. "There were some very pathetic cases,"[28] usually individuals detained for up to a decade because they lacked the money or social prestige to get bail or go to trial. After entering private legal practice, Nwankwo kept visiting prisons. He, his mentor Olisa Agbakoba (a leading Lagos-based attorney), and Abdul Oroh (at that time legal correspondent for *The Guardian*, a leading Lagos daily) agreed to establish the Civil Liberties Organisation in 1987. They decided at an early point to make prisoners' rights a major focus of their activity, both in study and in *pro bono* legal assistance. They had to counter a wall of negative public opinion. In Nwankwo's view, Nigerian society is biased against those in jail, since they are presumed guilty even if not yet tried.[29]

Prisoners are one of the most afflicted but least prominent groups in contemporary Africa. Those in jail (even if detained for years before trial) are forgotten by all save close relatives. Yet they have rights that must be respected. Careful analyses by Nigerian human rights NGOs, including the CLO, the CRP, and the Nigerian Institute of Advanced Legal Studies (NIALS), reveal distressing facts. A NIALS study, funded by the Ford Foundation and carried out by two members of the Institute, found that in June 1989, about 58,000 prisoners were being housed in prisons meant for 28,000 inmates, under "highly unacceptable conditions." The average prisoner on remand was indigent, drawn from lower social classes, always hungry, and deprived of clean clothing and medical attention.[30] This publication was followed by others. *Behind the Wall*, a publication of the CLO, "generated lots of controversy" upon its release in 1991.[31] The report documented even worse conditions than those detailed in the NIALS book. In particular, thousands were being held without trial, long beyond what jail sentence they might possibly have received had their guilt been proven in court. The Nigerian government set up a commission to investigate these disturbing findings. Over 13,000 prisoners were granted amnesty, the CLO executive director claimed, as of January 1992. In addition, feeding allowances were increased, repairs made to broken water systems within jails, and a German grant provided for medicine and foodstuffs within jails. Unfortunately, it must also be reported, Nigeria's worsening economic condition and exhaustion of the grant meant prison conditions once again have deteriorated.

Of far more immediate importance to the Nigerian populace — indeed, to citizens of all African countries—are police actions. As the NIALS authors aptly noted, given the country's slide toward anarchy and official lawlessness in the late 1980s and early 1990s, "the fundamental rights of the citizen are more often and more directly affected by police activities than by those of any other institution. Abuse of these powers invariably results in the violation of one or the other of the fundamental rights of the citizen. The right to personal freedom seems the worst affected because wrongful arrests and detentions abound."[32] In even stronger words, the CRP (in a USAID-sponsored report) branded the Nigerian police force as perceiving itself "as an occupying force — a bully, that has a duty to compel obedience to the authority of the State, an authority that the police believes [sic] should be unquestionable and obeyed at all times."[33] These strong words were fully justified, given what careful research uncovered. A few examples should be useful.

How much do arrested persons in Nigeria get to know about the grounds for their arrest and their rights? Perceptions differ markedly. One author noted that police, "relying on the wide powers conferred upon them by the Police Act, perpetrate inhumanities in the name of arrest," and constantly ignore their requirement to inform arrested persons promptly of the cause of arrest.[34] According to the NIALS analysis, a mere eight percent of arrestees knew of their right to remain silent. (By contrast, no less than 82.2 percent of the police interviewed said arrested persons were immediately notified of the grounds for arrest; a mere 20.4 percent of the accused said that was the case.[35]) Ill-treatment at the time of arrest was common: 48.7 percent of the detained persons interviewed for the NIALS book said their arrest involved insult or abuse by police; 35.9 percent were rough-handled or slapped.[36] The CRP study (in which 298 members of the public were surveyed) showed equally worrisome trends. More than three-quarters of the respondents saw police attitudes as cruel, inhuman, and/or corrupt; just over one-fifth found them kind and helpful.[37] Ill-treatment or torture to extract confessions, the CRP report commented, "has indeed become a regular feature of the police law enforcement system."[38] As the NIALS authors aptly concluded, "the above figures . . . depict a sad state of affairs which calls for immediate remedial action. . . . This cannot be achieved unless there is a radical change in police appreciation of their role towards suspects in the administration of criminal justice."[39]

One of the most important changes would be reduced corruption within the police force. To cite once again the NIALS analysis,

The image of the Nigeria Police is very poor. . . . Many factors are responsible. . . . Most important of these is corruption. It is now taken for granted that provided he can pay his way through, a citizen can manipulate the police as he wishes. Corruption seems to have become institutionalised by policemen at checkpoints. . . .

Every checkpoint became by itself a toll gate, especially for commercial vehicles, but with the difference that the proceeds went into private pockets.[40]

How can the rule of law be established if the major agents are themselves so corrupt, manipulable, and ill-trained? What are the consequences when "the experience and perception of certain institutions of the criminal justice system by ordinary citizens are negative and unpleasant"[41]? The answers are unpleasant to consider.

The Nigerian analyses just cited are not unique[42]; however, they were unusual in the late 1980s–early 1990s for the range and quality of their research. NIALS, the CLO, and the CRP provided important data that both confirmed popular awareness (say, of police brutality and corruption and of abysmal prison conditions), and challenged the government to respond. The Babangida regime did not do so, at least in lasting, effective terms. Its authoritarian nature intervened. Without human rights being a priority at the top, other institutions remained unreformed. Alas, documentation by itself had not changed, by mid-1994, the self-serving, corrupt, and overbearing conduct of Nigerian police. Nor had prison conditions improved; at best, they were poor, at worst, they were unlivable. Nigeria's economic anemia, political drift, and increasing violence had worsened the human rights climate as a whole. In the absence of broader changes in the national political and economic context, the studies of the CLO, CRP, and NIALS remained pieces of paper. The organizations pinpointed problems and suggested solutions. They helped prepare Nigerian public opinion for reform. They provided further confirmation of the already well-known professional ineptitude of the police. But political will (linked to democratization) and greater resources (tied to development) were essential. These matters belonged in the government's court, not the NGOs'. Documentation is necessary, but not sufficient, for improved protection of human rights. As two Nigerian authors concluded, "Therefore, the most important remedy against breaches of fundamental rights by the police and the enforcement of such rights by the courts, is the enthronement of a truly liberal democratic government in the country."[43]

Documentation as End or Means?

The continuous monitoring and documenting of human rights issues is, accordingly, a central task for NGOs. They play a crucial role, given the failings of the state-centered reporting system championed earlier by the UN Commission on Human Rights. It is now well accepted that both official reports and NGO reports are essential. They are complementary.[44]

NGO documentation has steadily increased in quality and quantity. Greater knowledge, growing links among NGOs, and better forms of measurement have helped both governments and NGOs. But existing documentation remains liable to many weaknesses. As one practitioner wrote, "human rights reporting is frequently episodic, incidental, sporadic and spotty. . . . Despite the many agencies and organizations involved in monitoring human rights and reporting on abuses, much of this collection is done according to self-defined mandates, using self-defined criteria and terms, and reporting primarily to internal or already-committed organizational constituents."[45] In other words, this author suggests, clear, universally-accepted standard definitions do not exist in a way that eases documentation.

I disagree. Much of the Universal Declaration of Human Rights has passed into the exalted realm of customary international law, many scholars argue. Its broad statements have been periodically reaffirmed in the face of challenges to its global nature, most recently at the 1993 World Conference on Human Rights. The committees established by the ICCPR and ICESCR have elaborated reporting guidelines that, over time, have resulted in more detailed, more consistent reports. Other human rights treaty bodies have developed formats that facilitate gathering information. Experienced NGOs such as Amnesty International have established and maintained high standards with their monitoring and documentation. African human rights NGOs (despite their problems with funding and staff) increasingly tap into global norms, for which quantitative measures have been defined. Basic economic and social data have become available, particularly through the World Bank, UNICEF, and UNDP (United Nations Development Program) annual publications.[46] Regular exchanges through workshops have markedly enhanced the consistency of information. Inadequate conceptualization and insufficient data may have excused pre-1990s comparative analysis of human rights. They are not excuses now.

Looking ahead, one could envisage the following important uses of human rights documentation:

- in pinpointing areas of potential future difficulty, using indicators of abuses drawn from prior studies of human rights abuses;
- in bringing to trial persons responsible for widespread or massive violations, both nationally and internationally;
- in providing yardsticks to governments for improving their performance in various policy areas;
- in better informing public opinion, leading to higher levels of human rights awareness.

These are assuredly *not* unrealizable dreams. They are well within the realm of present achievement. NGOs are central to the task. Whether the chief strategy be education, empowerment or enforcement, documentation gathered, evaluated, and disseminated by NGOs rests at the heart of the effort.

Documentation of human rights issues has become the primary objective for some NGOs; it is a necessary goal for all. End for some, means for all: that is the chief conclusion we can reach. Seeing how documentation is linked with democratization and development forms the subjects of the next two chapters.

Notes

1. Anne F. Bayefsky, "Making the Human Rights Treaties Work," in Louis Henkin and John Lawrence Hargrove, eds., *Human Rights: An Agenda for the Next Century* (Washington, DC: American Society of International Law, 1993), pp. 232–34.

2. Laurie S. Wiseberg, "Defending Human Rights Defenders: The Importance of Freedom of Association for Human Rights NGOs" (Montreal: International Centre for Human Rights and Democratic Development, 1993), pp. 5–6.

3. The exception is the International Committee of the Red Cross, which has developed, over time, a finely-calibrated system of working with both governmental and insurgent forces to ensure humanitarian norms are upheld. The ICRC maintains a policy of official silence about abuses it observes, going public very rarely. For details about its development, see David Forsythe, *Humanitarian Politics: The International Committee of the Red Cross* (Baltimore: Johns Hopkins University Press, 1977). Without doubt, the ICRC is a "special case," as Forsythe notes elsewhere (in *Human Rights and World Politics* [Lincoln: University of Nebraska Press, 1988, 2nd edition revised], p. 85).

4. George A. Lopez, "Data Sources and Data Needs in Human Rights Monitoring," in Alex P. Schmid and Albert J. Jongman, eds., *Monitoring Human Rights Violations* (Leiden: Center for the Study of Social Conflicts, 1992), pp. 47–62.

5. Source: George A. Lopez, "Data Sources and Data Needs in Human Rights Monitoring," p. 49. Minor typographical errors corrected.

6. Lopez limits his category here to civil and political rights, in part in keeping with the organizations with which he is concerned. However, given the interdependence of rights, such a limitation strikes me as inappropriate.

7. Information in this and the following two paragraphs comes from an interview October 7, 1993 with Ya Nangolah, subsequent discussions with other Namibians, and perusal of NSHR publications.

8. See note 27, Chapter 6. Ya Nangolah's purple prose also may affect his credibility. Take, for example, the opening sentences of the NSHR's report on children: "Despite the apparent dramatic changes and rapid transformation in the political, economic, social and cultural structures on the continent, in reality African societies and Namibian society is no exception, continued to be dominated by the partriarchal [sic] supreme guides of the revolution, fathers of the nation and other rapacious vampires whose insatiable lust for political power and opulence continue to make the 'dark' Continent a cesspool of human catastro-

phe." "The Namibia Country Report on the Status of the UN Convention on the Rights of the Child: A Critical Analysis" (Windhoek: NSHR, 1992), p. i.

9. Interview, EHRCO office, November 8, 1883. As Mesfin wrote in his book,

> The ghastly scene of famine left its indelible imprint on my mind. That experience convinced me personally of the urgent need to do something about famine. But the fact that I could not even have the description of the famine in Tigray printed in any of the newspapers, together with the long delay in delivering relief aid to the victims, cast a shadow of doubt in my mind, a doubt whether famine is really a consequence of natural phenomena such as drought or locust invasion, or whether it is the failure of the socio-economic system.

Mesfin Wolde-Mariam, *Rural Vulnerablity to Famine in Ethiopia 1958–77* (London: Intermediate Technology Publications, 1986), p. ix.

10. ". . . famine is fundamentally a result of socio-economic disorganization and political irresponsibility. . . . Government, government officials, traditional patrons, landlords, rich farmers, and merchants created the disorganized, illiterate, weak and voiceless mass of peasants. . . . For too long, the rural people of Ethiopia have been the victims of perhaps well-meaning but ill-advised tyrants of every kind" (ibid., pp. 15, 16, 184).

11. Mesfin Wolde-Mariam, *Suffering Under God's Environment: A Vertical Study of Peasants in North-Central Ethiopia* (Berne: African Mountains Association, Geographica Bernensia, 1991).

12. "Transitional Period Charter of Ethiopia," Article 1.

13. Ethiopian Human Rights Council, "Fourth Report on the Human Rights Situation in Ethiopia," January 21, 1993, p. 1.

14. The first four EHRCO reports did not result in any detailed commentary from the government. The fifth report, dated June 3, 1993, occasioned a lengthy rebuttal six weeks later from the Office of the Coordinator of the Police and Prisons Administration (see *Ethiopian Herald*, 18 July 1993). As should be expected, officials proved defensive about their actions, dismissive of EHRCO's reports.

> It is an unfortunate truth that human beings, including police officers, err. When accidents happen, this is a cause for grave and public concern. However, it is unjustifiable to refer to such incidents without any clarification of the circumstances, without any reference to corrective measures taken to guard against repetition of such accidents, and to confuse human error with deliberate human rights abuses. . . .
>
> Given all the above, we must, reluctantly, express serious dobuts [sic] about the EHRC as a genuine human rights organisation, and ask whether their operations do not reflect their own political activities and agenda rather than sincere commitment to human rights.
>
> The process of human rights monitoring is a very important part of the democratisation process in Ethiopia, and must be approached with integrity, in a serious, responsible, and genuine manner. We have yet to see the Ethiopian Human Rights Council demonstrate such an approach. (*Ethiopian Herald*, 18 July 1993)

Doth the government protest too much? Or was publication of these comments in the *Ethiopian Herald* a step toward dialogue between the regime and human rights activists? Such tension is a normal part of human rights monitoring. Charges and counter-charges should be expected. EHRCO provided its response a month later; little media attention was given to it. Ethiopian Human Rights Council, "Response to the Comment on the Fifth Report Given by the Office of the Coordinator of the Police and Prisons Administration of the Ministry of Internal Affairs," 16 August 1993.

Government-sponsored media naturally defend their employers. I learned an interesting lesson in the mores of the Fourth Estate when lecturing in Addis Ababa in November 1993 on freedom of expression, under EHRCO sponsorship. I drew largely on American experience in preparing the talk. My remarks were larded with citations from Supreme Court decisions interpreting the First Amendment. I argued, forcefully I believed, for very wide scope of tolerance for the press. Better to have multiple publications and problems of inaccurate reporting than to cut off the flow of ideas vital to democracy, I argued. In the concluding two minutes of my 50-minute presentation, I also noted that journalists must be careful to verify their information. These few final paragraphs were all the official media chose to report, totally omitting what I thought was ringing, well-informed prose about avoiding limits on freedom of the media.

15. Robert L. Hovde, "Democracy and Governance in Ethiopia: A Survey of Institutions, Issues, and Initiatives in the Transitional Period," unpublished paper presented at the XIIth International Conference of Ethiopian Studies, September 5–10, 1994, Michigan State University, pp. 26–27.

16. Interview with Aryeh Neier, HRW New York Office, June 2, 1993.

17. "Rapport de la Commission Internationale d'Enquête sur les Violations des Droits de l'Homme au Rwanda depuis le 1er Octobre 1990 (7–21 janvier 1993)" (Paris: Fédération Internationale des Droits de l'Homme [FIDH]; New York: Africa Watch; Ouagadougou: Union Interafricaine des Droits de l'Homme et des Peuples [UIDH]; Montreal: Centre International des Droits de la Personne et du Développement Démocratique [CIDPDD], 1993).

18. This is a particularly complicated matter, given the importance attached to cultural legitimation for human rights expressed by Abdullahi An-Na'im, director of Human Rights Watch/Africa. In his many writings, and notably in his books on reform in Islam and on cross-cultural perspectives, he has emphasized, "the merits of a reasonable degree of cultural relativism are obvious, especially when compared to claims of universalism that are in fact based on the claimant's rigid and exclusive ethnocentricity." Abdullahi Ahmed An-Na'im, "Toward a Cross-Cultural Approach to Defining International Standards of Human Rights: The Meaning of Cruel, Inhuman, or Degrading Treatment or Punishment," in An-Na'im, ed., *Human Rights in Cross-Cultural Perspectives: A Quest for Consensus* (Philadelphia: University of Pennsylvania Press, 1992), p. 25; also see his book, *Toward an Islamic Reformation: Civil Liberties, Human Rights, and International Law* (Syracuse: Syracuse University Press, 1990).

19. All quotes in this paragraph from "Future Directions and Development," unpublished memorandum from An-Na'im, August 29, 1993.

20. Information about Human Rights Watch/Africa is based largely from personal observation (I have served on the Board of HRW/Africa since its inception) and several interviews with its leaders and staff members (including former HRW director Aryeh Neier, New York, June 2, 1993).

21. However, given the number of states involved, some researchers cover as many as eight. Interview with Mike Dotridge (head, Africa section of Amnesty International), London, October 4, 1993.

22. Note must be duly taken of GONGOs—government-sponsored human rights "NGOs"—that benefit from official sponsorship. In large part to fend off criticism, many African governments have established national human rights commissions, charged with investigating alleged abuses, holding colloquia, and enhancing popular awareness. My contacts with these groups did not make me sanguine about their ability to change official policy or to carry out truly disinterested analyses of domestic human rights issues. However, is such lip service not a step in the right direction?

23. Personal communication from Abdullahi A. An-Na'im, Director of Human Rights Watch/Africa, November 1994.

24. The wave of democratization in tropical Africa has entailed large-scale efforts at election monitoring, in which numerous African NGOs have participated. Conferences on democratization, promotion and protection of human rights, obstacles to development, and the like have provided both experience and funding for these NGOs. Skeptics assert, with some justification, that organizational priorities have become unduly skewed, and that some NGOs, focused on "hot" topics, are established largely with the hope of attracting external grants. Such blanket indictments must be tested against reality. Some human rights NGOs I studied seemed more concerned with scrambling for grants on plausible topics than with directly promoting and protecting human rights. Some resources are wasted. I do not consider the problem grave, however. Given that few African human rights NGOs have annual budgets much over $50,000, given the importance of bolstering human rights awareness in Africa by a variety of means, and given the natural turnover in organizations (see concluding chapter), a few bad investments should be expected. African human rights NGOs generally operate on budgets that are small fractions of those for Human Rights Watch, Amnesty International or Anti-Slavery International, and must scramble for funds. "Faddism" is, thus, an inherent consequence of the current conditions south of the Sahara, and for human rights in general.

25. For details, see the following three publications, all appearing in 1993 from the organization: *HURIDOCS Standard Formats: A Tool for Documenting Human Rights Violations; HURIDOCS Supporting Documents;* and *Information for Human Rights: A HURIDOCS Reader for Information Workers,* edited by Agneta Pallinder. Computer software is also available. For an earlier analysis of HURIDOCS' efforts, see Judith Dueck, "HURIDOCS Standard Formats as a Tool in the Documentation of Human Rights Violations," in Thomas Jabine and Richard Claude, eds., *Human Rights and Statistics: Setting the Record Straight* (Philadelphia: University of Pennsylvania Press, 1992), pp. 127–58.

26. Interview with Berth Verstappen, HURIDOCS, Geneva, May 31, 1994. Kofi Kumado of Ghana chairs the organization.

27. Interview with Todd Howland, Special Prosecutor's Office, Addis Ababa, November 9, 1993.

28. Interview with Clement Nwankwo, CRP office, Lagos, February 3, 1993.

29. Ibid. Nwankwo left the CLO in February 1990 because of differences about how the organization should focus its efforts. Following an internship in London with Interrights and Human Rights Watch/Africa, he returned to Lagos and founded the Constitutional Rights Project. The CRP has established an excellent reputation for its research. Its major funders have included the Ford Foundation, the Friedrich Naumann Foundation, and USAID. It is less identified than the CLO with Nigeria's turbulent efforts to achieve democratization, as spearheaded by the Campaign for Democracy (CD). For details, see Chapter 8.

30. M. Ajo Ajomo and Isabella Okabue, *Human Rights and the Administration of Criminal Justice in Nigeria* (Lagos: Nigerian Institute of Advanced Legal Studies, 1991), pp. 183, 194.

31. Interview with CLO executive director Abdul Oroh, Lagos, February 8, 1994. Relevant CLO publications include *Behind the Wall: A Report on Prison Conditions in Nigeria and the Nigerian Prison System* (Lagos: CLO, 1991) and *Prisoners in the Shadows: A Report on Women and Children in Five Nigerian Prisons* (Lagos: CLO, 1993).

32. Ajomo and Okabue, *Human Rights and the Administration of Criminal Justice in Nigeria*, p. 98. The practices highlighted in the late 1980s had not disappeared in early 1994, much to the disappointment of the investigators. Interview with Isabella Okabue, Lagos, February 4, 1994.

33. Clement Nwankwo, Dulue Mbachu, and Basil Ugochukwu, *Human Rights Practices in the Nigerian Police* (Lagos: Constitutional Rights Project, 1993), p. 77. Also see Lawyers Committee for Human Rights, "The Nigerian Police Force: A Culture of Impunity" (New York: Lawyers Committee, 1992).

34. S. G. Ehindero, *Police and The Law in Nigeria* (Lagos: Times Press, 1986), p. 129.

35. Ajomo and Okabue, *Human Rights and the Administration of Criminal Justice in Nigeria*, pp. 111, 107.

36. Ibid., p. 122.

37. Nwankwo et al., *Human Rights Practices*, p. 28.

38. Ibid., p. 37.

39. Ajomo and Okabue, *Human Rights and the Administration of Criminal Justice in Nigeria*, p. 122.

40. Ibid., p. 126.

41. Ibid., pp. 126, 277.

42. See, for example, "Prison Conditions in Zaire" (New York: Human Rights Watch/Africa, January 1994). Human Rights Watch established its Prison Project in 1988, cutting across the five regional divisions of HRW.

43. Ajomo and Okabue, *Human Rights and the Administration of Criminal Justice in Africa*, p. 129.

44. Indeed, many governments have gone as far as urging that NGOs participate in some fashion directly in United Nations bodies, even including the Security Council! Pauline Comeau, "Mood is positive as the UN begins review of NGO status," *Human Rights Tribune* 2, 4 (September/October 1994), 24–27.

45. Gregg A. Beyer, "Human Rights Monitoring and the Failure of Early Warning: A Practitioner's View," *International Journal of Refugee Law* 2 (1990), 56–82; republished in Alex P. Schmid and Albert J. Jongman, eds., *Monitoring Human Rights Violations* (Leiden: Centre for the Study of Social Conflicts, 1992), citations from pp. 113, 117; footnote omitted from quotation.

46. A note of caution should be sounded, however. Many figures from sub-Saharan Africa are estimates. As one analyst noted in mid-1994, half the countries of the region had not measured their child death rates by any direct method for at least the last 10 years; 15 of them were still using data from the 1970s. Confidence cannot be high in the absence of statistical confirmation. In Adamson's mordant words,

Many of these social statistics, it is true, are regularly massaged in an effort to keep them alive, and some are permanently hooked up to life-support machines, computers which busily interpolate and extrapolate in order to produce signs of statistical life. Fresh-looking figures are therefore generated and published annually in most fields of social development, but faith in this process cannot be absolute when it leads the United Nations family to publish steadily declining under-five mortality rates which then have to be reversed when real measurements are taken.

Peter Adamson, "Statistical Arthritis," *West Africa* (27 June–3 July 1994), 1137.

Chapter 8
Democratization and the Search for Civil Society: Political Pressures in Nigeria

> Every citizen shall have the right and the opportunity . . .
> (a) To take part in the conduct of public affairs, directly or through freely chosen representatives;
> (b) To vote and to be elected at genuine periodic elections which shall be by universal and equal suffrage and shall be held by secret ballot, guaranteeing the free expression of the will of the electors;
> (c) To have access, on general terms of equality, to public service in his country.
> — International Covenant on Civil and Political Rights, Article 25

> . . . periodic and genuine elections are a necessary and indispensable element of sustained efforts to protect the rights and interests of the governed. . . . [A]s a matter of practical experience, the right of everyone to take part in the government of his or her country is a crucial factor in the effective enjoyment by all of a wide range of other human rights and fundamental freedoms, embracing political, economic, social and cultural rights.
> — General Assembly resolution 46/137, 17 December 1991

> 1.-(2) The Federal Republic of Nigeria shall not be governed, nor shall any person or group of persons take control of the Government of Nigeria or any part thereof, except in accordance with the provisions of this Constitution. . . .
> 14.-(1) The Federal Republic of Nigeria shall be a State based on the principles of democracy and social justice.
> — Constitution of the Federal Republic of Nigeria, 1979

A wave of democratization swept over Africa in the early 1990s. Some countries were drenched; many remained dry. In all, the climate for human rights and NGO activity was affected.

The "second independence," as it has been called, in fact left many countries untouched, rhetorical commitment notwithstanding. Single-party and one-man regimes did collapse or were replaced in nearly a dozen countries. But more remained under authoritarian rule. Faced with possible transfer of power to others, incumbents dug in their heels. They found many ways to manipulate the more open electoral processes they had been pressed to concede. Sitting presidents such as Jerry Rawlings (Ghana), Omar Bongo (Gabon), Paul Biya (Cameroon), Daniel arap Moi (Kenya), Lansana Conté (Guinea), and Gnassigbé Eyadéma

(Togo) quickly protected themselves from defeat. They did not wish to repeat the electoral losses of such men as Mathieu Kérékou (Benin), Kenneth Kaunda (Zambia), Pierre Buyoya (Burundi), or Pascal Lissouba (Congo-Brazzaville).

In many respects the most elaborate charade of democratization was played out in Nigeria. President Ibrahim Babangida (despite many personal and institutional reservations) found that claims to be protecting human rights and to be preparing to transfer power played well in the public arena. He followed the flow — that is, until an oft-postponed electoral process turned up with a victor "IBB" and his close advisers would not accept. Then his true unwillingness to democratize surfaced, with results already discussed earlier in this book. He and his successor General Sani Abacha felt, in the final analysis, that only the military could successfully rule in turbulent Nigeria.

I propose in this chapter to examine two approaches to democratization as they played out in the aborted 1993 Nigerian presidential election. I shall argue that the military incumbents committed significant financial resources to a controlled process of democratization from above, but were reluctant to accede to pressures from below. They tolerated political parties organized to their specifications up to the time when one of them, having received a popular mandate, demanded it receive the power it had democratically won. When citizen groups banded together, human rights NGOs playing a prominent role, the armed forces lashed out to protect their position. Military leaders denied the results of the secret ballot. Aborted popular choice posed serious strategic questions for human rights groups. Should they enter the political arena directly to counteract the oppressive military presence? Should they stand aside from the fray, using their resources in other ways?

Recall the history recounted in Chapter 1. If there were to be disengagement from politics, the military would march out in accordance with its own timetable and priorities. Most important in the controlled process were the two parties, the NRC (National Republican Convention) and the SDP (Social Democratic Party). They were heavily funded and tightly regulated by the government. Despite assertions about the "grassroots democracy" they embodied, neither had significant freedom of action until well-off political aspirants — the sort of persons supposedly *not* to be encouraged by the new system — started actively to campaign. Both parties were established to advance "newbreed" politicians, free from the crass self-seeking and narrow parochialism of earlier politicians. These attitudes were to be inculcated by the Government-sponsored Centre for Democratic Studies (CDS). Its training and research programs were intended to create a behavioral foundation for democracy among party officials and candidates. CDS was a GONGO, a government-organized non-governmental organization. Its ideals were unimpeachable, the realities of its accomplishments more debatable. To a substantial extent, the CDS helped the NRC and SDP develop their own structures and ways of proceeding. The CDS acted, in its Director-General's description, as "an institutionalized bi-partisan agency of government . . . much in the same manner that the National Endowment for Democracy (NED) in Washington is an agency of US governments."[1] The CDS also took the leading role in monitoring the aborted 1993 presidential election. Given the attention paid to the electoral process, the annulment came as all the greater surprise. Thereafter, the CDS fell from government favor, its activities (like many other politically related activities in Nigeria) coming under the pall of renewed military authoritarianism.

Efforts for democratization from above in Nigeria were complemented, and in central respects far surpassed, by attempts at democratization from below. This type of grassroots action rested on extant political and economic consciousness, enhanced first by the stirrings of the 1993 presidential campaign, later widened by the self-proclaimed effort of M. K. O. Abiola to assume the position to which he had been elected. NGOs were caught in the swirl. Human rights activists faced critical choices. Some opted to enter the political fray directly; others were more tentative. Recall the two vital tasks for human rights NGOs identified by Wiseberg: 1) information gathering, evaluation, and dissemination; 2) keeping the political process open, or creating political space for democratic forces.[2] Did this latter goal entail direct alliances of NGOs with the parties struggling for votes? close links with trade unions and other groups mobilizing against the Babangida and Abacha governments? only tacit support for various movements critical of the military's annulment of the election? or relative disengagement from the entire electoral process, in order to concentrate on human rights education or enforcement rather than empowerment? The strategic choices were important, particularly given the rocky road competitive elections have followed in Nigeria.

Political and human rights awareness in Nigeria is vigorous, at times turbulent, especially in the southwest. NGOs had taken root in the Lagos area well before the aborted June 1993 election. The first explicit human rights groups, the Civil Liberties Organisation (CLO) and Constitutional Rights Project (CRP), appeared in the late 1980s. Much of their work followed the strategy of enforcement, based on documentation (see Chapters 1, 6, and 7). But enforcement depends on courts of law able to reach independent judgments, based on constitutionally- and treaty-defined rights. These in turn rest on the rule of law — itself the fundament of democracy. Therefore, it stands to reason, NGOs should seek responsible, accountable, transparent forms of governance. Without democratization, they cannot function highly effectively. It would appear

NGOs cannot stand aside from politics. Where enforcement of human rights is manifestly impossible or is seriously impeded (for example, by "ouster" clauses that bar judges from overruling even patently unconstitutional military decrees, by bureaucratic inertia, judicial timidity, police corruption, or other ills), a different approach may be needed. If the fault lies in the entire system, why work within it? Why not change it in toto? To many, the "trouble with Nigeria" (as noted author Chinua Achebe entitled a prescient book[3]) lay with its government, as well as with widespread attitudes about the objectives and means of politics. Clearly, the military regime was inherently unable to preside over its own demise. Only with popular mobilization and ouster of the ruling junta, so it appeared, could the will of the people in fact be achieved.

The Campaign for Democracy (CD) was an umbrella organization.[4] A majority of self-styled human rights groups—certainly most of those in the Lagos area—cooperated in its establishment. The activists knew one another. They recognized the overarching obstacle to human rights represented by the Armed Forces Ruling Council and by General/President Babangida and Abacha in particular. They bent their efforts to democratization from below. The CD sought to oust the military from power by peaceful means, including public protest. When this effort collided with the wishes of senior officers of the armed forces, the coalition started to come apart. Within nine months of the aborted election, CD had to face a fundamental, and potentially crippling, set of decisions about what to do next.

Thus a GONGO and a composite NGO approached democratization from different perspectives. Both worked with nascent political parties, created by a vacillating military regime. The experiences of the Centre for Democratic Studies and the Campaign for Democracy merit recounting, for they illustrate some fundamental obstacles to democratization and the protection of human rights in contemporary Africa.

"Grassroots Democracy": Rhetoric and Reality at the CDS

Nigeria's experiment in democratization from above mixed serious efforts at creating and sustaining political institutions, high-sounding verbiage about transition, hundreds of millions of naira in expenses, and multiple twists and turns. Its failure was predicted, albeit cautiously, by several observers.[5] In the final analysis, the circuitous path followed between 1985 and 1993 led only to the non-disengagement of the Nigerian military from politics. It was not for lack of serious efforts by the CDS, the political parties it helped nurture, and the popular mobilization encouraged by the Campaign for Democracy, however.

The Centre for Democratic Studies was a direct creation of the Babangida government. In the eyes of its critics, the Centre was a façade to give the impression of action; in the view of its supporters, the establishment and funding of CDS substantiated the president's commitments both to return the armed forces to the barracks and to bequeath Nigeria a substantially revised political system. The CDS did enjoy substantial autonomy in designing and implementing programs. It was an object of pride to its creators, staff, and supporters (outside as well as within Nigeria), controversial to some, an unnecessary luxury to others, an important (if seemingly little-used) undertaking to most. Because the military failed to honor its promises to disengage, the CDS was saddled with part of the blame. Had Babangida et al. returned to the barracks, I suspect the Centre would have been honored as an important part of the transition. Any writing about it (at least so close to the aborted 1993 election) is thus bound to be controversial. It is also tragic in many respects.

For professor and political-activist-cum-intellectual Dr. Omo Omoruyi, CDS offered an extraordinary pulpit from which to reform Nigerian politics.[6] It is with him that this tale must begin.

The seeds of CDS were planted in 1979–80, when both Omoruyi and Babangida attended NIPSS, the Nigerian Institute for Policy and Strategic Studies. The two men became friends; indeed, the future president looked to the seconded professor as an intellectual mentor. The friendship bore fruit. Their personal relationship eased the establishment of the Centre for Democratic Studies; it also bequeathed it an ambiguous status. For, while able to bask in the power and resources its attachment to the Presidency permitted, CDS also carried the burden of organizing and rationalizing Babangida's hesitant commitment to democracy. The Centre was linked in the minds of many to Babangida's increasingly erratic political course. Nonetheless, the CDS sought to become an independent force for change. Its research and training programs, designed to create "newbreed" politicians, mixed ivory-tower detachment, political pragmatism, and a definite element of idealism, with clear appreciation of where power lay in Nigerian politics. Its electoral monitoring was without doubt on a par with similar efforts elsewhere in tropical Africa.

CDS was, obviously, not an independent NGO, but a GONGO. The overwhelming majority of its funding came directly from the Nigerian government—specifically, from the Presidency, to which it was administratively attached. The Centre focused its initial programs on support for two government-created entities: the National Republican Convention (NRC) and the Social Democratic Party (SDP). As should be recalled from Chapter 1, both were ordained by President Babangida in October 1989 with the establishment of parties "a little to the left/right of centre." Babangida wanted to control the terms of military disengagement. He was profoundly concerned about the possible re-emergence of ethnic separatism and of discredited (though often still respected) former politicians. His sleight-of-hand reflected his acute instinct for the unpredictable, as well as his increasingly ill-concealed desire to stretch out his stay in office as long as possible.

When the two parties were founded, almost every aspect of their organization was government-regulated: their platforms were drafted by civil servants; their internal statutes were prepared by CDS staff, with some advice from former politicians; federal funds were allocated so that party buildings could be constructed in all state capitals and even local government areas. (To this I must add that awarding construction contracts is a special pet of Nigerian leaders, since kickbacks are invariably provided. Little wonder that the parties attracted cash-hungry followings.) It was not easy to establish the NRC and SDP as autonomous entities within Nigerian civil society. Electoral rules were prescribed centrally, but seemingly changed capriciously in accordance with both Babangida's whims and genuine abuses. For example, party-conducted primaries in 1992 were disallowed, on grounds they had been corrupted. Indeed, some argue that the two parties could not claim an independent existence until they had nominated their 1993 presidential candidates, respectively Alhaji Bashir Tofa and M. K. O. Abiola. Both were wealthy Muslim businessmen able to carry substantial personal financial burdens; both apparently had the blessing of the military brass.

What functions, then, did the CDS carry out? Basically, it was envisaged as a training school for aspirant politicians (the "newbreed"), as a center for various groups of civil society,[7] as a focus for research and publication, and as the locus of domestic election monitoring.[8] Director-General Omoruyi described its duties thus: "CDS was envisaged to play a 'service role' in the evolution and nurturing of the two political parties into institution-hood. CDS's role for Policy Briefing of Politicians must be situated in the context of its larger responsibility, namely 'to homogenize the bureaucrats of political parties using short term training, Workshops, Seminars and Conferences.' "[9] As the presidential election neared, its duties were broadened to include coordination of domestic monitoring and accreditation of external observers. Critics called the CDS "Omoruyi's empire." It was an accusation he deeply resented.

The CDS provided a haven for many Nigerian intellectuals and bureaucrats. They worked on a campus near the center of the sprawling Federal Capital Territory, where facilities were gradually constructed for some staff and the participants in short-term courses. Working conditions at the Centre were notably better than at demonstration- and strike-torn Nigerian universities, or within the sclerotic public service. Although there was no academic tenure, and the same salary schedule was used as in universities, staff entry points were enhanced. Service there hence became a plum. As the CDS campus took shape, increasingly impressive training programs and research activities were established. Even the United States Government took notice, funneling a major grant through the "Nigeria Democracy Initiative" to the Centre and the noted Institute of Social Research at the University of Michigan.

Not immodestly, CDS sought to create a new model of Nigerian politics and politicians. The Presidential speech of October 7, 1989, announcing its establishment was grandiosely entitled, "The Dawn of a New Socio-Political Order." Significantly, this was the same date on which the two-party system was decreed. The high-flying title Babangida gave to his remarks had many parallels in the Centre's own public statements. The following excerpts from Centre publications suggest the earnestness, even fervor, with which CDS staff persuaded themselves of the value of its Centre's goals, and pursued the transformation of aspirant Nigerian democrats. That there is hyperbole should not be surprising, for

the experiment wih two grassroots political parties represents a major contribution to the theory of the origins of political parties. . . . the experiment remains unique and evidently instructive of a deliberate attempt by "incumbency" to create groups that will not only succeed it but will also in the Transition period be a rival source of power in the political system.[10]

Reshaping the foundations of a governance culture for 100 million vibrant Nigerians cannot be less daunting than successfully landing men on the moon. . . . Nigeria is obviously set to give democracy a new lease of life on the continent of Africa. . . . It is obvious that the success that has attended the implementation of the transition programme is largely attributable to government's positive disposition, and its flexibility and responsiveness to the imperatives of grassroots democracy.[11]

Grassroots Democracy which the Babangida Administration is determined to bequeath to this nation, is aimed at giving the vast majority of our country men and women the **fullest** opportunity to participate in shaping the political destiny of Nigeria. It tries to correct the ills of the past Republics by making it mandatory for any political aspirantt [sic] to get the genuine mandate of his people at the grassroots level, starting from the Ward.[12]

For the retired military officer, identifiable constraints to successful partisan politicking can be overcome through a carefully articulated social conversion programme which puts him in the right frame of mind to serve the peasant farmer and the urban wage earner in the truest spirit of grassroots democracy.[13]

The grand strategy for disengagement and democratization, insofar as it can be deduced from Babangida's blizzard of decrees and the workings of the CDS, involved four elements. First, there was profound distrust of previous political leaders. As already noted, wholesale disqualification of former officials of the First and Second Republics was ordained. Second, in their place, a new generation of civilian politicians would be called into existence, intimately linked to local ("grassroots") concerns and effectively trained by CDS. Centre programs were based on theories of political socialization (on which Omoruyi had written his doctoral dissertation), notably adult learning. Third, the Centre would coordinate the immense monitoring task for the June 1993 presidential election, involving more than 110,000 polling places. These three elements worked to the advantage of the Centre. The fourth did not. Though never publicly stated, the IBB administration, and notably Babangida himself, became increasingly hesitant about returning to the barracks. Legitimated to a substantial extent by its announced steps toward elections, the Armed Forces Ruling Council could not disavow the entire disengagement process without risking widespread domestic and international condemnation. But its delaying actions in the run-up to the presidential election made clear its reluctance; the cancellation of the electoral results put paid to any lingering doubts. The ultimate responsibility for the 1993 failure of democratization in Nigeria lay in the conduct of a clique of military officers.

The pro-democratization rhetoric of the Babangida administration, which the CDS tried to put into practice, thus presumed that a top-down strategy in creating political parties, could be transmogrified into a bottom-up "grassroots" approach. In theory, within the NRC and SDP, political reform would start within the villages and urban wards, toward whose interests the "new-breed" politicians would be oriented. Many Nigerians considered the hope doomed from the start. Such an approach flatly contradicted the realities of political life under military rule, and, I must add, long-term practices in Nigeria. Earlier, when the country was "democratic," "big men" with ample resources and limited local support vied for top posts and distributed favors to their followers. Popular participation was often channelled along ethnic lines. For most of its history, Nigeria was governed by military officers, who also doled out resources to stay in power, and who likewise drank deeply at the public trough for personal wealth. The man at the top occupied the crucial spot. From 1985 on, President Babangida tightly gripped the reins of power, his claims about military disengagement from politics notwithstanding. Success for the "grassroots" conception espoused by the CDS required that the two mandated parties themselves evoke support from below, that they build political foundations independent of ethnicity, and that a fair electoral process be permitted to reach its logical conclusion. To a significant extent, this effort succeeded. Neither the NRC nor the SDP was dominated by a single part of the country or by one religious faith. They recruited thousands of persons new to organized politics, whom the staff members of the Centre for Democratic Studies processed through their training courses. Pro-democracy attitudes were instilled. However, one person did not attend. The man who really counted, Ibrahim Badamosi Babangida, became increasingly closeted with a coterie of "hawks" opposed to handing over power. He and his immediate cronies must be blamed for halting the democratization process on which CDS had embarked in conjunction with the two political parties and other parts of civil society, and for which the Campaign for Democracy, to which we shall turn shortly, pressed from below.

In taking the leading role in organizing election monitoring, the Centre for Democratic Studies responded to a direct mandate. On November 17, 1992, President Babangida not only cancelled the just-held presidential primaries, but also directed the CDS "to put together, train and coordinate a group to monitor the Presidential elections . . . of representatives of professional groups, labour unions, business organisations and human rights groups."[14] The directive was inspired in part by international interest in the balloting, but was drawn mostly from recognition by Omoruyi and others that the credibility of the elections rested on a substantial, Nigerian-organized effort at independent observation. The task was immense, since there were more than 110,000 polling places!

The international wave of democratization has meant a boom in work by election observers, both domestic and international. The Vienna World Conference on Human Rights took note, declaring:

> Special emphasis should be given to measures to assist in the strengthening and building of institutions relating to human rights, strengthening of a pluralistic civil society and the protection of groups which have been rendered vulnerable. In this context, assistance provided upon the request of Governments for the conduct of free and fair elections, including assistance in the human rights aspects of elections and public information about elections, is of particular importance.[15]

United Nations efforts were crucial in the 1989 Constituent Assembly election in Namibia, important in the contested balloting in Angola three years later, and significant in Lesotho in 1991 and 1992, and in the replacement of the authoritarian government of Malawi in 1993, among others. A full-fledged Electoral Assistance Unit (EAU) functions within the UN's labyrinthine structure.[16] Where political tensions and the need for credibility are high, international monitors provide legitimation for the process, lending a patina of global approval to the balloting.[17] However, only a fraction of elections have extensive UN involvement.[18] Most are carried out by national personnel, with monitoring provided by existing parties. Even so, a place exists for international monitors in independently certifying the honest conduct of elections.

Nigerian human rights NGOs participated directly in the monitoring group established under CDS auspices. Human Rights Africa, the Citizenship Rights Society of Nigeria, Community Action for Popular Participation, the International Federation of Women Lawyers (FIDA), and the Institute of Human Rights and Humanitarian Law were among the 23 organizations explicitly involved. They and other NGOs had the advantages of presumed non-partisanship and detailed knowledge of the Nigerian political terrain. But what would they know about the duties and responsibilities of monitors? Here the Centre for Democratic Studies turned its expertise in training to advantage. CDS staff schooled hundreds of "trainers of trainers," who in turn trained thousands of specific monitors: 31 state coordinators, 346 local government trainers and supervisors, 4,312 ward supervisors and monitors, and 69,036 polling unit monitors went through the program in a frantic three-week period![19]

All, it seems, for naught. The annulment of the election came as a tremendous surprise and disappointment. The scenario was familiar in the annals of recivilianization. Military-based regimes have rarely disengaged in a smooth, tension-free way.[20] They become anxious about their fate as the handover date approaches, uncertain whether the successor governments will support and honor the claims of the post-disengagement officer corps. The heating-up of political tensions, inevitable in electoral campaigns, reinforces officers' doubts about the wisdom of leaving power. Unless understandings are reached, the proposed return to the barracks may well never occur. Babangida was initially believed to be seriously committed to democratization; his actions proved differently. Let me cite an indictment recently delivered by retired General Obasanjo, who successfully led the 1976–79 disengagement:

[In annulling the election results in 1993] Babangida came out in his true colours, demonstrating again and again that he is a great master of intrigue, mismanagement, corruption, manipulation, deceit, settlement, cover-up and self-promotion at the expense of almost everybody else and everything else. . . . I need only to add at this juncture that General Babangida is the main architect of the state in which the nation finds itself today, and that General Abacha was his eminent disciple, faithful supporter, and beneficiary.[21]

The Centre for Democratic Studies survived (at least temporarily) the purge of institutions unleashed by the Abacha government. It had done a commendable job, under difficult circumstances, in encouraging new patterns of political behavior and in preparing for the aborted presidential election. The two political parties were not so fortunate. They were disbanded, their offices closed and quickly stripped of their furnishings. Would the CDS have a role to play in the future? Its contribution to democratization cannot be assessed with complete objectivity at this point, given the Babangida *coup de grâce* and continuing uncertainties about the possibilities for democracy in Nigeria. Nonetheless, it clearly was a crucial participant in a complex process that almost succeeded. The approach of the Centre for Democratic Studies, working within the system, contrasted sharply with the confrontation tactics pursued by the CD, whose life history nearly coincided with that of the CDS, and to which we must now turn.

Democratization from Below: The Campaign for Democracy

Another major protagonist in Nigeria's democratization effort adopted a fundamentally different approach. Dr. Beko Ransome-Kuti, a slender, soft-spoken physician from one of the country's most prominent families,[22] would seem to be an unlikely candidate for combative politics. MDs usually minister to the ills of the body, not of the body politic. The training they receive and the demands of their profession incline them toward treating individual patients rather than entire societies. Yet Ransome-Kuti entered the tumultuous Nigerian political arena in the 1980s, a result, I am tempted to speculate, of both the occasion and his upbringing. We should start with his home environment, then shift to the broader national scene.

As a young child, Ransome-Kuti witnessed his mother's efforts to organize women in Abeokuta, a relatively prosperous Yoruba town with a long-standing tradition for leadership. As one source recounts, "[Mrs. Ransome-Kuti's] elite ladies' club was transformed into the Abeokuta Women's Union in 1946 and drew into its fold both the educated and the illiterate market women. A campaign was launched against unjust enforcement of women's taxation and the highhandedness of the Alake of Abeokuta who had become the mouthpiece of the British administration."[23] Like mother, like son? Both studied in Manchester (she in the 1920s, a time when the number of Nigerian women studying in England may have numbered less than 10; he in the late 1950s); she took a prominent role in partisan politics, joining an NCNC delegation to London in 1948 demanding rapid moves to self-government, and serving as the party's national treasurer; he in the late 1980s, as a leader of popular mobilization against the armed forces' rule.

Ransome-Kuti profited from an excellent education, knowing international standards of medical practice and the realities of his own country. He returned from medical training in Great Britain in 1963, again in 1965, and focused his practice in Lagos. Ransome-Kuti found the state's medical service, which had been "reasonable," gradually being deteriorated by government inattention. Poor pay for physicians, lack of drugs and telephones for emergencies, and the like impeded good health practices. He became increasingly vocal in his protests. As chairman of the Lagos State Junior Doctors, then of the Lagos State branch of the Nigerian Medical Association (NMA), and later as Secretary-General and First Vice-President of the NMA, he held positions that commanded respect. Ransome-Kuti and other medical activists pressed the military for change; the armed forces reacted. When the NMA declared a strike in February 1985 and criticized the Government for importing cattle for a religious festival rather than medicinal drugs, General Buhari proscribed the association. For the first time in his life, Ransome-Kuti was jailed. His political martyrdom had started.

Ransome-Kuti's major human rights work began in spring 1989, when friends of a detained member of the Nigerian Labour Congress approached him for assistance. A committee was formed under Ransome-Kuti's guidance which went to court, held rallies, and wrote letters to gain the labor leader's release. Nigeria's rapidly deteriorating political, economic, and security situations drew Ransome-Kuti and others into more militant actions. In May 1989, riots erupted against the IMF-ordained Structural Adjustment Program; many were killed, hundreds arrested. At this point, Ransome-Kuti formed the Committee for the Defence of Human Rights (CDHR). The quiet physician had taken the crucial step toward political activism. He had moved beyond pressure for his profession to pressure for his entire society.

The CDHR used the courts to highlight cases and, in Ransome-Kuti's words, "harass judges here and there."[24] It focused attention on the "ouster" clauses favored by the military regime. In a series of decrees, the Buhari and Babangida governments had suspended major constitutional provisions, notably the ability of courts to review specified acts. Among their major enactments were the following:

- Federal Military Government Constitution (Suspension and Modification) Decree No, 1, 1984: "No question as to the validity of this or any other Decree or Edict shall be entertained by any court of law in Nigeria"; the Decree also vested the Armed Forces Ruling Council with powers to appoint judges to state and federal courts.[25]
- State Security (Detention of Persons) Decree 2 of 1984 permitted detention without judicial review.[26]
- Recovery of Public Property (Special Military Tribunal), Decree 3 of 1984: This provided for special tribunals "to ascertain whether any public officer has been engaged in corrupt practices or has corruptly enriched himself or any other person or has by virtue of abuse of his office contributed to the economic adversity of Nigeria"; military officers rather than seasoned judges ran the tribunals.
- Public Officers (Protection Against False Accusation) Tribunal, De-

cree 4 of 1984, allowed a trial for any person "who publishes in any form whether written or otherwise, any message, rumor, report, or statement which is false in any material particular or which brings or is calculated to bring the Federal Military Government, or the government of a state or a public officer to ridicule or disrepute." In a chilling reversal of accepted international practice, Section 3(1) provided, "The burden of proving that the subject matter of the charge is true in every material particular shall, notwithstanding anything to the contrary in any enactment or rule of law, lie on the person charged."[27]

- Federal Military Government (Supremacy and Enforcement of Powers) Decree 13 of 1984: This indicated that "No civil proceedings shall lie or be instituted in any court or on account of or in respect of any act, matter or thing done or purported to be done under or pursuant to any Decree or Edict, and if any such proceedings are instituted before or after the commencement of this Decree, the proceedings shall abate, be discharged and made void." Cutting through the fog of legalese, this edict precluded judicial action on essentially any action of the military government.

- Special Tribunal (Miscellaneous Offence) Decree 20 of 1984: This provided the death penalty for numerous offenses including arson, tampering with oil pipelines or electric or telephone cables, importing or exporting mineral oil or ore, dealing in cocaine, etc.[28]

- Decree No. 9 of 1990: This gave the President, Vice President, and state military governors immunity from civil or criminal liability for any action they might have taken in their personal or official capacity during their tenure of office, "notwithstanding anything to the contrary in the constitution of the Federal Republic of Nigeria 1979, as amended."

- Decree No. 55 of 1992: "For the avoidance of doubt, if any law enacted before 31st December 1983, including the Constitution of [the] Federal Republic of Nigeria 1979, is inconsistent with any Decree promulgated by the Federal Military Government, the Decree promulgated by the Federal Military Government shall prevail and that other law shall to the extent of the inconsistency be void."

- Treason and Treasonable Offences Decree of 1993: Although not officially published, this would have permitted the government to prosecute "anyone who acts alone or conspires with anybody in Nigeria or outside, either by word or publication of any material capable of disrupting the general fabric of the country or any part of it. . ."[29] The death penalty could be utilized. However, in response to a storm of criticism, the government announced May 22 (three weeks after publication of the Decree) that it was being "set aside." Note the terminology: it was not repealed, and was in fact utilized to bring Abiola to trial in July 1994 for treason (Abiola had proclaimed himself president on June 12, 1994, one year after the aborted election).

Such draconian powers made mockery of the rule of law. Judicial independence was sapped by timidity and the appointment of pro-regime persons to the bench, many drawn from the civil service.[30] Nigeria's constitution was shelved in almost all important respects. Human rights groups worked assiduously to find chinks in the government's legal armor; as rapidly as they were discovered, another official decree (often with retrospective effect) would be issued. Some victories were won, to be certain, and are discussed elsewhere in this book. But generally on the legal front, the picture was bleak. A "political" as contrasted with a "legal" approach seemed necessary to bring change.

The Campaign for Democracy emerged, as one should expect, through a series of discussions and compromises. In Ransome-Kuti's words, "We convinced ourselves for need to broaden organizational efforts." Should an existing organization be transformed, or a new one formed? Nothing crystallized until early 1990, when Babangida "flew a kite" about holding a national conference to consider the French model of government (which includes, it will be recalled, both a president and a prime minister). Although this "National Consultative Forum" never got off the ground, it sparked discussion among human rights activists and politicians disqualified by decree from participating in political activities. They agreed on the sickness of the Nigerian political system. The chief problem was not the constitution, but controversial revenue allocation formulas, weakness of the rule of law, lack of democracy, and, in particular, the stifling continued presence of the military government. Several meetings were held to prepare an open forum, about which senior officers became increasingly concerned. The forum's organizers started to get threats three to four days before the meeting was due to be held. On the night before the public session was to occur, Attorney-General Bola Ajibola (later elected to the International Court of Justice despite strong opposition from human rights groups) threatened sentences of up to five years might be imposed on organizers under the Transition to Civil Rule decree. Armed police were deployed around the hall. The situation seemed ominous. The Babangida government made clear it would brook little questioning of its supposed master plan for disengagement. (At that point, the Armed Forces Ruling Council officially backed competitive elections between the two officially-recognized parties, and made no secret of its distaste for mass mobilization such as the Campaign for Democracy was to advocate.)

Despite these pressures, the delegates gathered at the venue. They could not gain entrance because of the police blockade and the meeting was thus aborted. However, the pressures for change were not released, and the organizers pushed ahead. On November 11, 1991, the CD was launched, composed of eight organizations (including the National Consultative Forum, the Campaign for the Defense of Human Rights [CDHR], the CLO, National Association of Democratic Lawyers [NADL], the Gani Fawehinmi Solidarity Association [GFSA], the National Association of Nigerian Students [NANS], Women in Nigeria [WIN], and the National Union of Journalists [NUJ]). Its objectives were clear and unambiguously political: military rule must be terminated and popular sovereignty restored.[31] Ransome-Kuti was elected chair at its first convention, held in June 1992. The government moved quickly to head off this threat. He and other activists were detained for six weeks just after the CD's launching. Paradoxically, Ransome-Kuti's imprisonment helped to project CD more widely by evoking agitation for his release and publicizing the organization. The quiet physician had become a focus for political agitation. The CD marched at the head of organizations demanding an end to military rule. The umbrella group would be satisfied with nothing less than the armed forces' rapid return to the barracks and installation of a popularly elected government.

The real test for the CD came shortly after the annulment of the presidential election. The public protests it evoked were the largest in the country's history. But the demonstrations proved to be a double-edged sword. Their massive nature gave the CD a sense of power, believing the regime should knuckle under. On the other hand, the concentration of the demonstrations in the southwest enabled critics to deem them narrowly tribalistic.

The massive upwelling of support surprised all concerned: CD organizers, government officials, and the participants themselves. July 5, 1993, the first day of protests, was marked by a curious paralysis of the regime in the face of a general strike and "stay-at-home." On the second day, government forces moved into action. Shooting started, with up to 168 persons (by count of CD supporters) killed. Urban toughs took advantage of the tumult to loot. The combination of fear from the official crackdown and increased lawlessness meant the political goals the CD espoused were overshadowed. Tensions escalated dangerously. After three days, the demonstrations subsided. The public protests, though confined to Lagos, had sent a clear message. Until Babangida left office, serious discontent would continue to simmer.

The most important reason that the demonstrations were confined to southwestern Nigeria lay in the CD's organization. Although it had attracted supporters from throughout the federation, most of the participating groups were based in Lagos State. The Lagos urban populace and the communities of nearby states had long histories of popular mobilization. Political consciousness was and is high. Local sensitivity in Lagos was heightened by the presence of many ethnic groups. The economic pressures of structural adjustment were especially marked in Lagos. (An estimated three-quarters of Nigeria's non-oil industrial establishments are located in the area. The sputtering economy meant few factories were working at more than one-third capacity and unemployment was rampant.) As a result, local anger against Babangida was extremely high. Opposition to the regime was thus the major rallying point for CD supporters. That a Yoruba businessman had won the election added to—but certainly did not cause—the popular discontent. (Indeed, Abiola had won majority support in 20 of Nigeria's 31 states and federal capital territory, and had even carried Kano, the home state of his opponent.) The CD called for public protest. Only in Lagos, however, were its preparations far advanced and the crowds large.

Although Babangida bought himself some time by repressing the demonstrations, he eventually resigned under strong pressure from the military hawks who had earlier urged him to annul the June 1993 election. On August 26, the anniversary of his 1985 seizure of power, he officially retired. A civilian named Ernest Shonekan (from the same Nigerian city as Abiola) assumed the reins of control—in theory, at least. The armed forces remained the real power, although there was only one military member of the cabinet, Minister of Defence Abacha. *Plus ça change. . . .* In the face of popular discontent and close military surveillance, the Shonekan government dithered. Protests continued, although at a considerably reduced level. As Ransome-Kuti commented, "We had to carry on with protest."[32] But the CD started to splinter. With its *bête noire* sidelined, and with government efforts to depict the CD as a cabal of power-hungry, aggrieved Yoruba, constituent units began to peel away. A serious set of blows came to the CD when Ransome-Kuti made contact, through respected intermediaries (firebrand Lagos lawyer Gani Fawehinmi and soon-to-be Attorney General/Minister of Justice Olu Onagoruwa), with the successor Shonekan government. The contacts failed to produce any concrete result, and opened a serious credibility gap. Several members of the CD accused Ransome-Kuti of failing to consult and of unilaterally overriding the organization's basic principles, which included no contact with the military regime. They argued that, despite their civilian veneer, Shonekan and his colleagues were stooges for the armed forces; the fight would have to continue. The charges came largely from younger officers of the CD, many of them former student activists and most born outside the Yoruba heartland.[33]

What appeared to be a schism based on ethnicity was in large part a contest over basic strategy. Should there be any collaboration with any government other than a duly-elected one? If there appeared to be a reasonable prospect for a negotiated settlement, should the opportunity be passed up? In the end, amidst significant recriminations, the Campaign for Democracy split in February 1994. By a 45–21 vote, the CD's second convention rejected a motion criticizing Ransome-Kuti. The critics (led by the general secretary and treasurer) walked out, and announced they might set up a rival organization.[34] The voice of the CD had not been stilled, but had been considerably muted.

The dilemma facing the CD epitomizes the major strategic issue democratization-oriented NGOs confront. They are neither political parties nor guerrilla resistance movements. As publicly-functioning, nongovernmental organizations, they are ill-equipped to deal with governments that are politically clever or able to play upon latent divisions. If they advocate empowerment, particularly for ethnic minorities, they risk being banned or combatted. If they transform themselves into vote-seeking machines, they are inherently partisan. "Success" in democratization requires that the NGOs themselves become highly organized and politicized — but in so doing, they run the risk of forfeiting their claims as disinterested, neutral watchdogs. They may attract strong negative pressure from the incumbents. If they become identified with a narrow ethnic, class, or regional base in a divided society, NGOs confront serious issues of credibility. Recall Bratton's observations about the delicacy of NGO-government relations, summarized in Chapter 2.

Although the CD brought together a large number of human rights organizations under its umbrella, some remained outside. The CRP (Constitutional Rights Project, which, as shown in the preceding chapter, has published several careful analyses of human rights in Nigeria[35]) and the LRRDC (Legal Research and Resource Development Centre, information about which appeared in Chapter 3) did not participate; nor did Human Rights Africa, which took a pro-Government line and which was active in the CDS-trained election monitoring group. Other organizations that had indicated they supported the CD diminished their levels of activity as time passed. For example, representatives of the NLC (Nigerian Labour Congress) and ASUU (Academic Staff of Universities Union) did not call for coordinated strike action after the July 1993 events in Lagos, and played little part in the acrimonious debates leading to the CD's split.

Ultimately, the CD was not organized to take power. It did provide a platform on which grievances could coalesce. It could demonstrate that thousands of Nigerians were willing to forgo pay and risk personal safety by joining a general strike. But these considerable accomplishments, the CD's president recognized, were born of particularly intense circumstances. Its "larger than life image,"[36] resulting from the July 1993 Lagos demonstrations, concealed a loose structure and serious tactical and strategic differences about the best way to proceed.

Democratization from below through the Campaign for Democracy thus seemed to fail in its critical moment in 1993. Although the protest far outstripped its organizers' estimates, the Babangida government was not be moved by what it perceived as posturing by a ethnically-inclined radical group. The regime's characterization was incorrect, I hope preceding paragraphs have shown. But the inherent problem for coalitions of NGOs remains. Rare indeed are the circumstances in which they could attempt to gain power, for that is not their forte. The mass demonstrations of summer 1994, spearheaded by striking oil and gas workers, posed more serious problems for the military junta.

Concluding Observations

The chapter to this point has presented an overly neat picture in certain respects. On one side stood the Centre for Democratic Studies, seeking to inculcate behavior in activists of the two recognized parties that would make "grassroots democracy" possible, and using election monitoring to legitimate transition. On the other side stood the Campaign for Democracy, aggregating popular discontent with the military regime to demand its immediate withdrawal and installation of the elected government. The failure of peaceful change through the official process opened the door to mass civil disobedience from below. Watching over both was the authoritarian regime of Babangida, determined to maintain its power. It would appear that neither a "top-down" nor a "bottom up" strategy worked in the face of military intransigence. This conclusion, however, would be premature. In fact, the work of both the CDS and the CD provided important lessons about democratization as a requisite and goal for human rights NGOs.

First, and most important, political struggles are best carried out by political bodies — but parties organized for elections cannot immediately transform themselves into something else. The real loser from the annulment was the SDP, whose free-wheeling presidential candidate had made a real impression. Abiola was denied the electoral victory he and the SDP won. Should efforts be made to revive the party in some fashion? Had the experiment with two parties met the hopes of its creators and trainers? Did Abiola make an appropriate gamble in proclaiming himself president a year after his aborted triumph, as a result of which he was jailed and brought to trial for treasonable behavior? Did his martyr-like imprisonment bring Nigeria to a necessary height of confrontation? Whatever judgment history may hold, the 1993–94 period was one in which the Nigerian political situation seemed to reach new heights, and new depths.

The CD faced critical decisions as to its future. Quite possibly this would lie in non-partisanship, trying to serve as a monitor to the political movements that, inevitably, will feature again in Nigerian politics. Human rights groups lack many of the skills requisite for political campaigns. They risk their independence in becoming formally linked to parties. Hence, efforts by human rights groups to pressure governments to democratize inevitably confront difficulty at critical periods of transition. Human rights NGOs may be weakened if they do not press for greater democratization; they similarly may be weakened if they become too partisan.

The Centre for Democratic Studies likewise had to reassess its role following the annulment (assuming, to be certain, that the government continued to fund it). With political parties, the major instruments of transition, having been swept away, should the Centre continue its research and programs for other parts of civil society? Great disappointment marked the CDS when the elections were aborted. Yet the immediate setbacks did not mean its efforts were in vain. When the military government of General Abacha collapses (as it inevitably will, as I write these words in August 1994), some CDS-trained "newbreed" politicians may emerge to chart a new course. Democratization requires a substantial foundation in all parts of civil society. CDS programs directed toward the media and civil servants could help the difficult transition, when it comes. The thousands of election monitors may once again find a brief but important task to perform.

Second, the annulment was a Pyrrhic victory for Babangida. His senior military colleagues would not permit him to remain atop the political heap. The concept that rule by the armed forces would be enlightened, rational, or disinterested suffered (I believe) a death blow. To be certain, members of the military backpedaled vigorously, to avoid identification with the nearly universally condemned Babangida regime. The president's action in annulling the 1993 election was a bad decision, undoing years of careful effort that might have made Nigeria a model for political transition. The successor military regime had clear warning that Nigerian patience was near the breaking point. The rancorous debate in early 1994 over a "constitutional" or a "national" conference, and the major strike led by oil and gas workers in July 1994, signaled the near-collapse of any lingering legitimacy for the Abacha government.

Third, the speed with which the CD's protests were dismissed by Babangida and later by Abacha as Yoruba sour grapes showed that the ethnic trump card can still be played in Nigerian politics. The sweeping national victory of the SDP was overlooked; the location and origins of the chief protestors were emphasized instead. Ethnicity continues to provide a political faultline in Nigeria, and in varying degrees in practically all African states. Not only, then, are there problems in establishing a "human rights culture"; there are issues in reinforcing a "national" political culture. Human rights NGOs tend to be clustered in African cities; certain groups tend to be overrepresented in their leadership, relative to their proportions in the overall population; attacks on their motives may play well in some quarters if tied to ethnicity. Is tribalism the last refuge of the scoundrel?

Finally, the aborted transition process reinforced a basic truth about liberalization and democratization in authoritarian systems: the most critical period comes in the final moments of transfer of power. Thirty-plus years ago, S. E. Finer observed that military regimes were caught in a fundamental dilemma. They could "neither stay nor go."[37] Human rights NGOs should expect attacks during the politically tortured setting of military disengagement from politics. Those that march at the head of demonstrations may be persecuted, just as those who cooperate may be blamed if the effort fails. Democratization involves high stakes risks. Some governments in Africa and elsewhere seem ready to put people's lives on the line. Are NGOs themselves willing and prepared to face that danger? How far will or should they go to open up the political process?

Democratization is thus both an end and a means for human rights NGOs. They can survive, with difficulty, under authoritarian governments, but they can flourish under democratic ones. The greater the need, the harder the functioning. NGOs contribute to civil society in large part through their documentation. If their message is to reach citizens generally, freedom of information is needed. If national policies that abridge human rights are to be changed, political parties must compete in free elections. Democracy does not spell an automatic end to abuses, but it does facilitate open discussion of them.

In the wave of the "second independence," unrealizably high expectations surfaced. Free elections were perceived by many (including, perhaps most notably, enthusiastic purveyors in the United States) as the Open Sesame. "Seek ye first the competitive balloting, and all things shall be added unto it," they asserted. Wrong! Although multi-partyism is generally accepted in principle, and often carried out in practice, several post-1990 elections in sub-Saharan Africa have disappointed both external observers and, far more important, domestic advocates of change.[38] Competitive balloting (particularly after long periods of one-party rule or military government) is hard to organize. New electoral registers must be compiled. Parties must have adequate opportunities to campaign, including in government strongholds. All groups must be willing to accept the results, even if they lose. Hastily called and ill-prepared elections, as Ethiopia in mid-1992 indicated, can impede rather than advance democracy. Pseudo-competitive elections, especially when given a veneer of legitimacy by independent observers, mock the democratization process.[39] The electoral triumphs of Presidents Biya (Cameroon), Bongo (Gabon), Conté (Guinea), Diouf (Senegal), Eyadéma (Togo), and others were vitiated by blatant pro-government maneuvers, as noted at the start of the chapter. Multi-partyism and competitive balloting are, in reality, parts of a far broader process.

Human rights NGOs should identify themselves with democratization and the deepening of civil society. They can facilitate, or keep more honest, the preparation for competitive elections. In the face of authoritarianism, they should struggle for openness. NGOs can utilize all the major strategies discussed in this book. They can educate the public about elections and the other trappings of democracy; they can seek to empower groups, with the related risks; they can use the courts, to enforce the laws needed for "genuine periodic elections which shall be by universal and equal suffrage and shall be held by secret ballot," as the International Covenent on Civil and Political Rights indicates.

Without question, the "second independence" of the early 1990s improved the climate for African human rights NGOs, often dramatically. The number of countries untouched by the wave of democratization as of mid-1994 could be counted on the fingers of one hand: Equatorial Guinea, Liberia, Mauritania, Sierra Leone and Sudan were the most likely suspects. Civil society had gained; so too had NGOs. Non-governmental organizations flourish as democratic practices increase. Civil and political rights, the rule of law, and the involvement of citizens in public affairs are all enhanced through democratization.

But in closing this chapter, I must underscore a major lesson. So-called first generation rights, such as freedom from torture, trial before an independent court, or freedom of the press, are not cost-free. Properly prepared elections are expensive undertakings. Democracy, and more broadly the protection of human rights as a whole, are facilitated by economic and social development. Africa's continuing struggle to escape from the calamitous results of poverty is a legitimate concern for human rights NGOs. Africans prefer freedom in poverty to riches in chains, Sékou Touré argued before the 1958 reference in Guinea—although he then bequeathed the people of his country both poverty and authoritarianism. Democratization and development go hand-in-hand. Both are important targets for NGO activity. But, as we shall see shortly, development-oriented NGOs in Africa have been more reluctant than democracy-oriented NGOs to use the language and institutions of human rights. This does not make them any less important, however.

Notes

1. Personal fax from Director-General Omo Omoruyi, July 27, 1994.
2. Laurie S. Wiseberg, "Defending Human Rights Defenders: The Importance of Freedom of Association for Human Rights NGOs" (Montreal: International Centre for Human Rights and Democratic Development, 1993), pp. 6–7.
3. Chinua Achebe, *The Trouble with Nigeria* (London: Heinemann, 1984).
4. Omoruyi described it as "a highly fluid mass-based umbrella social movement, specially geared toward the role of confrontation to authoritarian rule rather than of sustained democratic mobilization" (personal fax, 27 July 1994). I doubt that Beko Ransome-Kuti would disagree with this characterization.
5. Including myself, who, in May 1990, spoke at the Centre for Democratic Studies and predicted a less than even chance for success. Claude E. Welch, Jr., "Military Rule and the Imperatives of Democracy" (Abuja: Centre for Democratic Studies, 1992), p. 18. To quote Claude Ake, a well-known Nigerian political scientist,

the phenomenon of the coup has become part of the country's political equation. Even now, as Nigerians prepare for another transition, few believe that the Third Republic (1992?–) will survive longer than the First (1960–6) and the Second (1979–83).

Quoted in Julius Ihonvbere, "A Critical Evaluation of the Failed 1990 Coup in Nigeria," *Journal of Modern African Studies* 29 (1991), 608.
6. Omoruyi was a high-profile political scientist who, after receiving his doctorate at SUNY/Buffalo in 1970, returned to Nigeria and taught first at the University of Ibadan (incorrectly stated as Ife in the *Newswatch Who's Who*), then the University of Benin, where he had become Deputy Vice-Chancellor by late 1988. His research focused on political socialization. To him, "democracy is a learned or acquired behavior. How this is done and done effectively is an empirical question for learning experts" (personal fax, 27 July 1994). In the military disengagement of the late 1970s, Omoruyi served in the Constituent Assembly 1977–78, then briefly left the academic environment and plunged into politics, being named general secretary of the Nigerian Peoples Party. This scarring experience (about which he has written a lengthy, unpublished apologia and which is not mentioned in his *Who's Who* entry) nonetheless gave him a taste for the broader challenges of the public arena. His personal links with General Babangida, as will be shown shortly, facilitated the establishment of CDS, but also heightened suspicion about its potential subservience to the head of state. Such a political high profile had its costs. A few days before I flew to Abuja to interview Dr. Omoruyi, he was the target of an assassination attempt in his home city, Benin. That he escaped immediate death was itself a miracle. The dialogue I had hoped to carry out face-to-face in Nigeria instead became a series of telephone calls and faxes, based on an earlier version of this chapter.
7. Examples include newspaper editors, political correspondents of print and electronic media, women's NGOs, a research committee of the International Political Science Association, civil servants, female political activists, and election monitors. Omoruyi envisaged "empowerment through organized groups as opposed to empowerment through the street masses," an obvious contrast between the CDS and the Campaign for Democracy (personal fax, 27 July 1994).

8. Among publications of the Centre were the following: *State of the Nation: Policy Briefs for Politicians* (1992); J. A. A. Ayoade, Elone J. Nwabuzor, and Adesina Sambo, eds., *Grassroots Democracy and the New Government System in Nigeria* (n.d.); J. A. A. Ayoade, Elone J. Nwabuzor, and Adesina Sambo, eds., *Political Parties and the Third Republic* (1991); J. A. A. Ayoade, Elone J. Nwabuzor, and Adesina Sambo, eds., *Women and Politics in Nigeria* (1992); Omo Omoruyi, "The Reformed Civil Service in the Transition Period and Beyond" (1992) and "From Khaki to Agbada" (1992); Welch, "Military Rule and the Imperatives of Democracy" (1992); Larry Diamond, "Globalization of Democracy: Trends, Types, Causes and Prospects" (1992). In addition, through the Nigerian Democracy Initiative funded by USIS (United States Information Service), the highly respected University of Michigan and the CDS were to develop joint research on political participation and electoral behavior, train Nigerian participants in advanced research and analytical methods, and publish results. UM Professor Ronald Inglehart had scarcely arrived in Abuja when the bombshell annulment was announced, calling the entire project into question. However, an extensive data base was compiled about the "newbreed" politicians, who seemed to represent a different social foundation than earlier generations of Nigerian leaders. Analysis of these data, when complete, could be interesting to scholars of democratization.

9. Centre for Democratic Studies, *State of the Nation: Policy Briefs for Politicians* (Abuja: CDS, 1992), p. vii.

10. W. A. Sambo, "Party Administration in a Democratic Setting," in J. A. A. Ayoade et al., *Political Parties and the Third Republic*, p. 38.

11. Baba Gana Kingibe, "Closing Speech," in ibid., p. 108. Kingibe, then National Chairman of the SDP, was narrowly defeated in his bid to become the party's presidential standard-bearer in the 1993 election; he later joined the Abacha government as Minister of Foreign Affairs.

12. Elone A. Nwabuzor, "The Meaning and Purpose of Grassroots Democracy," in Ayoade et al., *Grassroots Democracy and the New Local Government System in Nigeria*, p. 12. Boldface in original.

13. Omoruyi, "From Khaki to Agbada," p. 6.

14. Cited in Ada Okwuosa, "The Nigerian Election Monitoring Group (NEMG): Structure and Functioning," in Omo Omoruyi, W. A. Sambo, and Ada Okwuosa, eds., *Parties, Elections and Election Monitoring in Nigeria 1993* (Abuja: Centre for Democratic Studies, in press).

15. "Vienna Declaration and Programme of Action," UN Document A/CONF.157/23, 12 July 1993, Part II, para. 67.

16. For details, see *Human Rights and Elections: A Handbook on the Legal, Technical and Human Rights Aspects of Elections* (New York and Geneva: United Nations, 1994).

17. Conversely, withdrawal of planned international monitoring sends a clear message. I had been selected as one of roughly a dozen monitors for the August 1993 presidential election in Togo. Jimmy Carter was to head the team. Twelve hours before my scheduled departure for Lomé, Carter's office called. The mission had been scrubbed. President Eyadéma was not living up to prior agreements about electoral procedure; most opposition candidates had withdrawn; the presence of Carter and others could have been interpreted as tacit approval of an obviously-flawed process. When I came to Togo six months later to speak on the role of armed forces in democratic systems, I was strongly advised not to discuss this cancellation. See the concluding footnote in this chapter for additional details.

18. Five conditions must be satisfied: formal request from the state concerned; broad public support for UN involvement; sufficient advance time; a clear international dimension to the situation; and a favorable decision by the General Assembly or Security Council. United Nations, *Human Rights and Elections*, p. 2.

19. Figures from Akwuosa, "The Nigerian Election Monitoring Group." Coverage of every polling place was manifestly impossible, so various criteria of political sensitivity were used. Thirteen states had full coverage, eighteen states and the Federal Capital Territory partial coverage. Each monitor (one per polling place) was required to be the first to leave the polling station at the end of counting, to report results to the ward level, thence to local government, state, and national levels. The NEMG publicly posted the results it received, confirming the huge lead SDP candidate Abiola built up. The annulment of the election should not be attributed to shortcomings in monitoring, but to trepidation within senior ranks of the military and in some Northern areas.

In addition to national monitors, international observers took part. The CDS sent invitations to 71 embassies and high commissions to send observers, but under specific requirements. The monitors would have to be sponsored by their missions in Nigeria; not question the electoral method adopted by Nigeria nor speak with the press; maintain liaison with the Nigerian Election Monitoring Group; submit reports to their home governments; and not issue a joint statement. Some 105 foreigners, drawn mostly from developed countries (for example, 24 from Great Britain, 30 from the United States) were represented. Figures from Omo Omoruyi, "The International Observer Group and the Presidential Election," in Omoruyi et al., eds., *Parties, Elections and Election Monitoring*.

20. As examples of the growing literature, see Claude E. Welch, Jr., *No Farewell to Arms? Military Disengagement from Politics in Africa and Latin America* (Boulder, CO: Westview, 1987); and Guillermo O'Donnell, Philippe C. Schmitter, and Laurence Whitehead, eds., *Transitions from Authoritarian Rule* (Baltimore: Johns Hopkins University Press, 1986).

21. Keynote address delivered at the Arewa House conference, Kaduna, on "State of the Nation: Which Way Forward?" 2 February 1994.

22. His eldest brother, Dr. Olikoye Ransome-Kuti, served as Minister of Health in the Babangida government (and his biography in *Who's Who in Nigeria*, at nearly three full columns, is longer than that of any living Nigerian head of state); his half-brother, Fela Anikulapo-Kuti, is a flamboyant musician who founded a short-lived movement in 1978 called New Men of the People; his mother, Funmilayo Ransome-Kuti, took a crucial leadership role in Nigerian women's movements. See text below. Biographical details on Olikoye and Bekololari can be found in *Newswatch Who's Who in Nigeria* (Lagos: Newswatch, 1990), pp. 699–700.

23. Bolanle Awe, "Women and Politics in Historical Perspective," in Ayoade et al., *Women and Politics in Nigeria*, p. 32.

24. Interview with Beko Ransome-Kuti, Lagos, February 9, 1994.

25. As the Constitutional Rights Project aptly noted, "The effect of this is that most of those appointed into judicial office are those seen by the military government as being unlikely to be engaged in 'undue radical' decisions, which accounts for most of the judges being picked from the various ministries of justice. . . . Clearly the powers of the AFRC over the judiciary cannot be exaggerated." *Rights at Risk* (Lagos: Constitutional Rights Project, 1990), pp. 55–56.

26. I agree with the Civil Liberties Organisation, which found Decree No. 2 "the greatest single threat to civil liberties in Nigeria." Chukwuemeka Gahia, *Human Rights in Retreat* (Lagos: Civil Liberties Organisation, 1993), p. 98.

27. This tribunal and decree setting it up were abrogated by Babangida in August 1985, part of his public relations blitz to "prove" his dedication to civil liberties.

28. This decree represented, in the CRP's judgment, the "most draconian and unjust piece of retroactive legislation in Nigeria's legal history," since three persons arrested for cocaine dealing *before* the decree was promulgated were arraigned, convicted, sentenced to death, and publicly executed. Clement Nwankwo, Dulue Mbochu and Basil Ugochukwu, "Nigeria: The Limits of Justice" (Lagos: Constitutional Rights Project, 1993), p. 43.

29. Quoted in "Nigeria, Threats to a New Democracy: Human Rights Concerns at Election Time" (Washington, DC: Africa Watch, 1993), p. 22.

30. As the CLO aptly noted, "Very few members of the bench were able to show the courage required by that duty [to proclaim "any order whatever" in the interest of justice] with respect to several of the major constitutional and human rights issues that came up. Most judges were only too willing to abdicate responsibility, often using as an excuse, the exclusionary provisions of such absolutist decrees as Nos. 1 and 13 of 1984. . . . In effect, most judges totally refused to scrutinize the ouster clauses and inadvertently [sic] or otherwise acquiesced in the emasculation of the judiciary." *Human Rights in Retreat*, p. 109.

31. The seven goals included: "1) the restoration of the sovereignty of the Nigerian people to self-determination, to choose how to be governed, who governs them and the procedure or process through which they will be governed; 2) the rights of the People to form their own Political parties without interference; 3) the termination of Military Rule; 4) the replacement of imposed Transition agencies with independent and impartial ones including the immediate establishment of impartial electoral bodies; 5) respect for fundamental human rights, the rule of law and abrogation of rule by Decree; 6) termination of economic policies which have caused the people hardship, poverty, disease, hunger, unemployment, retrenchment and illiteracy; 7) to ensure that the Military hands over power by October 1992." Cited in *A Harvest of Violations: Annual Report on Human Rights in Nigeria, 1991* (Lagos: Civil Liberties Organisation, 1992), p. 61; capitalization as in original.

32. Interview, February 9, 1994.

33. Interviews in Abuja, Kaduna and Lagos February 8–23, 1994 with several persons on both sides of the CD divide.

34. "The Enemy Within," *Tell*, February 21, 1994, pp. 23–24; interviews.

35. These include, inter alia, *The Bail Process and Human Rights in Nigeria* (1992), *The Crisis of Press Freedom in Nigeria* (1993), and *Human Rights Practices in the Nigerian Police* (1993), in addition to a quarterly journal and newsletter. Funding for these studies and others still in process has come from sources such as the Ford Foundation, the National Endowment for Democracy, the Norwegian Human Rights Fund, and the European Economic Community. Interview with Clement Nwankwo, Lagos, February 3, 1994.

36. The phrase is Gani Fawehinmi's; in interviews (Lagos, February 8 and 18, 1994), he asserted that leaders "must be willing to put their lives on the line." Yet Fawehinmi had also urged in private that the CD approach the Shonekan government!

37. S. E. Finer, *The Man on Horseback: The Role of the Military in Politics* (London: Pall Mall, 1962), p. 243.

38. Various interviews, most notably with Grace Githu (Chair, National Elec-

tion Monitoring Unit), Nairobi, November 3, 1993, and Ethiopians who wish not to be identified (Addis Ababa, November 1993).

39. As indicated in an earlier footnote, one of the anticipated highlights of my work in sub-Saharan Africa was to be participation in the small team of international observers, headed by former President Jimmy Carter, for the Togolese Presidential elections of 25 August 1993. The National Democratic Institute (NDI) prepared an extensive briefing book, replete with details of what Gnassigbé Eyadéma (ruler of Togo since a military coup of January 1967) had accepted as conditions, through negotiation with opposition groups. NDI sent field workers well in advance of the scheduled date. They saw, at first hand, the incredible obstructions to a genuine competitive election undertaken by the regime. Opposition candidates pulled out. The international mission was cancelled, since Eyadéma and company had not honored their commitments and the "election" was going to be a farce. The international boycott was not complete, however, due to the presence of some observers from France considered sympathetic to the government.

Chapter 9
Development and the Quest for Social Equity

> ... human rights NGOs in developing countries face a major challenge; their operational strategies must be directed towards elevating social and economic rights beyond the fanciful rhetoric of charters and conventions. For it is these rights that are, to all intents and purposes, more meaningful to their undernourished and illiterate populace rather than [the] class of civil and political rights which make little sense to the man whose lot is starvation, or who lives under the bridge for want of a better accommodation; or the university graduate who has become disillusioned and frustrated by the fruitlessness of his search for subsistence.
>
> — Olisa Agbakoba[1]

> To the large majority of people who are living in almost sub-human existence in conditions of abject poverty and for whom life is one long, unbroken story of want and destitution, notions of individual freedom and liberation, through representing some of the most cherished values of a free society, would sound as empty words bandied about in the drawing rooms of the rich and well to do, and the only solution for making these rights meaningful to them was to re-make the material conditions and usher in a new social order where socio-economic justice will inform all institutions of public life so that the preconditions of fundamental liberties for all may be secured.
>
> — Judge P.N. Bhagwati[2]

> The right to development is an inalienable human right by virtue of which every human person and all peoples are entitled to participate in, contribute to, and enjoy economic, social, cultural and political development, in which all human rights and fundamental freedoms can be fully realized. . . . States have the primary responsibility for the creation of national and international conditions favourable to the realization of the right to development.
>
> — Declaration on the Right to Development, Articles 1, 3[3]

If human rights in Africa are to be meaningfully enhanced, major efforts for economic development must come in the villages. This has not occurred, at least in a significant, direct way. Struggles for human rights have been concentrated in cities, and have tended to focus on the International Covenant on Civil and Political Rights. The NGOs of this book work primarily in Addis Ababa, Dakar, Lagos, or Windhoek. Once dusty tracks replace paved (or pot-holed streets), involvement by them and other "classic" human rights NGOs drops off sharply. And, when it comes to pressure for less inequitable allocation of resources, or for satisfaction of basic human needs, many human rights organizations seem to shrug their shoulders, for they already have more than enough to do. Leave these matters to development-oriented groups or community organizations. The job is important, but not for us.

The capital-centric nature of most African human rights NGOs arises in large part from necessity. It is far easier to find rights-active lawyers where the major courts are located, educators near the Ministry of Education, politically-oriented groups where the government sits. Basic strategy, particularly for civil and political rights, dictates a focus on the center. The "victories" won in the major towns can change national policies. The impact (at least in theory) can thus be enormous. However, if you accept two basic arguments of this book — that effective promotion and protection of human rights rest in the final analysis on informed public opinion, and that the so-called "generations" of rights are interdependent — then the efforts of human rights NGOs must be broadened considerably. They must, over time, have an impact on the conditions that militate against the dignity, worth, and rights of the rural majority. Accordingly, issues concerning them ought to move to center stage. But what, more precisely, are the best ways to reach the rural majority? Not only by political pressure at the center, but by economic development at the periphery, I argue in this chapter.

Africa is a continent plagued with underdevelopment, notably outside the cities. Villages (where the majority of Africans continue to live, although the demographic balance is shifting rapidly toward urban areas) exhibit many marks of neglect, even exploitation. A patina of dust, kicked up by gaunt herds of cattle or blown from distant arid areas, covers most surfaces. A few signs of prosperity — a bicycle here, a galvanized iron roof instead of thatch there — accentuate the picture of general poverty. The villages' populations are often skewed. Large numbers of adult males have gone to earn money in the towns, some permanently, many on long-term bases. Listless, swollen-bellied boys lie in the shade, lacking energy for games or access to education. Their mothers and often their sisters spend endless hours in their quests for firewood and water, whose sources may be miles from their homes. Human potential lies untapped.

One of the tropical Africa's most thoughtful political leaders expressed the problem thus:

What freedom has our subsistence farmer? He scratches a bare living from the soil provided the rains do not fail; his children work at his side without schooling, medical care, or even good feeding. Certainly he has freedom to vote and to speak as he wishes. But these freedoms are much less real to him than his freedom to be exploited. Only as his poverty is reduced will his existing political freedom become properly meaningful and his right to human dignity become a fact of human dignity.[4]

I argue in this chapter that a major avenue to human dignity, and essential parts of a "culture" of human rights, comes from development. Improved economic and social conditions represent, without hesitation, a cardinal need and paramount desire of contemporary Africans. For them, human rights in the villages begin with breakfast. To them, rights mean access to education, health services, and bacteria-free water. The quest for development finds expression through "grass-roots" participation in an increasing number of organizations focused on economic improvement. Such NGOs have proliferated in Africa, and often preceded human rights NGOs as known in the West. Their successes and failures teach an immense amount about the roles of citizen groups in the promotion and protection of human rights.

Development, like democratization, facilitates the achievement of a broad range of rights. And, for a large number of NGOs that promote and protect human rights in Africa, development forms their *raison d'être*. Their efforts must be included in a survey of this type. For reasons briefly explored in Chapter 2, evocation of the "right to development" has emerged as a "specifically African contribution to the international human rights discourse."[5] Hence, following the pattern of other chapters in which I utilize a specific NGO or group of NGOs to exemplify the particular issue, I shall begin in the Senegalese village of Kër Simbara, where "Tostan" — "breakthrough" or, literally, "the hatching of an egg" in the Wolof language — has established a noteworthy project focused on illiterate adult women. What they learn undergirds human rights consciousness. The chapter concludes with broader reflections on the obstacles to development *conceived of as a human right.*

Tostan and Kër Simbara: A Particular View

Similar to the other NGOs in *Protecting Human Rights in Africa,* Tostan was the brainchild of a specific individual, in this case a non-African who over 20 years has moved fully into African society. Molly Melching's hegira to rural Senegal began with study at the University of Dakar (as Cheikh-Anta Diop University was then entitled), and continued with a Peace Corps stint. She started her work in Dakar with a team of Senegalese. They soon recognized that educational programs needed to be established outside the capital. Melching focused on indigenous languages as the key to development. Her interests came to fruition with American, Canadian, and UNICEF funding for basic educational programs carried out in six Senegalese tongues, rather than in the official language, French. By taking her approach to rural areas, Melching arrived at the heart of the development problem.

Kër Simbara is a village of approximately 150 persons in the region of

Thiès, about 80 kilometers east of the capital, Dakar. There, change from below is making an impact. "Participatory development" has started to transform Kër Simbara from within. The village itself follows a typical Sahel plan. Most of the thirty or so homesteads are constructed of sun-dried mud and brick, though corrugated iron has replaced thatch atop most. Homesteads generally include several huts, surrounded by a light wall of woven reeds. A large tree provides welcome shade in a central part of the village. People, livestock, and hounds contend for space under it. Narrow paths lead off from the dusty track that connects Kër Simbara to the city of Thiès, only six kilometers away. No cars, even bicycles, are in evidence, however, although horses are obviously used. People converse in Wolof. Though French is the official tongue of Senegal, few villagers have functional literacy or communicative ability in it. Women and children are far more in evidence than adult males. Relatively easy access to Thiès and Dakar has taken a toll, for paying jobs cluster in the cities. What Senegalese deem the *malaise paysanne*—rural malaise—has spread through this area. In Kër Simbara, this means a steady effusion of the young, able, and ambitious, unable to earn enough cash in the farming community. Villages show little in the way of development. Light at night comes from kerosene lanterns or cooking fires. By 9 p.m., quiet has descended. The village sleeps, but not for long. As roosters crow in the pre-dawn coolness, women of the village head out to obtain water and firewood. Another day has started, in all likelihood little different from the ones that preceded it.

Yet there are major changes afoot. The discerning eye will see differences between Kër Simbara and many other Senegalese villages. A large windmill to pump water spins beside a well-tended vegetable garden, filled with lettuce, cabbage, onions, eggplant and bright red peppers. Much cooking is done in fuel-efficient clay stoves, rather than over open fires between the traditional three stones. Some people in the shade are reading. A few homes have been built of cement, rather than of the traditional sun-dried mud. And, most important, a beehive-shaped structure stands at the village heart. Benches line its inside walls; above them are carefully lettered posters, in Wolof, with the names of village children, check lists, and key words. A blackboard with stubs of chalk stands between the two doors, for in Kër Simbara Tostan's basic education program is in full swing, designed to enhance development and knowledge of human rights. Central to its philosophy is use of the indigenous (or, in Senegalese terms, the "national") language, utilized for an 18-month curriculum of vital skills.[6]

Melching and her associates founded the "Demb ak Tey" ("Yesterday and Today") resource center in the mid-1970s to promote non-formal education for Senegalese children, based on their home languages.

Demb ak Tey challenged much of orthodox Senegalese thinking about education. The official curriculum bore a strong colonial imprint. Formal education in the country emphasized knowledge of French, which was held to be the key to further learning. Use of indigenous tongues was strongly discouraged, presumably in the interest of national unity and access to wider learning outside Senegal. Classroom instruction, given in a language few children understood, stressed pronunciation and character recognition. The depth of education was open to question. Most children who visited Demb ak Tey, even if they had formally attended school, could neither read nor write in either French or Wolof, the lingua franca of Dakar. Their exposure to education had not been sufficient to give them functional literacy. And, without this basic skill, they were likely limited to dead-end menial jobs, assuming these were available. Allegedly schooled Senegalese youngsters received enough training to want to leave the village, but not enough to survive well in the urban environment.

Demb ak Tey, as already mentioned, received much of its initial impetus from an outsider deeply interested in Senegalese culture. As a student of African civilization in Dakar in the mid-1970s, Melching probed into various languages. She was astounded — appalled might be a better word — by the limited amount of material published in Wolof, the most widely spoken language in the country.[7] To reach children and awaken in them a thirst for further learning, she recognized, they should be approached in their mother tongues. Melching was well aware of research showing the greater efficacy of instruction in native languages. Children and adult learners as well could develop skills far more rapidly when taught in their own tongues. The Peace Corps, which she joined as a volunteer, and the Spencer Foundation of Chicago, provided funds for Melching's work for three years. She created the Demb ak Tey resource center in the teeming medina of Dakar. Melching and her Senegalese collaborators Bollé Mbaye and Malick Pouge utilized puppetry, games, art, theatre, and booklets in Wolof to attract children's interest. Achieving literacy was the major goal — but it was ability to read and write in Wolof, not in French. Though this effort ran against the grain of Senegalese policy, the government-sponsored Center for Civilization Studies (significantly, under the Ministry of Culture rather than the Ministry of Education) provided official support. Demb ak Tey took to the airwaves as well. A weekly two-hour children's show in Wolof ran from 1978 to 1982, directed at the rural areas. As Melching wrote subsequently,

Because of the difficult conditions facing the children interviewed in villages throughout Senegal, the program initiators decided to include messages of health, the environment and other community development issues in the stories, songs, games, and theaters. This effort to give children access to more information and knowledge through use of cultural traditions was extremely popular.[8]

Melching is a passionate, persuasive advocate, with a crucial understanding of local needs. Central to her concerns, as should now be apparent, are linkages between specific skills and the use of indigenous languages — in the politically correct Senegalese usage, "national" languages. There are six: Diola, Fulaani, Pulaar, Serer, Soninké, and Wolof. Few families in Senegal use French, the official language, in household conversation. Children thus encounter French when (if!) they attend school. Formal learning in Senegal (whether primary or aimed at illiterate adults) still focuses on literacy in French, in the belief knowledge of it would open magic casements, giving the new readers access to necessary information. It does not always do so. As one specialist noted in 1982,

Although literacy training is not interchangeable with basic education, many planners have conceived it as such. They have associated the need for literacy training with the objective of spreading developmental knowledge, when in fact they should have linked the need for a fuller, basic education with development. To this way of thinking, literacy training soon became an absolute prerequisite for acquiring knowledge that would lead to development. In the absence of a comprehensive, widespread motivation to acquire literacy skills, the literacy campaigns mounted by planners of this opinion turned into iron gates, barring the attainment of the developmental knowledge that the learner so urgently needs for survival in an ever more highly competitive and economic world. This narrow view of education and development, albeit well intentioned, ultimately proved self-defeating.[9]

Formal classroom learning in Senegal is not easy under any circumstances. Conditions are far from optimal. Classes are large, teachers heavily burdened, school supplies difficult to obtain. I have seen many classrooms in the country each with 70 students, 10 shared books, and no writing materials. The curriculum, despite some adaptation since independence, remains heavily based on French academic models ill-adapted to Senegalese needs. The educational pyramid, relatively broad at its base, narrows sharply, particularly for rural women for whom marriage at a relatively early age is common.[10] Classroom skills gained in French atrophy, and in fact disappear for many, in a matter of months after leaving school. Functional illiteracy in *any* language thus results, since the training in French is not carried over readily into ability to read one of the indigenous languages. More important, it seems not to transfer into the types of basic education that undergird village-level development.

Tostan's approach started from a fact of life in rural Senegal — and, for that matter, a truth in most of contemporary Africa. Most village women have not attended primary school, or, if they have, they have little opportunity to use the reading and mathematical skills they supposedly gained. Their training is maladapted to the environment in which they live. A program meaningful to them, *and likely to promote self-sustaining development and human rights consciousness within rural settings*, would have to be designed on different presumptions. All rhetoric about "participation" and "grassroots" efforts must be tested against the realities of village life. And, for persons in rural Senegal, problems of water, health, hygiene, the environment, limited roles for women, and the exodus to the cities were (and are) severe problems.[11] Why not, Melching and her colleagues reasoned, design an educational program that would help adult learners resolve these issues? Why not promote development through teaching basic skills in immediately applicable ways?

Hence basic education via the Tostan curriculum differs from literacy training in Senegalese schools. Perhaps the most salient contrasts include its 1) being taught entirely in indigenous tongues, 2) being focused on adults (especially women), 3) taking up practical issues of rural life, 4) following a detailed program (based on two-month modules) with guides for each session, 5) using consultations with coordinators and trainers linked to regular evaluation, and 6) linking class learning with problem-solving skills. As obvious as these may seem, such objectives have not characterized most education in Senegal.

The real world of the villagers lies at the heart of the program. Let me provide some examples. Basic reading and writing skills are applied to clear and present problems: transmission of germs, dehydration (a leading cause of death of children under five), immunization, and (with their new math skills) management of village projects. Immediate application in the rural setting is always sought. Learning numbers from 10 to 100 is linked with calendars, telling time, and developing planning skills and agendas for action. A "whole language" approach is used, rather than a narrow focus on isolated fragments (i.e., individual letters or phonemes). Knowledge is reinforced in several ways: through flip charts, discussion, specially-designed card games,[12] theater, poetry, etc. Traditional roles based on sex are called into question. Why should men automatically expect to lead?

Formal evaluations of the Tostan basic education program show intriguing, nay encouraging, results. In the experimental phase, 512 Fulaani speakers from 19 villages in the Kolda region of southeastern Senegal enrolled in 38 classes. The drop-out rate over the three-year period was a surprisingly low 12 percent. Class members were both interviewed and evaluated on their cognitive knowledge. According to one summary, "The majority of participants felt that their personal and village health and hygiene practices had changed more than anything else . . . they are now able to manage their millet machines, their financial resources, as well as other projects and small businesses . . . Reading and writing have changed the way the way the participants view the world — they claim to have more confidence when faced with new situations or projects."[13] And if emulation is the highest compliment, the fact that 72 villages in the region officially requested the basic education program, even collecting their own funds to start it, provides proof.

The objectives of the Tostan program may appear restricted, but they are not. The learning modules focus on skills vital to strengthening human rights in Africa. Participants gain knowledge in key areas, such as management skills, critical reasoning, and problem-solving. They are "enabled" or "empowered," to use recently fashionable verbs. Village women thereby can enhance their commercial acumen. They can cope better with the demands of contemporary life, raise healthier children, and speak with greater authority in that male-centered society. These skills may not be the stuff of habeas corpus, competitive elections, freedom from torture, or effective non-discrimination laws. To the great majority of Senegalese rural dwellers, nonetheless, they make for a better life. Their human dignity is advanced.

Let me go further, however, and argue that their human rights are advanced as well. Development that promotes equity, higher standards of living (measured by indices such as lower infant mortality rates, improved access to education or nearby sources of clean water), and the belief all members of society must benefit from change, are valuable in and of themselves. The inhabitants of Kër Simbara enjoy a stronger foundation for a human rights culture than do those of most other African villages.

This is not an argument for a hierarchy of rights. I am not asserting that economic improvements should precede civil and political rights; there are complex interconnections among them, recognized by all serious students of the subject. Global human rights conferences have regularly linked civil and political rights, and economic, social, and cultural rights. Important to both are personal attributes. Self-esteem, confidence, awareness of community obligations, involvement in group activities: these hard-to-measure attitudes fall into the realm I am describing. Rural dwellers in tropical Africa, particularly women, face massive difficulties in developing these attitudes. Programs such as Tostan, in focusing on development as well, in fact bring education and empowerment, thereby giving human rights a stronger foundation.

Two paragraphs of personal testimony surely belong here. I saw, and was impressed by, the effects of Tostan-style basic education. It was late April 1994, my last day of field work in tropical Africa. I arrived in Kër Simbara in mid-afternoon. My thoughts were on the immense tasks remaining for the remaining few months of sabbatical leave. These distractions quickly vanished. The enthusiasm of the villagers captivated me. Twenty-five children were gathered in the village's community hall; they were singing an alphabet song, clapping vigorously. *Toubabs* (white persons) did not come often.[14] And when they do, the questions they pose may be odd. What did the children hope would be achieved in the next few years?, I asked. Some wanted electricity for lights (a small solar generator atop the community hall is the only source of current), so that roving thieves wouldn't take cattle. Others called for a new millet machine, a toilet, a boutique, even a bread stand. They talked of possible careers as a teacher, hairdresser, journalist, maid, or leader. The kids were delighted to show their skills in printing and mathematics. They were fortunate. Without the external funding obtained through Melching's enthusiasm and proven approach, their thirst for learning would have gone unslaked. The government of Senegal provides schooling for barely half the country's youth; these do not include those of Kër Simbara.

And what of their parents? A score of them gathered later in the community center, most of them women, many with infants still in tow. Almost all had been illiterate in any tongue. Now they could decipher texts in Wolof. Their education had affected their basic outlooks. They were ready (much like Lerner's Middle Eastern villagers)[15] to move full-tilt into the modern world. Some were anxious to move on to French. The village chief (a vigorous man in his early 70s) contrasted the exploitation of the colonial period with villagers' rapidly growing awareness of rights. "It's our responsibility to respect others," he stated. Much to my surprise (and to the delight of Melching, who was interpreting the spirited flow of Wolof), the women showed their awareness of leadership. Formerly, several said, they would have been silent in such meetings. Now, they spoke up. The village head had to seek consensus. Children were better treated. "We are learning to vote for people who have the interests of all in mind, not just themselves," one woman opined. As she spoke, Melching called my attention to the check-list over the speaker's head: it listed qualities of leadership such as dynamic, visionary, competent, patient, kind. No longer could men expect automatic deference.[16]

Kër Simbara is a village changing largely from within. To be certain, the proximity of Dakar and Thiès has an impact. Cash-paying jobs can be found there. But self-sustaining development requires more than the ebb and flow of urban workers. A flow to the cities means rural areas lose out. Villages are deprived of skilled persons, even if enriched by their remitted earnings. Programs are required for those who remain behind, primarily women and children. When these efforts work, wider recognition should be given. What villagers have learned and put into practice in terms of health, leadership, computation, and reading has already made a discernible impact. The inhabitants of Kër Simbara have recognized that they have the ability to help create a better future for themselves, in which the rights of others figure prominently.

It may seem modest to talk about changed attitudes about a toilet or a bread stand for a village, in a book devoted to larger issues of human rights. Kër Simbara is not racked by ethnic violence or arbitrary killings; slave-like practices have disappeared; Senegal has adhered to a regular schedule of reasonably open elections, even if the opposition has good reason to complain[17]; few prisoners languish for years in a lock-up while awaiting trial. The crucial issues of human rights in Kër Simbara are subtle rather than shocking. Through basic education, the attitudinal and cultural foundations for rights are being strengthened. Progress has been measured and real.

"Development" as a "Human Right"

Through much of Africa, regretfully, the modest economic and social advances discernible in Kër Simbara cannot be found. Poverty has worsened. It is appropriate to recall and extend points made in Chapter 2 about Africa's economic condition:

- as part of the global economy, Africa's position has declined in recent decades, the result of both rapid growth elsewhere and negative trends in prices for primary products on which the economies of many African countries depend;
- what are for many countries impossibly high mountains of debt hang over their economies; periodic reschedulings postpone and compound (rather than resolve) the problem;
- structural adjustment plans have resulted in major trimming of public payrolls (both of "ghost workers" and regular employees), privatization of many parastatal enterprises, removal of barriers protecting local industries, and reductions of subsidies; unemployment and underemployment rates have worsened; the impact is particularly severe on urban residents, but rural dwellers are also affected;
- devaluation or free-floating of currencies has often exacerbated inflation, cost run-ups for imported goods, and unemployment;
- gaps continue to widen between rural and urban areas, for even with a third or more of the population unemployed or under-employed in the cities, conditions are even worse in the countryside;
- cutbacks in public services have had marked effects on education and health care, among others;
- increased conditionalities for international financial assistance have been imposed, including greater democratization/better governance, enhanced environmental protection, and stamps of approval

from the International Monetary Fund (IMF) prior to major disburse-
ments—all valuable long-term goals, but serious in their short-term
impact.

In brief, economic decline and marginalization have become hall-
marks of contemporary Africa. Retrogression, not development, marked
almost all African countries from the late 1970s well into the mid-1990s.
What had been billed as "development decades" proved instead to be
traumatic times. Only the privileged political class (including senior
members of the security establishment) and a few bankers, traders, or
entrepreneurs escaped the general impoverishment. For the populace as
a whole, conditions generally worsened. Quite a change, it is clear in
historical retrospect, from the rosier political and economic conditions
in the first decade-plus of independence.

The "right to development" formed part of the early 1970s political
agenda. The Third World majority in the United Nations sought to revise
the distribution of global economic power. Development was very much
the watchword. Was it a "right"? Its articulation by Kéba Mbaye in 1972[18]
coincided with discussion of important General Assembly resolutions on
permanent sovereignty over natural resources, the "New International
Economic Order," and the Charter of Economic Rights and Duties of
States. Although it was not until 1986 that the General Assembly adopted
the Declaration on Development by an overwhelming margin—the
United States cast the only negative vote, eight other Western industrial
countries abstained, 146 countries voted in favor[19]—it had its roots in
heated north-south (rather than east-west) debates over the disjuncture
between political power within the United Nations (and especially in the
General Assembly) and economic affluence. That divide was, and remains, a powerful factor in contemporary international politics. It meant
that development became prominent in human rights discourse at a
tender period in interstate relations.

Enunciation of the right to development by Mbaye also coincided with
the height of drought and famine in the Sahel and parts of southern
Africa. Thousands of African families and their herds had to leave their
traditional grazing grounds or farming areas in the early 1970s. Des-
ertification advanced. Millions of acres lay parched. Relief became an
urgent, immediate need. A series of NGOs sprang up, both in the West
and in Africa, to cope with this human and environmental tragedy.
Hopes for development in many areas lay shattered; survival itself was
difficult. Many of what today are development-oriented NGOs in Africa
were born at that time as food-distribution and disaster-relief organizations.

Third, the economic debate of the early 1970s overlapped the start of an immense (if short-lived) transfer of resources from developed to oil-producing states. OPEC price escalations of 1973–74, and again in 1979, meant a handful of countries profited. Petrodollars sloshed around the world banking system; many of them were invested in economically marginal undertakings in Africa. This surge of borrowed funds in the late 1970s and into the 1980s brought a patina of temporary prosperity to some African countries (Côte d'Ivoire is an excellent example), at the cost of later bankruptcy. That was far from the only consequence. The shocks to the global economy were immense, as is well-known. Recession in the west reduced demand for petroleum; high prices for it spurred production from alternative sources; overproduction became a fact of life, with sharp falls in price. The illusion of development was accordingly overshadowed by the mid-1980s by the reality of economic stagnation.[20] No wonder, then, that development became "the most pressing issue" Third World countries confronted.[21]

In other words, the right to development was initially articulated at a time when the gap between Western industrial and African countries was starting to widen. Aspiration and reality went in opposite directions. Evidence increased during the 1980s of how Africa was falling behind most other parts of the Third World and developed states. The effects were widespread. Economic malaise contributed directly to the 1990s wave of democratization south of the Sahara. If authoritarian governments proved unable to break the cycle of impoverishment, perhaps elected governments could. Certainly there might be less temptation for corruption or conspicuous consumption by a small group. Transparency and accountability became viewed as central to economic development, as well as to democratic rule.

Few human rights NGOs have dealt explicitly and easily with the right to development. To many, most notably certain international NGOs, the issue has been perceived as a distraction from seemingly more important tasks. The classic focus for human rights activists has been the state, and in particular its acts against individual citizens. Acts of commission by responsible authorities are central to their crusades. Detention without trial, torture, arbitrary execution, denial of political access on the basis of ascriptive characteristics: these are the types of rights issues familiar in the west as requiring NGO attention, and implicitly or explicitly adopted as a model for human rights work elsewhere. To summarize perhaps to the point of caricature, a state that enslaved or tortured children would be culpable — but a government that failed to inoculate infants against deadly infectious diseases would not. That was a classic view, in which prohibition of certain actions by governments was the watchword for action. "Negative" rights were preferred to "positive" rights. It was a message strongly amplified in the 1980s by Cold War tensions. Civil and political rights were held to be conceptually distinct from economic, social and cultural rights: terms such as "first" and "second" generation, or "negative" and "positive" rights, were bandied about.

Rights are indivisible and interdependent, despite arguments to the contrary. The case has been eloquently, indeed conclusively, argued by Shue.[22] Nonetheless, disquiet remains. As van Boven observed, a "structural" approach—one that links human rights to major worldwide patterns and issues, identifies root causes of violations, assesses human rights in the light of concrete contexts and situations, and recognizes the diversity of political and social systems, cultural and religious pluralism, *and different levels of development*—caused "a great deal of uneasiness in the traditional human rights community."[23] The right to development is, as Alston has argued, "the single most important element in the launching of a structural approach to human rights at the international level."[24] By rooting abuses in economic disparities as well as in governmental actions, this approach broadens the scope of action. The struggle for human rights becomes far more complex, perhaps impossibly so, if it means revising international economic policies in addition to combatting domestic governmental actions.

In Chapter 7, note was made of Human Rights Watch. Its careful documentation and good media contacts have significantly advanced American awareness of human rights abuses. Human Rights Watch does not argue along "structural" lines as just summarized. HRW addresses the development issues raised in this chapter only indirectly. Lack of transparency and accountability means governments not only infringe on civil and political rights, but also fail to promote economic rights. Development thus falls victim as well to political issues. But development does not figure among the human rights HRW was established to promote. Its mandate is directed toward rights of the person[25] and toward civil and political rights. Nor does Amnesty International concentrate on development, its limited mandate being directed toward prisoners of conscience, torture, and the death penalty.[26] Pressure for development as a human rights issue has come largely from within Africa. To a substantial extent, it reflects the economic disappointments of the 1970s and 1980s, in which relief was a major element. Of the international NGOs, one of the most consistent advocates of the need for development has been Oxfam. On the global level, it has paralleled the changes of many NGOs in Africa. Started as relief organizations, they have moved toward sustained development. Many have profited from partnerships with Western governments and NGOs, partners in the quest for better lives in rural areas.

From Relief to Development

The rich, complex history of African-based, development-oriented NGOs lies outside the scope of this volume. Among their sources are voluntary associations, thousands of which sprang up in African cities as part of the rural-urban movement,[27] religious-inspired organizations, frequently drawing from missionary impulses, and secular groups, often established with external funding. They are older in many cases than the NGOs to which attention was given earlier. They came to the fore shortly after independence, as popular demand grew for economic advance to complement political advance.

For obvious reasons, opportunities for development-oriented NGOs in Africa increased dramatically after 1960. The end of colonialism meant that a wider variety of international groups could seek access. No longer was most of the continent the *chasse gardée* (private preserve) of the Belgians, British, or French. USAID started to operate south of the Sahara, extending the work of the Commonwealth Development Corporation or the *Fonds d'Aide et de Coopération.* World Bank (and later African Development Bank) loans began to flow to the new governments. With 1960–1970 designated as the "Development Decade," and with a generally buoyant outlook about economic growth, African countries started their independent histories in an optimistic atmosphere.

The crushing droughts of the early 1970s and the shock of the OPEC price increase undercut this optimism. Famine opened the door for dramatically greater NGO activity. Food relief was imperative. International agencies — the International Committee of the Red Cross, Oxfam, CARE, religiously-inspired groups — swung into action. They relied heavily on local affiliates, workers, and other groups to distribute food, medicine, and other necessities. Indigenous NGOs gained from the experience. They proved themselves to be able partners.[28] Indeed, with their greater responsiveness to local needs, lower overhead costs, and better knowledge of prevailing conditions in the field, African groups outperformed the quasi-official, expatriate-dominated counterparts in many respects. Private organizations also stepped up their fund-raising efforts. As a result, grants from NGOs in developed countries became an important part of development assistance, while major aid-donors channeled significant parts of their funds through NGOs.

Tables 5 and 6 indicate the importance of private grants through NGOs as part of official development assistance.

Clark puts these figures in perspective: NGOs of developed countries ("northern") collectively transfer more funds to developing countries ("the south") than does the entire World Bank group.[29] And, it stands to

TABLE 5.   Private Grants by DAC-Country NGOs[30]
(Millions of U.S. dollars/percentage of official development assistance)

Country	1970	1980	1985	1992
Canada	$51.60/15.32%	$102/9.49%	$171.0/10.48%	$270/10.73%
France	$6.30/0.86%	$35.7/1.24%	$64.77/2.07%	$302.25/3.65%
Germany	$77.77/12.98%	$420.71/11.8%	$423.78/14.4%	$856.03/11.29%
Japan	$2.90/0.63%	$26.38/0.79%	$101.44/2.67%	$190.35/1.71%
Sweden	$25.19/21.53%	$59.0/6.13%	$77.57/9.24%	$130/5.29%
United Kingdom	$33.60/6.97%	$120.16/6.48%	$168.5/11.02%	$437.98/13.62%
United States	$598.0/18.97%	$1,301/18.23%	$1,513/16.09%	$2,812/24.02%
Total	$859/12.81%	$2,386.3/9.11%	$2,883.7/10%	$5,933.84/9.47%

reason, non-governmental organizations work more closely with citizens' groups than do official, government-to-government entities such as USAID, or inter-governmental organizations such as the African Development Bank. Note how practices differ markedly among countries. France, for example, steers its assistance overwhelmingly through governments; the United States both uses NGOs as subcontractors in various programs, and provides most resources as food aid rather than cash.[31]

To illustrate the evolution of development-oriented NGOs, complementing the analysis of Tostan in Senegal earlier in this chapter, a few final paragraphs on Ethiopia are appropriate. Recall the devastation wrought in the early 1970s by drought: hundreds of thousands of persons displaced and government capacities taken to the breaking point. The imperial court sedulously avoided public discussion of the rural disaster, at least until dramatic TV footage belied Haile Selassie's belief that all was well. A similar scenario prevailed in the early 1980s, when drought once again afflicted the north and the authoritarian government was shamed into accepting external assistance. Private agencies, mostly Western and many religiously-oriented, swung into action. Helping the hungry became a type of "feel good" activity. The first of what became a series of highly successful rock concerts raised funds for Ethiopian relief. The problems were enormous. Millions of dollars of food aid surged into the country without adequate means of distribution. (I recall being told, during my first visit to Ethiopia in December 1973, that because more than half the rural population lived over a day's walk from the nearest road, thousands starved because they were too weak to reach feeding stations, or too proud to leave their homesteads.) Some Western-based relief agencies mounted their own efforts. Many turned to local NGOs as partners. Whatever strategy was followed, the need for coordination was immense. Precious funds should not be wasted because of inadequate communication.

The Christian Relief and Development Association (CRDA) took

TABLE 6. Net Grants from DAC Governments to DAC-Country NGOs[32]
(Millions of U.S. dollars/percentage of official development
assistance)

Country	1980	1985	1992
Canada	$60/5.58%	$128.6/1.71%	$252.32/10.03%
France	$3.45/0.12%	$42.51/1.36%	$25.89/n.a.
Germany	$198.37/5.56%	$162.9/5.54%	$206.83/2.73%
Japan	$26.89/0.80%	$41.31/1.09%	$107.22/0.96%
Sweden	$49.17/5.11%	$32.96/3.92%	$137.07/n.a.
United Kingdom	$3.45/0.19%	$13.23/0.86%	$19.18/0.60%
United States	$640.7/8.47%	$802.77/8.54%	($1,100)/n.a.
Total	$1,126.89/4.30%	$1,461.85/5.08%	($2,314.23)/3.69%

Figures in brackets provisional

shape initially in 1973 as an informal grouping of church and mission
representatives combatting famine in Welo and Tigray provinces (northern Ethiopia).[33] CRDA remains in existence as of mid-1994. Its diverse
members — some 77 organizations as of the end of 1991, 90 by late 1993[34]
— share the common goal, in Hovde's words, "of providing material relief in times of emergencies and supporting the rehabilitation and development of Ethiopian society."[35]

Obviously, there were and are many ways to reach this broad objective.
The great majority of CRDA member organizations focused initially on
saving the starving. NGOs in Ethiopia distributed nearly two-thirds of all
relief food during emergency years.[36] The emergency, however, was
largely a result of government policies. The Derg under Mengistu consciously used starvation as a means of control.[37] Relief-oriented NGOs
were cowed into silence about the misdirected actions of Mengistu and
his henchmen — or, perhaps more likely, the NGOs believed their mission
of mercy meant they should avoid "politics." Hovde relates that, during
the five years he served as director of the Mennonite mission in Ethiopia,
he never once heard an NGO publicly challenge the government's human rights record, its policies, its cover-up of the cholera epidemic, or its
conduct of the civil war in the north; *Médecins sans frontières*, which did
raise a critical voice over the Derg's resettlement policy, was expelled.[38]
Given the despotic nature of Mengistu and his colleagues, and given the
ravages of the civil war, was silence the correct policy? The CRDA director
strongly believes that silence was necessary under the prevailing circumstances.[39] Mass starvation was avoided where affiliates were permitted to
operate. Even under the Derg, CRDA membership grew; hundreds of
thousands of hungry were fed. Was this avoidance of widespread death an
adequate reason to avoid speaking out? When should human rights advocates remain silent in the face of injustice? If publicity about abuses is one

of their few weapons, should NGOs risk being closed or ousted by revealing the facts to various publics?

Widespread famine may again threaten Ethiopia. Population continues to increase rapidly (as through the rest of the African continent). Many areas remain susceptible to drought. Although extensive arable land is available, the complexities of the new regions and other administrative reorganization complicate awarding of title. Recall as well Mesfin Wolde-Mariam's argument (chapter 7) that starvation in Ethiopia is a concomittant of authoritarianism. Without responsive government and better protection of human rights, he and the Ethiopian Human Rights Council assert, widespread disasters could recur. Of course, they may also recur without rural development. Especially needed is recognition of the interdependent nature of democratization, development, and a culture of human rights. In this task, as the concluding chapter points out, NGOs will play the key roles.

Notes

1. Olisa Agbakoba, "The Role of Non-Governmental Organisations in the Development and Protection of Individual Rights," in M. A. Ajomo and Bolaji Owasanoye, eds., *Individual Rights Under the 1989 Constitution* (Lagos: Nigerian Institute of Advanced Legal Studies, 1993), pp. 145–46. Agbakoba co-founded and (as of mid-1994) continues to lead the Civil Liberties Organisation of Nigeria.

2. From a 1980 judgment handed down in the Supreme Court of India in 1980; quoted in ibid., p. 142.

3. UN Resolution 41/128, 4 December 1986.

4. Julius K. Nyerere, "Stability and Change in Africa," originally published in 1969; quoted in Issa G. Shivji, *The Concept of Human Rights in Africa* (London: CODESRIA, 1989), p. 26. One could question how widespread the right to vote actually was in Africa when President Nyerere wrote; one could also cavil about the likelihood the person working in the field would be female rather than male. Nonetheless, the intent of "Mwalimu's" message is clear, and its basic sentiments widely shared.

5. Shivji, *Concept of Human Rights in Africa*, p. 29. He goes on, however, to argue against pressing for the right to development rather than self-determination. "Conceptually the right to development has very weak foundations. Development itself has either been expanded to include everything (and therefore nothing!) as in the UN Declaration, or more often narrowly to economic development in its economistic, and increasingly, even econometric sense. Either way it blunts, if not eliminates, the ideological and political sting and sharpness which are central to the concept of self-determination." Ibid., p. 82. Footnote omitted from citation.

6. Frequently, Senegalese contrast "national" tongues (such as Wolof or Fulaani) as based on *culture*, with the official language (French) leading to *promotion*.

7. Information about Demb ak Tey, Tostan, and Kër Simbara comes from interviews with Ms Melching and staff (Dakar, March 9, 1994; Kër Simbara April 26, 1994), and from personal observation in the village itself.

8. "Beyond Literacy: The TOSTAN Basic Education Program" (Thiès: TOSTAN, n.d.), pp. 3–4.

9. Abdun Noor, "Managing Adult Literacy Training," *Prospects: Quarterly Review of Education* 12 (1982), 165; quoted in Tostan, "Beyond Literacy," p. 6.

10. Indeed, there is pressure in Senegal to lower the age of school entrance from six or seven to perhaps five for girls — not because they are more ready than boys for education at that age, but because they could complete the primary school cycle before being married at age 13!

11. Gouvernement du Sénégal, *Analyse de la situation de la femme et de l'enfant au Sénégal*, cited in Tostan, "Beyond Literacy," p. 9.

12. Take, for example, the Oral Rehydration card game. The deck includes 50 drawings of positive and negative hygiene habits. Participants are given seven cards; to win, they must throw away "bad" cards, explaining why the practice can lead to diarrhea, and get four "good" cards plus the three oral rehydration cards (one liter of water, eight cubes of sugar, one teaspoon of salt). You can see villagers playing the game outside the teaching area; they learn and enjoy simultaneously.

13. Tostan, "Beyond Literacy," p. 23. This internal evaluation was complemented in November 1992 by an assessment by CIDA (Canadian Agency for International Development), "Projet TOSTAN — Education non-formelle pour le développement — Evaluation en cours d'exécution" (1993), and in February 1991 by ANAFA (National Association for Literacy and the Training of Adults), "Etude d'experiences d'alphabétisation en langues nationales" (1992). Copies on file in the Tostan office.

14. The villagers have been getting far more, however, as information about Tostan's successes spreads. UNICEF, the chief external funder, cited Tostan early in 1994 as one of four innovative programs it intended to highlight. UNICEF agreed to provide around $1.8 million, enabling Tostan to continue its program for more than 6,000 persons. Increasing numbers of observers are flocking to the Thiès area, or requesting copies of the Tostan curriculum.

15. Daniel Lerner, *The Passing of Traditional Society* (New York: Free Press, 1958).

16. In one Tostan village, for example, a new millet machine was obtained through women's efforts. Efforts by men to control it were quickly rebuffed by the women, an act practically unthinkable a few years earlier.

17. For an excellent recent perspective on Senegalese democracy, see Babacar Kanté, "Senegal's Empty Elections," *Journal of Democracy* 5, 1 (1994), 96–108.

18. Kéba Mbaye, "Le droit de développement comme un droit de l'homme," *Revue des Droits de l'Homme* 5 (1972), 503–534. Mbaye's analysis was not the first along these lines, although it was highly influential. See Michel Virally, "Vers un droit international du développement," *Annuaire Français de Droit International* 11 (1965), 3–12. Proponents of what some French scholars call the "droit international de développement" (DID) also suggest a major reworking of international law. They see classic international law "as positively instrumental in the process which has enabled the rich minority of nations to accumulate wealth at the expense of the poor majority — the international law of under-development. The object of DID therefore is to transform and harness international law into an active instrument in the reversal of this process and thus *la reduction des inégalités du développement*." Peter Slinn, "Differing Approaches to the Relationship between International Law and Development," in Francis Snyder and Peter Slinn, eds., *International Law of Development: Comparative Perspectives* (London: Macmillan, 1991), p. 29; French as in the original.

In terms of the origins of the "right to development," the noted Austrian scholar Ginther has also pointed to the 1944 Declaration of Philadelphia as adumbrating the right to development: Konrad Ginther, "The domestic policy function of a right of peoples to development: popular participation[,] a new hope for development and challenge for the discipline," in Subrata Roy Chowdhury, Erik M. G. Denters and Paul J. I. M. de Waart, eds., *The Right to Development in International Law* (Dordrecht: Martinus Nijhoff, 1992), pp. 63–64.

19. Declaration on the Right to Development (UNGA resolution 41/128), adopted 4 December 1986.

20. Richard Sandbrook, *Africa: The Politics of Economic Stagnation* (Cambridge: Cambridge University Press, 1985).

21. Roland Rich, "The Right to Development: A Right of Peoples?" in James Crawford, ed., *The Rights of Peoples* (Oxford: Clarendon Press, 1988), p. 40.

22. Henry Shue, *Basic Rights: Subsistence, Affluence, and U.S. Foreign Policy* (Princeton, NJ: Princeton University Press, 1980).

23. Theo van Boven, "Human Rights and Development: The UN Experience," in David P. Forsythe, ed., *Human Rights and Development: International Views* (New York: St. Martin's, 1989), p. 123.

24. Philip Alston, "Development and the Rule of Law: Prevention versus Cure as a Human Rights Strategy," quoted in Rich, "The Right to Development: A Right of Peoples?" p. 42.

25. Articulated by Secretary of State Cyrus Vance in 1977, and utilized in Department of State *Country Reports*, these include rights based on the integrity of the body, such as freedom from torture, freedom from slavery, and freedom from arbitrary or summary execution.

26. Peter R. Baehr, "Amnesty International and its Self-Imposed Limited Mandate," *Netherlands Quarterly of Human Rights* 12 (1994), 5–22.

27. As examples of early writings, see Kenneth Little, *West African Urbanization: A Study of Voluntary Associations* (Cambridge: Cambridge University Press, 1965) and P. C. Lloyd, *Africa in Social Change: West African Societies in Transition* (New York: Praeger, 1968).

28. Willard R. Johnson and Vivian R. Johnson, *West African Governments and Volunteer Development Organizations: Priorities for Partnership* (Lanham MD: University Press of America, 1990).

29. "General Review of Arrangements for Consultations with Non-Governmental Organizations," UN Document E/AC.70/1994/5, 26 May 1994, pp. 67–68. Figures are provided by the Development Assistance Council of the Organization for Economic Cooperation and Development — the major Western donors.

30. Ibid.

31. John Clark, *Democratizing Development: The Role of Voluntary Organizations* (London: Earthscan, 1991), p. 3. Measured in real terms, the amount available through NGOs doubled between 1975 and 1985, during which time official aid rose 39 percent (p. 47).

32. Ibid., p. 49. A host of interesting details about American policy toward PVOs ("private voluntary organizations") can be found in Ian Smillie, "United States," in Ian Smillie and Henny Helmich, eds., *Non-Governmental Organisations and Governments: Stakeholders for Development* (Paris: OECD, 1993), pp. 303–18.

33. Robert L. Hovde, "Nongovernmental Organizations: Development and Advocacy in Changing Political Environments," unpublished paper, p. 4. Hovde (as of mid-1994 a staff member at Illinois State University) had considerable experience in Ethiopia: as a Peace Corps volunteer 1967–69, as field director for

the Mennonite Mission 1983–88, and as part of the American observer team for the June 1992 election.

34. Interview with Brother Gus O'Keefe, executive director of CRDA, Addis Ababa, November 18, 1993. In a sense, his placement in Ethiopia was providential. He and many other Irish Catholic missionaries were ordered out of Nigeria after the civil war. Placed "temporarily" in January 1972 in Ethiopia, so he thought, O'Keefe became CRDA head in January 1977. His activities thus started with the collapsing regime of Haile Selassie, continued through the tumultuous rise of the Derg and its collapse under EPRDF pressure in the civil war, and witnessed the installation of the Transitional Government with its promises of human rights.

35. Hovde, "Nongovernmental Organizations," p. 5.

36. Ibid., p. 20.

37. Africa Watch (Alex de Waal), *Evil Days: 30 Years of War and Famine in Ethiopia* (New York: Human Rights Watch, 1991).

38. Ibid., p. 35, n. 9.

39. Interview, Addis Ababa, November 18, 1993.

Chapter 10
The "NGO Revolution"

It is now time to draw together the threads of argument in this book, and indicate what the various organizations and strategies tell us more generally about human rights and change in contemporary Africa.

I started with thumbnail sketches of four countries, chosen to represent diverse backgrounds and different parts of the continent, then continued with broad strategies human rights NGOs employ. The middle section of *Protecting Human Rights in Africa* explored, in greater detail through case studies, how education, empowerment, and enforcement approaches were utilized, in conjunction with documentation, democratization, and development, to promote and protect human rights. I offered some preliminary judgments on the effectiveness of the various organizations and strategies, but deferred final judgment until now. "Strength" of NGOs could not be assessed until we became aware of their resources, both local and global, and their relative political power and influence. Now, we are in a better position to determine the nature and limits of NGO action.

This conclusion attempts the following:

- to draw a balance sheet, suggesting the limits of what could be accomplished by NGOs on the basis of their resources;
- to determine why and how changes in NGO strength, spread, and objectives have occurred in recent years;
- to suggest steps whereby NGOs could better promote and protect human rights in Africa; and
- to indicate the key lessons of this study for both contemporary Africa and human rights.

Assessing the Strength of African Human Rights NGOs

The unpleasant facts must be faced first. Human rights violations continue in Africa — often massively — despite the efforts of NGOs. The problems sketched in Chapter 1 remain largely unresolved. Infant mortality statistics (probably the best single measure of the most basic of human rights, that of survival) are grim. Millions of refugees and displaced persons eke out wretched lives in squalid camps. African women continue to labor longer and with far less reward than African men. Rural development of the Tostan sort remains confined to a few villages. Clogged court systems seem to apply one brand of justice for the few who can afford lawyers, another brand for the many with limited funds or knowledge. Despite veneers of democratization, transparency and accountability in government operations remain limited. Almost everywhere, the unresolved problems far outnumber the successful solutions.

It would have been impossible for human rights NGOs to have corrected all these situations. That is not their responsibility. Their major tasks are to document and publicize problems and to press for an open political process through which the issues could be addressed. "Solutions" should be sought by governments. But it is not easy. African governments themselves face major obstacles, given their limited resources, given the short period of time during which human rights has been prominent on their political agendas, and given the links between many issues and deep-rooted cultural norms (for example, early marriages and other harmful traditional practices leading to higher rates of maternal and infant mortality; limited employment opportunities interacting with family obligations that exacerbate corruption). I am not sanguine, however, that all governments in Africa can effectively and rapidly create rights-protective settings. But the attempt needs to be made. The crucial point is to see them launched in the directions pointed by NGOs, international treaties, and (increasingly) the desires of their citizens.

Human rights NGOs work at the margins, in gradual, cumulative ways. Small groups with handfuls of staff laboring mostly in the capital cities cannot transform popular attitudes and governmental practices in a short time. Let us be realistic. African human rights NGOs ameliorate rather than transform situations. They monitor and analyze, rather than achieve rapid, blanket changes. They take gradual steps rather than massive leaps. Their consciousness-raising and help for individual victims can have cumulative effects, however. Over time, the reforms they encourage may add up to a fundamental change in attitude and practices. The "NGO revolution" — in the sense of their contribution to human rights — merits our attention.

Rather than point to weaknesses and problems, accordingly, I prefer to accentuate strengths and possibilities. In preparing this book, I became convinced that the positive results of NGO activity were harbingers of an improved future. I was struck by the transformation of beliefs about the importance of human rights groups in a relatively brief period. Organizations like the Ethiopian Human Rights Council, the Nigerian Legal Research and Resources Development Centre, or RADI (*Réseau africain pour le développement intégré*) of Senegal did not come into existence until late in the 1980s. The atmosphere is improving, despite the enervating economic decline of much of Africa. Civil society has become strengthened south of the Sahara, as witnessed by the creation of these organizations. Documentation skills have improved and networks of activists have been established. NGOs enjoy greater scope for action. The bugaboos of domestic sovereignty and cultural relativism have somewhat diminished, certainly compared to the early 1980s. Democratization has been accepted (at least verbally) throughout the continent.

What are specific signposts by which to measure the achievements of African human rights NGOs?

First, there are explicit references by African governments to human rights and to human rights groups. Relations between them remain tender in many instances. The Abacha government of Nigeria, with its military underpinnings, has little love for the Campaign for Democracy; the Zenawi government of Ethiopia, born of lengthy guerrilla struggle against authoritarianism, dislikes the Ethiopian Human Rights Council, which publishes reports of alleged arbitrary arrests or disappearances; the government also would prefer that the Oromo Liberation Front work more actively in national reconstruction, less for autonomy; the Diouf regime of Senegal would prefer to plow resources into the government-sponsored Institute for Human Rights and Democracy rather than listen to RADDHO (La Rencontre Africaine pour la Défense des Droits de l'Homme); the Namibian National Society for Human Rights is accused of pursuing a narrow, anti-SWAPO agenda. However, these organizations are tolerated, given modest coverage even in the government-controlled press,[1] and regularly visited by external diplomats and scholars concerned with human rights.

Second, the formal end of both apartheid and the Cold War have removed two massive complicating factors in assessing human rights throughout Africa. More honesty and attention are possible, both domestically and internationally. With institutionalized racism the official policy in South Africa, African governments could focus their criticisms on this massive abuse of human rights, while minimizing the extent of problems at home. In the view of national leaders, apartheid, belated independence for Namibia, and deliberate destabilization in Southern Africa meant that Africa as a whole was not free. Until it was, action to protect human rights internally seemed a lower priority than pursuing change south of the Limpopo River. The revolution in international relations wrought by the collapse of the Soviet Union (and preceded by Gorbachev's reforms) had extraordinary impact.[2] During the Cold War, the two superpowers had competed in part through different ideal models of human rights. Understandable historical and ideological reasons led the United States to emphasize civil and political rights, the Soviet Union economic, social, and cultural rights. The interdependence — nay, indivisibility—of both types was overshadowed in the competition. By the time of the 1993 Vienna world conference on human rights, the debate had quieted down considerably. "Generations" of rights seemed in some fashion a historical artifact rather than a matter of current concern. All governments had to recognize that human rights represented an item of legitimate interest of all states.

Further, improvements can be found in reports to, and discussions by, international human rights treaty bodies. Members of treaty bodies are demanding greater detail and providing clearer guidelines. Any state claiming ignorance of what a report should include will receive little sympathy in Geneva (or, for that matter, in Banjul). The learning curve can be steep. The UN Centre for Human Rights offers special colloquia and technical missions to assist countries with little experience in reporting; HURIDOCS, Human Rights Internet, and other entities offer special courses in documentation. To be certain, problems remain, as shown in Chapter 5, while others will be dealt with shortly. Nonetheless, the quality of human rights monitoring, through government-generated reports, NGO-generated counter-reports, and associated public examination, has increased. Such consciousness should not be underestimated.

Fourth, concealment of human rights abuses has become increasingly difficult. The transformation wrought by satellite dishes and mobile television cameras has clearly impacted on human rights. Instantaneous communications mean a young man halting a tank column in central Beijing, or troops deployed to remove demonstrators, can be viewed globally. Refugees attract attention, their plight a sign of terrible maladjustments at home. For proof, consider the attention given to the 1994 slaughter in Rwanda, contrasted with the inattention given to the 1972 massive killings in Burundi.

Fifth, quantitative measurements of human rights show improvements in many areas.[3] Certainly documentation has increased and become more sophisticated. Steps toward democratization for many African countries have meant indicators used by the Carter Center and Freedom House, for example, have moved upwards. On the other hand, presumed "gains" in political performance have been countered by serious declines in economic and social measurements. The Human Development Index used by UNDP (United Nations Development Programme), the PQLI (physical quality of life index), and UNICEF's statistics on conditions for children show chilling declines. With these statistics, however, governments are on notice about the need for change. As discussed in Chapter 7, HURIDOCS (Human Rights Documentation) has developed the basis of computerized information on human rights violations. Computerization enabled the United Nations special commission on El Salvador to build legal briefs against alleged perpetrators of disappearances;

its techniques are being employed by the Special Prosecutor's Office in Ethiopia to bring former Derg officials to trial.

Perhaps most impressive, human rights activists are calling for "early warning systems." Global monitoring should be encouraged through the new UN High Commissioner for Human Rights.[4] Assessments of government performance are becoming increasingly sophisticated and utilized as a basis for protection. These efforts are both cumulative and accelerating. World Bank, UNDP, and UNICEF figures can be used by human rights NGOs as statistical bases to assess how their countries stand. The figures may be based on flawed or incomplete information ("Lies, damn lies, and statistics," as Mark Twain complained), but corrections are made. With comparative and global performance statistics in hand, human rights NGOs have access to important additional information.

Sixth, the notion that internal human rights practices should not be the subject of international inquiry has been significantly weakened. Domestic sovereignty was, after all, the screen behind which South Africa and many other rights-abusing countries hid. For years, South Africa protested that its apartheid laws (including their application to Namibia) could not be legitimately discussed and criticized by the United Nations. The UN Charter, it asserted, precluded international involvement in matters "essentially in the domestic jurisdiction" of its members. The global interest shown in apartheid belied this interpretation. It was not only South Africa that concealed distasteful internal practices behind claims of sovereignty. The Organization of African Unity was founded on the principle of non-intervention into internal matters. This "see no evil" attitude meant the OAU remained silent in the face of massive violations of human rights in the 1970s, such as in Burundi or Uganda. One might argue that the weaknesses in the African Charter on Human and Peoples' Rights were deliberate, to provide a veneer of legitimation and a shield against external criticism. Certainly there was little evidence that several African governments took the Charter's obligations seriously, at least until NGO pressures and greater democratization brought human rights to their attention. And, in the United States, concern about weakening constitutional protections and opening American courts to claims has resulted in numerous reservations to the few human rights treaties the US has ratified.[5]

Claims about domestic sovereignty, frequently expressed as the notion that each society should determine how to measure human rights rather than use international criteria, considerably complicated the 1993 world conference. The compromise finally reached in Vienna was tortuous, but ultimately an advance relative to the stances of many African (and especially Asian) governments. No longer can it be claimed that human rights are exclusive matters of domestic jurisdiction. They are legitimate matters for the international community.

Related claims about cultural relativism have been advanced, and partially resolved. The "international bill of rights" had its origins in the West, but it is not an unmitigated imposition of alien values on other societies. The Universal Declaration of Human Rights is now far more global in its reach and recognition than when the United Nations General Assembly adopted it. To a very substantial extent, the standards of international treaties are accepted as legitimate goals for all societies, toward which serious progress must be made. Issues remain, nevertheless. Arguments continue about the best ways to achieve human rights, notably under economically constrained conditions. The once-flourishing academic enterprise of ferreting out human rights protection in "traditional" African cultures and of arguing there was no need for even the modest claims of the African Charter on Human and People's Rights has shriveled, though not disappeared. I regard the muting of debate over the source and content of rights as a significant advance. In a sense, the relative silence over domestic sovereignty and cultural relativism is eloquent testimony to the spread of universal human rights ideals.

Ultimately, the seventh and most important measurement of strength comes not from the NGOs but from civil society. How widespread and relevant are broad social understandings of human rights? Has a significant "human rights culture" emerged in any of the four countries under review, or elsewhere in Africa? Are favorable situations primarily the result of idiosyncratic factors and leaders, or symptomatic of a broader trend through the continent? Here, the auguries are, at best, more mixed.

Change here could be measured more readily if polling firms had been in existence south of the Sahara for several years, and if they had been asking the appropriate questions. For a variety of obvious reasons, public opinion about human rights has rarely been sampled in Africa. Neither baseline nor trend data exist, at least to my present knowledge. In interviews, I asked each NGO leader how he or she assessed the organization's "success." The evidence they provided was invariably anecdotal, or based on personal surmise. Such information should not be dismissed as unscientific or shallow, although it tended toward the impressionistic rather than the quantitative. These judgments, in the aggregate, showed a definite trend toward greater popular awareness. Can I dispute Dr. Irene Thomas's judgment that knowledge of the harmful effects of female genital mutilation has changed practices in parts of Nigeria? I cannot— but I felt also more comfortable with figures she provided demonstrating a marked decline in maternal mortality following training programs for traditional birth attendants. Relying hence on reports from persons with an interest in fostering a "human rights culture," I conclude that there has been change within a relatively brief period of time. It is a wave that preceded the "second independence" of democratization in some states, while elsewhere it has been facilitated by the emergence of civil society.

Ideally, one would want to measure declines in documented human rights abuses in order to assess NGO impacts. Modern technology gives governments extraordinary measures for investigating and repressing persons. It is how these powers are *not* used against rights-seeking critics, and how they are used to achieve rights goals, that are the significant measures. This cannot be done with precision. Consciousness of what is and what isn't an "abuse" changes over time. Yesteryear's accepted practice may become today's inappropriate behavior. (Witness the recognition of sexual harassment, a phenomenon of long history but only recent disapprobation.) And how can events that do not occur be tabulated? More meaningful a measure, I believe, would be long-term research into attitudes about "rights" held by the public, into legislation and law enforcement practices, and into the breadth and depth of international reporting. I assume that acceptance of "rights" involving expectations of both public and private actions is fundamental. This is what I mean by "human rights consciousness." Changes in it — historically, for example, in accepting that slavery was morally wrong — could be assessed over time. Related questions can be posed. What laws are on the books about violations? How often and effectively are they enforced? Patterns of arrests and prosecutions could illustrate changing mores. Are the courts being used increasingly to enforce laws adopted as part of human rights campaigns? Do governments take care in meeting their reporting obligations? Do they seek to change practices on the basis of "constructive" dialogue with NGOs and expert bodies? What are the results of content analysis of major newspapers and government publications? Such research will be partly historical, partly quantitative, ultimately reflecting attitudes within civil society.

This book was written in the relative youth of African human rights NGOs. The problems I have highlighted might be short-term in nature. We must turn again to the causes of abuses, implicit in the seven signposts just examined.

Why Do Human Rights Abuses Continue?

If "human rights consciousness" and NGO strength are increasing, why do serious violations continue? Admittedly, the four countries given detailed attention in this book did not, during the field work period, suffer at the levels of war-torn Liberia, Sierra Leone, Somalia, or Sudan. Namibia and Senegal indeed scored high, as it were, in State Department country reports and other global scorecards. Despite the manifest problems Nigeria and Ethiopia encountered in making transitions to lesser levels of authoritarianism, the conditions in both could be described as difficult rather than critical. Activists could rest in none of these states, however—for the tasks of human rights monitoring know no cease. Eternal vigilance is the price . . .

Possible reasons for continued violations can be found in cultural, economic and political realms.

"Human rights consciousness" rests on culture. Well-informed scholars, and perhaps most notably Howard and Donnelly, have argued that African cultures were oriented toward dignity rather than rights.[6] What an individual enjoyed was not his or hers by birth, nor provided equally to all. Rather, ascriptive factors—gender, age, membership in an ethnic group—determined what and how much could be expected. Relativism and differentiation, rather than universalism and equality, provided the foundations. Beliefs of this sort, deeply engrained in social awareness, will inevitably persist for long periods of time.

Earlier in this book, I discussed the efforts of the Inter-African Committee on Traditional Practices Affecting the Health of Women and Children. The IAC operates from the premise that a series of related discriminatory attitudes must be changed. The task is enormous. Nutritional taboos, or the sense that initiation into adulthood requires severe genital mutilation, are central beliefs in some societies. Gender-based role differentiation is accepted throughout Africa. A trivial example should suffice. No self-respecting Amhara man would enter the kitchen; that is a woman's realm. Better he go hungry, I was told many times, than he challenge the "natural" order. Would a male who refuses to play any role in the preparation of food act on the belief that all persons enjoy equal rights irrespective of sex? He might argue, to use a hoary phrase, that rights and roles could be "separate but equal." The logic is not persuasive. However, the attitudinal fact remains. In Africa, as elsewhere in the world, the initial and most widespread battle for many human rights occurs in individual psychology.

Economic factors complicate the quest for human rights. The struggle for daily existence throughout almost all of Africa absorbs persons' energies. Low levels of development and the widening gaps between Africa and developed countries (and, for that matter, between African states and other "developing" states) are distressing, unavoidable facts. The appeal of the "right to development" reflects an unfortunate reality. It is more difficult to promote and protect the full range of human rights when the people have very limited resources. Getting the next meal or the week's rent or the term's school fees loom far larger to them than trial by jury or the right to periodic paid holidays. Limited resources affect even what Shue deemed basic rights. Insufficient national spending on immunizations or schooling or police protection mock the commitments made in treaties and, more important, made in electoral campaigns to the increasingly aware citizens of African states. High rates of infant mortality, violent crime, and low rates of literacy, are serious, though far from inevitable, consequences of poverty. They assuredly are violations of basic rights. Not having resources is not an acceptable argument for governments' failing to take steps to protect rights. It is important to know how they expend their funds (hence the importance of accountability and transparency). Quantitative reporting of government expenditures gives evidence of how they are directed. Growing attention of reporting bodies and especially of monitoring groups as to how resources are used is thus commendable.

Some of the valuable work of NGOs involves issues removed from public consciousness, or perhaps thoroughly unpopular, in much of Africa. Take, for example, the exposés of prison conditions done by several human rights groups.[7] These publications have been valuable if largely unread documents. The immediate effects have been limited; jails remain human hellholes. Improving prison conditions has run up against both financial and cultural issues: governments have higher priorities than housing and feeding prisoners and detainees; to many in the general population, that persons are in jail is sufficient evidence of their wrong-doing. Under such conditions, the NGOs' research must be seen as a long-term investment in building human rights awareness. Culture affects the ways in which prisoners are viewed.

For African human rights NGOs, the combined effect of the cultural and economic factors noted thus far should be obvious. The NGOs depend heavily on external resources and low-cost or volunteer internal expertise. They work in milieus in which their goals may not be widely shared. Human rights NGOs are founded and directed by unusual persons, some of whom we have met in this book. They do not enjoy unconditional social respect. Most lead rather abstemious lives, with personal danger, vilification by unsympathetic media, and numerous disappointments in their professional work. The demands on them are high. As a result, personal burn-out is a frequent consequence. Individual NGOs may be ephemeral entities: not fully accepted in the culture; not adequately supported in their tasks; confronted with public apathy and government opposition. For, ultimately, effectiveness rests on political factors.

The most serious immediate obstacles to African human rights NGOs result from government actions. Many of the organizations are, in the eyes of political leaders, destructive. NGOs argue against steps governments deem essential. If a regime feels (as Nkrumah wrote shortly before Ghana's independence) that the country must be "jet-propelled" to development, and that "emergency measures of a totalitarian kind"[8] are justified, then rights-protecting groups are bound to protest, and in turn likely to be assailed. The contest over political space, to which I shall return in this conclusion, can be literally a life-or-death matter to some NGOs.

Does this mean that democratization south of the Sahara will directly facilitate human rights by enhancing civil society? A perceptive Ghanaian social scientist has argued that one need not bring the other.[9] Aidoo's caution is an important one. Increased transparency, accountability, and choice are not automatically translated into more effective protection of human rights. A necessary part of the translation, this book has argued, is NGOs. We need, accordingly, to look to the future, based on the evidence presented in earlier pages.

Assessing the Future of African Human Rights NGOs

Few of the national organizations sketched in this book have a history of more than five years. Most African human rights NGOs have yet to make the crucial transition from leadership by the "founding father" or "founding mother" to selection of new heads and directions without organizational collapse. The first generation of chairs/presidents remains in control. To a substantial extent, the organizations are personalized: "Phil" or "Clement" or "Tokunbo" or "Professor Mesfin" remains at the center and sets the agenda. When they leave for international conferences, the pace of activity slows. Their staffs rarely number as many as eight. Yes, decisions may be made relatively rapidly with a small cadre, but all the necessary skills (especially in budget control and documentation) cannot be carried by an individual. Broadening and deepening of leadership are essential.

There will be increasing organizational turnover. The NGO scene is a shifting, dynamic one, in which collapse of many (or, more likely, their progressive inanition) should be expected. The half-life of African human rights NGOs likely is less than five years. Personal burn-out, drying up of resources, and shifting goals of funders will cause attrition in NGOs' ranks. This, I stress, is natural. Long term success for NGOs qua organizations will rest on their success in becoming better bureaucratized or institutionalized. NGOs must become true organizations.

Recall Huntington's four factors of organizational strength: adaptability, autonomy, coherence, and complexity.[10] Judging by them, African human rights NGOs have made variable progress. They have shown adaptability in both tactics and strategy. On the other hand, almost all have yet to experience generational change of leadership. (The transition from David Smuts to Andrew Corbett at the LAC is a major exception.) Financial autonomy has remained an impossible dream. Organizational coherence has been difficult to achieve for some. The blame is not just theirs; it is an inescapable dilemma resulting from how funding can be obtained. Apart from small seed money grants, generalized office support is difficult for donors to justify in terms of their goals, hence difficult to receive. Major funders like the Ford Foundation, USAID, or the Friedrich Naumann Foundation,understandably prefer to support specific undertakings — a booklet on this, a workshop on that, a program designed to provide prescribed numbers of persons with specific skills. Assistance without "strings" is rare, and invariably limited in amounts. The siren call of resources, even though tied to specific projects at the fringes of the group's major emphasis, has proved hard to resist. Organizational diffuseness resulting from over-expansion to obtain earmarked funds thus is a danger. And, finally, complexity will not be readily achieved, as long as resources are straitened and responsibilities tightly defined. For the foreseeable future, most African human rights NGOs will remain relatively personalized, small, lightly funded entities. It is almost a miracle that they exist at all.

The climate for human rights NGOs assuredly will be affected by the extent of democratization, though probably not as much by the level of economic development. Well-off countries may not have human rights groups, but democratic states, whether rich or poor, have human rights organizations. Thus, if "sequencing" is a matter of concern, a case could be made for creating conditions of civil society first. From the evidence I gathered in writing this book, as well as from prior research on human rights in Africa, I believe that poverty is a far from insuperable obstacle to the establishment and effective functioning of human rights NGOs, in part because external funding can usually be found for specific tasks. Authoritarianism is a more fundamental obstacle. Political leaders such as Lee Kuan Yew of Singapore or Mahathir bin Mohamed of Malaysia can argue that human rights overall would be bolstered by stability and economic growth rather than by partisan democracy — but they cannot argue that case for NGOs. The strength of civil society, rather than the level of economic development, is the critical variable.

On the other hand, NGOs are not mere dependent variables. Their presence and activity reinforce civil society. Skills increase, if not by a multiplier effect, at least with an additive effect. Increased numbers of organizations that engage in education, empowerment, and enforcement build civil society. Informed, active citizens do not operate in vacuums, but through groups. Skills increase; successful examples can be followed. It is in part through NGO action that human rights abuses can be corrected and democratization enhanced. As noted above, governments must take the crucial steps, but they may be unlikely to do so without the prodding and documentation of NGOs.

Broadly speaking, human rights in Africa (and elsewhere, it should be added) can be enhanced in three ways. Abuses can be diminished, with corrective government actions the major but not the sole focus. NGOs can be strengthened as monitors. Popular awareness can be increased, so that mobilized, informed opinion, the core of civil society, accepts protection of human rights as a valued goal. These three—reducing abuses, strengthening NGOs, and increasing awareness—should be pursued in tandem. Each must be seen as an objective, requiring both short- and long-term steps.

Let us turn first to the short term. *Lessening abuses* requires identifying their causes, then moving to effective programs. Ill-trained military and police forces constitute one of the most obvious causes of poor human rights records. Their unprofessional actions—arbitrary arrests, use of torture to extract "confessions," excessive force in confronting demonstrators, poor preparation of cases for presentation in court, gross favoritism based on bribes—have been documented extensively, especially by Nigerian NGOs.[11] Without doubt, "law and order" is a term of mockery when their major agents are chief contributors to violence and corruption. Reform of public safety practices should include better pay and working conditions (thereby diminishing the temptation to extract bribes), mandatory and more effective training programs, vigorous efforts to root out corrupt and other unprofessional practices (requiring independent as well as in-house investigations and prosecutions of guilty officers), and conscious inculcation of higher standards of behavior. The costs of action are not low; however, the costs of inaction are higher. The abuses pointed out by NGOs must be solved by governments.

Here as elsewhere, external funding may be appropriate, indeed necessary. Is it advisable for major donors to assist with police and military training? The dilemma, moral and political, does not seem difficult to resolve. It is appropriate for funders to advance human rights through training of security forces. Effective use of non-lethal force, improved investigative techniques, and ethical standards (among others) are always appropriate items for implementation, regardless of the source of funding. Affluent countries should be generous in the areas just listed. That Senegalese from the military, gendarmerie, and police have been trained by US military justice specialists is important as a sign of what is needed.

Relevant international norms should be *incorporated* by governments into national law and, more important, into national practice. The International Convention on Civil and Political Rights, the Geneva Conventions and their protocols, the Convention Against Torture, international minimum standards for treatment of prisoners, and similar documents set forth standards which all African military and police forces should attain. Ratification of these agreements is itself a modest, simple act of political will. Implementation of them is a complex, lengthy, costly series of actions. But the journey begins with the first step. In the short run, legislative steps can readily be taken; in the long run, practices can be improved.

How efficacious are human rights "strings" to aid in improving human rights performance? I have some qualms about conditions on specific forms of foreign assistance, for the flow of wealth out of Africa has recently exceeded the return of funds. "Reparations" is an issue around which Africans rally, including that multi-millionaire paragon of business acumen, M. K. O. Abiola, Nigeria's one real example of military disengagement from politics, Olesegun Obasanjo, and Africa's most noted academic, Ali Mazrui. The strong case they present must not be dismissed in the industrialized north. It is morally, politically, and economically wise for "the West" to assist Africa in far less niggardly fashion. Modest investments in oral rehydration for sick children, genetic engineering to improve crop yields, or enhancement of rural infrastructure, can dramatically improve chances for life itself. Such aid should be given generously and without strings. Humanitarianism carries its own rewards. It can, and should, come from private as well as governmental sources.

More difficult questions arise over conditions on general economic assistance. On balance, I have little hesitation personally in linking government-to-government aid with relatively detailed specifications about human rights performance, especially if foreign governments recognize the sensitivities of Africans to external *dictats*, and the possibility (likelihood?) that some of these specifications may be inappropriate unless certain conditionalitiess exist. The U.S. Congress was correct in establishing the policy that denies economic and military assistance to states with consistent patterns of gross violations of human rights, unless the President gives specific authorization; it was the execution of this policy that became unduly politicized and inconsistently applied. The emphasis on democratization discussed earlier in this book also has merit, although the virtues of specific Western models have been overstated. (For example, overly hasty moves to elections, as shown in Ethiopia, may have hindered rather than assisted democratization. On the other hand, SWAPO's victory over the DTA in Constituent Assembly elections, or the dramatic South African elections of April 1994, showed that a largely illiterate public could cast meaningful votes and support important political compromises.) Factors specific to each case must be carefully examined within the overall context of conditionalities. If the results are mutually satisfactory, greater generosity by donors should result.

"Development" aid ought to be directed at numerous modest, grass-roots programs, some on the Tostan model. Though administrative costs may seem higher as a percentage of total budgets, multiple approaches would seem wiser. NGOs should be factored into the equation. As Clark recently argued, "democratizing development" entails recognizing a greater role for voluntary organizations.[12] The interdependence among democratization, development, and human rights is apparent. More equitable distribution of resources, made possible by diverse projects, manifestly promotes human rights. In the short run, relief programs in areas of critical need may be most important; in the long run, self-sustaining development programs, in which human rights are integral, are unquestionably necessary.[13]

Strengthening human rights NGOs forms another short-term strategy, in addition to improved practices by security forces and sensitive use of aid conditionalities. Realistically, the major financing for these groups will continue to be external. At the present time, there are neither sufficient resources nor requisite levels of public understanding within Africa to enable them to stand fully on their own. The costs are not great relative to the benefits (at least for those NGOs that focus their work domestically, and avoid the siren calls of international junkets or costly, low-impact programs).

Once again, however, the economic facts of life collide with political realities. The "success" of human rights NGOs ultimately depends on their being accepted as necessary, valued national institutions. They must not be perceived as exotic transplants, fertilized and watered by distant outsiders. They should not pursue the wisp of external funding at the cost of adopting projects with limited relevance to their societies' needs. I recognize that words such as these are cheap to write, the consequent practices difficult to implement when jobs, indeed institutional survival, may be at stake. (I interviewed the executive director of one human rights NGO a few days after he had laid off a third of the staff. Anticipated grants had not come through, and he was bitter. But he was also coming to terms with the fact that his organization was losing its focus and diffusing its expertise in its race for funds. It was a poignant, thought-provoking discussion.) Ideal would be endowment grants for groups that have proven their objectivity and commitment, permitting them to meet basic expenses from a steady, assured source; more realistic would be three- to five-year grants, based on carefully developed action programs, with regular reviews.[14]

The chronic insufficiency of resources can be countered, to some measure, by NGO networking and coordination. African human rights organizations profit from meetings. They learn from each other, reducing the sense of isolation their leaders often experience. The ICJ- and African

Commission-sponsored workshops provide stimulating lessons in the value of discussion. More such opportunities should be provided (with the related caveats that too much time at international confabs can take a toll on institutional effectiveness, in light of the small staffs, and that yet another workshop rounding up the usual suspects incurs high travel costs for limited results). Perhaps the most successful example of networking comes with the IAC. The Geneva office works on general strategy for combatting harmful traditional practices, handles major financial matters, produces materials, and lobbies international organizations for support; the Addis Ababa office coordinates efforts across Africa; national committees undertake programs adapted to their special needs. Active IAC groups have made significant progress. On the other hand, weak or inactive national committees contribute little. The IAC illustrates as well that the more focused the area of NGO activity, the easier the coordination among levels.

Many explicit continent-wide networks of African human rights NGOs have yet to "take off." Are their goals too diffuse? Are the benefits of international coordination uncertain? Given the realities of politics, isn't a primary focus on national issues most promising? One activist in Namibia complained vigorously about the problems she confronted in getting support for the continent-wide linkages she envisaged, but it was by no means clear what direct positive results would occur if her network came into existence. The Banjul-based African Centre for Democracy and Human Rights Studies carries out worthwhile research, yet has not (as of late 1994) catalyzed widespread coordinated human rights action. The matter remains open for discussion. At this point, however, I am more impressed by the problems of networking than heartened by the opportunities for coordinating.

Networks based on specific issues stand a better chance of short-run success than generalized networks for broad human rights or development matters, or politically-motivated institutes that proclaim human rights more in their titles than in effective programs of action. Networking proceeds better, to restate this point, if the central coordinating body has a focused agenda, expertise, sufficient financial resources, and good political contacts. Entities focused on specific UN human rights treaties seem especially well-placed to maximize the benefits of networking. I have not examined organizations such as IWRAW (International Women's Rights Action Watch, based in Minneapolis and focused on CEDAW), ARIS (Anti-Racism Information Service, based in Geneva and focused on CERD), or Defence of Children International (DCI, a highly successful INGO, based in Geneva and focused on the Convention on the Rights of the Child, in whose drafting DCI took a major role. Another book could, and should, be written on the roles of these INGOs. A focus on Africa as a whole seems to have come best through the continuing efforts of the International Commission of Jurists and the African Commission, or through the coordinating actions of specialized groups such as the Inter-African Committee on Traditional Practices. And special mention must be made of Human Rights Internet (HRI), the grandmother and in many respects the role model for keeping human rights NGOs in touch with each other. Internet's publications have brought the accomplishments of NGO researchers to wide audiences. The Director's incessant travels, the business cards she collects and enters into her data base, and her personal contacts provide an important glue. I hope Laurie Wiseberg will someday take time to chronicle HRI's history; its record of achievement is extraordinary.[15]

A different set of issues exists on the national level. GONGOs (government-sponsored "non-governmental" organizations) have sprouted. Was it accidental that the Senegalese government announced with pride that the "African Institute for Democracy" would be established in Dakar, its membership comprised almost exclusively of francophone states, and its director a political crony of President Diouf? GONGOs dilute the impact of the human rights NGO community, to the extent that they rationalize government inaction and absorb resources. Their establishment pays lip service to human rights ideals; their functioning leaves much to be desired. With such semi-official bodies in existence, governments can control genuine NGOs through restrictive legislation.[16] Nonetheless, GONGOs should not automatically be eliminated from consideration. As suggested in Chapter 8, the Centre for Democratic Studies gave "new-breed" politicians broadened understanding. GONGOs must be carefully studied; some may make substantial contributions to developing a "human rights culture."

So much for objectives in the short run. What features should mark long run programs?

They must also aim at diminishing abuses, strengthening NGOs, and building human rights consciousness. The last seems the most essential, as well as the most complex to achieve. Human rights consciousness means that awareness of human rights and human wrongs rests in citizens. They then become the true guardians of the dignity and worth of individuals. Ultimately, the highest form of protection comes through personal behavior throughout society, through the actions of individuals multiplied million-fold: in respect for all persons; in efforts at equitable economic and social development; in providing for periodic renewal of government personnel and policies through principled competitive elections and through well-established principles of accountability and transparency. Nothing is stronger, in the long term, than deeply-rooted popular support for human rights.

The conventional avenue for popular awareness lies through education. Hence, formal curricula at all levels should incorporate human rights, the "fourth R."[17] Some examples were given in Chapter 3; others can be offered at this time. Many means must be utilized and adapted to individual societies. The efforts need not be confined to schools, of course. In Senegal, RADI *(Réseau africain pour le développement intégré,* African Network for Integrated Development) has prepared calendars with monthly messages about women's rights in readily-understood French; in Nigeria, the Legal Research and Resources Development Centre published booklets on topics highly relevant to daily life; in Ethiopia, SAHRE (Society for Human Rights Education) has started to press the Ministry of Education for a place for rights issues; in Namibia, the Legal Assistance Centre cooperates in publishing newspaper features, "Know Your Rights." All media should be used to convey messages that are appropriate to local concerns and knowledge, but that are based on fundamental, global, human rights principles.

Effective implementation of international treaty obligations will assuredly diminish the number and severity of abuses over time. As already pointed out, ratification is but the first step, however. National laws and practices must be adjusted, adapted, brought into conformity — a continuous, on-going process. Long-standing customs must be consciously changed. Thus, while there is a finite period for negotiating and ratifying a convention, the period for implementing it stretches into the indefinite future. What the treaty sets as goals must be translated as rapidly as possible into realities.

Strengthening NGOs will rest, in this long-term perspective, on the concurrent development of civil society. Vigorous associational life should emerge, free of the confining cocoons of jealous governments or narrow ethnicity. More human rights NGOs would help. The most effective results seem likely to emerge from multiplicity. Many organizations to promote and protect human rights would both broaden and deepen the basis for the "human rights consciousness" I have been advocating. Professional associations, women's groups, trade unions, cooperatives: the possibilities are endless. If human rights are seen as the exclusive province of self-defined organizations, they will suffer. Far better to have a profusion of NGOs with a broad basic consensus on human rights than a small number of highly focused organizations that risk being marginalized. Others may disagree; and certainly there will always be an important place for entities like the Constitutional Rights Project (Nigeria) or the Legal Assistance Centre (Namibia). But if the foundation of understanding is achieved, then a hundred diverse blooms (even including some weeds) will serve better than a few exotic, specialized plants.

This last statement rests on an important, and questionable, assumption. Does a widely accepted foundation for human rights exist for Africa? The simple answer is, yes; the more complex answer is, perhaps. Much more work must be done to extend this foundation.

The Universal Declaration of Human Rights constitutes the core of basic standards. The UDHR is explicitly mentioned in many African constitutions. Many of its provisions have been incorporated into customary international law. Though drafted by a small group of Western and Western-educated specialists, the Universal Declaration has, over time, achieved a distinctive status. It is as close to a global consensus about human rights as currently exists.

Yet the UDHR has, from African perspectives, some flaws. In particular, and at the risk of caricature, the Universal Declaration emphasizes individuals, minimizes responsibilities, and neglects groups. Non-discrimination constitutes the core value of the UDHR. Individuals, equal in worth and dignity, must not suffer from invidious discrimination based on race, sex, religion, or ethnicity. This ideal collides with the reality of deeply-rooted cultural assumptions about roles. In African societies (and, one should assume, in many other parts of the world) differentiation rather than equality is the starting point. There are different roles based on gender. Biology is destiny (even if sex and gender are separate concepts, the former being biologically determined, the latter culturally constructed). Roles and responsibilities vary in accordance with membership in groups. Groups are not just minorities, but potential building blocks of society. Vertical and horizontal associations contribute. Peoples and groups have the right to maintain their identities.

In the future, accordingly, African human rights NGOs should be expected to continue widening the ambit of civil society. Their efforts should result in increased awareness of human rights, primarily as set out in the UDHR and related international documents, but increasingly as enriched by African insights and experiences. Resources, in both funds and personnel, will remain limited, and international contributions highly important. These lessons, and others, can be derived from this book.

Lessons from This Study

Let us conclude by circling back to the start. Early in this book, I proposed four broad hypotheses about the strength and effectiveness of African human rights NGOs. To measure these, one would have to examine financial resources, popular support, societal diversity, and political space. The preceding chapters have provided data and preliminary observations. It is now appropriate to see how well the preliminary formulations square with the "real world" of NGO performance.

A consistent theme in *Protecting Human Rights in Africa* has been limited resources. The impacts were hypothesized as follows:

1. *Financial resources:* severe budget constraints affect all human rights NGOs based in Africa, making them heavily dependent on grants from (primarily) North American and northern European governments and foundations. This relationship has led to some negotiation of goals and strategies between African leaders and their external funders, and has accentuated civil and political rights linked to democratization. Far less stress has been laid on economic and social rights linked to development, and practically no attention given to group rights for sub-national groups, unless these are defined by gender or occupation.

Without question, the "NGO revolution" has been fiscally fueled in large part by extra-Africa sources. Decisions by largely Western governments and foundations facilitated the creation and/or expansion of human rights groups. Pioneering work by the Ford Foundation in legal aid (especially strong in South Africa, but with many parallels in tropical Africa and on other continents) made possible important expansion in the rule of law. Ford Foundation funds for studies of prison conditions or independence of the judiciary strengthened other parts of the legal system. Generous Scandanavian and Dutch support in southern Africa (such as scholarships for Namibians during the struggle for independence) helped form a cadre of persons aware of social democracy. Democracy and human rights funding, through Section 116e of the Foreign Assistance Act, meant the United States government assisted the creation or operation of many NGOs.[18] Mushrooming international election monitoring (shown in this book for Ethiopia, Namibia, and Nigeria) bolstered pro-democracy groups; and, despite the very mixed results of the Ethiopian and Nigerian balloting, external support for competitive elections in Africa seems likely to continue. The ICJ (International Commission of Jurists), the Inter-African Committee, ARIS (Anti-Racism Information Service), the World Council of Churches, HURIDOCS, DCI (Defence of Children International) and the dozens of other Geneva-based human rights NGOs draw almost exclusively on Western funds.

What is necessary for survival of most NGOs is also a bone of contention. Do human rights groups respond more to external rather than to internal concerns? Governments sensitive to criticisms from human rights groups often seek to deflect their charges by alleging that external funding makes the NGOs partisan.[19] This is a cheap criticism to make, but it has an immediate resonance in some quarters. NGOs indeed gain requisite space by requesting and receiving financial support. Most couldn't exist at their present levels without it. Consequent threats to NGOs' credibility exist, which their opponents can exploit.

Non-partisanship is obviously far simpler for groups focused on promotion rather than protection of human rights. Direct, street-level challenges to the government, such as mounted by the Campaign for Democracy against Babangida, may be met with police fire. Indirect challenges to the government through publications, such as distributed by the Ethiopian Human Rights Council or the Namibian National Society for Human Rights, might be countered by indifference, verbal rebuttal, impugning of motives, or even detention; not, however, by use of widespread force. On the other hand, well-documented analyses of prison conditions or gender inequalities or even detentions would not evoke the same level of government fear. Carefully-researched, documented studies may even move governments to positive action. By contrast, empowerment-oriented NGOs seeking greater ethnic autonomy will assuredly encounter sharp opposition. Their demands for self-determination raise fundamental fears about secession or a cascade of similar demands from other groups. Documentation free of manifest political bias, focused on areas where obligations exist, carries a subtle, long-term message, and avoids many accusations. There is a cost in separating promotion and protection, however, to which I shall return in discussing the final hypothesis.

Has the availability of funding influenced NGO priorities? Yes, it has. In each country in which I carried out research, I found one or more NGOs that had been conjured into existence because of external resources, or at least the hope these would be available. For example, the glossy, four-color brochures of the Namibia Institute of Democracy bore witness to the generosity of the Konrad Adenauer Foundation (linked to the German Christian Democratic Union and funded, like its counterparts linked to the SPD and Greens, by the government); the Senegal-based Institute of Democracy and Human Rights functioned with private government-influenced UNDP funding; SAHRE, the Ethiopian Society for the Advancement of Human Rights Education, made no secret of its hope for American resources; the Nigerian Civil Liberties Organisation and Constitutional Rights Project relied heavily on Ford Foundation funds for their several excellent studies, and hoped for further on-going support. The emphasis was not solely on civil and political rights. Development and relief activities also rested on partner NGOs. Recall, for example, the Christian Relief and Development Association of Ethiopia, whose creation was necessitated by the need to coordinate aid supplies under drought and civil war conditions. In Namibia, as Brown's excellent study illustrated, the NGO community was profoundly affected by the sources of support and the resulting objectives of the various groups.[20]

Have there been deleterious results from this "he who pays the piper" phenomenon? Critics naturally argue that there have been. Dependence has merely taken a new form. These voices have not gone unchallenged. Supporters state that the wave of democratization in Africa sprang largely from indigenous roots, and in particular from the failures of authoritarianism; they also comment that NGOs active in relief, development, women's rights, legal aid, and the like benefit large numbers of people. The resulting greater good of the greater number should be the criterion.

There are dangers in heavy reliance on external funds. Trendy issues can be seized upon and a plethora of otherwise-underemployed persons seek a better future. But blame should not be placed only on non-African supporters. Human rights GONGOs (governmental NGOs) and QUANGOs (quasi-governmental NGOs) exist in many African countries, as pointed out a few paragraphs back. They may be façades, intended far more to impress gullible outsiders than to challenge domestic policies. One must be cautious, and not assume that any group claiming to promote and protect human rights actually does so. Growing global awareness of human rights has meant a few spurious efforts. On the other hand, acceptance of government funds should not automatically count as a strike against an African NGO claiming to espouse human rights. It is their action (especially in documentation and promotion of democratization and/or development) that is important.

The first hypothesis distinguished, in effect, among the three "generations" of rights. In the perspective of recent years, NGOs with explicit agendas of civil and political rights, and in particular advancement of the rule of law, have increased in numbers. Their creation must not overshadow the earlier multiplication of NGOs linked to relief and development. Second generation economic and social rights have been pressed by scores of African groups. They are far more numerous than NGOs focused on first generation rights. A "right to development" is not accepted by major aid-givers, however. They do not accept the notion that "reparations" should be provided to atone for slavery and colonialism. By necessity, major aid-givers often work with and through development- and relief-oriented NGOs; they usually do not work with explicitly human rights groups. And, with respect to collective or third generation rights, some NGOs claiming self-determination turned out to be more significant than I had anticipated. MOSOP is a good example. By means of its links to international NGOs and its well-timed pressure on Geneva-based treaty bodies, the Movement for the Survival of the Ogoni People has catapulted the Ogonis to the front ranks of Nigerian human rights problems, at least in terms of global awareness.

Perhaps I should have given greater attention to the contributions of professional groups to human rights. Lawyers did indeed figure in the preceding pages, as did some journalists; physicians and professors

(Beko Ransome-Kuti; Mesfin Wolde-Mariam) also were prominent. Leadership by persons with such backgrounds differs in nature from the far more decentralized, village-oriented leadership found among factions of the MFDC, or the village women affected by Tostan education. Middle class professionals turn more readily to reform through legal challenges than to rebellion based on accumulated grievances. Villagers must learn to speak for themselves, but they need to form alliances with urban-based groups.

Does this mean that leaders can readily set the agendas for their groups? It would seem that the nature and extent of public support also plays a significant role. This leads us to the second hypothesis.

2. *Popular backing/membership:* to the extent that African human rights NGOs concentrate on civil and procedural rights involving extensive reliance on court systems, they draw their main support from urban, educated and legally-aware individuals. A different situation can be presumed to prevail among NGOs that focus on economic and social issues. To the extent they concentrate on subsistence rights and development, they draw support from more rural, less educated individuals. Success in gaining government action is far more likely with urban-based, middle-class backing than with rural, lower-class support.

This hypothesis combines different strands. "Backing" for an issue championed by an organization may differ radically from "membership" of the NGO. For example, demonstrations organized by Nigeria's Campaign for Democracy (CD) drew thousands into the streets of Lagos; the CD was itself an umbrella for different movements. Should the success of the CD's efforts be judged by the numbers who rallied against the Babangida government in July 1993 or against the Abacha government a year later, and who may have been mobilized only temporarily into action, or by the far smaller numbers who actually joined one of the constituent groups? Should human rights NGOs aim at becoming broad-based movements, or are they better served by concentration on a more limited group of supporters? Some answers may be implicit in the material we have already surveyed.

As organizations, many human rights groups follow rather narrow agendas. Their basic strategy impacts directly on what supporters they serve, and vice-versa. Their members will likely be few, although their supporters may be many in number. Severe obstacles stand in the way of transforming African human rights NGOs into large membership organizations. (Indeed, in the entire world of human rights NGOs, only Amnesty International can claim adherents in the many thousands.) Despite their small size, human rights NGOs are not necessarily limited in influence, however — at least for certain goals. Let us look at them once again from the perspective of their basic strategy.

Enforcement clearly depends on persons able to maneuver through court systems and comprehend the diplomatic jargon of international treaty bodies. It stands to reason that this strategy draws heavily upon lawyers. Lawyers in Africa are few in number, overwhelmingly concentrated in national capitals, probably more likely to be employed by the government than out in private practice, and not affected by extensive *pro bono* obligations. They enjoy significant prestige as a result of their education, affluence, and general political savvy. A single triumph in court, at least in a common law system, can set a precedent from which many can benefit. Hence, although small membership limits financial and advocacy resources, it does not preclude effectiveness. The protection of human rights through enforcement-oriented NGOs would seem to be an efficacious strategy with limited resources, *assuming that the requisite court system and independent judiciary exist.* Opposition to many government actions is part-and-parcel of such groups' operation. There should be no surprise, accordingly, when attorneys like Gani Fawehinmi (practically a one-man NGO) are rounded up.

Education as a choice of direction draws upon a much wider range of persons. Like their legal friends, educators are likely to rank high in prestige, based on their diplomas. Their impact will be far less immediate, however, than that of litigation-oriented groups. Education is the quintessential form of promotion. It is not protection. In other words, NGOs that seek to enhance human rights through formal and informal schooling do not pose immediate threats to skittish governments, although the messages they convey may ultimately subvert authoritarianism. Promotion of human rights through education is long-term, as already emphasized.

Few human rights NGOs deliberately seek political power. Those that favor confrontation face serious struggles with the government for political space, as will be discussed below. The MFDC, OLF, and MOSOP, please recall, ran up against strong opposition. Their objective of empowerment, using confrontation or violent struggle rather than peaceful electoral participation, waved a red cape before the incumbent regimes. The demands each made for autonomy were interpreted as claims for secession. The demonstrations each encouraged degenerated into violent confrontations. Such groups, I believe, moved increasingly away from the model implicitly espoused in this book. They seriously doubted whether open competition for votes would advance their causes. As permanent minorities (or, for the Oromos, as a plurality that lacked a strong sense of identity), the Diola, Ogoni and Oromos felt major political restructuring was necessary. They believed that simple documentation of group problems would not suffice to change long-standing government practices. Here, widespread popular support within the affected groups was critical for their success. A divided, weakly articulated social foundation could not realistically hope to achieve power, unless in combination with other forces of social change.

Documentation is a task par excellence for the better educated of society. They have the research skills and media contacts necessary for this approach. Yet analysis of human rights conditions lacks much of the excitement, urgency, and risk of protecting individual victims. Risk is not lacking, however. Inquiry into some subjects is difficult—perhaps most notably into ill-treatment by and corruption within security forces. As indicated earlier, prison conditions were not "popular" issues for NGOs, although analysis and criticism of police practices assuredly were. It seems clear that for documentation-oriented NGOs, widespread popular backing and membership are not requisite for their success. Careful study, networks to share information, and good links to the press certainly are essential, however.

Democracy and democratization are buzzwords of the 1990s. Unfortunately, some of the African NGOs with either term in their titles are hollow entities, created as façades to cover far more closed situations. They may be GONGOs or QUANGOs, pro-government fronts where authoritarianism lingers. Others are created to coax resources from willing donors who may bank on the hope that a title on the door eventually means advances on the floor. Such organizations do not claim to advance a full range of human rights. They focus, quite obviously, on civil and political rights. In Africa in the 1990s, no one can oppose, at least rhetorically, the importance of democracy. Election monitoring seems to be a favorite objective, given the external funding available. Does this entail a great deal of animosity between the relevant human rights NGOs and their governments?

With the obvious exception of the CD in Nigeria, I did not see significant levels of hostility between governments and pro-democracy NGOs in the four countries (assuming, to be certain, that they pressed for democracy on a country-wide basis, not merely for a single ethnic group). Quite the contrary. Namibian and Senegalese politicians appeared proud to associate themselves with internationally funded and attended colloquia on democracy. The CD itself was moving closer to becoming a specific political movement, although Ransome-Kuti hoped it would be non-partisan.[21] Wisely, human rights NGOs left to political parties the real struggle to mobilize popular opinion and elect candidates. Problems of strategy exist for empowerment oriented groups, however.

Development oriented NGOs advance certain rights, not others. They seek material underpinnings and social attitudes that ease the expansion of human rights. As is the case with documentation and democracy oriented NGOs, development oriented NGOs have a partial agenda; however, they have a different target group. More than any other strategy, development means working directly with the less privileged of society who might not seem to pose direct political threats to the powers-that-be. And, similar to democracy, no government officially opposes development. Development provides an essential long-term foundation for human rights. I regard the work of development oriented NGOs as essential, both in terms of enhancing cooperation between governments and NGOs and in correcting the mammoth abuses that exist in the impoverished villages and teeming cities.

I conclude that government action — both positive and negative — rests jointly on the strategic choices and the social underpinnings of the NGOs. Lawyers can advance human rights in ways that market women cannot. The prestige attached to education and wealth, and the greater political leverage the relatively privileged already enjoy, mean that organizations favoring enforcement of human rights through the legal system will be tolerated (or, perhaps more accurately, not as readily susceptible to regime pressures). So, too, will NGOs favoring documentation and education in human rights. Cooperation may in fact occur. However, empowerment oriented and potentially democratization oriented NGOs should expect strong resistance, especially if their numbers and support swell and their tactics embrace direct confrontation.

To summarize in a sentence the basic messages of this section: neither the size of membership nor backing seems to affect the efficacy of human rights groups, with the exception of those seeking direct political power. Social prestige and political acumen of leaders seem more important than popular participation. The strategy chosen determines to a substantial extent the nature of interactions between the NGO and the government, in particular the extent of hostility or cooperation.

3. *Societal diversity:* African human rights NGOs are profoundly affected by ethnic animosities within societies, the strength of which varies inversely with the political significance of their main supporters. Human rights may be needed most strongly by members of ethnic minorities who, for historical and cultural reasons, are scapegoated under conditions of national trauma. Thus, while it is generally assumed that "horizontal" associations are needed to strengthen civil society, "vertical" associations in fact also play an important role. A society based on pluralism of political and/or economic convictions may find compromise easier than a society marked by pluralism based on exclusive ethnic or religious identities.[22]

This proposition, like the preceding one, sought to explain how and why an NGO may be (in)effective in reaching its goals by reference to social background. I emphasized achievement factors (education, class) before; now I am stressing ascriptive factors (ethnicity, gender). The former social divisions are more "horizontal" than "vertical." There is no neat, clean distinction in real life, however. A poor person in Africa is far more likely to be rural, female, and illiterate than to be urban, male, and literate. Both need better protection of their human rights. All odds, however, are that the latter would be in a better position.

What about groups that feel discriminated against qua groups? How effectively can NGOs articulate and help achieve their interests? Three of the organizations I selected — MFDC, MOSOP, and OLF — are intensely political. The Oromo Liberation Front fought in guerrilla war and vied for power in Ethiopia, the Mouvement des Forces Démocratiques Casamançais stumbled into conflict against the Senegalese government, the Movement for the Survival of the Ogoni People manifested its antipathy against both the Nigerian government and its partner in oil exploitation, Shell. Common to all was the goal of greater autonomy. Claiming a right to self-determination, well aware of their economic marginalization, and resentful of their peripheral positions in the overall political structures, leaders of the three movements far exceeded what other groups did. Their quests for empowerment brought them into the political arena, where they pressed their agendas to differing extents.

NGOs claiming to represent ethnic minorities will in all likelihood receive a more sympathetic hearing outside rather than inside their own country. The primary question is whether external leverage may help accomplish what limited internal numbers in the face of marked government antipathy could not. MOSOP proved itself far and away the most skillful user of the international stage. Ken Saro-Wiwa's writings and travels brought his version of Ogoni grievances to global awareness. MOSOP's astute links to international NGOs concerned with indigenous rights were significantly more adept than Nigeria's defense of its actions. The weakest numerically of the entities demanding autonomy, the Ogoni could have taught (and may well yet teach) many lessons to the Diola and Oromos. The Oromos did profit from the Transitional Government's redrawing of regional boundaries; the Diola might benefit from Senegal's long-proposed but as-yet-unimplemented administrative decentralization; the Ogoni most certainly will derive more revenue from petroleum as allocation formulas are changed, and have pressed ethnic awareness closer to the heart of Nigerian politics. There can be no question, accordingly, that the "ethnic card" can be played to political advantage. Feelings of discrimination can be extended into broader claims for autonomy. Self-determination below the level of the state will, I am certain, become an increasingly vocal claim in coming years south of the Sahara. The vocabulary of human rights, and in particular of internal self-determination, will be heavily employed.

There is equally no question, however, that charges of narrow ethnicity can be utilized against human rights NGOs of almost any character. In other words, organizations need not seek empowerment of a specific ethnic group to feel the hot breath of government pressure. This takes the form of accusations that groups pursue a self-centered agenda, determined by the "tribal" background of their leaders. It is quite likely — indeed, it is almost inevitable — that human rights NGOs in contemporary Africa will be ethnically and socially skewed, strictly speaking. Their leaders are drawn from the ranks of the well-educated. Schooling is certainly not evenly distributed among ethnic groups in contemporary Africa. Their major issues (even one as broad as pressuring a recalcitrant military to honor election results) do not appeal equally to all social sectors. Strength will differ from one area to another, depending on local factors.

The significance of ethnicity as an explanation of political behavior south of the Sahara is debatable. A highly-respected French specialist recently opined,

Ethnicity cannot provide a basic reference point for postcolonial political areas, because it is itself constantly being formed and is largely mingled within the phenomenon of the State, for which it is supposed to provide the explanatory key. . . . In Africa ethnicity is almost never absent from politics, yet at the same time it does not provide its basic fabric. . . . In the context of the contemporary State, ethnicity exists mainly as an agent of accumulation, both of wealth and of political power. Tribalism is thus perceived less as a political force in itself than as a channel through which competition for the acquisition of wealth, power or status is expressed. . . . The generality of factional struggles and the important role of political entrepreneurs give us cause to doubt the absolute preeminence of communitarian organisations over individualised social relationships.[23]

Yet one must remember history. Three of the four states examined in this book experienced bloody internal wars in which ethnicity figured prominently, and the other (Senegal) suffered from rebellious flare-ups in the Casamance, based on Diola particularism and central government neglect or ignorance. Memories of civil conflict are vivid and, it stands to reason, are factors in domestic political perceptions. Prisoners of history like all human beings, African leaders are deeply concerned about national unity. They react strongly to assertions of ethnic autonomy, fearful lest a would-be timely concession turn into an incentive for further demands. This means they will be reluctant to decentralize political power in significant ways.

Bayart's analysis, quoted above, is timely and thought-provoking. His concerns with historic continuities, means of accumulation, and social inequalities within African states are valuable. He gives little attention to either human rights or NGOs, however, even in his discussion of civil society. Given his focus, the omission is understandable. But it means some weaknesses exist in using his framework to explain differential reactions to challenges from below. The evidence in this book tends to support the hypothesis as stated. Pluralism based on political or economic factors can achieve peaceful compromises and protect the rights of individuals more readily than can pluralism derived from ethnic or religious identities, which advance the claims of groups. Civil society seems more hospitable to the former than the latter. The reason can be found in the nature of political space, to which we must now turn.

4. *Political space:* a major change of political regime can rapidly open the political space necessary for human rights NGOs to press their agenda on a national basis. Absent such a shift, NGOs will cluster their activities in areas of immediate class or ethnic group concerns, treaty obligations, or availability of financial support, each of which provides a degree of political space.

In Chapter 2 I suggested a mnemonic, CUTS, with respect to political space: Created, Unoccupied, Taken, or Surrendered. Now is the opportunity to determine whether the way in which NGOs and governments interact has a discernible impact on the groups' effectiveness.

Strongly authoritarian governments make life difficult (but existence necessary) for human rights NGOs. The groups enjoy essentially no space, for they are regarded as opponents. If and when conditions are relaxed, human rights NGOs can spring up. Space can be surrendered by the regime or taken by the NGO. Sometimes additional space can be created through NGO-government cooperation.

The first and third patterns — those of creating and of taking space — was typified in this book by the Legal Assistance Centre of Namibia. The apartheid government's efforts after 1982 to achieve a figleaf of international legitimation facilitated the creation of the LAC. As David Smuts explained, he wanted to discover whether the government's rhetoric and political reality were congruent. The LAC *took* space prior to independence. At that time, the hostility between human rights NGOs and the South African-dominated territorial administration was sharp. After independence, the situation changed significantly. President Nujoma, Prime Minister Geingob, and others built bridges to NGOs, based upon their shared commitment to human rights. A significant degree of cooperation between government and NGOs could be noted. Space was, in this respect, *created* through their joint action.

The Civil Liberties Organisation of Nigeria provides an example, in its early years, of voluntary *surrender* of space. General Babangida had seized political power in 1985, riding a small wave of human rights actions to bolster his rule. The more open atmosphere encouraged CLO organizers to begin their work. Clement Nwankwo et al moved into political space in effect given up by the military rulers as they relaxed authoritarianism. Increasingly, however, Babangida's clutch on power led his regime to more resistance to NGOs. The pattern changed to struggle. In mid-1993 and again in mid-1994, the contest between them crested. The harsh confrontation between the regime and the Campaign for Democracy may have been won in the short run by the military clique in Abuja. In the long run, I believe, the cause of democracy was advanced, despite the widely-circulated (and, in parts of Nigeria, widely-accepted) canard about Yoruba exclusivism. The struggle kindled wider awareness of how far Nigeria remained from democratization and effective protection of human rights. As long as General Abacha et al continue to be hostile to demands for change, the Nigerian political scene will continue to be marked by confrontations over political space.

The most marked change in political regimes occurred in Ethiopia. When the Transitional Government issued its charter in July 1991, pledging adherence to major human rights treaties, the way seemed open for a multitude of NGOs to emerge. They did not. The Ethiopian Human Rights Council (EHRCO) continued its work, albeit on a much more open basis, yet it still encountered opposition from the regime. Despite the profusion of issues around which rights advocates could cluster, little appeared to be happening, with the exception of funding, to which we shall turn shortly. The complex political situation in Ethiopia, and in particular the ambiguous status of the Amhara relative to the Tigreans, led to caution. It seemed that only "Professor Mesfin," with the self-assurance that retired, urbane academics display, was publicly willing to criticize from within.[24]

Conversely, the relatively relaxed atmosphere in Senegal facilitated the creation of numerous groups, several of which appeared to be adrift and ineffectual. Though there were issues aplenty, Senegalese NGOs seemed to me as of mid-1994 to lack strong commitment to task relative to other organizations depicted in this book. The government and NGOs alike appeared passive; in Senegal, space was thus *unoccupied*. Tacit cooperation meant not rocking the boat. There was also conscious cooptation. Creation of the officially-sponsored African Institute for Democracy and Human Rights manifested at least to skeptics the Senegalese passion for pro-democracy rhetoric as a mask for limited action.

The table presented there thus might be filled as in Table 7.

How does the distribution of explicitly human rights oriented NGOs

TABLE 7. Government/NGO Relationships over Political "Space"

	NGO/government cooperation	NGO/government opposition
Government active	Space created	Space taken
	Namibia post-independence	Namibia pre-independence (LAC) Nigeria 1993–94 (CD) Ethiopia (EHRCO)
Government passive	Space unoccupied	Space surrendered
	Senegal	Nigeria 1987 (CLO)

vary in terms of issues? As pointed out a few paragraphs ago, lawyers and professors took the lead in creating these groups, drawing on their professional skills and interests. An urban, middle-class, civil and political rights orientation has been a natural consequence. Yes, these groups have pressed for prison reform, and certainly the overwhelming majority of prisoners and detainees south of the Sahara are not highly-trained professionals. More important, they seek to strengthen the legal system, using the courts to advance the "rule of law" and to enforce constitutionally- and treaty-guaranteed human rights. However, somewhat more attention to the needs of "ordinary" people seems to have been given by development oriented and women's groups. This is intended as an observation, not a criticism. The advances attorneys make in pressing for fair administration of bail or fewer restrictions on freedom of expression benefit societies as wholes. Most persons in sub-Saharan Africa encounter "the law" through the behavior of police (are they bribe-seeking? are they apt to use violence?), and accordingly might derive immediate benefits from better police training. Overall long-term benefits appear likely from reduction of gender differences and boosts in the standard of living; hence, development is important.

I have no doubt that external funding made possible the creation and sustaining of a substantial portion of Africa's human rights NGOs. I am equally convinced that resources have been requested, and on occasion received, by groups contributing only marginally to the protection of human rights. Some, admittedly, carry out promotion. They organize colloquia, seminars, workshops; they publish *comptes-rendus*, newsletters, studies; they thereby encourage the "human rights consciousness" I have frequently extolled in these pages. Such organizations are important, nay necessary. For example, despite its inherent Charter limitations, the African Commission on Human and People's Rights fills an important role. Its presence reminds governments of the binding pledges they made to protect human rights; its discussions and responses to communications manifest limits to domestic sovereignty. But talk or publication unaccompanied by action (including serious research) is sterile. A combination of promotion and protection based on a regular research program seems ideal. Hence I was attracted by the steps taken by the Nigerian Legal Research and Resources Development Centre. The LRRDC not only published booklets, encouraged studies, and established a library, but also trained paralegals for work outside Nigeria's major cities.

Are purposes diffused and "spread-too-thinnedness" increased if human rights NGOs undertake protection and promotion concurrently? No, *if* a broadening of activities is based on a commensurate increase in resources, based on prior careful assessment that the new work can be satisfactorily handled. No, *if* the NGO has started to achieve a track record, and can build on prior success. What is needed thus is time to see how the "NGO revolution" copes with the continuing needs of African societies.

We have traveled a long way through this book. The details were intended to deepen and enrich the overall picture. The struggle for human rights is, at the end of the day, an intensely personal effort, carried out through organizations, inspired by ideals, and only gradually moving to the center of political attention. We should now have greater understanding and respect for those engaged in the effort. The persons who help make human rights realities south of the Sahara are individuals worth of our attention and support.

Notes

1. Not always with the greatest accuracy, however, as noted earlier in this book. I gave a 50-minute lecture on freedom of expression under the auspices of the Ethiopian Human Rights Council; national television and the press covered the event. Only a minute part of my message was carried, however. Neither my pleading for the widest possible latitude of expression, that nor for the right to receive and impart information, received any attention from the official media; the government-employed media types were interested only in the two minutes during which I stressed the importance of accuracy and verification.

2. The noted Arusha conference on popular participation felt the full force of both events. As the Charter itself concluded,

> This Conference has taken place during a period when the world continues to witness tumultuous changes in Eastern Europe. Even more dramatically, this Conference has taken place during the very week when Nelson Mandela's release has exhilarated all of Africa, and galvanized the international community.
>
> There is an inescapable thread of continuity between those events and our Conference; it is the power of people to effect momentous change. At no other

time in the post-war period has popular participation had so astonishing and profound an impact.

"African Charter for Popular Participation in Development and Transformation," UN Document E/ECA/CM.16/11, paragraphs 27 and 28.

3. There is no question, however, that very serious deficiencies exist in current attempts to assess human rights performance by individual governments. Preceding pages have given examples. It is, naturally, my hope that this book suggests strategies for improvement.

4. Establishment of this office was a major objective of several Western powers for the Vienna conference. Although the final communiqué waffled on the issue, leaving it for study by the General Assembly, the UNGA surprised many observers by electing José Ayala Lasso of Ecuador as High Commissioner. It remains to be seen how successful he can be.

5. For historical background, see Natalie Hevener Kaufman, *Human Rights Treaties and the Senate: A History of Opposition* (Chapel Hill: University of North Carolina Press, 1990). The numerous reservations attached to Congressional implementation of the International Covenant on Civil and Political Rights shows that "Brickerism" remains alive in spirit.

6. Rhoda E. Howard and Jack Donnelly, "Human Dignity, Human Rights and Political Regimes," *American Political Science Review* 80 (1986), 801–17.

7. Civil Liberties Organisation, *Behind the Wall: A Report on Prison Conditions in Nigeria and the Nigerian Prison System* (Lagos: CLO, 1991); Civil Liberties Organisation, *Prisoners in the Shadows: A Report on Women and Children in Five Nigerian Prisons* (Lagos: CLO, 1993); Human Rights Watch, "Prison Conditions in Zaire" (New York: HRW/Africa Watch and Prison Project, 1994).

8. The phrase comes from the hardcover edition of his autobiography; it was deleted in later editions, although Nkrumah's basic attitude showed no sign of change. Kwame Nkrumah, *Ghana: The Autobiography of Kwame Nkrumah* (London: Nelson, 1957), p. x.

9. Akwasi Aidoo, "Africa: Democratization Without Human Rights?" *Human Rights Quarterly* 15, 4 (November 1993), 703–15.

10. Samuel P. Huntington, *Political Order in Changing Societies* (New Haven, CT: Yale University Press, 1968).

11. Clement Nwankwo, Dulue Mbochu and Basil Ugochukwu, *Human Rights Practices in the Nigerian Police* (Lagos: Constitutional Rights Project, 1993).

12. John Clark, *Democratizing Development: The Role of Voluntary Organizations* (London: Earthscan, 1991). For "just" development, Clark uses the acronym DEPENDS: Development of Infrastructure; Economic growth; Poverty alleviation; Equity; Natural-resource base protection; Democracy; Social justice. An approprite mnemonic!

13. See the compelling arguments and discouraging results reported by Katarina Tomaevski, *Development Aid and Human Rights Revisited* (London and New York: Pinter, 1993).

14. Particularly impressive to me, based on the field work for this book, are the procedures evolved by the Ford Foundation. Ford representatives work within relatively broad policy parameters. Dialogue with NGOs is central to the process. Foundation staff emphasize the importance of effective internal governance, involving clear definition of duties, staff development, and accountability. Grants are made on multi-year bases (up to five), with annual draw-downs. In special circumstances, after a lengthy period of success, Ford may consider special en-

dowment grants, in which interests and dividends from these one-time donations can be used for general NGO purposes. Interviews with Ford representatives Akwasi Aidoo (Dakar), Steve Lawry (Windhoek) and Mora McLean (Lagos).

15. This book is probably much too personal already. Yet I cannot resist inserting (if only in an obscure footnote) a few hints about Internet's fascinating history. It started with the mutual interest of political scientists Laurie Wiseberg and Harry Scoble, both teaching at the University of Illinois at Chicago in the mid-1970s. Both were interested in human rights, though from different backgrounds: Scoble from political activism on the American west coast, with freedom of expression a major concern; Wiseberg from her doctoral dissertation on the Nigerian civil war and the response of the international community. As husband and wife, they started to collect and categorize the ephemeral publications of NGOs, material most libraries discard in favor of "permanent" items like books or scholarly quarterlies. Internet was established as a section of the International Studies Association in March 1976, then separately incorporated November 1977 as a not-for-profit organization; the founders moved from Chicago to Washington, converting the basement of their crowded townhouse into a librarian's dream (or perhaps nightmare!) of files stuffed into boxes, spilling across the floor, crowded into corners. (I spent many delightful hours there, rooting through files in some of my early research on human rights in Africa.) Laurie and Harry (for I find it hard to call them by their surnames) attracted modest Ford Foundation support, then moved their increasingly sophisticated operation to Harvard Law School. Scoble died of emphysema; anticipated support did not materialize; Internet relocated to the University of Ottawa, then had to seek independent quarters. The organization continues to play a vital role, described in these words (as valid in the mid-1990s as in 1979): HRI aims to "fill the vacuum which existed between human rights organisations — so that one group knows what other groups are doing; between academics and activists in the human rights field — so that activists know what research is being carried out and scholars are aware of what activists are doing; and between both of these groups and policy makers." Marguerite Garling, compiler, *The Human Rights Handbook: A Guide to British and American International Human Rights Organizations* (London: Macmillan for Writers and Scholars Educational Trust, 1979), p. 204.

16. Laurie S. Wiseberg, "Defending Human Rights Defenders: The Importance of Freedom of Association for Human Rights NGOs" (Montreal: International Centre for Human Rights and Democratic Development, 1993), pp. 15–19.

17. For details of many successful approaches, see Richard Pierre Claude and George Andreopoulos, eds., *Human Rights Education Handbook* (Philadelphia: University of Pennsylvania Press, forthcoming).

18. Melanie Bixby, "The Democracy and Human Rights Fund for Africa: Institutional Impact and Lessons from the Field" (Washington, DC: Department of State, unpublished report, 1993).

19. Wiseberg, "Defending Human Rights Defenders," pp. 19–21.

20. Susan Brown, "Assessment of Popular Participation in the Formulation and Implementation of Development Policies and Programmes: A Case Study of Namibia," Windhoek: Namibian Economic Policy Research Unit (NEPRU), 1992.

21. Interview, Lagos, February 25, 1994.

22. The strategies for managing ethnic conflict outlined by Horowitz merit attention in this regard. Donald L. Horowitz, *Ethnic Groups in Conflict* (Berkeley and Los Angeles: University of California Press, 1985).

23. Jean-François Bayart, *The State in Africa: The Politics of the Belly* (London: Longmans, 1993), pp. 49, 55, 266 (originally published in 1989).

24. Having said this, however, I must immediately point out that Ethiopians in exile (of whom the overwhelming proportion appear to be Amhara) sharply criticize the Meles regime. Their overseas diatribes spice the political scene, and call attention to serious problems. Their credibility is (at least according to persons I interviewed in Addis Ababa) vitiated by distance.

Bibliography

Abayomi, Tunji. "Non-Governmental Organizations in the Protection and Promotion of Human Rights in Africa: Critique of Approach and Methods," in Awa U. Kalu and Yemi Osinbajo, eds., *Perspectives on Human Rights* (Lagos: Federal Ministry of Justice, 1992), pp. 173–95.

Abdalla, Raqiya H.D. *Sisters in Affliction: Circumcision and Infibulation of Women in Africa* (London: Zed, 1982).

Abdullah, Hussaina. "The Democratic Process and the Challenge of Gender in Nigeria," *Review of African Political Economy* 56 (1993), 28–37.

Addo, Michael K. "Political Self-Determination Within the Context of the African Charter of Human and Peoples' Rights," *Journal of African Law* 32 (1988), 182–93.

Adebayo, Okunade. "Human Rights and Trade Unionism in Africa: The Nigerian Experience," in David P. Forsythe, ed., *Human Rights and Development: International Views* (New York: St. Martin's, 1989), pp. 60–80.

Achebe, Chinua. *The Trouble with Nigeria* (London: Heinemann, 1984).

Africa Watch (Alex deWaal). *Evil Days: 30 Years of War and Famine in Ethiopia* (New York: Human Rights Watch, 1991).

—— (Richard Dicker). *Waiting for Accountability: Human Rights and the Transition to Democracy* (New York: Human Rights Watch, 1992).

——. "Where Silence Rules" (New York: Human Rights Watch, 1990).

Agbaje, Adigun. "In Search of Building Blocks: The State, Civil Society, Voluntary Action, and Grassroot Development in Africa," *Africa Quarterly* 30, 3–4 (1990), 24–40.

Agbakoba, Olisa. "The Role of Non-Governmental Organisations in the Development and Protection of Individual Rights," in M. A. Ajomo and Bolaji Owasanoye, eds., *Individual Rights Under the 1989 Constitution* (Lagos: Nigerian Institute of Advanced Legal Studies, 1993), pp. 141–58.

Agbese, Pita Ogaba. "The State Versus Human Rights Advocates in Africa: The Case of Nigeria," in Eileen McCarthy-Arnolds, David R. Penna, and Debra Joy Cruz Sobrepeña, eds., *Africa, Human Rights, and the Global System: The Political Economy of Human Rights in a Changing World* (Westport, CT.: Greenwood, 1994), pp. 147–72.

Aidoo, Akwasi. "Africa: Democracy Without Human Rights?" *Human Rights Quarterly* 15 (1993), 703–15.

Ajomo, M. Ayo and Isabella Okabue. *Human Rights and the Administration of Criminal Justice in Nigeria* (Lagos: Nigerian Institute of Advanced Legal Studies, 1991).

Ajomo, M. Ayo and Bolaji Owasanoye, eds. *Individual Rights Under the 1989 Constitution* (Lagos: Nigerian Institute of Advanced Legal Studies, 1993).

Akande, Jadsola. "A Decade of Human Rights in Nigeria," in M. Ayo Ajomo, ed., *New Dimensions in Nigerian Law* (Lagos: Nigerian Institute of Advanced Legal Studies, 1989), pp. 101–25.

Alexander, Yonah and Robert A. Friedlander, eds., *Self-Determination: National, Regional and Global Dimensions* (Boulder, CO: Westview, 1980).

All Africa Conference of Churches, Commission on International Affairs. *African Church Leaders' Human Rights Summit, Cairo, September 8–13, 1986* (Nairobi: AACC, 1986).

Allen, Chris, Carolyn Baylies, and Morris Szeftel. "Surviving Democracy?", *Review of African Political Economy* 54 (July 1992), 3–10.

Alston, Philip. "The Committee on Economic, Social and Cultural Rights," in Philip Alston, ed., *The United Nations and Human Rights: A Critical Evaluation* (Oxford: Clarendon Press, 1992), pp. 473–508.

———. "Effective Implementation of International Instruments on Human Rights, Including Reporting Obligations under International Instruments on Human Rights," UN Document A/44/688, 8 November 1989 (initial report); UN Document A/Conf.157/PC/62/Add.11/Rev.1, 22 April 1993 (interim report).

———. "Making Space for New Human Rights: The Case of the Right to Development," *Harvard Human Rights Yearbook* 1 (1988), 3–40.

———. "The Purposes of Reporting," in *Manual on Human Rights Reporting* (Geneva: United Nations Centre for Human Rights, 1991).

———. "Revitalising United Nations Work on Human Rights and Development," *Melbourne University Law Review* 18 (1991), 216–57.

———, ed. *The United Nations and Human Rights: A Critical Evaluation* (Oxford: Clarendon Press, 1992).

———. "The UN's Human Rights Record: From San Francisco to Vienna and Beyond," *Human Rights Quarterly* 16 (1994), 375–90.

Alubo, S. O. "Human Rights and Militarism in Nigeria," in George W. Shepherd, Jr. and Mark O.C. Anikpo., eds., *Emerging Human Rights: The African Political Economy Context* (Westport, CT: Greenwood, 1990), pp. 197–207.

Amnesty International. "Amnesty International's Observations on Possible Reform of the African Charter on Human and Peoples' Rights" (London: Amnesty International, June 1993; Document IOR 63/03/93).

———. *Annual Report* (London: Amnesty International, annual).

———. "Human Rights in Ethiopia, Memorandum to the Transitional Government of Ethiopia" (London: Amnesty International, November 1994).

———. "Senegal—Torture: The Casamance Case" (London: Amnesty International, 1990).

Amoah, Philip. "The African Charter on Human and Peoples' Rights," *African Journal of International and Comparative Law* 4, 1 (March 1992), 226–40.

An-Na'im, Abdullahi Ahmed, ed. *Human Rights in Cross-Cultural Perspectives: A Quest for Consensus* (Philadelphia: University of Pennsylvania Press, 1992).

———. *Toward an Islamic Reformation: Civil Liberties, Human Rights, and International Law* (Syracuse, NY: Syracuse University Press, 1990).

Anaya, S. James. "The Capacity of International Law to Advance Ethnic or Nationality Rights Claims," *Iowa Law Review* 73 (1990), 837–73.

Arat, Zehra F. *Democracy and Human Rights in Developing Countries* (Boulder, CO: Lynne Rienner, 1991).

Artz, Donna E. "The Application of International Human Rights Law in Islamic States," *Human Rights Quarterly* 12 (1990), 202–30.

Ati, Hassan Ahmed Abdel. "The Development Impact of NGO Activities in the Red Sea Province of Sudan: A Critique," *Development and Change* 24 (1993), 103–30.

Austin, Dennis. "Reflections on African Politics: Prospero, Ariel and Caliban," *International Affairs* 69 (1993), 203–21.

Awolowo, Obafemi. *Path to Nigerian Freedom* (London: Faber, 1966 [originally published 1947]).

Ayoade, J. A. A., Elone J. Nwabuzor, and Adesina Sambo, eds. *Grassroots Democracy and the New Government System in Nigeria* (Abuja: Centre for Democratic Studies, n.d.).

Ayoade, J. A. A., Elone J. Nwabuzor, and Adesina Sambo, eds. *Political Parties and the Third Republic* (Abuja: Centre for Democratic Studies, 1991).

Ayoade, J. A. A., Elone J. Nwabuzor, and Adesina Sambo, eds., *Women and Politics in Nigeria* (Abuja: Centre for Democratic Studies, 1992).

Azarya, Victor and Naomi Chazan. "Disengagement from the State in Africa: Reflections on the Experiences of Ghana and Guinea," *Comparative Studies in Society and History* 29 (1987), 106–31.

Badawi El-Sheikh, Ibrahim. "The African Commission on Human and Peoples' Rights: Prospects and Problems," *Netherlands Quarterly of Human Rights* 7 (1989), 272–83.

Baehr, Peter R. "Amnesty International and its Self-Imposed Limited Mandate," *Netherlands Quarterly of Human Rights* 12 (1994), 5–22.

——. "Human Rights, Development, and Dutch Foreign Policy: The Role of an Advisory Committee," in David P. Forsythe, ed., *Human Rights and Development: International Views* (London: Macmillan, 1989), pp. 154–70.

Barkan, Joel D., Michael L. McNutty, and M. A. O. Ayeni. " 'Hometown' Voluntary Associations, Local Development, and the Emergence of Civil Society in Western Nigeria," *Journal of Modern African Studies* 29 (1991), 457–80.

Barry, Boubacar. *La Sénégambie du XVe au XIXe siècle: Traite negrière, Islam et conquête coloniale* (Paris: L'Harmattan, 1988).

Barsh, Russel Lawrence. "Democratization and Development," *Human Rights Quarterly* 14 (1992), 120–34.

——. "The Right to Development as a Human Right: Results of the Global Consultation," *Human Rights Quarterly* 13 (1991), 322–38.

Baxter, Paul. "The Problem *of* the Oromo, or the Problem *for* the Oromo," in I. M. Lewis, ed., *Nationalism and Self-Determination in the Horn of Africa* (London: Ithaca Press, 1983), pp. 129–49. Originally published as "Ethiopia's Unacknowledged Problem: The Oromo," *African Affairs* 77, 208 (1978), 283–96.

——. "The Creation and Constitution of Oromo Nationality," in Katsuyoshi Fukai and John Markakis, eds., *Ethnicity and Conflict in the Horn of Africa* (London: James Currey, 1994), pp. 167–86.

Bayart, Jean-François. "Civil Society in Africa," in Patrick Chabal, ed., *Political Domination in Africa* (Cambridge: Cambridge University Press, 1986), pp. 106–25.

——. *The State in Africa: The Politics of the Belly* (London: Longmans, 1993).

Bayefsky, Anne F. "Making the Human Rights Treaties Work," in Louis Henkin and John Lawrence Hargrove, eds., *Human Rights: An Agenda for the Next Century* (Washington, DC: American Society of International Law, 1993), pp. 229–95.

Bebbington, Anthony and John Farrington. "Governments, NGOs and Agricultural Development: Perspectives on Changing Inter-Organisational Relationships," *Journal of Development Studies* 29 (1993), 199–219.

Bedjaoui, Mohammed. "The Right to Development," in Mohammed Bedjaoui, ed., *International Law: Achievements and Prospects* (Dordrecht: Martinus Nijhoff, 1991), 1177–1203.

Beigbeder, Yves. *The Role and Status of International Humanitarian Volunteers and Organizations: The Right and Duty to Humanitarian Assistance* (Dordrecht: Martinus Nijhoff, 1990).

Bello, Emmanuel G. "The African Charter on Human and Peoples' Rights: A Legal Analysis," *Recueil des Cours 194* (Dordrecht: Nijhoff), 9–268.

———. "Article 22 of the African Charter on Human and Peoples' Rights," in Emmanuel G. Bello and Prince Bola A. Ajibola, *Essays in Honour of Judge Taslim Olawale Elias* (Dordrecht: Nijhoff, 1992), pp. 447–75.

———. "The Mandate of the African Commission on Human and Peoples' Rights: Article 45 of the Charter," *African Journal of International Law* 1 (1988), 31–64.

Benedek, Wolfgang. "The African Charter and Commission on Human and Peoples' Rights; How to make it more effective," *Netherlands Quarterly of Human Rights* 11, 1 (1993), 25–40.

Bennett, Tom W. "Human Rights and the African Cultural Tradition," in Wolfgang Schmale, ed., *Human Rights and Cultural Diversity* (Goldbach: Keip, 1993), pp. 269–80.

Berg, Robert J. "Non-Governmental Organizations: New Force in Third World Development and Politics" (East Lansing, MI: Center for Advanced Study of International Development, CASID Distinguished Speaker Series No. 2, 1987).

Bettati, Mario and Pierre-Marie Dupuy, eds. *Les ONG et le Droit International* (Paris: Economica, 1986).

Beyani, Chaloka. "Toward a More Effective Guarantee of Women's Rights in the African Human Rights System," in Rebecca Cook, ed., *Human Rights of Women: National and International Perspectives* (Philadelphia: University of Pennsylvania Press, 1994), pp. 285–306.

Beyer, Gregg A. "Human Rights Monitoring and the Failure of Early Warning: A Practitioner's View," *International Journal of Refugee Law* 2 (1990), 56–82; republished in Alex P. Schmid and Albert J. Jongman, eds., *Monitoring Human Rights Violations* (Leiden: Centre for the Study of Social Conflicts, 1992), pp. 111–30.

Bienen, Henry. *Political Conflict and Economic Change in Nigeria* (London: Frank Cass, 1985).

Binder, Guyora. "The Kaplan Lecture on Human Rights: The Case for Self-Determination," *Stanford Journal of International Law* 29 (1993), 223–70.

Bixby, Melanie. "The Democracy and Human Rights Fund for Africa: Institutional Impact and Lessons from the Field" (Washington, DC: Department of State, unpublished report, 1993).

Bjornlund, Eric, Michael Bratton, and Clark Gibson. "Observing Multiparty Elections in Africa: Lessons from Zambia," *African Affairs* 91, 364 (July 1992), 405–32.

Blair, Harry. *Defining, Promoting and Sustaining Democracy: Formulating an A.I.D. Strategy for Development Assistance and Evaluation* (Washington, DC: USAID, 1992).

Blaser, Arthur W. "How to Advance Human Rights Without Really Trying: An

Analysis of Nongovernmental Tribunals," *Human Rights Quarterly* 14 (1992), 339–70.

——. "Human Rights in the Third World and Development of International Non-governmental Organizations," in George W. Shepherd, Jr. and Ved P. Nanda, eds., *Human Rights and Third World Development* (Westport, CT: Greenwood, 1985), pp. 273–85.

Blay, S. Kwaw Nyamkeke. "Changing African Perspectives on the Right of Self-Determination in the Wake of the Banjul Charter on Human and Peoples' Rights," *Journal of African Law* 29, 2 (1985), 147–59.

Bondzie-Simpson, E. "A Critique of the African Charter on Human and Peoples' Rights," *Harvard Law Journal* 31 (1988), 643–55.

Bratton, Michael. "Beyond the State: Civil Society and Association Life in Africa," *World Politics* 41, 3 (1989), 407–30.

——. "Civil Society and Political Transitions in Africa," in John W. Harbeson, Donald Rothchild and Naomi Chazan, eds., *Civil Society and the State in Africa* (Boulder, CO: Lynne Rienner, 1994), pp. 51–81.

——. "Non-Governmental Organizations in Africa: Can They Influence Public Policy?" in Eve Sandberg, ed., *The Changing Politics of Non-Governmental Organizations and African States* (Westport, CT: Praeger, 1994), pp. 33–58.

——. "The Politics of Government-NGO Relations in Africa," *World Development* 17, 4 (1989), 569–87.

Bratton, Michael and Nicolas Van de Walle. "Popular Protest and Political Reform in Africa," *Comparative Politics* 24, 4 (July 1992), 419–42.

—— and Nicolas Van de Walle. "Toward Governance in Africa: Popular Demands and State Responses," in Goren Hyden and Michael Bratton, eds., *Governance and Politics in Africa* (Boulder, CO: Lynne Rienner, 1992), pp. 27–56.

Brett, E. A. "Voluntary Agencies as Development Organizations: Theorizing the Problem of Efficiency and Accountability," *Development and Change* 24 (1993), 269–303.

Breytenbach, W. J. "Inter-Ethnic Conflict in Africa," in Willem A. Veenhoven, ed., *Case Studies on Human Rights and Fundamental Freedoms*, Vol. I (The Hague: Martinus Hijhoff, 1975), pp. 309–31.

Brown, Susan. "Assessment of Popular Participation in the Formulation and Implementation of Development Policies and Programmes: A Case Study of Namibia" (Windhoek: Namibian Economic Policy Research Unit [NEPRU], 1992).

Buchheit, Lee H. *Secession: The Legitimacy of Self-Determination* (New Haven, CT: Yale University Press, 1978).

Butegwa, Florence. "Using the African Charter on Human and Peoples' Rights to Secure Women's Access to Land in Africa," in Rebecca Cook, ed., *Human Rights of Women: National and International Perspectives* (Philadelphia: University of Pennsylvania Press, 1994), pp. 495–514.

Carleton, David and Michael Stohl, "The Role of Human Rights in Foreign Assistance," *American Journal of Political Science* 31 (1987), 1002–1018.

Carter Center of Emory University. *Beyond Autocracy in Africa: Working Papers for the Inaugural Seminar of the Governance in Africa Program* (Atlanta: The Center, 1989).

Carver, Richard. "Called to Account: How African Governments Investigate Human Rights Violations," *African Affairs* 89, 356 (1990), 391–415.

Carver, Richard and Paul Hunt. "National Human Rights Institutions in Africa" (Banjul: African Centre for Democracy and Human Rights Studies, 1991).

Centre for Democratic Studies. "Policy Briefs for Politicians" (Abuja: CDS, n.d.)

Chabal, Patrick. *Power in Africa: An Essay in Political Interpretation* (New York: St. Martin's, 1992).

Chazan, Naomi. "Africa's Democratic Challenge: Strengthening the State and Civil Society," *World Policy Journal* 9 (1992), 279–308.

———. "Engaging the State: Associational Life in Sub-Saharan Africa," in Joel S. Migdal, Atul Kohli, and Vivienne Shue, eds., *State Power and Social Forces: Domination and Transformation in the Third World* (Cambridge: Cambridge University Press, 1994), pp. 255–89.

Chazan, Naomi, John W. Harbeson, and Donald Rothchild, eds. *Civil Society and the State in Africa* (Boulder, CO: Lynne Rienner, 1993).

Chinje, Eric. "The Media in Emerging African Democracies: Power, Politics and the Role of the Press," *Fletcher Forum of World Affairs* 17 (1992/3), 49–66.

Chowdhury, Subrata Roy, Erik M. G. Denters, and Paul J. I. M. de Waart, eds. *The Right to Development in International Law* (Dordrecht: Martinus Nijhoff, 1992).

Civil Liberties Organisation. *Behind the Wall: A Report on Prison Conditions in Nigeria and the Nigerian Prison System* (Lagos: CLO, 1991).

———. *A Harvest of Violations: Annual Report on Human Rights in Nigeria, 1991* (Lagos: CLO, 1992).

———. *Human Rights in Retreat* (Lagos: CLO, 1993).

———. *Prisoners in the Shadows: A Report on Women and Children in Five Nigerian Prisons* (Lagos: CLO, 1993).

Clapham, Christopher. *Transformation and Continuity in Revolutionary Ethiopia* (Cambridge: Cambridge University Press, 1988).

Clark, John. *Democratizing Development: The Role of Voluntary Organizations* (London: Earthscan, 1991).

Clark, Roger S. "The International League for Human Rights and South West Africa 1947–1967: The Human Rights NGO as Catalyst in the International Legal Process," *Human Rights Quarterly* 3, 4 (1981), 101–36.

Claude, Richard P. "Human Rights Education in the Philippines" (Manila: Kalikasan Press, 1991).

Claude, Richard P. and Burns H. Weston, eds. *Human Rights in the World Community: Issues and Action* (Philadelphia: University of Pennsylvania Press, 1992, 2nd edition).

Claude, Richard P. and George Andreopoulos, eds. *Human Rights Education Handbook* (Philadelphia: University of Pennsylvania Press, forthcoming).

Clough, Michael. *Free at Last? U.S. Policy Toward Africa and the End of the Cold War* (New York: Council on Foreign Relations, 1992).

Cobbah, Josiah A.M. "African Values and the Human Rights Debate: An African Perspective," *Human Rights Quarterly* 9 (1987), 309–31.

Cohen, Cynthia Price. "The Role of Non-Governmental Organizations in the Drafting of the Convention on the Rights of the Child," *Human Rights Quarterly* 12 (1990), 137–47.

Cohen, Robin and Harry Goulbourne, eds. *Democracy and Socialism in Africa* (Boulder, CO: Westview, 1991).

Cohen, Robin, Goran Hyden, and Winston P. Nagan, eds. *Human Rights and Governance in Africa* (Gainesville: University Press of Florida, 1993).

Cohn, Cindy A. "The Early Harvest: Domestic Legal Changes Related to the

Human Rights Committee and the Covenant on Civil and Political Rights," *Human Rights Quarterly* 13 (1991), 295–321.

Comeau, Pauline. "Mood is positive as the UN begins review of NGO status," *Human Rights Tribune* 2, 4 (September/October 1994), 24–27.

Commins, Stephen K., ed. *Africa's Development Challenges and the World Bank: Hard Questions, Costly Choices* (Boulder, CO: Lynne Rienner, 1988).

Condamines, Charles. *L'aide humanitaire entre la politique et les affaires* (Paris: Harmattan, 1989).

Corbett, Andrew. "The Legal Assistance Centre in Transition," unpublished paper.

Coulon, Christian, "Senegal: The Development and Fragility of Semidemocracy," in Larry Diamond, Juan J. Linz, and Seymour Martin Lipset, eds., *Democracy in Developing Countries: Africa* (Boulder, CO: Lynne Rienner, 1988), pp. 141–78.

Cristescu, Aurelio. *The Right to Self-Determination: Historical and Current Developments on the Basis of United Nations Instruments* (New York: United Nations, 1981).

Crocker, Chester A. *High Noon in Southern Africa: Making Peace in a Rough Neighborhood* (New York: Norton, 1992).

daCosta, Peter. "Senegal: The Secessionist South," *Africa Report* 36, 1 (1991), 21–23.

Dale, Richard. "Melding War and Politics in Namibia: South Africa's Counterinsurgency Campaign, 1966–1989," *Armed Forces & Society* 20 (1993), 7–24.

Danielsen, Astrid. "The State Reporting Procedure under the African Charter" (Copenhagen: Danish Centre for Human Rights, 1994).

Danielsen, Astrid and Gerd Oberleitner. "16th Session of the African Commission on Human and Peoples' Rights," *Netherlands Quarterly of Human Rights*, in press.

Dankwa, E. V. O. "Commentary on the Rules of Procedure of the African Commission on Human and Peoples' Rights," *Proceedings of the Second Annual Conference of the African Society of International and Comparative Law in Annaba 1990* (London: The Society, 1990), pp. 29–34.

Darbon, Dominique. *L'Administration et le paysan en Casamance* (Paris: Pedone, 1988).

———. "Le culturalisme bas-Casamançais," *Politique Africaine* 14 (1984), 125–28.

De Mars, William. "Tactics and Protection: International Human Rights Organizations in the Ethiopian Conflict, 1980–1986," in Eileen McCarthy-Arnolds, David R. Penna, and Debra Joy Cruz Sobrepeña, eds., *Africa, Human Rights, and the Global System: The Political Economy of Human Rights in a Changing World* (Westport, CT.: Greenwood, 1994), pp. 81–106.

Decalo, Samuel. "The Process, Prospects, and Constraints of Democratization in Africa," *African Affairs* 91, 362 (1992), 7–35.

Degni-Segui, René. "L'apport de la Charte Africaine des Droits de l'Homme et des Peuples au droit internationale de l'homme," *African Journal of International and Comparative Law* 3 (1991), 699–741.

Descendre, Daniel. *L'autodétermination paysanne en Afrique: Solidarité ou tutelle des O.N.G. partenaires* (Paris: Harmattan, 1991).

———. *L'autodétermination paysanne en Afrique* (Paris: Harmattan, 1989).

Desouches, Christine. *Le Parti démocratique sénégalais: Une opposition légale en Afrique* (Paris: Berger-Levrault, 1983).

DeWaal, Alex. "Ethiopia: Transition to What?" *World Policy Journal* 9, 4 (1992), 719–38.

Diallo, Mamadou. *Le Sénégal* (Paris: EDICEF, n.d.).

Diamond, Larry. "Beyond Authoritarianism and Totalitarianism: Strategies for Democratization," *Washington Quarterly* 12 (1989), 141–63.

———. *Class, Ethnicity and Democracy in Nigeria: The Failure of the First Republic* (Basingstoke: Macmillan, 1988).

———. "Class Formation in the Swollen African State," *Journal of Modern African Studies* 23 (1985), 567–96.

———. "Nigeria: Pluralism, Statism, and the Struggle for Democracy," in Larry Diamond, Juan J. Linz, and Seymour Martin Lipset, eds., *Democracy in Developing Countries: Africa* (Boulder, CO: Lynne Rienner, 1988), pp. 33–91.

———. "Promoting Democracy," *Foreign Policy* 87 (Summer 1992), 25–46.

———. "Promoting Democracy in Africa: U.S. and International Policies in Transition," unpublished paper presented at the Fourth Annual East African-American Studies Colloquium, Kenya, July 19–23, 1993.

———. "The Second Wind of Change," *Times Literary Supplement* 4709 (July 2, 1993), 43–46.

Diamond, Larry, Juan J. Linz, and Seymour Martin Lipset, eds. *Democracy in Developing Countries: Africa* (Boulder, CO: Lynne Rienner, 1988).

Dicker, Richard. "Monitoring Human Rights in Africa," *Journal of Modern African Studies* 29 (1991), 505–10.

Dinstein, Yoram and Mala Tabory, eds. *The Protection of Minorities and Human Rights* (Dordrecht: Martinus Nijhoff, 1991).

Diop, Momar Coumba and Mamadou Diouf. *Le Sénégal sous Abdou Diouf: Etat et société* (Paris: Karthala, 1990).

Dlamini, C. R. M. "Towards a Regional Protection of Human Rights in Africa: The African Charter on Human and Peoples' Rights," *Comparative and International Law Journal of Southern Africa* 24 (1991), 189–203.

———. "The Violation of Human Rights in Africa: A Lesson for South Africa?" *South African Journal of Human Rights* 7 (1991), 291–303.

Donnelly, Jack. *International Human Rights* (Boulder, CO: Westview, 1993).

———. "International Human Rights: A Regime Analysis," *International Organization* 40 (1986), 599–642.

———. "Post-Cold War Reflections on the Study of International Human Rights," *Ethics and International Affairs* 8 (1994), 97–117.

———. "Repression and Development: The Political Contingency of Human Rights Trade-Offs," in David P. Forsythe, ed., *Human Rights and Development: International Views* (New York: St. Martin's, 1989), pp. 305–28.

———. "The 'Right to Development': How Not to Link Human Rights and Development," in Claude E. Welch, Jr. and Ronald I. Meltzer, eds., *Human Rights and Development in Africa* (Albany: State University of New York Press, 1984), pp. 261–83.

———. *Universal Human Rights in Theory and Practice* (Ithaca: Cornell University Press, 1989).

Doornbos, Martin. "The African State in Academic Debate: Retrospect and Prospect," *Journal of Modern African Studies* 28 (1990), 177–98.

Dore, Isak I. *The International Mandate System and Namibia* (Boulder, CO: Westview, 1985).

Dorkenoo, Efua and Scilla Elworthy. *Female Genital Mutilation: Proposals for Change* (London: Minority Rights Group International, 1994).

Dueck, Judith. "HURIDOCS Standard Formats as a Tool in the Documentation of Human Rights Violations," in Thomas B. Jabine and Richard P. Claude, eds.,

Human Rights and Statistics: Getting the Record Straight (Philadelphia: University of Pennsylvania Press, 1992), pp. 127–58.

Dugard, John. "Secession: Is the Case of Yugoslavia a Precedent for Africa?" *African Journal of International and Comparative Law* 5 (1993), 163–75.

———, ed. *The SouthWest Africa/Namibia Dispute* (Berkeley: University of California Press, 1973).

Egeland, Jan and Thomas Krebs, eds. *Third World Organisational Development: A Comparison of NGO Strategies* (Geneva: Henry Dunant Institute, HDI Series on Development No. 1, 1987).

Ehindero, S. G. *Police and The Law in Nigeria* (Lagos: Times Press, 1986).

Ehrlich, Haggai. *The Struggle over Eritrea 1962–1978: War and Revolution in the Horn of Africa* (Stanford: Hoover Institution, 1983).

Ekeh, Peter. "Colonialism and the Two Publics in Africa: A Theoretical Statement," *Comparative Studies in Society and History* 17 (1975), 91–112.

———. "Historical and Cross-Cultural Contexts of Civil Society in Africa," unpublished paper presented at the USAID workshop on Civil Society, Democracy and Development in Africa, Washington DC, June 9–10, 1994.

———. "The Structure and Meaning of Federal Character in the Nigerian Constitution," in P. Ekeh and E. Osaghae, eds., *Federal Character and Federalism in Nigeria* (Ibadan: Heinemann, 1989).

Elmadmad, Khadija. "Les droits de la femme dans la charte africaine des droits de l'homme et des peuples," *Afrique 2000: Revue africaine de politique internationale* 14 (1993), 21–37.

Erasmus, Gerhard. "The Namibian Constitution and the Application of International Law," *South African Yearbook of International Law* 15 (1989/90) (Cape Town: VerLoren van Themaat Centre for International Law, 1990), 81–110.

Ese, Osita C. "The Organization of African Unity and Human Rights: 25 Years After," *Nigerian Journal of International Affairs* 14 (1988), 154–88.

EyaNchama, C.M. *Développement et droits de l'homme en Afrique* (Paris: Publisud, 1991).

Falola, Toyin and Julius Ihonvbere. *The Rise and Fall of Nigeria's Second Republic* (London: Zed Press, 1985).

Feuer, Guy and Hervé Cassan. *Droit international du développement* (Paris: Dalloz, 1991, 2nd edition).

FIDH and others. "Rapport de la Commission Internationale d'Enquête sur les Violations des Droits de l'Homme au Rwanda depuis le 1er Octobre 1990 (7–21 janvier 1993)" (Paris: Fédération Internationale des Droits de l'Homme [FIDH]; New York: Africa Watch; Ouagadougou: Union Interafricaine des Droits de l'Homme et des Peuples [UIDH]; Montreal: Centre International des Droits de la Personne et du Développement démocratique [CIDPDD], 1993).

Fisher, Julie. *The Road from Rio: Sustainable Development and the Nongovernmental Movement in the Third World* ((Westport, CT: Praeger, 1993).

Flinterman, Cees and Evelyn Ankumah. "The African Charter on Human and Peoples' Rights," in Hurst Hannum, ed., *Guide to International Human Rights Practice* (Philadelphia: University of Pennsylvania Press, 1992, 2nd edition), pp. 159–69.

Forrest, Joshua Bernard. "Namibia—The First Postapartheid Democracy," *Journal of Democracy* 5, 3 (1994), 88–100.

———. "A Promising Start: The Inauguration and Consolidation of Democracy in Namibia," *World Policy Journal* 19 (1992), 739–53.

——. "The Quest for State 'Hardness' in Africa," *Comparative Politics* 20 (1988), 423–42.

Forsythe, David P. "Human Rights After the Cold War," *Netherlands Quarterly of Human Rights* 11 (1993), 393–412.

——. *Human Rights and World Politics* (Lincoln: University of Nebraska Press, 1989, 2nd edition, revised).

——. *Humanitarian Politics: The International Committee of the Red Cross* (Baltimore: Johns Hopkins University Press, 1977).

Forsythe, David P.. *The Internationalization of Human Rights* (Lexington MA: Lexington Books, 1991).

—— and Kelly Kate Pease. "Human Rights, Humanitarian Intervention, and World Politics," *Human Rights Quarterly* 15 (1993), 290–314.

Fosu, Augustin Kwasi. "Political Instability and Economic Growth: Evidence from Sub-Saharan Africa," *Economic Development and Cultural Change* 30 (1992), 829–42.

Fowler, Alan. "Distant Obligations: Speculations on NGO Funding and the Global Market," *Review of African Political Economy* 55 (1992), 9–29.

——. "Non-Governmental Organizations as Agents of Democratization: An African Perspective," *Journal of International Development* 5 (1993), 325–39.

——. "Non-Governmental Organisations in Africa: Achieving Comparative Advantage in Relief and Micro-Development" (Brighton: Institute of Development Studies, University of Sussex, Discussion Paper 249, 1988).

——. "The Role of NGOs in Changing State-Society Relations: Perspectives from Eastern and Southern Africa," *Development Policy Review* 9 (1991), 53–84.

Fox, Gregory H. "The Right to Political Participation in International Law," *Yale Journal of International Law* 17, 2 (1992), 539–607.

Franck, Thomas M. "The Emerging Right to Democratic Governance," *American Journal of International Law* 86 (1992), 46–91.

Freedom House. *Freedom in the World* (New York: Freedom House, annual).

Freeman, Marsha A. "Women, Law, and Land at the Local Level: Claiming Women's Human Rights in Domestic Legal Systems," *Human Rights Quarterly* 16 (1994), 559–75.

Fund for Peace. "Human Rights Education: Strategies for Fostering Participatory Democracy in Ethiopia" (New York: The Fund, 1993).

Gaer, Felice D. "First Fruits: Reporting by States under the African Charter of Human and Peoples' Rights," *Netherlands Quarterly of Human Rights* 10 (1992), 29–42.

Gahia, Chukwuemeka. *Human Rights in Retreat: A Report on Seven Years of Human Rights Violations by the Military Regime of General Ibrahim Babingida, August 1985 to August 1992* (Lagos: Civil Liberties Organisation, 1993).

Garber, Larry. "The OAU and Elections," *Journal of Democracy* 4 (1993), 55–59.

García-Amador, F.V. *The Emerging International Law of Development: A New Dimension of International Economic Law* (New York: Oceana, 1990).

Garling, Marguerite, compiler. *The Human Rights Handbook: A Guide to British and American International Human Rights Organizations* (London: Macmillan for Writers and Scholars Educational Trust, 1979).

Gashaw, Solomon. "Nationalism and Ethnic Conflict in Ethiopia," in Crawford Young, ed., *The Rising Tide of Cultural Pluralism: The Nation-State at Bay?* (Madison: University of Wisconsin Press, 1993), pp. 138–57.

Geschieri, Peter and Jos Van der Klei. "La relation état-paysans et ses ambivalences: modes populaires d'action politique chez les Maka (Cameroun) et les

Diola (Casamance)," in Emmanuel Terray, ed., *L'état contemporain en Afrique* (Paris: Harmattan, 1987), pp. 297–340.

Gezelius, Helena. "NGOs in Development and Participation in Practice: An Initial Inquiry" (Stockholm: Popular Participation Programme, working paper, 1988, vol. 3).

Gilkes, Patrick. *The Dying Lion: Feudalism and Modernization in Ethiopia* (London: Julian Friedmann, 1975).

Gillies, David and Clarence Dias. *Human Rights, Democracy and Development* (Geneva: UN Centre for Human Rights, 1992).

Gills, Barry and Noel Rocamora. "Low Intensity Democracy," *Third World Quarterly* 13 (1992), 501–23.

Ginther, Konrad. "The domestic policy function of a right of peoples to development: popular participation[,] a new hope for development and challenge for the discipline," in Subrata Roy Chowdhury, Erik M. G. Denters and Paul J. I. M. de Waart, eds., *The Right to Development in International Law* (Dordrecht: Martinus Nijhoff, 1992), pp. 61–82.

Glickman, Harvey. "Frontiers of Liberal and Non-Liberal Democracy in Tropical Africa," *Journal of Asian and African Studies* 23 (1988), 234–54.

Gonidec, P. F. "Démocratie et développement en Afrique: Perspectives internationales et nationales," *Afrique 2000* 14 (1994), 49–60.

Gorman, Robert F., ed. *Private Voluntary Organizations as Agents of Development* (Boulder, CO: Westview, 1984).

Gros Espiell, Hector. *The Right to Self-Determination: Implementation of United Nations Resolutions* (New York: United Nations, 1980).

Guest, Iain. *Behind the Disappearances: Argentina's Dirty War Against Human Rights and the United Nations* (Philadelphia: University of Pennsylvania Press, 1990).

Gupta, Dipak K., Albert J. Jongman and Alex Schmid. "Creating a Composite Index for Assessing Country Performance in the Field of Human Rights," *Human Rights Quarterly* 16 (1994), 131–62.

Gutto, Shadrack B. O. *Human and Peoples' Rights for the Oppressed: Critical Essays on Theory and Practice from Sociology of Law Perspectives* (Lund: Lund University Press, 1993).

——. "Non-governmental Organizations, People's Participation and the African Commission on Human and Peoples' Rights: Emerging Challenges to Regional Protection of Human Rights," in Bard-Anders Andreassen and Theresa Swinehart, eds., *Human Rights in Developing Countries Yearbook 1991* (Oslo: Scandinavian University Press, 1992), pp. 33–54.

——. "The Role of Mass Struggles in the Search for Popular Democracy and Integrated Human Rights in Africa: Aspects of Theory and Practice," *Review of the African Commission on Human and Peoples' Rights* 2, 1 & 2 (1992), 71–85.

Guy, Gran, ed. *Development by People: Grassroots Participation in the Third World* (New York: Praeger, 1983).

Gye-Wado, Onje. "The Rule of Admissibility under the African Charter on Human and Peoples' Rights," *African Journal of International and Comparative Law* 3 (1991), 742–55.

Hall, H. Duncan. *Mandates, Dependencies, and Trusteeships* (Washington, DC: Carnegie Endowment for International Peace, 1948).

Halliday, Fred and Maxine Molleyneaux. *The Ethiopian Revolution* (London: Verso, 1981).

Halperin, Morton. "Guaranteeing Democracy," *Foreign Policy* 91 (1993), 105–22.

Hamalengwa, M., C. Flinterman and E. V. O. Dankwa. *The International Law of*

Human Rights in Africa: Basic Documents and Annotated Bibliography (Dordrecht: Martinus Hijhoff, 1988).

Hannum, Hurst. *Autonomy, Sovereignty and Self-Determination: The Accommodation of Conflicting Rights* (Philadelphia: University of Pennsylvania Press, 1990).

——, ed. *Guide to International Human Rights Practice* (Philadelphia: University of Pennslyvania Press, 1992, 2nd edition).

Hansohm, Dirk. "The Role of African Non-Governmental Organizations in Development: An Introduction," in Karl Wohlmuth et al., eds., *African Development Perspectives Yearbook 1989*, Vol. I, Human Dimensions of Adjustment (Berlin: Schelzy and Jeep for Research Group on African Development Perspectives Bremen, 1990), pp. 563–74.

Hartmann, Lori. "Indigenous Rebellion in the Casamance," *Fourth World Bulletin* 3, 1 (December 1993), 14–16.

Hassan, Mohammed. *The Oromo of Ethiopia: A History 1570–1860* (Cambridge: Cambridge University Press, 1990).

Hay, Margaret Jean and Sharon Stichter, eds. *African Women South of the Sahara* (White Plains, NY: Longman, 1984).

Healey, John and Mark Robinson. *Democracy, Governance and Economic Policy: Sub-Saharan Africa in Comparative Perspective* (London: Overseas Development Institute, 1992).

Heilbrunn, John R. "The Social Origins of National Conferences: A Comparison of Benin and Togo," *Journal of Modern African Studies* 31 (1993), 277–299.

Helmich, Henny, Chantal Mohrmann, and Shamita Sharma. "Partners in Development, Democracy and Global Justice: Non-Governmental Organisations in OECD Countries Active in Human Rights, Refugee and Migrant Assistance and Development," in *Human Rights, Refugees, Migrants & Development: Directory of NGOs in OECD Countries* (Paris: OECD Development Centre, 1992), pp. 68–78.

Heraclides, Alexis. *The Self-Determination of Minorities in International Politics* (London: Cass, 1991).

Hess, Robert L. *Ethiopia: The Modernizing of Autocracy* (Ithaca, NY: Cornell University Press, 1970).

Higgins, Rosalyn. "Africa and the Covenant on Civil and Political Rights During the First Five Years of the *Journal,*" *African Journal of International and Comparative Law* 5, 1 (March 1993), 55–66.

Horowitz, Donald L. *Ethnic Groups in Conflict* (Berkeley: University of California Press, 1985).

Hosken, Fran P. *The Hosken Report: Genital and Sexual Mutilation of Females* (Lexington, MA: Women's International Network News, 1994, 4th revised edition).

Hovde, Robert L. "Democracy and Governance in Ethiopia: A Survey of Institutions, Issues, and Initiatives in the Transitional Period," unpublished paper presented at the XIIth International Conference of Ethiopian Studies, September 5–10, 1994, Michigan State University.

——. "Nongovernmental Organizations: Development and Advocacy in Changing Political Environments," unpublished paper.

Howard, Rhoda and Jack Donnelly. "Human Dignity, Human Rights and Political Regimes," *American Political Science Review* 80 (1986), 801–17.

——. *Human Rights in Commonwealth Africa* (Totowa, NJ: Rowman and Littlefield, 1986).

——. "Human Rights and Democratization in Nigeria, Comparison with Indonesia," *Netherlands Quarterly of Human Rights* 10 (1992), 414–46.

——. "Human Rights, Development and Foreign Policy," in David P. Forsythe, ed., *Human Rights and Development: International Views* (New York: St. Martin's, 1989), pp. 213–34.

Human Rights Internet. *Africa: Directory and Bibliography* (special issue of *HRI Reporter* 12, 4 [1988/89]).

———. "A Listing of Organizations Concerned with Human Rights and Social Justice Worldwide" (supplement to *HRI Reporter* 15, 1994).

Human Rights Watch. *Human Rights Watch World Report* (New York: Human Rights Watch, annual).

———. "Indivisible Human Rights: The Relationship of Political and Civil Rights to Survival, Subsistence and Poverty" (New York: Human Rights Watch, 1992).

Human Rights Watch/Africa. "Ethiopia: Reckoning Under the Law" (Washington, DC: Human Rights Watch/Africa, 1994).

———. "Nigeria, On the Eve of 'Change': A Transition to What?" (New York: Africa Watch, 1991).

———. "Nigeria, Contradicting Itself: An Undemocratic Transition Seeks To Bring Democracy Nearer" (Washington, DC: Africa Watch, 1992).

———. "Nigeria, 'The Dawn of a New Dark Age': Human Rights Abuses Rampant as Nigerian Military Declares Absolute Power" (Washington, DC: Africa Watch, 1993).

———. "Nigeria, Democracy Derailed: Hundreds Arrested and Press Muzzled in Aftermath of Election Annulment" (Washington, DC: Africa Watch, 1993.

———. "Nigeria, Threats to a New Democracy: Human Rights Concerns at Election Time" (Washington, DC: Africa Watch, 1993).

———. "Prison Conditions in Zaire" (New York: Human Rights Watch/Africa, January 1994).

Hunt, Paul. "Children's Rights in West Africa: The Case of The Gambia's *Almudos,*" *Human Rights Quarterly* 15, 3 (1993), 499–532.

Huntington, Samuel P. "How Countries Democratize," *Political Science Quarterly* 106 (1992), 579–616.

———. "Political Development in Ethiopia: A Peasant-Based Dominant-Party Democracy?" (unpublished paper submitted to the Constitutional Commission of Ethiopia, 1993; financed by USAID).

———. *Political Order in Changing Societies* (New Haven, CT: Yale University Press, 1968).

———. *The Third Wave: Democratization in the Late Twentieth Century* (Norman: University of Oklahoma Press, 1991).

HURIDOCS Standard Formats: A Tool for Documenting Human Rights Violations (Geneva: HURIDOCS, 1993).

HURIDOCS Supporting Documents (Geneva: HURIDOCS, 1993).

Hyden, Goren. *No Shortcuts to Progress* (Berkeley: University of California Press, 1983).

Ibidapo-Obe, Aki. "Remedies for Breach of Fundamental Rights," in M. A. Ajomo and Bolaji Owasanoye, eds., *Individual Rights Under the 1989 Constitution* (Lagos: Nigerian Institute of Advanced Legal Studies, 1993), pp. 84–96.

Ibidapo-Obe, Aki and Clement Nwankwo. "The Bail Process and Human Rights in Nigeria" (Lagos: Constitutional Rights Project, 1992).

Ihonvbere, Julius O. "A Critical Evaluation of the Failed 1990 Coup in Nigeria," *Journal of Modern African Studies* 29 (1991), 601–26.

———. "The Military and Political Engineering Under Structural Adjustment: The Nigerian Experience Since 1985," *Journal of Military and Political Sociology* 20, 1 (1992), 107–32.

Imam, Ayesha. "Democratization Processes in Africa: Problems and Prospects," *Review of African Political Economy* 54 (July 1992), 102–105.

Innes, Judith Eleanor. "Human Rights Reporting as a Policy Tool: An Examination of the State Department Country Reports," in Thomas B. Jabine and Richard P. Claude, eds., *Human Rights and Statistics: Getting the Record Straight* (Philadelphia: University of Pennsylvania Press, 1992), pp. 235–57.

International Commission of Jurists. *African Conference on the Rule of Law: A Report on the Proceedings* (Geneva: ICJ, 1961).

——. *Development, Human Rights and the Rule of Law: Report of a Conference held in The Hague on 27 April–1 May 1981* (Oxford: Pergamon Press, 1981).

——. *Human and Peoples' Rights in Africa and the African Charter* (Geneva: ICJ, 1986).

International Human Rights Internship Program and Swedish NGO Foundation for Human Rights. *The Status of Human Rights Organizations in Sub-Saharan Africa* (Washington, DC and Stockholm: 1994).

International Human Rights Law Group. *Ethiopia in Transition: A Report on the Judiciary and the Legal Profession* (Washington, DC: The Group, 1994).

International Human Rights Organisations: The Meaning of Their Work for Local Organizations with Case Studies from the Philippines, Indonesia and Sri Lanka (The Hague: NOVIB, 1992).

International Society for Human Rights. "No Escape from Misery? The Situation of SWAPO Detainees and Namibian Refugees in the Transitional Period towards an independent Namibia" (Frankfurt: The Society, 1989).

Irele, Abiola. "The Crisis of Legitimacy in Africa," *Dissent* 39 (1992), 296–302.

Iyob, Ruth. "Regional Hegemony: Domination and Resistance in the Horn of Africa," *Journal of Modern African Studies* 31 (1993), 277-99.

Jacobson, Jodi L. *Gender Bias: Roadblock to Sustainable Development* (Washington, DC: Worldwatch Institute, Paper 110, 1992).

Jalata, Asafa. *Oromia and Ethiopia: State Formation and Ethnonational Conflict, 1868–1992* (Boulder, CO: Lynne Rienner, 1992).

Jason, Karen J. "The Role of Non-Governmental Organizations in International Election Observing," *New York University Journal of International Law and Politics* 24 (1992), 1795–1843.

Johnson, Willard R. and Vivian R. Johnson. *West African Governments and Volunteer Development Organizations: Priorities for Partnership* (Lanham MD: University Press of America, 1990).

Jones, Dorothy V. "The League of Nations Experiment in International Protection," *Ethics and International Affairs* 8 (1994), 77–95.

Joseph, Richard. *Democracy and Prebendal Politics in Nigeria: The Rise and Fall of the Second Republic* (Cambridge: Cambridge University Press, 1987).

Kalu, Awa U. and Yemi Osinbajo, eds. *Perspectives on Human Rights* (Lagos: Federal Ministry of Justice, 1992).

Kamararotos, Alexander S. "A View into NGO Networks in Human Rights Activities: NGO Action with Special Reference to the UN Commission on Human Rights and its Sub-Commission" (Geneva: Graduate Institute of International Studies, 1993).

Kamminga, Menno T. *Inter-State Accountability for Violations of Human Rights* (Philadelphia: University of Pennsylvania Press, 1992).

Kannyo, Edward. "The OAU and Human Rights," in Yassin El-Ayouty and I. Willliam Zartman, eds., *The OAU After Twenty Years* (New York: Praeger, 1984), pp. 155–72.

Kanté, Babakar. "Senegal's Empty Election," *Journal of Democracy* 5 (1994), 96–108.

Karsai, Ferenc. "The Right of Self-Determination in Africa: A Contribution," *Africana Gandensia* 6 (1989), 75–103.

Kasfir, Nelson. "Popular Sovereignty and Popular Participation: Mixed Constitutional Democracy in the Third World," *Third World Quarterly* 13, 4 (1992), 587–605.

Katjavivi, Peter H. *A History of Resistance in Namibia* (London: James Currey, 1988).

Katjavivi, Peter H., Per Frostin, and Kaire Mbuende, eds. *Church and Liberation in Namibia* (London: Pluto, 1981).

Kaufman, Edy. "Prisoners of Conscience: The Shaping of a New Human Rights Concept," *Human Rights Quarterly* 13 (1991), 339–67.

Kaufman, Natalie Hevener. *Human Rights Treaties and the Senate: A History of Opposition* (Chapel Hill: University of North Carolina Press, 1990).

Keller, Edward. *Revolutionary Ethiopia: From Empire to People's Republic* (Bloomington: Indiana University Press, 1988).

Kerr, Joanna, ed. *Ours by Right: Women's Rights as Human Rights* (London: Zed, 1993).

Kiwanuka, Richard N. "The Meaning of 'People' in the African Charter on Human and Peoples' Rights," *American Journal of International Law* 82 (1988), 80–101.

Klabbers, J. and René Lefeber. "Africa: Lost Between Self-Determination and Uti Possidetis," in Catherine Bröhmann, René Lefeber and Marjoleine Zieck, eds., *Peoples and Minorities in International Law* (Dordrecht: Martinus Nijhoff, 1993), pp. 37–76.

Knight, David B. and Maureen Davies. *Self-Determination: An Interdisciplinary Annotated Bibliography* (New York: Garland, 1987).

Kodjo, Edem. "The African Charter on Human and People's Rights," *Human Rights Law Journal* 11 (1990), 271–83.

Konaté, Abdourahmane. *Le problème casamançais: mythe ou réalité? Un ancien préfet temoigne* (Dakar: The author, 1993).

Korten, David C. *Getting to the 21st Century: Voluntary Action and the Global Agenda* (West Hartford, CT: Kumarian Press, 1990).

Koso-Thomas, Olayinka. *The Circumcision of Women: A Strategy for Eradication* (London: Zed, 1992).

Koso-Thomas, Olayinka and Mabel E. Willoughby. "Report on Traditional Practices and their Influence on the Choice of Contraceptives among Women in Sierra Leone" (Geneva: WHO and IAC, 1994).

Kpundeh, Sahr J. and Stephen P. Riley. "Political Choice and the New Democratic Politics in Africa," *Round Table* 323 (July 1992), 263–72.

Kufuor, Kofi Oteng. "Safeguarding Human Rights: A Critique of the African Commission on Human and People's Rights," *Africa Development* 18 (1993), 65–77.

Kumado, Kofi and Nana K.A. Busia, Jr. "The Impact of Development in Eastern Europe on the Democratization Process in Africa: An Exploratory Analysis," in Bard-Anders Andreassen and Theresa Swinehart, eds., *Human Rights in Developing Countries Yearbook 1990* (Oslo: Scandinavian University Press, 1991), pp. 3–17.

Kumssa, Asfaw. "The National Question and the Right to Self-Determination in Ethiopia: The Case of the Oromo," in Marc A. Sills and Glenn T. Morris, eds.,

Indigenous Peoples' Politics: An Introduction (Denver: Fourth World Center for the Study of Indigenous Law and Politics, 1993), pp. 135–46.

Kunig, Philip. "The Protection of Human Rights by International Law in Africa," *German Yearbook of International Law* 25 (1982), 138–68.

Kunig, Philip, Wolfgang Benedek and Costa Ricky Mahalu. *Regional Protection of Human Rights by International Law: The Emerging African System* (Baden-Baden: Nomos, 1985).

Kuper, Leo. *Genocide: Its Political Use in the Twentieth Century* (New Haven, CT: Yale University Press, 1981).

Laing, Edward A. "The Norm of Self-Determination, 1941–1991," *California Western International Law Journal* 22 (1992), 209–308.

Landis, Elisabeth. "Namibia and Human Rights," *Revue de Droits de l'Homme, Droit International et Droit Comparé* 9 (1976), 283–339.

Lawyers Committee for Human Rights. "Malawi: Ignoring Calls for Change" (New York: The Committee, 1992).

——. "The Nigerian Police Force: A Culture of Impunity" (New York: The Committee, 1992).

Leary, Virginia. "The Asian Region and the International Human Rights Movement," in Claude E. Welch, Jr. and Virginia Leary, eds., *Asian Perspectives on Human Rights* (Boulder, CO: Westview, 1990), pp. 13–27.

——. "Lessons from the Experience of the International Labour Organisation," in Philip Alston, ed., *The United Nations and Human Rights: A Critical Evaluation* (Oxford: Clarendon Press, 1992), pp. 580–619.

——. "A New Role for Non-Governmental Organizations in Human Rights: A Case Study of Non-Governmental Participation in the Development of International Norms on Torture," in Antonio Cassese, ed., *U.N. Law/Fundamental Rights* (Alphen aan den Rijn: Sitjhoff and Noordhoff, 1979), pp.197–210.

Leatherbee, Leah and Dale Bricker. "Balancing Consensus and Dissent: The Prospects for Human Rights and Democracy in the Horn of Africa" (New York: The Fund for Peace, 1994).

Lemarchand, René. "Africa's Troubled Transitions," *Journal of Democracy* 3, 4 (1992), 98–109.

——. "Uncivil States and Civil Societies: How Illusion Became Reality," *Journal of Modern African Studies* 30, 2 (1992), 177–92.

Lerner, Natan. *Group Rights and Discrimination in International Law* (Dordrecht: Martinus Nijhoff, 1991).

Levine, Donald N. *Greater Ethiopia: The Evolution of a Multiethnic Society* (Chicago: University of Chicago Press, 1974).

——. *Wax and Gold: Tradition and Innovation in Ethiopian Culture* (Chicago: University of Chicago Press, 1967).

Lewis, Herbert S. "Ethnicity in Ethiopia: The View from Below (and from the South, East, and West)," in Crawford Young, ed., *The Rising Tide of Cultural Pluralism: The Nation-State at Bay?* (Madison: University of Wisconsin Press, 1993), pp. 158–78.

Lewis, Peter. "Political Transition and the Dilemma of Civil Society in Africa," *Journal of International Affairs* 27 (1992), 31–54.

Lighfoot-Klein, Hanny. *Prisoners of Ritual: An Odyssey into Female Genital Mutilation in Africa* (New York: Haworth Press, 1989).

Linares, Olga F. *Power, Prayer and Production: The Jola of Casamance* (Cambridge: Cambridge University Press, 1992).

Lipset, Seymour Martin, Kyoung-Ryung Seong and John Charles Torres. "A Comparative Analysis of the Social Requisites of Democracy," *International Social Science Journal* 136 (May 1993), 155–75.

Little, Kenneth. *West African Urbanization: A Study of Voluntary Associations* (Cambridge: Cambridge University Press, 1965).

Livezey, Lionel W. *Non-Governmental Organizations and the Idea of Human Rights* (Princeton: Center for International Studies, 1988).

——. "U.S. Religious Organizations and the International Human Rights Movement," *Human Rights Quarterly* 11, 1 (1989), 14–82.

Lopez, George A. "Data Sources and Data Needs in Human Rights Monitoring," in Alex P. Schmid and Albert J. Jongman, eds., *Monitoring Human Rights Violations* (Leiden: Centre for the Study of Social Conflicts, 1992), pp. 47–62.

Lopez, George A. and Michael Stohl. "Problems of Concept and Measurement in the Study of Human Rights," in Thomas B. Jabine and Richard P. Claude, eds., *Human Rights and Statistics: Getting the Record Straight* (Philadelphia: University of Pennsylvania Press, 1992), pp. 216–24.

Louis, William Roger. "African Origins of the Mandates Idea," *International Organization* 19 (1965), 20–36.

Luckham, Robin. *The Nigerian Military: A Sociological Analysis of Authority and Revolt, 1960–67* (Cambridge: Cambridge University Press, 1971).

Lush, David. *Last Steps to Uhuru* (Windhoek: New Namibia Books, 1993).

MacChesney, Alan. "The Promotion of Economic and Political Rights: Two African Approaches," *Journal of African Law* 24 (1980), 163–205.

Machida, Robert. *Eritrea: The Struggle for Independence* (Trenton, NJ: Red Sea Press, 1987).

Magnarella, Paul J. "Preventing Interethnic Conflict and Promoting Human Rights Through More Effective Legal, Political, and Aid Structures: Focus on Africa," *Georgia Journal of International and Comparative Law* 23 (1993), 327–45.

Mahmud, Sakah Saidu. "The State and Human Rights in Africa in the 1990s: Perspectives and Prospects," *Human Rights Quarterly* 15 (1993), 485–98.

Makonnen, Yilma. *International Law and the New States of Africa: A Study of the International Legal Problems of State Succession in the Newly Independent States of Eastern Africa* (Paris: UNESCO, 1983).

Mamdami, Mahmood. "Africa: Democratic Theory and Democratic Struggles," *Dissent* 39 (1992), 312–18.

Marcus, Harold. *Haile Selassie* (Berkeley and Los Angeles: University of California Press, 1987).

Marantis, Demetrios James. "Human Rights, Democracy, and Development: The European Community Model," *Harvard Human Rights Journal* 7 (1994), 1–32.

Markakis, John. *Ethiopia: Anatomy of a Traditional Polity* (Oxford: Clarendon Press, 1974).

——. *National and Class Conflict in the Horn of Africa* (Cambridge: Cambridge University Press, 1987).

Markakis, John and Nega Ayele. *Class and Revolution in Ethiopia* (Nottingham: Spokesman, 1978).

Mathews, K. "The OAU and Political Economy of Human Rights in Africa: An Analysis of the African Charter on Human and Peoples' Rights," *Africa Today* 34 (1987), 85–104.

Mbaya, Etienne-Richard. "The Compatibility of Regional Human Rights Systems with International Standards," in Asbjorn Eide and Bernt Hagtvet, eds., *Human Rights in Perspective: A Global Assessment* (Oxford: Blackwell, 1992), pp. 66–89.

Mbaye, Kéba. "Le droit de développement comme un droit de l'homme," *Revue des Droits de l'Homme* 5 (1972), 503–534.

——. *Les droits de l'homme en Afrique* (Paris: Pedone, 1992).

——. "Human Rights in Africa," in Karel Vasak and Philip Alston, eds., *The International Dimensions of Human Rights* (Paris: UNESCO, 1982), pp. 583–601.

McCorquodale, Robert. "Self-Determination Beyond the Colonial Context and Its Potential Impact on Africa," *African Journal of International and Comparative Law* 4, 3 (October 1992), 592–608.

McDougall, Gay J. "International Law, Human Rights, and Namibian Independence," *Human Rights Quarterly* 8 (1986), 443–70.

McFerson, Hazel M. "Democracy and Development in Africa," *Journal of Peace Research* 29 (1992), 241–48.

McGoldrick, Dominic W. *The Human Rights Committee: Its Role in the Development of the International Covenant on Civil and Political Rights* (Oxford: Clarendon Press, 1991).

Mesfin Wolde-Mariam. *Rural Vulnerablity to Famine in Ethiopia 1958–77* (London: Intermediate Technology Publications, 1986).

——. *Suffering Under God's Environment: A Vertical Study of Peasant in North-Central Ethiopia* (Berne: African Mountains Association, Geographica Bernensia, 1991).

Mgoqi, Wallace. "The Work of the Legal Resource Centre in South Africa in the Area of Human Rights Promotion and Protection," *Journal of African Law* 36 (1992), 1–10.

Micou, Ann McKinstry and Birgit Lindsnaes, eds., *The Role of Voluntary Organisations in Emerging Democracies: Experience and Strategies in Eastern and Central Europe and in South Africa* (New York and Copenhagen: Institute of International Education and Danish Centre for Human Rights, 1993).

Moore, Mick and Mark Robinson. "Can Foreign Aid Be Used to Promote Good Government in Developing Countries?" *Ethics and International Affairs* 8 (1994), 141–55.

Morrison, J. Stephen. "Ethiopia Charts a New Course," *Journal of Democracy* 3, 3 (July 1992), 125–37.

Motala, Ziyad. "Human Rights in Africa: A Cultural, Ideological and Legal Examination," *Hastings International and Comparative Law Review* 12 (1989), 373–410.

Mower, A. Glenn. "Human Rights in Black Africa: A Double Standard?" *Revue des Droits de l'Homme, Droit International et Droit Comparé* 9 (1976), 39–70.

Muller, Jean-David. *Les ONG ambigües: Aides aux États, aides aux populations* (Paris: Harmattan, 1989).

Namibia, Republic of. *National Programme of Action for the Children of Namibia* (Windhoek: Capital Press, 1991).

Nanda, Ved. "Self-Determination Under International Law: Validity of Claims to Secede," *Case Western Reserve Journal of International Law* 13 (1981), 257–80.

Nanda, Ved, George W. Shepherd, and Eileen McCarthy-Arnold, eds. *World Debt and the Human Condition: Structural Adjustment and the Right to Development* (Westport, CT: Greenwood, 1993).

National Democratic Institute for International Affairs and African-American Institute. *An Evaluation of the June 21, 1992 Elections in Ethiopia* (Washington: NDI, 1992).

——. *International Delegation Report on the October 11, 1992 Presidential Election in Cameroon* (Washington: NDI, 1992).

——. *The October 31, 1991 National Elections in Zambia* (Washington: NDI, 1992).

National Election Monitoring Unit (NEMU), *The Multi-Party General Elections in Kenya 29 December, 1992* (Nairobi: NEMU, 1993).

National Society of Human Rights. *'Etopola', The Practice of Torture and Other Cruel, Inhuman or Degrading Treatment or Punishment in Present-Day Namibia* (Windhoek: April 1, 1993).

———. *The Namibia Country Report on the Status of the UN Convention on the Rights of the Child: A Critical Analysis* (Windhoek: 1992).

———. *Annual Human Rights Report for 1992* (Windhoek: January 12, 1993).

Ndiaye, Birame. "The Place of Human Rights in the Charter of the Organization of African Unity," in Karel Vasak and Philip Alston, eds., *The International Dimensions of Human Rights* (Paris: UNESCO, 1982), pp. 601–16.

Nelson, Joan M., ed., *Economic Crisis and Policy Choice: The Politics of Adjustment in the Third World* (Princeton, NJ: Princeton University Press, 1990).

Nelson, Joan and Stephanie J. Eglinton. *Encouraging Democracy: What Role for Conditional Aid?* (Washington, DC: Overseas Development Council, 1992).

Neuberger, Benjamin. *National Self-Determination in Postcolonial Africa* (Boulder, CO: Lynne Rienner, 1986).

Ngom, Benoît. *Les droits de l'homme et l'Afrique* (Paris: Silex, 1984).

Ngoyi, Rev. Fr. John Patrick and Emma O'mano Edigheji. *The Church and Human Rights* (Lagos: Human Rights Committee, Ijebu-Ode Catholic Diocese and Civil Liberties Organisation, 1993).

Nguéma, Isaac. "L'Afrique, les droits de l'homme et le devéloppement," *Review of the African Commission on Human and Peoples' Rights* 1 (1991), 16–50.

———. "[La] Commission Africaine des droits de l'homme et des peuples," UN document A/CONF.157/PC/62/Add.2, 23 mars 1993.

———. "Contribution relative à la Commission africaine des droits de l'homme et des peuples," UN Document A/CONF.157/PC/62/Add.2, p. 3.

Nieman, Michael. "Regional Integration and the Right to Development in Africa," in Eileen McCarthy-Arnolds, David R. Penna, and Debra Joy Cruz Sobrepeña, eds., *Africa, Human Rights, and the Global System: The Political Economy of Human Rights in a Changing World* (Westport, CT.: Greenwood, 1994), pp. 107–127.

Nnaemeka-Agu, Justice Philip. "The Role of Lawyers in the Protection and Advancement of Human Rights," *Commonwealth Law Bulletin* 18 (1992), 734–46.

Nolotshungu, Samuel. "Africa in a World of Democracies: Interpretation and Retrieval," *Journal of Commonwealth and Comparative Political Studies* 30, 3 (1992), 316–64.

Nsereko, Daniel D. Ntanda. "The Police, Human Rights and the Constitution: An African Perspective," *Human Rights Quarterly* 15 (1993), 465–84.

Nwakwo, Arthur Agwuncha. *Nigeria: The Political Transition and the Future of Democracy* (Enugu: Fourth Dimension, 1993).

Nwankwo, Clement. "The OAU and Human Rights," *Journal of Democracy* 4 (1992), 50–54.

Nwankwo, Clement, Frank Aigbogun, Eluem Emeka Izeze, and Dulue Mbachu. "The Crisis of Press Freedom in Nigeria" (Lagos: Constitutional Rights Project, 1993).

Nwankwo, Clement, Dulue Mbochu, and Basil Ugochukwu. "Human Rights Practices in the Nigerian Police" (Lagos: Constitutional Rights Project, 1993).

Nwankwo, Clement, Dulue Mbochu, and Basil Ugochukwu. "Nigeria: The Limits of Justice" (Lagos: Constitutional Rights Project, 1993).

Nyang'oro, Julius E. "Reform Politics and the Democratization Process in Africa," *African Studies Review* 37 (1994), 133–49.

Nyong'o, Anyang P. "Political Instability and the Prospects for Democracy in Africa," *Africa Development* 13 (1988), 71–86.

——. "Democratization Processes in Africa," *Review of African Political Economy* 54 (July 1992), 97–102.

Oberleitner, Gerd and Claude E. Welch, Jr. "15th Session of the African Commission on Human and Peoples' Rights," *Netherlands Quarterly of Human Rights* 12 (1994), 331–34.

Obiora, Amede L. "The Little Foxes That Spoil the Vine: Re-Visiting the Feminist Critique of Female Circumcision in Africa," unpublished paper.

Odinkalu, Anselm Chidi. *Justice Denied: The Area Courts System in the Northern States of Nigeria* (Lagos: Civil Liberties Organisation, 1992).

——. "Proposals for Review of the Rules of Procedure of the African Commission on Human and Peoples' Rights," *Human Rights Quarterly* 15 (1993), 533–48.

O'Donnell, Guillermo, Philippe C. Schmitter, and Laurence Whitehead, eds. *Transitions from Authoritarian Rule* (Baltimore: Johns Hopkins University Press, 1986).

Ojo, Abiola. *Constitutional Law and Military Rule in Nigeria* (Ibadan: Evans Brothers, 1987).

Ojo, Olusola and Amadu Sesay. "The OAU and Human Rights: Prospects for the 1980s and Beyond," *Human Rights Quarterly* 8 (1986), 89–103.

Okere, B. Obinna. "The Protection of Human Rights in Africa and the African Charter on Human and Peoples' Rights: A Comparative Analysis with the European and American Systems," *Human Rights Quarterly* 6 (1984), 141–59.

Olagunjo, Tunji, Adele Jinadu and Sam Oyovbaire. *Transition to Democracy in Nigeria (1985–1993)* (Ibadan: Safari, 1993).

Olson, Mancur. "Dictatorship, Democracy, and Development," *American Political Science Review* 87 (1993), 567–76.

Omoruyi, Omo, W. A. Sambo, and Ada Okwuosa, eds. *Parties, Elections and Election Monitoring in Nigeria 1993* (Abuja: Centre for Democratic Studies, in press).

Oputa, Chukwudifu Akunne. *Human Rights in the Political and Legal Culture of Nigeria* (Lagos: Nigerian Law Publications, 1989).

Organisation for Economic Cooperation and Development. *Voluntary Aid for Development: The Role of NGOs* (Paris: OECD, 1988).

Osaghae, Eghosa E. "The Complexity of Nigeria's Federal Character and the Inadequacies of the Federal Character Principle," *Journal of Ethnic Studies* 16, 1 (1988), 1–25.

——. "Ethnic Minorities and Federalism in Nigeria," *African Affairs* 90 (1991), 237–58.

Othman, Shehu. "Nigeria," in Donal B Cruise O'Brian, John Dunn and Richard Rathbone, eds., *Contemporary West African States* (Cambridge: Cambridge University Press, 1989), pp. 113–44.

Ottaway, Marina and David, Ottaway. *Ethiopia: Empire in Revolution* (New York: Africana, 1978).

Ouguergouz, Fatsah. *La Charte africaine des droits de l'homme et des peuples: Une approche juridique des droits de l'homme entre tradition et modernité* (Paris: Presses Universitaires de France for the Institut Universitaire de Hautes Etudes Internationales Genève, 1993).

Owoade, M. Adekunle. "Human Rights and the Criminal Justice System in Nigeria: From Buhari to Babangida," *Human Rights Law Journal* 9 (1988), 181–203.

Owusu, Maxwell. "Democracy and Africa: A View from the Village," *Journal of Modern African Studies* 30 (1992), 369–96.

Oyediran, Oye and Adigun Agbaje. "Two-Partyism and Democratic Transition in Nigeria," *Journal of Modern African Studies* 29 (1991), 213–35.

Oyugi, Walter O., Atieno Adhiambo, Michael Chege, and Afrifa K. Gitonga, eds. *Democratic Theory and Practice in Africa* (Portsmouth, NH: Heinemann, 1988).

Pallinder, Agneta, ed. *Information for Human Rights: A HURIDOCS Reader for Information Workers* (Geneva: HURIDOCS, 1993).

Parpart, Jane L., ed. *Women and Development in Africa: Comparative Perspectives* (Lanham, MD: University Press of America, 1989).

——. "Women's Rights and the Lagos Plan of Action," *Human Rights Quarterly* 8 (1986), 180–96.

Parpart, Jane L. and Kathleen A. Staudt, eds. *Women and the State in Africa* (Boulder, CO: Lynne Rienner, 1988).

Paul, James C. N. "Participatory Approaches to Human Rights in Sub-Saharan Africa," in Abdullahi A. An-Na'im and Francis N. Deng, eds., *Human Rights in Africa: Cross-Cultural Perspectives* (Washington, DC: Brookings Institution, 1990), pp. 213–39.

——. "Rural Development, Human Rights and Constitutional Orders in Sub-Saharan Africa," *Third World Legal Studies* 1989, 57–84.

Paul, James C. N. and Christopher Clapham, eds., *Sourcebook of Ethiopian Constitutional Law* (Addis Ababa: Faculty of Law, Haile Selassie I University, n.d.)

Pélissier, Paul. *Les paysans du Sénégal: Les civilisations agraires du Cayor à la Casamance* (Saint-Yrieix: Imprimerie Fabrègue, 1966).

Pellet, Alain. *Le droit international du développement* (Paris: Presses Universitaires de France, 1987).

Perham, Margery. *The Government of Ethiopia* (New York: Oxford University Press, 1948).

Poe, Steven C. "Human Rights and Economic Aid Allocations under Ronald Reagan and Jimmy Carter," *American Journal of Political Science* 36 (1992), 147–67.

——. "Human Rights and U.S. Foreign Aid: A Review of Quantitative Studies and Suggestions for Future Research," *Human Rights Quarterly* 12 (1990), 499–512.

Pollack, Alexander J. "The South West Africa Case and the Jurisprudence of International Law," *International Organization* 23 (1969), 767–87.

Pomerance, Michla. *Self-Determination in Law and Practice: The New Doctrine in the United Nations* (The Hague: Nijhoff, 1982).

Poulton, Robin and Michael Harris, eds. *Putting People First: Voluntary Organisations and Third World Development* (London: Macmillan, 1988).

Pritchard, Kathleen. "Human Rights and Development: Theory and Data," in David P. Forsythe, ed., *Human Rights and Development: International Views* (New York: St. Martin's, 1989), pp. 329–45.

Przeworski, Adam and Fernando Limongi. "Political Regimes and Economic Growth," *Journal of Economic Perspectives* 7 (1993), 51–69.

Public Interest Law Around the World: Report of a Symposium Held at Columbia University in May, 1991 With Descriptions of Participating Legal Organizations From Twenty Countries (New York: Columbia Human Rights Law Review and the NAACP-LDF, 1992).

Quaye, Christopher D. *Liberation Struggles in International Law* (Philadelphia: Temple University Press, 1991).

Ramcharan, B. G. *The Concept and Present Status of the International Protection of Human Rights: Forty Years After the Universal Declaration* (Dordrecht: Martinus Nijhoff, 1989).

———. "Strategies for the International Protection of Human Rights in the 1990s," *Human Rights Quarterly* 13 (1991), 155–69.

———. "The Travaux Préparatoires of the African Commission on Human Rights," *Human Rights Law Journal* 13, 7–8 (1992), 307–14.

Rembe, Nasila Selasini. *Africa and Regional Protection of Human Rights: A Study of the African Charter on Human and Peoples' Rights; Its Effectiveness and Impact on the African States* (Roma Lesotho: Center for International Juridical Cooperation, 1985).

———. "The System of Protection of Human Rights under the African Charter on Human and Peoples' Rights: Problems and Prospects" (Roma Lesotho: Institute of Southern African Studies, National University of Lesotho, 1991).

Remmer, Karen L. "Democracy and Economic Crisis," *World Politics* 42 (1990), 315–35.

Rencontre Africaine pour la Défense des Droits de l'Homme [RADDHO]. "Observations sur la réplique du Ministère de la Justice de la République du Sénégal à la communication-plainte du RADDHO" (Dakar: RADDHO, n.d.).

———. "Rapport sur les evenéments de Kaguit Casamance Sénégal, Septembre 1992" (Dakar: RADDHO, 1992).

Rice, Andrew, ed. *The Role of Non-Governmental Organizations in Development Cooperation, Liaison Bulletin Between Development Research and Training* (Paris: OECD Development Center, 1983).

Rich, Roland, "The Right to Development: A Right of Peoples?", in James Crawford, ed., *The Rights of Peoples* (Oxford: Clarendon Press, 1988), pp. 39–54.

Riddell, J. Barry. "Things Fall Apart Again: Structural Adjustment Programmes in Sub-Saharan Africa," *Journal of Modern African Studies* 30 (1992), 113–40.

Riggs, Fred W. "Fragility of Third World's Regimes," *International Social Science Journal* 136 (May 1993), 199–243.

Riley, Stephen P. "Political Adjustment or Domestic Pressure: Democratic Politics and Political Choice in Africa," *Third World Quarterly* 13 (1992), 539–51.

Robertson, A. H. and J. G. Merrills. *Human Rights in the World* (Manchester: Manchester University Press, 1989, 3rd edition).

Robinson, Mark. "Aid, Democracy, and Political Conditionality in Sub-Saharan Africa," *European Journal of Development Research* 5 (1993), 85–99.

Robinson, Pearl. "Transnational NGO's: A New Direction for U.S. Policy," *Issue* 23 (1989), 41–46.

Rocha, Geise Maria. *In Search of Namibian Independence: The Limitations of the United Nations* (Boulder, CO: Westview, 1984).

Roche, Christian. *Histoire de la Casamance: Conquête et résistance 1850–1920* (Paris: Karthala, 1985).

Ronen, Dov. *The Quest for Self-Determination* (New Haven, CT: Yale University Press, 1979).

Ross, Stanley D. "The Rule of Law and Lawyers in Kenya," *Journal of Modern African Studies* 30 (1992), 421–42.

Rothchild, Donald and Naomi Chazan, eds. *The Precarious Balance: State and Society in Africa* (Boulder, CO: Westview), 1988.

Rovine, Arthur W. "The World Court Opinion on Namibia," *Columbia Journal of Transnational Law* 11 (1972), 203–39.

Rustow, Dankwart A. "Transitions to Democracy," *Comparative Politics* 2 (1970), 337–63.

Saglio, Christian. *Casamance* (Paris: Harmattan, 1984).

Salole, Gerry. "Not Seeing the Wood for the Trees: Searching for Indigenous Non-Governmental Organizations in a Forest of Voluntary Self-Help Associations," *Journal of Social Development in Africa* 6 (1991), 6–17.

Sandbrook, Richard. "Liberal Democracy in Africa: A Socialist-Revisionist Perspective," *Canadian Journal of African Studies* 22 (1988), 240–67.

———. *The Politics of Africa's Economic Recovery* (Cambridge: Cambridge University Press, 1993).

———. *The Politics of Africa's Economic Stagnation* (Cambridge: Cambridge University Press, 1985).

Sandberg, Eve, ed. *The Changing Politics of Non-Governmental Organizations and African States* (Westport, CT: Praeger, 1994).

——— and Carol L. Martin. "Namibia: An Institutional Analysis of a Consultative Model of Decision Making by a Democratizing State and Its NGOs," in Eve Sandberg, ed., *The Changing Politics of Non-Governmental Organizations and African States* (Westport CT: Praeger, 1994), pp. 169–192.

Sanderson, Lilian Passmore. "The Role of Anti-Slavery International (formerly the Anti-Slavery Society) in the Work for the Ultimate Elimination of All Forms of Female Genital Mutilation," *Anti-Slavery Reporter* (London: ASI, 1992), 41–57.

Saro-Wiwa, Ken. *Genocide in Nigeria: The Ogoni Tragedy* (London: Saros, 1992).

———. *Nigeria: The Brink of Disaster* (London: Saros, 1991).

———. *On a Darkling Plain: An Account of the Nigerian Civil War* (London: Saros, 1989).

Schatz, Sayre P. "Pirate Capitalism and the Inert Economy of Nigeria," *Journal of Modern African Studies* 22 (1984), 145–57.

Schmale, Matthias. *The Role of Local Organizations in Third World Development: Tanzania, Zimbabwe and Ethiopia* (Aldershot: Avebury, 1993).

Schmidt, Markus G. "Individual Human Rights Complaints Procedures Based on United Nations Treaties and the Need for Reform," *International and Comparative Law Quarterly* 41 (1992), 645–59.

Schmitz, Gerald and David Gillies. *The Challenge of Democratic Development: Sustaining Democratization in Developing Societies* (Ottawa: North-South Institute / Institut Nord-Sud, 1992).

Scoble, Harry M. "Human Rights Non-Governmental Organizations in Black Africa: Their Problems and Prospects in the Wake of the Banjul Charter," in Claude E. Welch, Jr. and Ronald I. Meltzer, eds., *Human Rights and Development in Africa* (Albany: State University of New York Press, 1984), pp. 177–203.

Sachs, Albie. *Protecting Human Rights in a New South Africa* (Cape Town: Oxford University Press, 1990).

Seck, Moustapha. "A Plea for Human Rights Education in Africa," *Human Rights Law Journal* 11 (1990), 283–29.

Selassie, Alemante G. "Ethnic Identity and Constitutional Design for Africa," *Stanford Journal of International Law* 29 (1992), 1–56.

Shaw, Timothy M. "Africa in the 1990s: Beyond Continental Crises to Sustainable Development — Structural Adjustment, Civil Society and NGOs," in Karl Wohlmuth et al., eds., *African Development Perspectives Yearbook 1990/91*, Vol. II, Industrialization Based on Agricultural Development (Research Group on African Development Perspectives Bremen, 1992), pp. 193–206.

———. "Popular Participation in Non-Governmental Structures in Africa: Implications for Political Development," *Africa Today* 37 (1990), 5–22.

Shivji, Issa G. *The Concept of Human Rights in Africa* (London: CODESRIA [Council for the Development of Economic and Social Research in Africa]), 1989.

Shue, Henry. *Basic Rights: Subsistence, Affluence, and U.S. Foreign Policy* (Princeton, NJ: Princeton University Press, 1980).

Shute, Stephen and Susan Hurley, eds. *On Human Rights: The Oxford Amnesty Lectures 1993* (New York: Basic Books, 1993).

Sikkink, Kathryn. "Human Rights, Principled Issue-Networks, and Sovereignty in Latin America," *International Organization* 47 (1993), 411–41.

Sirowy, Larry and Alex Inkeles. "Effects of Democracy on Economic Growth and Inequality: A Review," *Studies in Comparative International Development* 25, 1 (1990), 126–57.

Sklar, Richard. "Developmental Democracy," *Comparative Studies in Society and History* 29 (1987), 686–714.

Skogly, Sigrun I. "Human Rights Reporting: The 'Nordic' Experience," *Human Rights Quarterly* 12 (1990), 513–28.

——. "Structural Adjustments and Development: Human Rights, an Agenda for Change," *Human Rights Quarterly* 15 (1993), 751–58.

Slack, Alison T. "Female Circumcision: A Critical Appraisal," *Human Rights Quarterly* 10 (1988), 437–86.

Slinn, Peter. "Differing Approaches to the Relationship between International Law and Development," in Francis Snyder and Peter Slinn, eds., *International Law of Development: Comparative Perspectives* (London: Macmillan, 1991).

Slonim, Solomon. *South West Africa and the United Nations: An International Mandate in Dispute* (Baltimore: Johns Hopkins University Press, 1973).

Smillie, Ian. "Changing Partners: Northern NGOs, Northern Governments," in Ian Smillie and Henny Helmich, eds., *Non-Governmental Organisations and Governments: Stakeholders for Development* (Paris: OECD, 1993), pp. 13–43.

——. "The United States," in Ian Smillie and Henny Helmich, eds., *Non-Governmental Organisations and Governments: Stakeholders for Development* (Paris: OECD, 1993), pp. 303–18.

Smith, Brian H. *More than Altruism: The Politics of Private Foreign Aid* (Princeton, NJ: Princeton University Press, 1990).

Smuts, Dave. "Accounting for Violations in the Context of National Reconciliation," *Namibia Brief* 16 (March 1993), 12–13.

Snyder, Richard. "Explaining Transitions from Neopatrimonial Dictatorships," *Comparative Politics* 24 (1992), 379–400.

Sorensen, George. *Democracy and Democratization: Processes and Prospects in a Changing World* (Boulder, CO: Westview, 1993).

Sparks, Donald L. *Namibia: The Nation After Independence* (Boulder, CO: Westview, 1992).

Steiner, Henry. *Diverse Partners: Non-Governmental Organizations in the Human Rights Movement* (Cambridge, MA: Harvard Law School and Human Rights Internet, 1991).

Stepan, Alfred. *Rethinking Military Politics: Brazil and the Southern Cone* (Princeton: Princeton University Press, 1988).

Stewart, Frances. "Basic Needs Strategies, Human Rights, and the Right to Development," *Human Rights Quarterly* 11 (1989), 347–74.

Stiefel, Matthias and Marshall Wolfe. *A Voice for the Excluded: Popular Participation in Development, Utopia or Necessity?* (London: Zed, in association with United Nations Research Institute for Social Development, 1994).

Stoelting, David. "The Challenge of UN-Monitored Elections in Independent Nations," *Stanford Journal of International Law* 28 (1992), 371–424.

Stosic, Borko D. *Les organisations non-gouvernementales et les Nations Unies* (Geneva: Librarie Droz, 1964).

Stratton, Lisa C. "The Right to Have Rights: Gender Discrimination in Nationality Laws," *Minnesota Law Review* 77 (1992), 197–239.

Tandon, Yash. "Foreign NGOs, Uses and Abuses: An African Perspective," *IFDA Dossiers* 81 (1991), 67–78.

Tardu, Maxime. "The Effectiveness of United Nations Methods and Mechanisms in the Field of Human Rights: A Critical Overview," UN Document A/CONF.157/PC/60/Add.5, April 1, 1993.

——. *Human Rights: The International Petition System* (Dobbs Ferry, NY: York: Oceana, 1979–1985, three volumes).

Therien, J. 1990. "Non-governmental Organizations and International Development Assistance." *Canadian Journal of Development Studies* 12 (1990), 263–80.

Theunis, Sjef, ed. *Non-Governmental Development Organizations of Developing Countries: And the South Smiles . . .* (Dordrecht: Martinus Nijhoff for Novib, 1992).

Thiam, Awa. *Black Sisters Speak Out: Feminism and Oppression in Black Africa* (London: Pluto Press, 1986).

Third World Legal Studies, 1989. "Pluralism, Participation and Decentralization in Sub-Saharan Africa."

Thomas, Louis-Vincent. *Les Diola: essai d'analyse fonctionnelle sur une population de Basse-Casamance* (Dakar: Institut Français de l'Afrique Noire, 1959).

Thoolen, Hans and Berth Verstappen. *Human Rights Missions: A Study of the Fact-finding Practice of Non-governmental Organizations* (Boston: Martinus Nijhoff, 1986).

Thornberry, Patrick. "The Democratic or Internal Aspect of Self-Determination with some remarks on Federalism," in Christian Tomuschat, ed., *Modern Law of Self-Determination* (Dordrecht: Martinus Nijhoff, 1993), pp. 101–38.

——. *International Law and the Rights of Minorities* (Oxford: Clarendon Press, 1991).

Tirunchi, Andargachew. *The Ethiopia Revolution 1974–1987: A Transformation from an Aristocratic to a Totalitarian Autocracy* (Cambridge: Cambridge University Press, 1993).

Tobin, Jack and Jennifer Green. *Guide to Human Rights Research* (Cambridge: Human Rights Program, Harvard Law School, 1994).

Tolley, Howard B., Jr. *Global Advocates for Human Rights: The International Commission of Jurists* (Philadelphia: University of Pennsylvania Press, 1994).

——. "Popular Sovereignty and International Law: ICJ Strategies for Human Rights Standard Setting," *Human Rights Quarterly* 11 (1989), 561–85.

——. *The U.N. Commission on Human Rights* (Boulder, CO: Westview, 1987).

Tomaševski, Katarina. *Development Aid and Human Rights Revisited* (London and New York: Pinter, 1993).

——. *Women and Human Rights* (London: Zed Press, 1993).

Tomuschat, Christian, ed. *Modern Law of Self-Determination* (Dordrecht: Martinus Nijhoff, 1993).

TOSTAN. "Beyond Literacy: The TOSTAN Basic Education Program" (Thiès: TOSTAN, n.d.).

Toubia, Nahid. "Female Circumcision as a Public Health Issue," *New England Journal of Medicine* 331, 11 (September 15, 1994), 712–16.

———. *Female Genital Mutilation: A Call for Global Action* (New York: Women, Ink., 1993).

Trincaz, Jacqueline. *Colonisations et religions en Afrique Noire: L'exemple du Zinguin-chor* (Paris: Harmattan, 1981).

Tsanga, Amy S. and Olatokunbo Ige. "A Paralegal Trainer's Manual for Africa" (Geneva: ICJ, 1994).

Ukpong, Ebebe A. "The Constraints of NGOs' Operational Flaws on Rural Development Initiatives in Nigeria," *Journal of Social Development in Africa* 8 (1993), 51–72.

Ume, Fidelis Ejike. *The Courts and Administration of Law in Nigeria* (Enugu: Fourth Dimension, 1989).

Umozurike, U.O. "The Domestic Jurisdiction Clause in the OAU Charter," *African Affairs* 78, 311 (1979), 197–209.

———. "The Protection of Human Rights under the Banjul (African) Charter on Human and People's Rights," *African Journal of International Law* 1 (1988), 65–83.

———. *Self-Determination in International Law* (Hamden CT: Archon, 1972).

United Nations. "General Review of Arrangements for Consultation with Non-Governmental Organizations, Report of the Secretary-General." UN Document E/AC.70/1994/5, 26 May 1994.

———. *Human Rights and Elections: A Handbook on the Legal, Technical and Human Rights Aspects of Elections* (New York and Geneva: United Nations, 1994).

———. *Human Rights Bibliography: United Nations Documents and Publications 1980–1990* (New York: United Nations, 1993), five volumes.

———. *Non-Governmental Organizations and Sub-Sahara Africa: Profiles of Non-Governmental Organizations Based in Western Europe, Australia and New Zealand and Their Work for the Development of Sub-Saharan Africa* (Geneva: UN Non-Governmental Liaison Service, 1988).

———. *The Realization of the Right to Development: Global Consultation on the Right to Development as a Human Right* (New York: UN, 1991).

———. *United Nations Action in the Field of Human Rights* (New York: United Nations, 1988).

United Nations Centre for Human Rights and UNITAR. *Manual on Human Rights Reporting* (New York: United Nations, 1991).

United Nations Development Programme. *Human Development Report 1993* (New York: Oxford University Press, 1993).

United States. *Country Reports on Human Rights Practices* (Washington, DC: Government Printing Office for the Department of State, annual).

Unrepresented Nations and Peoples Organization. "Ogoni Background Material November 1993," The Hague: UNPO, 1993.

Uwazurike, P. Chudi. "Confronting Potential Breakdown: The Nigerian Redemocratization Process in Critical Perspective," *Journal of Modern African Studies* 28 (1990), 55–77.

van Boven, Theo. "Human Rights and Development: The UN Experience," in David P. Forsythe, ed., *Human Rights and Development: International Views* (New York: St. Martin's, 1989), pp. 121–35.

———. " 'Political' and 'Legal' Control Mechanisms: Their Competition and Coexistence," in Asbjorn Eide and Bernt Hagtvet, *Human Rights in Perspective: A Global Assessment* (Oxford: Blackwell, 1992), pp. 36–60.

———. "The Relations Between Peoples' Rights and Human Rights in the African Charter," *Human Rights Law Journal* 7 (1986), 183–94.

———. "The Role of Non-Governmental Organizations in International Human

Rights Standard-Setting: A Prerequisite of Democracy," *California Western International Law Journal* 20, 2 (1989), 207–25.

——. "The Role of Non-Governmental Organizations in the Promotion and Protection of Human Rights," in Johannes Chan and Yash Ghai, eds., *The Hong Kong Bill of Rights: A Comparative Approach* (Hong Kong: Butterworths Asia, 1993), pp. 279–95.

Verhaegen, Koenraad. *L'autodéveloppement: Un défi posé aux ONG* (Paris: Harmattan, 1991).

Virally, Michel. "Vers un droit international du développement," *Annuaire Français de Droit International* 11 (1965), 3–12.

Walle Engedayehu. "Ethiopia: Democracy and the Politics of Ethnicity," *Africa Today* 40 (1993, second quarter), 29–52.

Raoul Wallenberg Institute. Report No. 9, "Human Rights Workshop Namibia, 18–24 February 1991" (Lund: The Institute, 1991).

Waltz, Susan. "Making Waves: The Political Impact of Human Rights Groups in Northern Africa," *Journal of Modern African Studies* 29 (1991), 481–504.

Wanda, B.P. "The One-Party State and the Protection of Human Rights in Africa with Particular Reference to Political Rights," *African Journal of International and Comparative Law* 3 (1991), 699–741.

Wean, Deborah. "Real Protection for African Women? The African Charter on Human and Peoples' Rights," *Emory Journal of International Dispute Resolution* 2 (1988), 425–58.

Weinstein, Warren. "Africa," in Robert G. Wirsing, ed., *Protection of Ethnic Minorities: Comparative Perspectives* (New York: Pergamon, 1981), pp. 208–44.

——. "Human Rights and Development in Africa: Dilemmas and Options," *Daedalus* 112 (1983), 171–96.

Weissbrodt, David and Rose Farley. "The UNESCO Human Rights Procedure: An Evaluation," *Human Rights Quarterly* 16 (1994), 391–414.

Weissbrodt, David. "The Contribution of Non-Governmental Organizations to the Protection of Human Rights," in Theodor Meron, ed., *Human Rights in International Law: Legal and Policy Issues* (Oxford: Clarendon Press, 1984), pp. 403–37.

Welch, Claude E., Jr. "The African Commission on Human and Peoples' Rights: A Five-Year Report and Assessment," *Human Rights Quarterly* 14 (1992), 43–61.

——. *Anatomy of Rebellion* (Albany: State University of New York Press, 1980).

——. "Breaking New Ground," *West Africa* (9–15 November 1992), 1920.

——. "Changing Civil-Military Relations," in Robert O. Slater, Barry M. Schutz, and Steven R. Dorr, eds., *Global Transformation and the Third World* (Boulder, CO: Lynne Rienner, 1993), pp. 71–90.

——. "Civil-Military Agonies in Nigeria: Agonies of an Unaccomplished Transition," *Armed Forces & Society* 21, 4 (summer 1995), 593–614.

——. "Continuity and Discontinuity in African Military Organization," *Journal of Modern African Studies* 12 (1975), 224–45.

——. "Human Rights and African Women: A Comparison of Protection Under Two Major Treaties," *Human Rights Quarterly* 15 (1993), 549–74.

——. "Human Rights in Francophone West Africa," in Abdullahi Ahmed An-Na'im and Francis M. Deng, eds., *Human Rights in Africa: Cross-Cultural Perspectives* (Washington: Brookings Institution, 1990), pp. 184–212.

——. "The Military and Social Integration in Ethiopia," in Henry Dietz, Jerrold Elkin, and Maurice Roumani, eds., *Ethnicity, Integration and the Military* (Boulder, CO: Westview 1991), pp. 151–78.

———. "Military Rule and the Imperatives of Democracy" (Abuja: Centre for Democratic Studies, 1992).

———. *No Farewell to Arms? Military Disengagement in Africa and Latin America* (Boulder, CO: Westview, 1987).

———. "The OAU and Human Rights: Regional Promotion of Human Rights," in Yassin El-Ayouty, ed., *The OAU After Thirty Years* (Westport, CT: Praeger, 1994), pp. 55–74.

———. "The OAU and International Recognition: Lessons from Uganda," in Yassin El-Ayouty, ed., *The Organization of African Unity After Ten Years* (New York: Praeger, 1975), pp. 103–17.

———. "The Organization of African Unity and the Promotion of Human Rights," *Journal of Modern African Studies* 29, 4 (1991), 535–55.

———, ed. *Soldier and State in Africa* (Evanston, IL: Northwestern University Press, 1970).

Welch, Claude E., Jr. and Virginia Leary, eds. *Asian Perspectives on Human Rights* (Boulder, CO: Westview, 1990).

Welch, Claude E., Jr. and Ronald I. Meltzer, eds. *Human Rights and Development in Africa* (Albany: State University of New York Press, 1984).

Wellard, Kate and James G. Copestake. *Non-Governmental Organizations and the State in Africa: Rethinking Roles in Sustainable Agricultural Development* (London: Routledge, 1993).

Whelan, Anthony. "Wilsonian Self-Determination and the Versailles Settlement," *International and Comparative Law Quarterly* 43 (1994), 99–115.

Williams, David and Tom Young. "Governance, the World Bank and Liberal Theory," *Political Studies* 42 (1994), 84–100.

Williams, Donald C. "Accommodation in the Midst of Crisis? Assessing Governance in Nigeria," in Goran Hyden and Michael Bratton, eds., *Governance and Politics in Africa* (Boulder, CO: Lynne Rienner, 1992, pp. 97–121.

Wilson, Heather A. *International Law and the Use of Force by National Liberation Movements* (Oxford: Clarendon Press, 1988).

Wiseberg, Laurie S. "Defending Human Rights Defenders: The Importance of Freedom of Association for Human Rights NGOs" (Montreal: International Centre for Human Rights and Democratic Development, 1993).

———, rapporteur. "A Guide to Establishing a Human Rights Documentation Centre: Report of a UNESCO-UNU International Training Seminar on the Handling of Documentation & Information on Human Rights" (Ottawa: Human Rights Internet, 1990).

———. "Human Rights in Africa: Toward a Definition of the Problem of a Double Standard," *Issue* 6 (1976), 3–13.

———. "NGO Self-Examination is the Missing Link in ECOSOC Review," *Human Rights Tribune* 1 (1994), 11–13.

———. "Protecting Human Rights Activists and NGOs: What More Can Be Done?" *Human Rights Quarterly* 13 (1991), 525–44.

——— eds., "Monitoring Human Rights Violations: The Role of Non-Governmental Human Rights Organizations," in David P. Kommers and Gilbert D. Loescher, eds., *Human Rights and American Foreign Policy* (Notre Dame, IN: Notre Dame University Press, 1979), pp. 179–208.

Wiseberg, Laurie S. and Laura Reiner, eds. *Africa: Human Rights Directory and Bibliography* (Cambridge, MA: Human Rights Internet, 1989).

Wiseberg, Laurie S. and Harry M. Scoble, eds. *Human Rights Directory, Latin America, Africa, Asia: A Directory of Organizations in Latin America and the Caribbean,*

Africa, the Middle East, Asia, and the Pacific, Concerned with Issues of Human Rights and Social Justice (Washington, DC: Human Rights Internet, 1981).

Wiseman, John. *Democracy in Black Africa: Survival and Renewal* (New York: Paragon House, 1990).

———. "Early Post-Democratic Elections in Africa," *Electoral Studies* 11, 4 (December 1992), 279–92.

Woods, Dwayne. "Civil Society in Europe and Africa: Limiting State Power through a Public Sphere," *African Studies Review* 35, 2 (1992), 77–100.

World Bank, *Poverty: World Development Report 1990* (New York: Oxford University Press, 1990).

World Health Organization, Regional Office for the Eastern Mediterranean. "Traditional practices affecting the health of women and children: Female circumcision, childhood marriage, nutritional taboos, etc.: Report of a Seminar, Khartoum, 10–15 February 1979" (WHO/EMRO Technical Publication No. 2, 1979).

Wunsch, James and Dele Owolu, eds. *The Failure of the Centralized State: Institutions and Self-Government in Africa* (Boulder, CO: Westview, 1990).

Young, Crawford. "In Search of Civil Society," in John W. Harbeson, Donald Rothchild, and Naomi Chazan, eds., *Civil Society and the State in Africa* (Boulder, CO: Lynne Rienner, 1994), pp. 33–50.

Young, Crawford. *The Politics of Cultural Pluralism* (Madison: University of Wisconsin Press, 1976).

Young, Crawford and Babacar Kanté. "Governance, Democracy, and the 1988 Senegalese Elections," in Goran Hyden and Michael Bratton, eds., *Governance and Politics in Africa* (Boulder, CO: Lynne Rienner, 1992), pp. 57–74.

Zartman, I. William, ed. *Collapsed States: The Disintegration and Restoration of Legitimate Authority* (Boulder, CO: Lynne Rienner, 1994).

———. *Ripe for Resolution? Conflict and Intervention in Africa* (New York: Oxford University Press, 1989, updated edition).

Zewde, Bahru. *A History of Modern Ethiopia 1855–1974* (London: James Currey, 1991).

Zolberg, Aristide R. "The Specter of Anarchy: African States Verging on Dissolution," *Dissent* 39 (1992), 303–11.

Zuccarelli, François. *La vie politique sénégalaise (1940–1988)* (Paris: CHEAM, 1988).

Zuijdwijk, Ton J.M. *Petitioning the United Nations: A Study in Human Rights* (New York: St. Martin's, 1982).

Index

University of Pennsylvania Press
Pennsylvania Studies in Human Rights

Bert B. Lockwood, Jr., Series Editor

Professor and Director, Urban Morgan Institute for Human Rights,
University of Cincinnati
College of Law

Advisory Board

Marjorie Agosin
Philip Alston
Kevin Boyle
Richard P. Claude
David Weissbrodt

This book was set in Baskerville and Eras typefaces. Baskerville was designed by John Baskerville at his private press in Birmingham, England, in the eighteenth century. The first typeface to depart from oldstyle typeface design, Baskerville has more variation between thick and thin strokes. In an effort to insure that the thick and thin strokes of his typeface reproduced well on ppaer, John Baskerville developed the first wove paper, the surface of which was much smoother than the laid paper of the time. The development of wove paper was partly responsible for the introduction of typefaces classified as modern, which have even more contrast between thick and thin strokes.

Eras was designed in 1969 by Studio Hollenstein in Paris for the Wagner Typefoundry. A contemporary script-like version of a sansserif typeface, the letters of Eras have a monotone stroke and are slightly inclined.

Printed on acid-free paper.